REFORMATION UNBOUND

Fundamentally revising our understanding of the nature and intellectual contours of early English Protestantism, Karl Gunther argues that sixteenth-century English evangelicals were calling for reforms and envisioning godly life in ways that were far more radical than have hitherto been appreciated. Typically such ideas have been seen as later historical developments, associated especially with radical puritanism, but Gunther's work draws attention to their development in the earliest decades of the English Reformation. Along the way, the book offers new interpretations of central episodes in this period of England's history, such as the "Troubles at Frankfurt" under Mary and the Elizabethan vestments controversy. By shedding new light on early English Protestantism, the book ultimately casts the later development of puritanism in a new light, enabling us to re-situate it in a history of radical Protestant thought that reaches back to the beginnings of the English Reformation itself.

KARL GUNTHER is an assistant professor of history at the University of Miami.

CAMBRIDGE STUDIES IN EARLY MODERN BRITISH HISTORY

Series editors

John Morrill, *Professor of British and Irish History, University of Cambridge, and Fellow of Selwyn College*

Ethan Shagan, *Professor of History, University of California, Berkeley*

Alexandra Walsham, *Professor of Modern History, University of Cambridge, and Fellow of Trinity College*

This is a series of monographs and studies covering many aspects of the history of the British Isles between the late fifteenth century and the early eighteenth century. It includes the work of established scholars and pioneering work by a new generation of scholars. It includes both reviews and revisions of major topics and books which open up new historical terrain or which reveal startling new perspectives on familiar subjects. All the volumes set detailed research within broader perspectives, and the books are intended for the use of students as well as of their teachers.

For a list of titles in the series go to
www.cambridge.org/earlymodernbritishhistory

REFORMATION UNBOUND

Protestant Visions of Reform in England, 1525–1590

KARL GUNTHER

University of Miami

CAMBRIDGE
UNIVERSITY PRESS

CAMBRIDGE
UNIVERSITY PRESS

University Printing House, Cambridge CB2 8BS, United Kingdom

Cambridge University Press is part of the University of Cambridge.

It furthers the University's mission by disseminating knowledge in the pursuit of education, learning and research at the highest international levels of excellence.

www.cambridge.org
Information on this title: www.cambridge.org/9781107074484

First published 2014

Printed in the United Kingdom by Clays, St Ives plc

A catalogue record for this publication is available from the British Library

Library of Congress Cataloguing in Publication data
Gunther, Karl, 1979– author.
Reformation unbound : Protestant visions of reform in England, 1525–1590 / Karl Gunther, University of Miami.
pages   cm. – (Cambridge studies in early modern British history)
Includes bibliographical references and index.
ISBN 978-1-107-07448-4 (hardback)
1. Reformation – England.   2. Protestantism – England – History – 16th century.
3. England – Church history – 16th century.   I. Title.
BR375.G86   2014
274.2′06–dc23
2014027871

ISBN 978-1-107-07448-4 Hardback

For Wendy, Graham, and Nina

Contents

Acknowledgments

It is a pleasure to begin this book by acknowledging the many people and institutions who have played such an important role in making it possible. Mark Noll kindled my fascination with the English Reformation as an undergraduate, and Jay Wood provided much encouragement at an early stage. I had exceptional teachers as a graduate student at Northwestern, where I was fortunate to study with Bill Heyck, Richard Kieckhefer, Robert Lerner, William Monter, Ed Muir, Regina Schwartz, and Ethan Shagan. I could not have asked for a better advisor than Ethan, who from the start has been extraordinarily generous with his time and knowledge. Thank you. I would also like to thank my colleagues at Northwestern for their friendship and support, especially Nic Baker, Justin Behrend, Will Cavert, Elise Lipkowitz, Brian Maxson, Peter Mazur, Matt Miller, Lonnie Robbins, Jarod Roll, Sarah Ross, Owen Stanwood, Rhiannon Stephens, and Matt Sterenberg. Thanks too to many friends from Illinois, especially Wendy and Stephen Taylor; Renee and Kent Richter; Sandy and Ian Richter; Mary, Peter, and Betsy Welander; Nate Lee; and Rob and Kate Lee Noll. Thank you all for making this such an enjoyable period in my life and for making the countless hours on the train to and from Evanston well worth it.

Many scholars have graciously shared their knowledge with me, and I would especially like to thank David Como, Liz Evenden, Tom Freeman, Polly Ha, Paul Lim, Diarmaid MacCulloch, Peter Marshall, Michael Questier, Richard Rex, David Trim, Nicholas Tyacke, and Brett Usher for conversations and assistance with a wide range of questions. I owe a special debt of gratitude to Peter Lake for reading drafts of many chapters and for his encouragement and invaluable advice throughout the course of this project. Bill Bulman, Brett Foster, Rebecca Goetz, and Robert Ingram have shared their scholarly expertise and their friendship, while Luke Harlow has cheerfully endured innumerable drafts and been a constant friend over the years. I have had wonderful colleagues, first in the Department of History at Rice University and now for the past several years in the Department of History at the University of Miami, who have provided a great deal of intellectual and moral support as I completed this book. Special thanks to Hugh Thomas for reading the manuscript in full and for his helpful advice. I am also thankful for the opportunities I have had to present portions of the book to learned audiences who provided valuable feedback at the Sixteenth Century Society Conference, the Midwest and Southern Conferences on British Studies, the Institute for Historical Research, a conference on "Anti-Popery: The Transatlantic Experience" sponsored by the McNeil Center for Early American Studies at the University of Pennsylvania, the Folger Shakespeare Library, Princeton University, Rice University, Vanderbilt University, and the University of Miami. Last, but not least, I would like to thank the anonymous readers for Cambridge University Press for reading the manuscript with great care and for offering insightful and constructive criticism that has improved the book immensely. The errors and faults that remain are, of course, entirely my own responsibility.

This book would not have been possible without a wide range of institutional support. My research as a graduate student was generously funded by grants and fellowships from Northwestern University, the English-Speaking Union of Illinois, and the Dolores Zohrab Liebmann Fund. The Folger Shakespeare Library awarded me a short-term research fellowship and provided an extraordinary environment in which to work, and I would like to thank Carol Brobeck and the librarians at the Folger for all their assistance. The University of Miami has been enormously supportive, and I would like to express my gratitude for two Max Orovitz Research Awards to work on this book, as well as a junior research leave. I was also fortunate to receive a Research Fellowship from the University of Miami's Center for the Humanities, and I would like to thank the Center and its director, Mihoko Suzuki, for their support and for creating such a vital hub for humanistic scholarship in Miami. At Cambridge University Press, I would like to thank the series editors, as well as Elizabeth Friend-Smith, Rosalyn Scott, and Sunita Jayachandran, who have been a pleasure to work with during the book's final stages. Portions of this book appeared in an earlier form in "Rebuilding the Temple: James Pilkington, Aggeus and Early Elizabethan Puritanism" *Journal of Ecclesiastical History* 60:4 (October 2009), 689–707 and "Protestant Radicalism and Political Thought in the Reign of Henry VIII" (co-authored with Ethan H. Shagan) *Past and Present* 194 (February 2007), 35–74. I am grateful to these journals, Cambridge University Press, and Oxford University Press for permission to republish this material.

My greatest debts are to my family. Bruce, Elizabeth, and David Gunther have been endlessly encouraging through many highs and lows. Chin-Fang and Susan Chen have welcomed me into their family, and I thank all of the Chens and the Lins for their support over the years. Wendy has been there from this book's beginnings, and I cannot thank her enough for everything she has done for me. Graham and Nina love books, and I hope that one day they will know how much they did to help me finish this one.

Introduction: Remembering the Tuesday Sabbath

In a book about baptism, written in 1533 while he was imprisoned in the Tower of London on charges of heresy, an English evangelical named John Frith made a startling suggestion. Instead of observing the Sabbath on Sunday as Christians had done for a millennium and a half, the English should start observing it on Monday or Tuesday. According to Frith, this reform was essential to combat the superstition that the medieval church had implanted in the hearts of the English people. The day on which the Sabbath was observed was *adiaphora*, a "thing indifferent" like many other ceremonies and orders that in themselves made Christian worship "nether the better nor worse of a myte."[1] While God had commanded the Jews to celebrate the Sabbath on Saturdays, Christians were not commanded to observe the Sabbath on any specific day. The leaders of the early church were free to observe the Sabbath whenever they wanted and they *could* have continued to observe it on the same day as the Jews, but they changed the Sabbath day to Sundays "to be a perpetuall memorye that we are fre and not bound to any daye but that we may do all lawful workes to the pleasure of God & profyt of our neighboure."[2] The Catholic church, however, had led the English people into bondage, teaching them that it was necessary for Christians to observe the Sabbath on Sundays, an erroneous and legalistic belief implying that salvation depended on ceremonial observance rather than on faith in Christ alone.[3] Because so many people held such "supersticious" and dangerously self-destructive views of ceremonies – especially after they had been warned against such errors – Frith argued that "the

---

[1] John Frith, *A myrroure or lokynge glasse wherin you may beholde the sacramente of baptisme described Anno. M.D.xxxiii. Per me I.F.* (London, 1548; STC 11391), c2v. Original spelling and punctuation have been retained throughout, with abbreviations expanded, "j" substituted for "i," and "v" for "u" where appropriate.

[2] Frith, *A myrroure or lokynge glasse*, c4v-c5r.

[3] On the late medieval church's sabbatarian teaching, see Kenneth Parker, *The English Sabbath: A study of doctrine and discipline from the Reformation to the Civil War* (Cambridge, 1988), 8–23; Frith also might have been specifically responding to the claims of his *bête noire*, Thomas More: *The Complete Works of St. Thomas More*, vol. 6 (New Haven, CT, and London, 1981), 149.

Seniours and ministers of the congregations" ought "to abrogate or alter those cerimonies or elles they can not escape the wrathe of God."[4] Because the English were now "as supersticious in the Sonday as they [the Jews] were in the Satterdaye, yea, & we are moche madder," it was "at this tyme very expedyent yet ones agayne to over set our Sabbaoth which is the Sonday (because the ignorante people do count it as necessary) unto the mondaye or tewysday."[5] The English were "moche madder" than the Jews because whereas the Jews had direct biblical warrant for the Saturday Sabbath, Christians had no biblical warrant at all for the Sunday Sabbath.[6]

Needless to say, even though Henry VIII pruned the number of holy days in the 1530s, the English Reformation did not usher in a Tuesday Sabbath. Evangelical leaders like Thomas Cranmer did not seek a change in the Sabbath day, and the formularies of the Henrician and Edwardian Church of England increasingly moved in the opposite direction, defending the Sunday Sabbath as a signifier of Christ's resurrection on a Sunday.[7] In 1548, the year in which Frith's pamphlet was first published, John Hooper not only defended the custom of Sunday Sabbath observation but argued that Sunday was mandated as the Sabbath day for Christians by Scripture. Frith was a leading figure within the early evangelical movement and celebrated as a martyr after his execution in 1533, but his proposal to transfer the Sabbath day to Monday or Tuesday was deemed so unacceptable by John Foxe that when the great martyrologist edited and reprinted Frith's works in the early 1570s, he deleted it. Foxe's Frith was a supporter of the Sunday Sabbath – the margin read "Sabaoth kept on the Sonday" where Frith's radical proposal would have appeared – and merely an opponent of superstitious attitudes about it.[8] Thomas Russell perpetuated this distortion by employing Foxe's emended edition when he reprinted Frith's writings in 1831, and the reliance of modern scholars on these editions continues to perpetuate this omission.[9]

[4] Frith, *A myrroure or lokynge glasse*, c3r-v.   [5] Frith, *A myrroure or lokynge glasse*, c5r.

[6] Frith was not the only English Protestant to advocate such views: two years earlier, his close friend and fellow exile William Tyndale had gone even further when he argued that Christians might not only change the Sabbath day but also observe the Sabbath on a ten-day or a biweekly schedule, or simply abandon its observance entirely. William Tyndale, *An answere unto Sir Thomas Mores dialoge* (Antwerp, 1531; STC 24437), 59v.

[7] Parker, *The English Sabbath*, 36–40.

[8] *The Whole workes of W. Tyndall, John Frith, and Doct. Barnes* (London, 1573; STC 24436), PP6v. N. T. Wright noted these omissions in his 1978 edition of Frith's works, although the omitted sentence is unfortunately tucked away in an endnote: N. T. Wright (ed.), *The Work of John Frith* (Appleford, 1978), 52–53, 579n14.

[9] See Thomas Russell (ed.), *The Works of the English Reformers: William Tyndale and John Frith*, vol. 3 (London, 1831), 295; Parker, *The English Sabbath*, 34.

Frith's call for a Tuesday Sabbath reveals one way in which evangelicals could call for a radical reformation in Tudor England, and it provides a particularly striking example of how radical visions of reform in the early English Reformation have been obscured from the historical record. Historians do not typically place early English evangelicals among the radicals of Reformation Europe. The word "radical" is notoriously slippery, but it has taken on a largely fixed meaning for historians of the Reformation: it is typically used to refer to Anabaptists, who rejected not only infant baptism but also the "magisterial" reformers' project of forming state churches, embracing instead a sectarian vision of the church as a separated community of true believers.[10] Radicalism in this sense of the word was exceedingly rare in the English Reformation, and English evangelicals (Frith included) regularly proclaimed their hostility to Anabaptism and their commitment to a national church under royal authority.[11] A more useful way of thinking about Reformation radicalism rejects essentialist definitions of what constituted radicalism and instead adopts a contextual and relative use of the term to describe ideas, attitudes, or behaviors that fundamentally challenged the status quo in ways that were more extreme and/or extensive than those adopted by other reformers.[12] Conceived in this way, reform programs that sought an alliance with secular authorities could be every bit

---

[10] Roland H. Bainton, "The Left Wing of the Reformation," in *Studies on the Reformation* (Boston, 1963), 119–129; Ernst Troeltsch (trans. Olive Wyon), *The Social Teaching of the Christian Churches*, 2 vols. (New York, 1960); Hans J. Hillerbrand (ed.), *Radical Tendencies in the Reformation: Divergent Perspectives* (Kirksville, MO, 1988); Michael G. Baylor (ed. and trans.), *The Radical Reformation* (Cambridge, 1991); George Huntston Williams, *The Radical Reformation*, 3rd edn. (Kirksville, MO, 2000); Michael Driedger, "Anabaptism and Religious Radicalism," in Alec Ryrie (ed.), *Palgrave Advances in the European Reformations* (Basingstoke, 2006), 212–231; C. Scott Dixon, *Protestants: A History from Wittenberg to Pennsylvania 1517–1740* (Chichester, 2010), 7.

[11] For studies of Anabaptism and sectarian movements in England, see Irvin Buckwalter Horst, *The Radical Brethren: Anabaptism and the English Reformation to 1558* (Nieuwkoop, 1972); John F. Davis, *Heresy and Reformation in the South-East of England, 1520–1559* (London, 1983); D. Andrew Penny, *Freewill or Predestination: The Battle over Saving Grace in Mid-Tudor England* (Woodbridge, 1990); M. T. Pearse, *Between Known Men and Visible Saints: A Study in Sixteenth-Century English Dissent* (Cranbury, NJ, 1994). On evangelical hostility to Anabaptism, see especially Diarmaid MacCulloch, *Thomas Cranmer: A Life* (New Haven, CT, and London, 1996) and Catharine Davies, *A religion of the Word: The defence of the reformation in the reign of Edward VI* (Manchester, 2002), ch. 2.

[12] For helpful discussions of the term "radical," see Adolf Laube, "Radicalism as a Research Problem in the History of the Early Reformation," in Hillerbrand (ed.), *Radical Tendencies*, 9–23; Hans J. Hillerbrand, "Radicalism in the Early Reformation: Varieties of Reformation in Church and Society," in Hillerbrand (ed.), *Radical Tendencies*, 25–41; Glenn Burgess, "Introduction," in Burgess and Matthew Festenstein (eds.), *English Radicalism, 1550–1850* (Cambridge, 2007); David R. Como, "Radical Puritanism, c. 1558–1660," in John Coffey and Paul C. H. Lim (eds.), *The Cambridge Companion to Puritanism* (Cambridge, 2008), 242; Ariel Hessayon and David Finnegan, "Introduction: Reappraising Early Modern Radicals and Radicalisms," in Hessayon and Finnegan (eds.), *Varieties of Seventeenth- and Early Eighteenth-Century English Radicalism in Context* (Farnham, 2011), 1–30.

as radical in their vision for change as programs that rejected the religious authority of the magistrate.[13] In both senses of the term, however, radicalism was treated as a foreign concept in A. G. Dickens's classic *The English Reformation*, which proclaimed that "modest and mundane reforms sprang naturally from our Tudor age, with its deep aspirations to good order in Church, commonwealth and society at large."[14] English Protestantism – or rather Anglicanism – was a *sui generis* form of Christianity according to Dickens, one that charted a theological middle way between Catholicism and Protestantism, since the English "have scarcely grasped the deepest implications of either Catholicism or Protestantism; we have tended to avoid the peaks and the abysses of both, and our greatest men have seldom found it easy to operate within the framework of either."[15] The institutional expression of this *via media* was the Church of England, an inclusive state church born out of "a Reformation of compromise and detachment, partly because these attitudes come naturally to the English temperament, partly in consequence of a patriotic distrust for foreign models, partly since both Catholic and Lutheran powers failed to comprehend our situation, most of all because the divisions between Englishmen made it safer to attempt a settlement based on balance and comprehension rather than upon a narrow orthodoxy."[16] Roland Bainton took a similar view of the English reformers, remarking that the English were "not passionately stirred over confessional issues" in the sixteenth century and aimed instead to draw as much of the population as possible into a state church that made "minimal and ambiguous demands."[17] From this perspective, the English desired a reformation that was not only *not* radical; it was inherently antiradical.

---

[13] On this point, see Laube, "Reformation as a Research Problem," 17; Ethan H. Shagan, "Clement Armstrong and the godly commonwealth: radical religion in early Tudor England," in Peter Marshall and Alec Ryrie (eds.), *The Beginnings of English Protestantism* (Cambridge, 2002), 60–83; Diarmaid MacCulloch, *The Reformation* (New York, 2003), 161–2.

[14] A. G. Dickens, *The English Reformation*, 2nd edn. (University Park, PA, 1989), 204–5.

[15] Dickens, *The English Reformation*, 205.

[16] Dickens, *The English Reformation*, 206. As Dickens put it elsewhere, "[t]he English may have been spiritually incapable of grasping the genius of Catholicism or that of Protestantism, but at least they knew how to dethrone pseudo-logic, overdogmatic theology and various sorts of clerical messiahs." A. G. Dickens, "The Reformation in England," in Joel Hurstfield (ed.), *The Reformation Crisis* (New York, 1966), 56. On the subject of English exceptionalism and the Reformation, however, it is worth remembering that E. G. Rupp argued in 1947 that "We shall be wise if we refuse to imitate those historians who loved to glorify some imaginary and splendid isolation of the English Church, as though there were something inherently disreputable in borrowing from abroad, and who shied at the word 'Continental' with something of the blushing aversion for the word of a traditional spinster. The Reformers happily were without such odd parochialism." E. G. Rupp, *Studies in the Making of the English Protestant Tradition* (Cambridge, 1947), 47.

[17] Roland H. Bainton, *The Reformation of the Sixteenth Century* (Boston, 1952), 183.

The "myth" of moderate Anglicanism has been subject to devastating critiques from a variety of perspectives over the past several decades.[18] As scholars like Eamon Duffy and Christopher Haigh have forcefully shown, the destructive agents of English Protestantism looked decidedly immoderate when viewed from the perspective of the practitioners of traditional religion in England – the members of the parish gilds at Morebath, for instance, or the monks dwelling in Syon Abbey.[19] Scholars have also powerfully disproved the notion that English reformers aimed at a *via media* between Catholicism and Protestantism, and they have emphasized the deep interconnections between English and continental reformers, identifying the theology of the earliest English evangelicals with Lutheranism and then, especially from the reign of Edward VI onward, with a full-blooded Reformed theology that would forge a "Calvinist consensus" in the Elizabethan Church.[20] This body of scholarship has transformed our understanding of sixteenth-century English Protestantism, but radical visions of reform within English Protestantism have nevertheless remained marginal to our understanding of the early English Reformation.[21] This has largely been a matter of focus. Several scholars have shown that early English evangelicals could advocate sweeping social and economic reforms, but much of the finest scholarship on early English reformers has focused on figures who were decidedly evangelical, yet moderate in their inclinations and approach to reforming the

---

[18] Diarmaid MacCulloch, "The Myth of the English Reformation," *Journal of British Studies* 30:1 (January 1991), 1–19; Nicholas Tyacke, "Anglican attitudes: some recent writings on English religious history, from the Reformation to the Civil War," in *Aspects of English Protestantism, c. 1530–1700* (Manchester, 2001), 176–202; Ethan H. Shagan, *The Rule of Moderation: Violence, Religion and the Politics of Restraint in Early Modern England* (Cambridge, 2011).

[19] Eamon Duffy, *The Stripping of the Altars: Traditional Religion in England c. 1400–c. 1580* (New Haven, CT, and London, 1992); Christopher Haigh, *English Reformations: Religion, Politics, and Society under the Tudors* (Oxford, 1993); Duffy, *The Voices of Morebath: Reformation and Rebellion in an English Village* (New Haven, CT, and London, 2001).

[20] Such a list must necessarily be incomplete, but would include Andrew Pettegree, *Foreign Protestant Communities in Sixteenth-Century London* (Oxford, 1986); Nicholas Tyacke, *Anti-Calvinists: the Rise of English Arminianism, c. 1590–1640* (Oxford, 1987); MacCulloch, *Thomas Cranmer*; MacCulloch, *The Boy King: Edward VI and the Protestant Reformation* (New York, 2001); Philip Benedict, *Christ's Churches Purely Reformed: A Social History of Calvinism* (New Haven, CT, and London, 2002); Davies, *A religion of the Word*; Alec Ryrie, "The Strange Death of Lutheran England," *Journal of Ecclesiastical History* 53:1 (Jan. 2002), 64–92; Ryrie, *The Gospel and Henry VIII* (Cambridge, 2003); Carrie Euler, *Couriers of the Gospel: England and Zurich, 1531–1558* (Zurich, 2006); Torrance Kirby, *The Zurich Connection and Tudor Political Theology* (Leiden, 2007); Diarmaid MacCulloch, "Sixteenth-century English Protestantism and the Continent," in Dorothea Wendebourg (ed.), *Sister Reformations: The Reformation in Germany and in England* (Tübingen, 2010), 1–14.

[21] Indeed, the most recent studies of "radicalism" in early modern English history have focused overwhelmingly on the seventeenth and eighteenth centuries: see Burgess and Festenstein (eds.), *English Radicalism, 1550–1850*; Hessayon and Finnegan (eds.), *Varieties of Seventeenth- and Early Eighteenth-Century English Radicalism in Context*.

church.[22] Diarmaid MacCulloch has commented on the absence of "fiery clerical reformers independently spearheading the changes which transformed the English Church. There was no Luther to arouse the nation against the Pope, no Zwingli to turn the eating of a sausage into the downfall of a city's traditional faith, and among the rather thin and muted ranks of English religious radicalism, no Thomas Müntzer to face death for a revolutionary new Jerusalem."[23] The leader of English Protestantism was instead Archbishop Thomas Cranmer, an extremely cautious (albeit sometimes ruthless) reformer who hated radicals even more than conservatives, remained within the boundaries set by Henry VIII while the old king lived, and then pursued gradual reform under Edward VI in ways that aimed at "change accomplished with decency, order and the maximum possible degree of popular consent."[24] In his study of late Henrician evangelicalism, Alec Ryrie has argued that the radical evangelical exiles of the 1540s were a "sideshow" and that the "real centres of English evangelicalism" were to be found among those who remained in England and pursued reform in less confrontational ways within the boundaries of the Henrician Church of England – an argument and focus that fit closely with the emphasis that he and other scholars have recently placed on compromise, dissimulation, and Nicodemism within English Protestantism.[25]

Radical visions of reform did develop within English Protestantism, of course, but they are typically treated as later developments in the course of the English Reformation. Mary Tudor's reign proved to be a cradle of radical Protestant thought, as the experience of persecution and the restoration of Catholicism created circumstances in which "many of the habits and attitudes that belonged to life in an established Church – the

---

[22] On social and economic radicalism, see Shagan, "Clement Armstrong and the godly commonwealth"; Ryrie, *The Gospel and Henry VIII*, chs. 4–5; MacCulloch, *The Boy King*, ch. 3; Davies, *A religion of the Word*, ch. 4.

[23] Diarmaid MacCulloch, "England," in Andrew Pettegree (ed.), *The Early Reformation in Europe* (Cambridge, 1992), 168.

[24] Diarmaid MacCulloch, *Thomas Cranmer*, 144–146, quote at p. 483; also see Susan Brigden, *New Worlds, Lost Worlds: The Rule of the Tudors, 1485–1603* (New York, 2000), 196.

[25] Ryrie, *The Gospel and Henry VIII*, 112; Luc Racaut and Alec Ryrie (eds.), *Moderate Voices in the European Reformation* (Aldershot, 2005); Susan Wabuda, "Equivocation and Recantation During the English Reformation: The 'Subtle Shadows' of Dr Edward Crome," *Journal of Ecclesiastical History* 44:2 (April 1993), 224–242; Andrew Pettegree, "Nicodemism and the English Reformation," in *Marian Protestantism: Six Studies* (Aldershot, 1996), 86–117; Norman Jones, *The English Reformation: Religion and Cultural Adaptation* (Oxford, 2002); Angela Ranson, "Sincere Lies and Creative Truth: Recantation Strategies during the English Reformation," *Journal of History and Cultures* 1 (2012), 1–18; Jonathan Michael Gray, *Oaths and the English Reformation* (Cambridge, 2012), ch. 6. Also see Lucy Bates, "The Limits of Possibility in England's Long Reformation," *Historical Journal* 53:4 (2010), 1058–70; Alec Ryrie, *Being Protestant in Reformation Britain* (Oxford, 2013), 6–9.

habits of centuries – were temporarily discarded."[26] While the vast majority of Protestants conformed to the Marian Church, waiting for better days, the most radical Protestants waged a fierce written campaign against Nicodemism, denouncing it as a heinous sin against God and one's neighbors. Fleeing the Marian Church, they formed separatist congregations in England or exile churches in the more hospitable environs of Frankfurt, Wesel, Strassburg, Zurich, and Geneva. Notoriously, some of these exiles not only demanded separation from the Marian Church but also called for active resistance to the Marian regime and death to the queen herself. Mary's reign was short-lived, however, and the development of radical visions of reform within English Protestantism has been identified above all with the development of puritanism. During Edward VI's reign, "cracks in the edifice of evangelical unity began to appear" when John Hooper was appointed Bishop of Gloucester but refused to wear traditional vestments at his consecration.[27] Hooper's principled stand is widely taken to mark the "first signs of the gap in comprehension" within English Protestantism between "puritans" and "conformists," as it raised questions among English Protestants about the proper pace of reform, the locus of religious authority, and "the Church's freedom to choose to retain institutions and observances not explicitly commanded by the Word of God."[28] While proto-conformists like Archbishop Cranmer and Bishop Nicholas Ridley viewed the external forms of the church as "things indifferent" that the monarch could order as he or she saw fit, proto-puritans like Hooper demanded the elimination of ceremonies that they deemed harmful, arguing that the use of "things indifferent" was to be governed by rules regarding offense and edification laid down in Scripture. The division that Hooper's intransigence opened up would deepen in a series of escalating controversies, next over the use of the Book of Common Prayer among the Marian exiles at Frankfurt in 1554–1555 and then again over clerical garb a decade later in the vestments controversy of 1565–1566. By the 1570s the

---

[26] Patrick Collinson, *The Elizabethan Puritan Movement* (Oxford, 2000), 24.

[27] Peter Marshall, *Reformation England, 1480–1642*, 2nd edn. (London, 2012), 73.

[28] Diarmaid MacCulloch, *The Later Reformation in England, 1547–1603*, 2nd edn. (Basingstoke, 2001), 69; Marshall, *Reformation England*, 89. Also see Dickens, *The English Reformation*, 345; Alec Ryrie, *The Age of Reformation: The Tudor and Stewart Realms, 1485–1603* (Harlow, 2009), 191–192; Marshall, *Reformation England*, 131; John Craig, "The growth of English Puritanism," in Coffey and Lim (eds.), *The Cambridge Companion to Puritanism*, 37; Collinson, *Elizabethan Puritan Movement*, 72; Ronald Vander Molen, "Anglican Against Puritan: Ideological Origins during the Marian Exile," *Church History* 42:1 (March 1973), 45; Scott Wenig, *Straightening the Altars: The Ecclesiastical Vision and Pastoral Achievements of the Progressive Bishops under Elizabeth I, 1559–1579* (New York, 2000), 75; Claire Cross, *Church and People: England 1450–1660*, 2nd edn. (Oxford, 1999), 107.

conflict had reached new heights, with the most radical puritans not only criticizing the Book of Common Prayer but turning their sights on the church's government and calling for the abolition of episcopacy and a revolutionary restructuring of the Church of England along presbyterian lines. As Patrick Collinson put it, these mid-Tudor arguments over *adiaphora* and church order "began a debate which lasted intermittently for more than a century," fracturing English Protestantism and marking the point where "the geological fault-line between Anglicanism and Nonconformity, Church and Chapel, began."[29]

The development of radical views of godly activism and identity within English Protestantism also tends to be associated with the puritans. Elizabethan puritans practiced a "singular" style of piety or voluntary religion, marked by their zealous devotion to sermon gadding and fasting – among other pious behaviors – which sometimes ostentatiously distinguished them from their less zealous neighbors.[30] They engaged in distinctive social behavior, segregating themselves from those they deemed ungodly and waging war on sin and idolatry in their communities and the nation as a whole. Puritans, as Ethan Shagan has vividly put it, were people who felt a "positive obligation to pick fights with their reprobate neighbours," courting confrontation all in the name of producing godly order in church and society.[31] Local circumstances and personal temperaments obviously played a significant role in determining the level of conflict that puritans experienced, and Peter Lake especially has drawn our attention to the ways in which "moderate Puritans" avoided conflict within the Elizabethan Church and also to the ways in which "Puritanism had within it integrative and ameliorative, as well as polarising and fissiparous, impulses."[32] Yet the puritans embraced an embattled mentality and tended to view conflict as a godly and necessary part of Christian life. As Lake has argued, "[i]t was perhaps the defining characteristic of puritanism that it did not shirk, indeed welcomed, the disruptive, discomforting effects of protestant doctrine on the lives of

---

[29] Collinson, *English Puritanism* (London, 1983), 15–16.

[30] Collinson, *English Puritanism*, 19–20; Christopher Durston and Jacqueline Eales (eds.), *The Culture of English Puritanism, 1560–1700* (New York, 1996), 20–23.

[31] Shagan, *The Rule of Moderation*, 160; also see Alexandra Walsham, "The godly and popular culture," in Coffey and Lim (eds.), *The Cambridge Companion to Puritanism*, 290.

[32] Peter Lake, "The historiography of Puritanism," in Coffey and Lim (eds.), *The Cambridge Companion to Puritanism*, 356. Also see Peter Lake, *Moderate puritans and the Elizabethan church* (Cambridge, 1982); Lake, "Defining Puritanism – again?" in Francis J. Bremer (ed.), *Puritanism: Transatlantic Perspectives on a Seventeenth-Century Anglo-American Faith* (Boston, 1993), 18; Lake, *The Antichrist's Lewd Hat* (New Haven, CT, and London, 2002), 520.

individuals and on the life of the whole social organism."[33] Puritans embraced "an extraordinarily polarised view of the social world" in which they were, as Collinson put it, "constrained by their own principles to relate to the community at large in a manner which, in principle, maximised social stress."[34]

Beginning with Henrician evangelicals like John Frith and ending with the Elizabethan puritans, *Reformation Unbound* revisits the development of radical visions of reform and godly activism during the English Reformation. It argues that there were early English evangelicals who were envisioning the reformation in ways that were far more radical than we have hitherto recognized, and that radical ideas and attitudes that typically have been viewed as later developments had been part of the English Reformation at its start. Revisiting some of the most radical aspects of Marian Protestant thought, it argues that these ideas continued to shape the thought and activism of the hotter sort of Protestants under Elizabeth in ways that we have not previously appreciated. All of this not only revises our understanding of the intellectual boundaries of early English Protestantism, but it also has implications for how we view the development of puritanism in Elizabeth's reign. It is undoubtedly the case that "puritanism as an historical phenomenon and episode was rooted in the particularities of the Elizabethan church settlement," profoundly shaped by the unique political, polemical, ecclesiastical, intellectual, and social circumstances of Elizabethan England.[35] Indeed, as Chapters 5 and 6 argue, we still have a great deal to learn about the divisions that emerged within English Protestantism over "things indifferent" and about the circumstances that produced these divisions during the 1550s and 1560s. But by expanding our understanding of early English Protestant radicalism, this book enables us – indeed, requires us – to view some of the most radical ideas about "further reformation" and the nature of godly life that developed during Elizabeth's reign in a new light: not as fundamentally new departures within English Protestantism, but as the continuation (and in some cases) the reappearance of ideas and tensions that had been developing within the English Reformation from its start.

The book begins by examining the ways in which evangelicals envisioned a reformed church during the reign of Henry VIII. Historians

---

[33] Lake, *Moderate puritans*, 129.
[34] Peter Lake, "'A Charitable Christian Hatred': The Godly and their Enemies in the 1630s," in Durston and Eales (eds.), *The Culture of English Puritanism*, 156; Patrick Collinson, *The Birthpangs of Protestant England: Religious and Cultural Change in the Sixteenth and Seventeenth Centuries* (New York, 1988), 143.
[35] Collinson, *English Puritanism*, 13.

widely view early English evangelicals as relatively unconcerned with issues of church government, seeing calls for root-and-branch reform of the church's government as a new development – indeed, a quintessentially presbyterian development – within Elizabethan Protestantism. Chapter 1 shows, however, that there were some Henrician evangelicals – including a figure of no less importance than William Tyndale – who were calling in print for sweeping changes to the church's polity, advocating the abolition of diocesan episcopacy, clerical hierarchy, canon law, ecclesiastical courts, and the exclusion of the clergy from any role in secular governance. A properly biblical church, these evangelicals claimed, would have a bishop in every city or parish, the election of clergy, and the parochial exercise of church discipline. A reformation of this sort would have transformed the English Church beyond all recognition and, needless to say, Henry VIII did not enact these proposed reforms, leaving the polity and governance of the newly formed Church of England largely unchanged from that of its medieval predecessor. These radical visions of ecclesiastical reform stood in stark contrast to the views outlined in official and quasi-official publications from the 1530s and early 1540s, which not only legitimated the Church of England's essentially unreformed polity but also denied that the New Testament established binding rules or models for the church, investing the monarch instead with wide-ranging authority to regulate the church's government and its external forms as he saw fit. Importantly, this was also the view held by Archbishop Cranmer, but the chapter shows how it would come under sharp attack in the 1540s by radical evangelicals who denounced it for merely cloaking "popery" under the veil of royal "policy." In many respects, then, Chapter 1 significantly revises our understanding of the intellectual contours of early English Protestantism, revealing sweeping visions of ecclesiastical change and calls for reform that are typically associated with Elizabethan presbyterians, not Henrician evangelicals. It also shows that fundamental disagreements about the government of the church, religious authority, and *adiaphora* were not later developments in the history of the English Reformation, but were developing and being openly canvassed at its very start.

Chapter 2 traces a variety of ways in which Henrician and Edwardian evangelicals envisioned the English Reformation as bringing not "peace, but a sword" (Matt. 10:34). In a culture that was deeply devoted to the ideals of peace and unity, the division and conflict produced by the Reformation were widely taken to be great evils that needed to be eradicated. Henry VIII envisioned the establishment of a national church under royal authority as a way to restore peace and unity among his subjects and to bring an end to religious strife and contention. Indeed, the establishment of religious peace and unity were intrinsic to the idea of the national church. As this chapter argues, however, many (although not all) evangelicals took the view that preaching the gospel and living according to Christ's teaching would – indeed, *should* – scandalize the ungodly and produce a state of permanent strife between the followers of Christ and the children of Satan. Evangelicals who took this view developed highly agonistic visions of the reformation, the church, and Christian life in which ungodly peace would be broken up by godly conflict as the gospel went forth in a hostile world. This was not the only sense, however, in which some early English evangelicals envisioned reformation as bringing "a sword." In ways that we do not associate with early English evangelicalism, some evangelicals urged the monarch to take violent action against the enemies of the gospel, cleansing the land of persecutors, punishing idolaters, and imprisoning or executing enormous numbers of "popish" priests. These violent and polarizing visions of godly reformation all sat uncomfortably with alternative visions of the English Reformation that aspired to establish religious peace and unity through the national church. These radical evangelicals did not reject the notion of a national church under royal authority, but they envisioned it as a battleground and hoped that the monarch would be a powerful, partisan ally who would join their struggle against the forces of Antichrist in England.

While Chapters 1 and 2 draw attention to ideas and tensions regarding reform and the nature of godly life that have been neglected within early English Protestantism, Chapters 3 and 4 turn to some very well-known radical ideas on these subjects in the thought of Marian Protestants, arguing that we still have much to learn about the lasting power of these ideas within English Protestantism. Chapter 3 focuses on the anti-Nicodemite ethos that coursed through the veins and the pens of the most radical Marian Protestants. Anti-Nicodemism has been closely studied, and historians have understandably assumed that dissimulation was only a matter of concern for early modern Christians during periods of persecution. As this chapter reveals, however, anti-Nicodemite anxieties and attitudes would powerfully shape the thought of the hotter sorts of Protestants throughout Elizabeth's reign. Protestants continued to produce explicitly anti-Nicodemite literature into the 1590s and, in ways that sometimes sharply divided them, continued to identify Nicodemism as an ongoing problem that must be addressed at court, in the church, and in society at large. Anti-Nicodemite concerns and arguments were prevalent among the hottest Elizabethan Protestants, underwriting nonconformity in the Elizabethan Church, the separatists' refusal to participate in that church at all, and the ostentatious public repudiation of sin and sinners that virtually defined "puritans" in the eyes of many Elizabethans.

Chapter 4 similarly traces the continuing purchase of Marian "resistance theory" after Elizabeth's accession. An older historiographical tradition assumed that the ideas of the Marian resistance theorists lost their relevance with the accession of a Protestant monarch and the restoration of a Protestant national church. Yet just as scholarship on monarchical republicanism has stressed the ongoing relevance of resistance theory in debates surrounding the Elizabethan succession crisis, this chapter argues that it also continued to shape Elizabethan Protestant thought regarding religious reform. It does so through a close, contextual reading of one of the earliest calls for further reformation in the Elizabethan Church: a 1560 commentary on the book of Haggai by James Pilkington, a former Marian exile and leading figure at Cambridge, who was soon to become the Bishop of Durham. As Pilkington glossed Haggai's call for the Jews to rebuild the temple after the Babylonian exile, he made arguments and redeployed themes that had been at the heart of Marian resistance theory, repeatedly arguing that God commanded all of his people to build the temple and that the opposition of rulers (or their failure to establish true religion) did not excuse their subjects from the task of temple building. This view of religious authority and reform, the chapter argues, not only found expression in Pilkington's call-to-arms but would also continue to inform the widespread nonconformity practiced by Elizabethan puritans (often with the connivance of sympathetic bishops like Pilkington), the independent "temple-building" initiatives pursued by alliances of godly magistrates and ministers, and especially the willingness of Elizabethan separatists from the mid-1560s onward to complete the reformation without tarrying for the magistrate.

While these chapters highlight the persistence of these radical ideas within Elizabethan Protestantism, the next two chapters significantly revise our understanding of the divisions that emerged within English Protestantism during the 1550s and 1560s over "things indifferent" and the need for further reformation. Chapter 5 revisits the "Troubles at Frankfurt" in 1554–1555, the debate among the Marian exiles about the use of the Book of Common Prayer that has been widely viewed as continuing the debate sparked by Bishop-elect Hooper under Edward VI and presaging the division between puritans and conformists over *adiaphora* and religious authority in the Elizabethan Church. The debate at Frankfurt took place in a very different political and polemical environment than did earlier Edwardian or later Elizabethan debates over *adiaphora*, however, and the chapter offers a new account of the controversy, which argues that the issues dividing the exiles at Frankfurt were very different from the issues that would divide puritans from conformists. Neither party at Frankfurt adopted a "conformist" view of *adiaphora* and while the two factions at Frankfurt did take different views of "things indifferent," the arguments made by *both* sides would later be made by puritans *against* the use of vestments in the 1560s. Rather than revealing a deepening divide between puritans and conformists during Mary's reign that naturally carried over into Elizabeth's reign, then, the chapter argues that the positions staked out at Frankfurt instead foreshadowed the broad-based commitment among the returning exiles to abolish the "remnants of popery" in the Elizabethan Church – an interpretation of the controversy that fits much better with our current understanding of the widespread Protestant desire for further reformation in the early years of Elizabeth's reign.

Chapter 6 then turns to the first great Elizabethan debate between puritans and conformists: the vestments controversy of 1565–1566. The chapter begins by arguing that it was not simply a debate among English Protestants. Catholic voices are almost entirely absent from existing accounts of this well-known controversy, which treat it as a wholly Protestant affair, yet the chapter shows that Catholics were aggressive and crucially important participants in the public debate over vestments, *adiaphora*, and religious authority in the mid-1560s. Puritans were deeply concerned about the dire effects they expected the vestments to have on the English population – anxieties that were powerfully confirmed for them by Catholics' public statements about the vestments. Building on the previous chapter's analysis, then, it goes on to show how the puritans' opposition to the vestments was based on ideas and concerns that had been influential within Marian and early Elizabethan Protestantism, highlighting the extent to which the conformist defense of vestments was (while hardly without precedent) significantly out of step with these recent trends in Protestant thought. Indeed, the conformist case for wearing vestments was far more expansive than we have previously recognized, as Archbishop Parker not only defended the use of vestments as a matter of obedience in "things indifferent" but argued that they would provide a powerful tool for drawing Catholics into the Church of England. These chapters give us a new and much richer understanding of the divisions that formed over "things indifferent" within mid-Tudor Protestantism, therefore, and like the preceding two chapters, they also point to significant continuities between the thought of radical Marian Protestants and Elizabethan puritans.

Claims to continuity with the Protestant past played an important role in the debates between puritans and conformists during Elizabeth's reign. When puritans criticized the use of vestments in the 1560s, and then especially as presbyterians rejected episcopacy and began to demand sweeping changes to the church's government in the early 1570s, they were regularly confronted by their opponents with the examples of early English Protestants like Archbishop Cranmer and Bishop Ridley. These heroic martyrs, they were reminded, had written the Book of Common Prayer, defended the wearing of vestments, and occupied episcopal office: did nonconformists and presbyterians condemn them? Chapter 7 examines the ways that puritans attempted to respond to these accusations, shedding light on developing notions of historical identity among the puritans. Historians have hitherto argued that the puritans responded to these attacks by claiming to have received "further light" from God than early English Protestants, but this chapter reveals the development of a different puritan view of the English Reformation's history – and their place in it – among presbyterians and separatists in the last decades of Elizabeth's reign. Mining the printed works of early English Protestants in search of ancestors, these radical puritans found leading figures who had denounced episcopacy, clerical hierarchy, the civil employment of the clergy, and ecclesiastical courts. Mustering an ever-expanding array of quotations from Henrician and Edwardian texts, these puritans turned the conformists' historical denunciations on their head, arguing that *they* were the true heirs of the English Protestant tradition, and that it was the conformists and the Elizabethan Church who had departed from the original reforming spirit of English Protestantism.

In their quest to define early English Protestantism as "conformist" or "puritan," both sides ignored inconvenient facts and glossed over important differences that distinguished them in certain ways from early English Protestants. The entire question of whether an early English evangelical like William Tyndale would have been a puritan or a conformist, moreover, was fundamentally anachronistic and unanswerable. Nevertheless, the Elizabethan battle for early English Protestantism reveals an important historical reality, one that neither side appreciated or was interested in acknowledging but that this book seeks to elucidate. Seeing the ways in which Elizabethan conformists, presbyterians, and separatists could pit different early English Protestants against each other (and sometimes against themselves at different points in time) further highlights the fact that the early English Reformation had contained a spectrum of voices – and not only on the issue of the church's government. Competing visions of the church and reformation, some of them very radical, had been part of the English Reformation from the start. It is to those visions of reform that we now turn.

CHAPTER I

Radical Reformation and the Henrician Church

When Walter Travers wrote a defense of presbyterianism in 1574, just two years after the *Admonition to Parliament* created a furor with its call to abolish episcopacy and establish a presbyterian church polity, he reflected on the history of the English Reformation and on the priorities of his Protestant predecessors. According to Travers, English Protestants had not always shared the presbyterians' concerns about church discipline and polity. The reformers under Henry VIII had attempted to revive a church that was practically dead, but Travers claimed that they "were so wholy bent unto the doctrine, that they never thowght off Discipline and so reteined yt still almost wholie suche, as it was amonghest the Papistes."[1] Under Edward VI, godly reformers like Martin Bucer "did exhorte to abolishe that popishe tyrannye which then was still remayning in the pollicie off the Churche, and to place in steade theroff a just and lawfull manner off government according to the worde off God," but this enterprise had failed. The entire English Reformation had foundered during Mary's reign, and the early years of Elizabeth's reign "hath not as yet bene any more happie towching the restoring of discipline then were the former tymes."[2]

Few historians would accept Travers's claim that early English Protestants never gave the church's discipline or government a thought, but modern scholars have offered a similar account of early English Protestant priorities. Protestant ecclesiology writ large has been viewed as gradually moving from an early indifference regarding the external forms and governance of the church (especially in Luther's early thought), through a mediating period where increasing attention was paid to these issues by Melanchthon, Bucer, and Calvin, and finally culminating in an

---

[1] Walter Travers (trans. Thomas Cartwright), *A full and plaine declaration of Ecclesiasticall Discipline owt off the word off God, and off the declininge off the churche off England from the same* (Heidelberg, 1574; STC 24184), 15–16.
[2] Travers, *A full and plaine declaration*, 4–5.

intense focus on these aspects of the visible church by Beza and his followers in "the later Reformed and puritan tradition with its stress on discipline."[3] A similar progression is both implicit and explicit in the historiography of English Protestantism. While histories of the Elizabethan Church of England have rightly devoted significant attention to debates over church government and discipline, histories of the early English Reformation have focused instead on evangelical efforts to achieve doctrinal and liturgical reform. On the one hand, surveys of the English Reformation emphasize early evangelicals' commitment to the doctrine of justification by faith and the English Bible, while on the other hand they stress evangelicals' intense opposition to purgatory and prayers for the dead, images and the cult of the saints, clerical celibacy, and – above all else – their hatred for the Mass.[4] When historians have addressed divisions within the early evangelical movement, they have focused primarily on Eucharistic theology and the question of Christ's presence in the Eucharist. It is of course a commonplace that evangelicals were among the staunchest supporters of Henry VIII's break with Rome and his assertion of royal supremacy over the Church of England – hardly an insignificant point of ecclesiastical governance – but beyond support for the abolition of papal authority, it has been assumed that the "nature of the external government of the church had not been a topic of much significance for early English protestants."[5] Only after achieving doctrinal and liturgical reformation in the reign of Edward VI, it has been argued, did Protestants then go further and hesitantly begin to consider reforming the church's governance and discipline.[6] This

---

[3] Paul D. L. Avis, *The Church in the Theology of the Reformers* (Atlanta, 1981), 35. When discussing English Protestantism, Avis treats concern with discipline as an Edwardian and Marian development, fully flourishing then among the Elizabethan presbyterians and separatists (pp. 61–66).

[4] See Dickens, *The English Reformation*; Marshall, *Reformation England*; Ryrie, *The Age of Reformation*; Ryrie, "The Strange Death of Lutheran England"; Benedict, *Christ's Churches Purely Reformed*, ch. 8; Duffy, *Stripping of the Altars*, pt. 2; Felicity Heal, *Reformation in Britain and Ireland* (Oxford, 2003), esp. 333, 347. Doctrine is the focus of William A. Clebsch, *England's Earliest Protestants, 1520–1535* (New Haven, CT, and London, 1964). Carl R. Trueman, *Luther's Legacy: Salvation and English Reformers, 1525–1556* (Oxford, 1994) revises and supersedes Clebsch's study in a variety of important ways, but focuses entirely on soteriology.

[5] Peter Lake, *Anglicans and Puritans? Presbyterianism and English Conformist Thought from Whitgift to Hooker* (London, 1988), 1. Importantly, however, Lake has also argued that the presbyterian platform advanced in Elizabeth's reign should be seen "not merely as a foreign import grafted on to a native protestant tradition which was ill suited to receive it, but as the product and extension of long term trends and tendencies within English protestant thought and feeling." Peter Lake, "Presbyterianism, the Idea of a National Church and the Argument from Divine Right," in Peter Lake and Maria Dowling (eds.), *Protestantism and the National Church in Sixteenth Century England* (London, 1987), 195.

[6] Catharine Davies, "'Poor Persecuted Little Flock' or 'Commonwealth of Christians'; Edwardian Protestant Concepts of the Church," in Lake and Dowling (eds.), *Protestantism and the National*

Edwardian turn has been depicted as something that would have been virtually unthinkable during the reign of Henry VIII. The Protestant doctrinal reformation had not yet been achieved, and the "psychological climate" produced by the Erastianism of the Henrician Royal Supremacy was so smothering that Protestants needed the freedom of a royal minority in order "to approach the problem of trying to bring the Church into line with pure, apostolic models," even in extremely limited ways.[7]

As I argue in this chapter, however, there were many prominent Henrician evangelicals who were not only deeply concerned with the reform of the church's government and discipline, but who called for sweeping changes in these areas. For many evangelicals, doctrinal and liturgical reformation needed to be accompanied – or even preceded – by a drastic reconfiguration of the church's offices, institutions, and structures of power. In the first part of the chapter, I examine influential printed texts from the 1520s and 1530s written by English evangelicals like William Tyndale and Robert Barnes, as well as translations made by English evangelicals of texts by Martin Luther, Wolfgang Capito, and François Lambert. These Henrician authors and translators articulated visions of the true church that demanded the elimination of all ecclesiastical offices except bishops (reenvisioned as parish ministers) and deacons. This would require an end to diocesan episcopacy and clerical hierarchy, with every city, village, or even parish having its own bishop and possibly electing him. Pastoral ministry would not merely be the *primary* activity of these clerics, but their *only* task: "bishops" would be prohibited from sitting in parliament or performing any civil duties for the crown, whether it was serving on the privy council, in the great offices of state, or as ambassadors. Ecclesiastical courts would be abolished and the church would no longer possess a judicial apparatus or function, with the business of the church courts handed over to laymen. Ecclesiastical discipline would be practiced vigorously by parish priests – not magistrates or diocesan officials – who would excommunicate impenitent sinners and ban them from the fellowship of the parish.

Church, 89–95. Davies writes that "It must be remembered that (Hooper apart) calls for discipline only started in the second half of the [Edwardian] reign" and that they were "to a large extent, limited by the essentially erastian framework set up by the Henrician reformation" (94).

[7] Catharine Davies and Jane Facey, "A Reformation Dilemma: John Foxe and the Problem of Discipline," *Journal of Ecclesiastical History* 39:1 (January 1988), 37–38. J. William Black has problematically criticized Davies and Facey for neglecting the disciplinary schema of Martin Bucer, who he (echoing Travers) deems to be "the first Protestant in England to argue for a revision of parish discipline in light of reformation priorities" and whose "significance to any further discussion of later Elizabethan and Stuart efforts to reform the church's discipline cannot be overstated." J. William Black, "From Martin Bucer to Richard Baxter: 'Discipline' and Reformation in Sixteenth- and Seventeenth-Century England," *Church History* 70:4 (December 2001), 647.

These were radical calls for institutional reformation that would have transformed the English Church beyond all recognition, but they were by no means the only vision of what a post-papal church would be like in Henrician England. The radical reformation envisioned in these texts went far beyond the view taken by the regime and by other evangelicals who argued that a reformed Church of England could properly retain the offices, internal governance, and disciplinary structures of the pre-reformation church. These different visions of a properly reformed church of England reflected the existence of significant ideological tensions that developed in the earliest years of the English Reformation. Did Scripture provide a binding model for the structure and governance of the church, or were these matters left to the discretion of Christians – or more specifically, Christian monarchs – to determine? In precisely which ways had the papal Antichrist corrupted the church and to what extent had he succeeded? These were open questions among advocates of reformation in the 1530s, and tensions over these issues were already coming to the surface during the 1540s. As we will see, evangelicals like Henry Brinkelow, John Bale, and William Turner not only continued to call for radical institutional reform during the last decade of Henry VIII's reign but also began to critique the ways in which "popery" was being retained within the Church of England as a matter of royal "policy."

Therefore, whereas these sorts of proposals for institutional reform and these sorts of disagreements about reform and religious authority are typically seen as later developments in the history of the English Reformation, this chapter argues that they had been present from its very start. This forces us to reassess not only our understanding of the early evangelical movement and the ideological development of Protestantism in Tudor England but also broader notions about the nature of English Protestantism. The presbyterian view of church government in Elizabeth's reign – with its claim to possess a strict biblical mandate and its rejection of episcopacy and clerical hierarchy – has been depicted as a "dogmatic" departure from the "original protestant tradition," which adopted a far more pragmatic approach to the subject and sought to reform (rather than remove) the traditional institution of diocesan episcopacy.[8] This chapter argues that both sorts of visions of a reformed church had been part of early English Protestantism, articulated by figures who were central to the making of English Protestantism and its

---

[8] Patrick Collinson, "Episcopacy and Reform in England in the Later Sixteenth Century," in Collinson, *Godly People: Essays on English Protestantism and Puritanism* (London, 1993), 161.

identity. English Protestantism had been divided over these issues at its very beginning.

When early English evangelicals discussed the church and its reform, they were not writing in a vacuum, and their views of the church's institutions and officers were very much shaped by their own experiences. The most prominent evangelical writers of the 1520s and early 1530s – William Tyndale, John Frith, and Robert Barnes – had little reason to view bishops in a positive light. Tyndale had unsuccessfully sought support from Bishop Tunstall in 1523 for his translation of the New Testament, only to find his translation later denounced and burned by Tunstall in London, an event that naturally disgusted the evangelical exiles.[9] It was the bishops who played the leading roles in the repression and prosecution of heresy during the later 1520s, and virtually all of the evangelical exiles had personal experience with persecution at the hands of prelates such as Wolsey, Fisher, and Tunstall.[10] Barnes was an Augustinian friar who had been charged with heresy in 1526 for a Christmas Eve sermon he had preached at Cambridge the preceding year. Tried before a panel of bishops in London, he was publicly denounced at his abjuration in a sermon by Fisher and then imprisoned by Tunstall before making his escape to the Continent.[11] Frith had his own brush with heresy prosecution at the hands of Cardinal Wolsey in 1528 when he was arrested and imprisoned along with other evangelical canons at the Cardinal's Oxford college for possessing a wide range of reformist texts. While he fled to the Continent shortly thereafter, he would again face trial and then execution only five years later under the oversight of an evangelical Archbishop, Thomas Cranmer.[12]

Given the complexion of the episcopal bench in the late 1520s and evangelicals' experiences with the bishops, therefore, it is hardly surprising that they often issued sweeping denunciations of bishops and the episcopal estate. In books like Frith's *A pistle to the Christen reader* (1529) and Tyndale's *The obedience of a Christen man* (1528), bishops were denounced as persecutors in an undifferentiated mass alongside the cardinals and the pope.[13] Frith straightforwardly explained to his evangelical readers that "all

[9] David Daniell, *William Tyndale: A Biography* (New Haven, CT, and London, 1994), 190–195; on reaction to this event, see Jerome Barlow and William Roy, *Rede me and be nott wrothe* (Strassburg, 1528; STC 1462.7), c2r.

[10] Craig W. D'Alton, "The Suppression of Lutheran Heretics in England, 1526–1529," *Journal of Ecclesiastical History* 54:2 (April 2003), 228–253.

[11] Korey D. Maas, *The Reformation and Robert Barnes: History, Theology and Polemic in Early Modern England* (Woodbridge, 2010), 17–21.

[12] Clebsch, *England's Earliest Protestants*, 78–81.

[13] William Tyndale, *The obedience of a Christen man* (Antwerp, 1528; STC 24446), 4v, 6r, 7v-8r, 9v.

the Popes, Cardinalles, Busshopes and their adherentes, be Ismael, the reprobate, and Antichristes."[14] While the papacy was certainly denounced as Antichrist in Tyndale's *Obedience*, it was the bishops who were specifically depicted as the root of all evil, since "there is no myscheve or disorder, whether it be in the temperall regimente or else in the spirituall where of they are not the chefe causes and even the very founteyne & springes & as we saye, the well heed so that it is impossible to preach agenste any mischeve excepte thou begynne at them or to sette any reformacion in the worlde excepte thou reforme them fyrst."[15] According to Tyndale, then, the government of the church would have to be reformed first, before any doctrinal progress could be made. John Bale would make the same case in the 1540s when he wrote that the church "shall not folowe Christe in fayth and in doctrine, tyl it apere lyke that churche which he left here behynde him whan he ascended. And that is not lyke to be yet."[16]

Criticism of the clergy was, of course, nothing new. The clergy and particularly bishops had long been subject to criticism by reformers like John Colet, whose famed sermon of 1512 calling for "reformation of the churche" was reprinted in 1530 by the royal printer, Thomas Berthelet.[17] Colet indicted the clergy for their greed, which manifested itself in pluralism, a lust for promotion, and "suynge for tithes, for offrynge, for mortuaries, for delapidations, by the right and title of the churche."[18] The clergy were also chastened for lording over their brethren within the church, with Colet citing Matthew 20:25–28, a passage to which we will return throughout this chapter: "The princis of people (sayth he) have lordshyp of them: and those that be in auctorite have power: but do ye nat so: but he that is greatter amonge you, let him be minister. He that is highest in dignitie, be he the servant of all men."[19] Colet extensively denounced the "secular occupation" of clergy, who were so busy with secular business that they had become "the servantes rather of men than of god."[20] Quoting Paul's teaching in 2 Timothy 2:4 that "No man beinge goddes soudiour, turmoyle hym selfe with seculare busynes," Colet argued that the clergy were to occupy themselves with prayer, study of the Scripture, preaching, ministering the sacraments, and doing "sacrifice for the people, and to offre hostis for their sinnes" as "mediatours and meanes unto

[14] John Frith, *A pistle to the Christen reader* (Antwerp, 1529; STC 11394), 9v.

[15] Tyndale, *The obedience*, 156r.

[16] Bale, *The Image Of bothe churches* (London, 1548; STC 1297), i[1]4v.

[17] John Colet, *The sermon of doctor Colete, made to the Convocacion at Paulis* (London, 1530; STC 5550), a2v.

[18] Colet, *The sermon*, a7r-v.   [19] Colet, *The sermon*, a5v.   [20] Colet, *The sermon*, a8r.

god for men."[21] This work was so all-consuming that it left no time for other activities. The apostles had refused to provide food for the poor – "a great worke of vertue" – because it would distract them from their divinely appointed tasks.[22] The clergy should not be engaged in secular business, therefore, and when they were so involved, a number of "evils do folowe." The clergy, who were of greater dignity than "kynges or emperours," were dishonored by bothering themselves with mere "erthly thinges," and their participation in this realm of life effaced the proper distinction between "pristis and lay people."[23] When bishops and priests handled secular business, "the beautiful ordre, and holy dignite in the churche, is confused, whan the highest in the churche do meddle with vile and erthly thynges: and in theyr stede, vile & abjecte persons do exercise hygh and hevenly things."[24]

Evangelicals like Tyndale would continue to voice many of the same criticisms in the 1520s and 1530s, albeit shorn of Colet's claims regarding the superiority of the clergy over the laity or the sacrificial nature of the clergy's activity. In Tyndale's famous *The obedience of a Christen man* (1528), a text that aimed to outline the biblical duties and responsibilities of all members of society toward each other, he argued that the clergy must not occupy civil offices: kings ought to "rule their Realmes them selves with the helpe of laye men that are sage wise, lerned & experte."[25] Surely writing with Cardinal Wolsey foremost in mind, Tyndale argued that it was "a monstrous thinge that no man shulde be founde able to governe a worldly kingdome save Bisshopes and prelates."[26] It was impossible for a cleric to serve both the church and state properly: "To preach Gods worde is to[o] moch for half a man. And to minister a temporall kingdome is to[o] moch for half a man also. Ether other requireth an hole man. One therfore can not well doo both."[27] Tyndale was quite specific about the offices that the clergy should not be occupying, complaining that clergy abandoned their divine duties when they served as the keepers of the privy seal and the great seal, as president of the "princes councell," as ambassadors, and as members of the privy council. This was disastrous, for "Woo is unto the Realmes where they are of the councell."[28] Peter would have been woefully unprepared for clerical life in England, Tyndale noted sarcastically, since "thou wast to[o] longe a fysher, thou wast never brought uppe at the arches, nether wast master of the Rolles, ner yet chaunceler of Englonde."[29] Tyndale returned to this theme two years

---

[21] Colet, *The sermon*, a8v.   [22] Colet, *The sermon*, b1r.   [23] Colet, *The sermon*, b1r-v.
[24] Colet, *The sermon*, b1v.   [25] Tyndale, *The obedience*, 55r.   [26] Tyndale, *The obedience*, 55r-v.
[27] Tyndale, *The obedience*, 55v; on papal supremacy, see 102v, 111–112.
[28] Tyndale, *The obedience*, 105v.   [29] Tyndale, *The obedience*, 75r.

later in *The practyse of Prelates* (1530), arguing that those who have "oversight of his [Christ's] flocke maye be none emperours, kinges, dukes, lordes, knyghtes, temporall judges, or any temporall officer, or under false names have any soche dominion or ministre any soch office as requyreth violence."[30]

Tyndale's friend and fellow exile Robert Barnes likewise denounced the employment of the clergy in civil offices in his 1531 *Supplicatyon* addressed to Henry VIII, a text published at Antwerp, in which Barnes complained about "the intollerable injuries, wronges and oppressions where wyth the bisshoppes of youre royalme vexe and have vexed ... not onlye me but also all true preachers and professours of the same."[31] Making a move sure to appeal to Henry VIII, Barnes rejected the clergy's traditional claim to possess temporal jurisdiction independent of the prince, since "oure master Christ, and all hys holy apostles were subject, bothe in bodye and goodes to temporall princes, And toke no temporall rule nor jurisdiccyon on them."[32] Clergy should not usurp temporal authority, just as the laity should not usurp spiritual authority, and "youre grace must have fulle power over al worldlye coursis, and the bysshops allonly mynistracion of the worde of God: and as youre grace maye not usurpe to preache the worde of god, no more maye they usurpe any power that belongeth to youre swerde."[33] But like Tyndale, Barnes was not just criticizing the clergy's claim to possess *independent* authority or earthly jurisdiction simply by virtue of their sacerdotal status. More sweepingly, he was also rejecting the notion that clergy could serve as royal officers at the king's order. If the king found himself unable to administer the commonwealth himself, he might deputize officers to assist him, but not from among the clergy. Civil officers "may not be of all maner of sortys, but they must be suche men as god hathe ordenyd there unto, and that have no nother particular adminystracion. As Dukys Erlys, Barons and suche temporall lordes whych be ordenyd of god for that same purpose to helpe youre grace in alle suche temporall causes."[34] Just as it would be wrong for the king to appoint a duke to preach a sermon, it would be equally wrong for "a bysshop to be a Judge in westmynster halle. For the office of a bisshop is onlye to preache godes worde and there in to be a faythefull minister."[35] Barnes was calling for a radically restricted role for the

[30] William Tyndale, *The practyse of Prelates* (Antwerp, 1530; STC 24465), a7r. Violence was a crucial issue here: "none that beareth rule in it [Christ's kingdom] maye have any temporall jurisdiction or ministre any temporall office that requyreth violence to compell with all" (a8v).

[31] Robert Barnes, *A supplicatyon made by Robert Barnes doctoure in divinitie, unto the most excellent and redoubted prince kinge henrye the eyght* (Antwerp, 1531?; STC 1470), 2r.

[32] Barnes, *A supplicatyon*, 14v.   [33] Barnes, *A supplicatyon*, 16r.   [34] Barnes, *A supplicatyon*, 16v.

[35] Barnes, *A supplicatyon*, 16v-17r.

clergy in English civil life when he wrote that bishops "ought not to be lordes of the parlament, nor to have no place of worldly honour amonge the people nor to have dominion over them," and that they should not "medyll in ony causes but alonly in reding and preachinge of the worde of god, wyth greate studye diligence and labour."[36]

Tyndale and Barnes not only rejected the clergy's exercise of authority in the temporal sphere; they also challenged the way the clergy exercised authority within the church. Whereas Colet's critique of clerical lordliness had focused on denouncing sinful attitudes and behaviors, Tyndale's critique of clerical lordliness was part of a structural critique of clerical hierarchy itself, a critique that often focused on the papacy but that also spilled over into a broader analysis of the clergy and the church's governance. In the *Obedience*, Tyndale challenged claims that Peter possessed "moare auctoritie and power" than the other apostles.[37] Christ not only forbade the apostles from claiming power over temporal lords; he forbade them "to exalte them selves one above a nother in the kingdome of God."[38] There was no lordship among the apostles, or in the early church, nor would the church fathers have approved of it. The apostles collectively chose Judas's successor (not Peter alone), and Augustine, Jerome, Cyprian, Chrysostom and Bede "knew of none auctoritie that one Bishope shuld have above a nother, nether thought or once dreamed that ever any soch shuld be."[39] Even when authority was offered to saintly fathers like St. Gregory, he "wolde receave no soch auctoritie above his brethren when it was proferd him."[40] Tyndale railed against the titles of lordship claimed by these "monstres," asking, "What names have they? my lorde prior, my lorde abbot, my lorde Bisshope, my lorde Archbisshope, Cardinal & legate: yf it please youre fatherhode, yf it please your lordschip, yf it please your grace, if it like your holynes and innumerable soch like."[41] Such titles had no place in the church of Christ.

---

[36] Barnes, *A supplicatyon*, 3r-v.   [37] Tyndale, *The obedience*, 40v.

[38] Tyndale, *The obedience*, 56r. Also see Tyndale, *The practyse of Prelates*, b1r.

[39] Tyndale, *The obedience*, 147v; Tyndale had made the same claim earlier in the book, where Ambrose and Origen were added to the list of church fathers who "never one knew of any auctoritie that one Bisshope shulde have above a nother" (62v). Dean Smeeton has stressed the similarities between this view and Lollard notions that "there was no rank within the priesthood," although it is unclear whether Tyndale was influenced by Lollard views on this point. Donald Dean Smeeton, *Lollard Themes in the Reformation Theology of William Tyndale* (Kirksville, MO, 1986), 185. However, while not discussing Tyndale's ecclesiology specifically, Richard Rex has firmly rejected the likelihood of Lollard influence on Tyndale's theology: Richard Rex, "New Light on Tyndale and Lollardy," *Reformation* 8 (2003), 143–171.

[40] Tyndale, *The obedience*, 62v.   [41] Tyndale, *The obedience*, 84r.

Tyndale offered a more elaborate critique of clerical lordship two years later when he discussed the proper government of the church in *The practyse of Prelates* (1530), an exposé targeting Cardinal "Wolfsee" and detailing the antichristian machinations of the clergy. Tyndale argued in this text that children provided the best model for rule within the church because they "beare no rule one over a nother, but all is felowshipe amonge them."[42] Noting that his readers would see this as hopelessly naive, Tyndale wrote, "Thou wilt saye: thou canst not se how there shuld be any good ordre in that kyngdome where none were better then other and where the superior had not a lawe and authoryte to compelle the inferior with violence."[43] This was how authority functioned in the world, because "The worlde trulye can se no nother waye to rule then with violence," and it was how authority functioned in the worldly "popes kingdome" that was governed by hierarchies: "there one sorte are youre grace, youre holynesse, youre fatherhod: Another, my lorde bysshope, my lorde Abbot, my lord pryor, Another, master doctor, father, bacchelare, master person, master vicar, and at the last cometh in simple syr Jhonn."[44] This hierarchy ruled the church with coercion and violence, as "everye man raygneth over other with might and have everye rular his preson his jayler, his chaynes his tormentes ... They rule over the bodye with violence and compell it whether the harte will or not, to observe thinges of their awne makinge."[45] All of this marked the kingdom of the pope as hopelessly mired in the world, but Christ's kingdom "is all to gether spirituall, and the bearynge of rule in it is cleane contrarye unto the bearinge of rule temporallye."[46] Rule within Christ's kingdom was counterintuitive to worldly spirits: the Holy Spirit gave Christians "lust unto the lawe of god, and love compelleth them to worke, and love maketh every mans good and all that he can do commune unto his neyghbours neade."[47] In the kingdom of Christ, the strong took the weak by the hand or carried them on their shoulders, and "to do servyce unto the weker, is to beare rule in that kyngdome."[48]

What is most remarkable about this account of church governance is the way in which Tyndale so explicitly insisted that the government of the church must *not* reflect the government of society at large. These two bodies were fundamentally different and operated according to fundamentally different rules, rules which were wholly appropriate in their own spheres

---

[42] Tyndale, *The practyse of Prelates*, a7v-a8r. Tyndale seems to have had limited experience with children.

[43] Tyndale, *The practyse of Prelates*, b1r.   [44] Tyndale, *The practyse of Prelates*, b1r.

[45] Tyndale, *The practyse of Prelates*, b1r-v.   [46] Tyndale, *The practyse of Prelates*, a8v.

[47] Tyndale, *The practyse of Prelates*, b1v.   [48] Tyndale, *The practyse of Prelates*, b1v.

but which must not be confused with each other. Given that a congruence between the government of the church and the government of the state was a Tudor orthodoxy and later a point of much controversy – no bishop, no king – it is important to recognize that Tyndale argued that church and state *must* operate according to distinct forms of governance. To Tyndale, Scripture was the "rular" of the church and Christ was its "heede," while all Christians were "brethren."[49] While some men might be called heads within the church, this was only due to their faithful custody of the true rule of Scripture – "because of the worde which they preach" – and their headship lasted only so long as they faithfully proclaimed the word.[50] Indeed, Scripture was practically the head officer of the church according to Tyndale, since the "worde is the chefest of the apostles and pope and christes vicare and hed of his church and the hed of the generall counsell."[51]

If Tyndale viewed the church as a spiritual kingdom, how then did he envision its polity? Tyndale addressed this question directly in *The practyse of Prelates* in a section entitled "What officers the apostles ordened in christes chirche & what their offices were to do."[52] Tyndale made it clear that this was a matter of doctrine, not an indifferent matter that might vary according to time and place: apostolic practice was divinely inspired and therefore binding on all Christians, since the apostles were "folowing & obeying the rule doctrine & commaundment of oure saviour Jesus Christ their master."[53] The apostles ordained only two offices in the church and instituted no "ceremony at all required in makynge of oure spirituall officers, then to chose an able person and then to reherse him his dutie and geve hym his charge and so to put hym in his rowme."[54] The first officer had many names: in Greek he was called a "bisshop" or "preast," whereas in English he was called "an oversear" or an "elder . . . because of his age discrecion & sadnesse."[55] As Tyndale explained in the *Obedience*, an elder was charged "to preach Gods worde unto the paresh" and "to minister the sacramentes which Christe ordeyned, which is also nothynge but to preach Christes promises."[56] This overseer or elder was to be resident in a single congregation: as he would argue against Thomas More in 1531, "those oversears which we now call bisshopes aftir the greke worde, were all waye bydynge in one place, to governe the congregacion there."[57] An elder was to be free from civil occupations, since he "put his handes unto the plowe of

---

[49] Tyndale, *The practyse of Prelates*, b2v.   [50] Tyndale, *The practyse of Prelates*, b2v.
[51] Tyndale, *The practyse of Prelates*, i8r-v.   [52] Tyndale, *The practyse of Prelates*, b4r.
[53] Tyndale, *The practyse of Prelates*, b4r.   [54] Tyndale, *The obedience*, 94r.
[55] Tyndale, *The practyse of Prelates*, b4r.   [56] Tyndale, *The obedience*, 72r, 92r.
[57] Tyndale, *An answere unto Sir Thomas Mores dialoge* (Antwerp, 1531; STC 24437), 8v.

goddes worde and fed Christes flocke and tended them only without loking un to any other busynesse in the worlde."[58] In his 1533 commentary on the Sermon on the Mount, Tyndale wrote that these overseers should be selected by their congregations. While all people had the duty to share God's Word, "no man maye preache openly save he that hath the offyce commytted unto him," which occurred when he "is called and chosen therto by the commen ordynaunce of the congregacyon."[59] The second officer was called a "deacon" in Greek and a "servaunte or a minister" in England, and his duty was to "ministre the almes of the ryche unto the poore," and he was assisted by widows who would "tende the syke."[60]

There was no place for hierarchy within Tyndale's model for church government. It has been widely claimed that English Protestants accepted "the subordination of one minister to the permanent oversight of another" until the advent of the presbyterian movement in the 1570s, an ecclesiological development that was the result of Theodore Beza's influence and was "foreign to earlier protestant teaching."[61] Bishops "belonged to the hierarchical arrangement of Tudor society, and it was more natural to think of them as instruments of reform than as an insuperable obstacle."[62] Yet in *The practyse of Prelates*, Tyndale depicted the present-day distinction between bishops and priests as a perversion of the biblical equality of bishops and their congregational ministry. Hierarchy was not ordained by Christ or the apostles, but developed when some greedy clergymen decided to seize the title of "bishop" for themselves and create a subordinate class of "priests."[63] Tyndale argued that in the early church, Christians faced such grievous persecution that few men were willing to become bishops "save he only which loved christ better then his awne liffe."[64] But as the church's earthly fortunes changed and wealthy converts entered the church, they gave great sums for "the mayntenaunce as well of the clergye as of the

---

[58] Tyndale, *The practyse of Prelates*, b4v.

[59] Tyndale, *An exposicion upon the v. vi. vii. chapters of Mathew* (Antwerp?, 1533?; STC 24440), 29r-v. Donald Smeeton has noted that this "democratic suggestion" echoed Lollard views of the ministry: Smeeton, *Lollard Themes*, 174. Also see Tyndale's claim in *The obedience* that "where a congregation is gathered to gether in Christ one be chosen after the rule of Paul, and that he only preach, and else no man openly: but that every man teach his housholde after the same doctrine" (112v).

[60] Tyndale, *The obedience*, 72r; Tyndale, *The practyse of Prelates*, d4v.

[61] Collinson, "Episcopacy and Reform," 161. In this important essay, Collinson was making the valuable point that presbyterianism was not "the only alternative to uncritical acceptance of the *status quo* of the Anglican settlement" (161).

[62] Collinson, "Episcopacy and Reform," 168.

[63] In debate with Sir Thomas More a year later, Tyndale would emphasize that "all that were called elders (or prestes if they so will) were called bisshopes also, though they have divided the names now," and he pointed to Titus 1 and Acts 20 as proof. Tyndale, *An answere unto Sir Thomas Mores dialoge*, 8v.

[64] Tyndale, *The practyse of Prelates*, b6r.

poore . . . then the bisshopes made them substitutes under them to helpe them, whiche they called preast, and kepte the name bisshope unto them selves."[65] The deacons also played a role at this fatal moment. Indeed, Tyndale claimed that "out of the deacons sprange all the mischefe."[66] Because the deacons were the ones who dispensed money to both the bishops and to the poor, "they were in favoure with great & smal," and when the office of bishops "began to have rest & to be honorable, then the deakons thorow favoure and giftes clam [i.e., climbed] up therunto."[67] This invasion of deacons into the ranks of the bishops was a disaster for the church, because deacons were "more subtyle and worldlye wyse then the olde bisshoppes and lesse lerned in goddes worde" and began to enrich themselves and to neglect the poor.[68] As a result, "faith waxed feble and fayntye, love waxed colde, the scripture waxed darcke Christ was no moare sene."[69] Hierarchy proceeded to spread like a cancer through the church, as the newly elevated bishops began to compete with each other for primacy, leading to the development of the patriarchates and ultimately the papacy.[70]

For Tyndale, then, the church's hierarchical polity – down to the most basic distinction between "bishop" and "priest" – was not the divinely ordained structure of Christ's kingdom on earth, but instead a perversion of true church government motivated by worldly clergymen's desire for wealth and superiority over their brethren. The papacy was ultimately a symptom of this problem, not its root. Tyndale was not alone among early English evangelicals in espousing such radical views. A similar analysis of the distinction between bishops and priests would be advanced in *A comparison betwene the Olde learnynge & the Newe* (1537), a frequently republished translation by the Cambridge evangelical William Turner of Urbanus Rhegius's *Novae doctrinae ad veterem collatio* (1526).[71] This text, which cast evangelical doctrine as the "old learning" of Christ and the apostles, briefly discussed the old and new teaching regarding bishops amid other doctrinal, ceremonial, and institutional matters. The "new" teaching of the

---

[65] Tyndale, *The practyse of Prelates*, b6r.   [66] Tyndale, *The practyse of Prelates*, b6r.

[67] Tyndale, *The practyse of Prelates*, b6r-v.

[68] Tyndale, *The practyse of Prelates*, b6v. Tyndale would later complain about this again in *An answere unto Sir Thomas Mores dialoge*, 93v.

[69] Tyndale, *The practyse of Prelates*, b7r.

[70] Tyndale, *The practyse of Prelates*, b7r-v. The pope subsequently created the myriad suboffices of the church, making "one a patriarcke, a nother Cardinall, a nother Legate a nother Primate, a nother Archesbisshope a nother Bisshoppe, a nother Deane, a nother Archdeacon and so forthe as we nowe se" (d2r).

[71] Turner's translation would be published in 1537 (STC 20840, 20840.5), 1538 (STC 20841), and again in 1548 (STC 20842).

pope's church held that "A Byshop is of hyer authorite then a symple prest, and hath the reservacyon and kepynge behynde to hym of certayne causes: for the hyer that the degre is, the greater and more is the power."[72] The old learning of Christ and the fathers was rather different, making no distinction of authority or power between priests or bishops. Rhegius noted that when Christ sent his disciplines into the world before his ascension, "he made no defference of the power of the Apostles," but told them all "equally" to preach throughout the world: "Where is ther here ony kepynge behynde of certayne causes, and that great dyfference amonge the mynisters of the worde?"[73] The early congregations "were governed by the commune counsell of prestes," and the distinction between priests and bishops arose gradually, although the unwitting human actors who instituted this division possessed good intentions.[74] In order "that the plantes of discencyon myght be plucked up by the rootes, al the care was devolved and brought unto one man," and priests were subordinated to the authority of a bishop.[75] Rhegius specifically addressed this historical digression to contemporary priests and bishops, so that they should know that their institutional hierarchy was "more by costume, then by the truthe of the ordynaunce of God, and that the church ought to be ruled of them altogether alyke, folowynge Moses, which whan he had alone the power and rule over the chyldren of Israel, he chose. lxx. persones, with whom he myght judge the people."[76]

Collapsing even the jurisdictional distinction between priests and bishops like this obviously had radical implications for how the church ought to be governed. Tyndale clearly envisioned bishops or overseers as pastors who ministered within a parochial or congregational context, rather than as pastors who administered a large diocese. When discussing bishops and the guidelines for their conduct laid down in 1 Timothy 3, for instance, Tyndale complained that "we have above twenty thousande that know no moare scripture then is written in their portoves," which was obviously a reference to England's lower clergy rather than its twenty-one diocesan "bishops."[77] Tyndale also argued that a bishop/overseer was entitled to tithes "because he was taken from his awne busynes and laboure, to preach

[72] Urbanus Rhegius (trans. William Turner), *A comparison betwene the Olde learnynge & the Newe. Translated out of Latyn in Englysh by Wyliam Turner* (London, 1537; STC 20840.5), f2v-f3r. This aspect of the text is not mentioned in discussions of the translation by Whitney R. D. Jones, *William Turner: Tudor Naturalist, Physician and Divine* (London and New York, 1988), 140–141, or Celia Hughes, "Two Sixteenth-Century Northern Protestants: John Bradford and William Turner," *Bulletin of the John Rylands University Library of Manchester* 66 (1983), 131.
[73] Rhegius, *A comparison*, f3v.   [74] Rhegius, *A comparison*, f4r.   [75] Rhegius, *A comparison*, f4r.
[76] Rhegius, *A comparison*, f4r.   [77] Tyndale, *The obedience*, 71v.

Gods worde unto the paresh," and therefore he "hath ryght by the auctorite of his office, to calenge an honest lyvinge of the paresh."[78] This reconceptualization of the bishop's office would require a massive and disruptive structural reorganization of the English Church. As Patrick Collinson has noted, the immense size of most English dioceses was a cause of concern to later reformers who sought to improve the bishop's pastoral abilities: during Mary's reign, John Knox suggested that each diocese be divided into ten smaller units, and William Turner would propose four bishops per shire, while Elizabethan Protestants like Hugh Stoughton proposed the creation of hundreds of new dioceses.[79] The presence of these arguments in Mary's reign has been taken to mark an ideological watershed within English Protestantism, with Turner "groping for the as yet unformulated presbyterian polity" and producing "the first of a long line of proposed Puritan disciplines for the English church."[80] These were not the first proposals along these lines, however, as Henrician evangelicals had previously urged the establishment of hundreds (if not thousands) of bishops in England. In his 1531 *Supplicatyon* to Henry VIII, Barnes had argued that every city, or perhaps even every church, should have its own bishop. Barnes had been accused of heresy in 1526 for claiming in a sermon at Cambridge that (among other things) "I wille never beleve nor I can never beleve that one man may be by the lawe off God a bysshop of ii. or iii. Cyttys ye of an holle contry, for yt is contrary to S. Paule whyche saythe, I have lefte the behynde to set in everye cityе a bysshop [Titus 1]. And if you fynde in one place of scripture that they be callid Epyscopi, thou shalt fynd in dyvers other places that they be callid contrary wyse presbiteri."[81] Cardinal Wolsey had responded to Barnes's claim by arguing that in the time of the apostles a single bishop was placed in charge of large cities (six or seven miles across) as well as their suburbs, just like a Tudor "bisshop hath but one Cytie to his Cathedrall churche and the contry about yt was as subbarbis un to it."[82] Barnes responded that this was "farfetchyd," asserting that there was no evidence for it either in Scripture or the testimonies of the church fathers.[83] Barnes went even further, however, suggesting that not only every city but also every church should have its own bishop. Chrysostom "wolde not that a

---

[78] Tyndale, *The obedience*, 72r.
[79] Collinson, "Episcopacy and Reform," 169–170. As Richard Rex has noted, the diocesan structure of the English Church "stood in clear need of rationalisation," and Wolsey had been pursuing a plan to create additional dioceses before his fall in 1529: Richard Rex, *Henry VIII and the English Reformation*, 2nd edn. (Basingstoke, 2006), 30.
[80] Collinson, "Episcopacy and Reform," 169; M. M. Knappen, *Tudor Puritanism* (Chicago, 1939), 113. On the "pioneering" nature of Turner's Marian arguments, also see Jones, *William Turner*, 174.
[81] Barnes, *A supplicatyon*, 27v.   [82] Barnes, *A supplicatyon*, 27v.   [83] Barnes, *A supplicatyon*, 27v.

wholle contre shulde be permyttyd un to one man," since pastoral ministry would be easier and more effective "yf the teachers were not distract with the governyng of meny churchys but had cure and charge of one church only &c."[84] Barnes dismissively told the Cardinal that he could have "alle these cytis," but insisted that his own claim was valid and "yet can you make it none heresy" since the evidence Barnes had presented "be playne wordes and able to move a man to speke as muche as I dyde."[85]

Tyndale and Barnes were among the most influential figures in the early evangelical movement, and their writings had a formative impact on the evangelical community in England.[86] Both offered sweeping accounts of how Antichrist had infiltrated the Christian Church in which they called not only for a theological and devotional reformation but also for a radical reconfiguration of the church's structure, government, and offices. When Tyndale and Barnes wrote in the late 1520s and early 1530s, of course, they had little reason to expect that the inhabitants of the episcopal bench or the bureaucrats in diocesan administrations would become allies in the cause of reformation. With the fall of Wolsey and the rise of the Boleyns and Cromwell, however, the situation began to change. Thomas Cranmer's surprising appointment to Canterbury in 1533 produced great hopes among the evangelical exiles. George Joye, presumably expressing a sentiment common among his fellow exiles, urged Hugh Latimer to "animate him [Cranmer] to his office. He is in a perilous place, but yet in a glorious place to plant the Gospel."[87] With Henry VIII turning against the papacy and with defenders of the traditional order like Bishop Fisher and Sir Thomas More not only falling from power but going to the block, the political fortunes of the gospel seemed to be providentially improving. Thanks to Anne Boleyn's patronage, nearly all of the episcopal nominees during her brief reign were men of evangelical convictions.[88] Evangelicals like Cranmer and Latimer were catapulted to the church's highest offices and able to wield the power of episcopal office to pursue reformation, promote fellow evangelicals, and frustrate, harass, and punish their opponents.[89]

It might be expected that the ascension of evangelical reformers in both church and court would have brought an end to evangelical criticism of

---

[84] Barnes, *A supplicatyon*, 28r.   [85] Barnes, *A supplicatyon*, 28r.
[86] Haigh, *English Reformations*, 65–67; Maas, *The Reformation and Robert Barnes*, 23–24.
[87] Quoted in MacCulloch, *Thomas Cranmer*, 101.
[88] Rex, *Henry VIII and the English Reformation*, 115.
[89] MacCulloch, *Thomas Cranmer*; Susan Wabuda, "Setting Forth the Word of God: Archbishop Cranmer's Early Patronage of Preachers," in Paul Ayris and David Selwyn (eds.), *Thomas Cranmer: Churchman and Scholar* (Woodbridge, 1993), 75–88.

episcopacy and the church's government, or tempered it at the very least. For Robert Barnes, it partially did. In the early 1530s, Barnes's personal friendship with Martin Luther made him useful to the regime as an ambassador to the German Lutherans regarding the King's Great Matter. In 1534, Barnes decided to publish a revised edition of his *Supplicatyon*. Douglas Parker has argued that whereas the 1531 edition was shaped by "the trials, heartaches, and incarcerations he endured under English prelates and Cardinal Wolsey," Barnes revised the text in 1534 in order to ingratiate himself to Henry VIII and pursue further advancement, a decision that he undertook "almost certainly at Cromwell's instigation," according to Korey Maas.[90] Barnes toned down his aggressive attacks on the bishops and focused his criticism on the papacy, a move sure to appeal to Henry VIII, but also a change that may have been influenced by his friendship with figures like Archbishop Cranmer and the hope that evangelical bishops offered. For example, Barnes deleted the statements from the 1531 edition regarding bishops being prohibited by Scripture from serving as "lordes of the parlament" and not meddling with "ony causes but alonly in reding and preachinge of the worde of god."[91] By the following year, Barnes was working in a theological and preaching capacity for Cranmer, and his diplomatic usefulness earned him a royal chaplaincy. By early 1536, his stock had risen so high that it was rumored that Henry had offered Barnes a bishopric.[92]

It is noteworthy, however, that Barnes did not entirely expurgate his earlier radical claims regarding episcopacy, and his argument that a bishop ought to govern only a single church remained in his 1534 edition of the *Supplicatyon*.[93] Nor did the preferment of evangelicals at church and court prevent other evangelicals from calling for sweeping reforms to the church's government. An extremely radical view of bishops was advanced in a 1536 book entitled *The images of a verye Chrysten bysshop, and of a couterfayte bysshop*, a translation of Martin Luther's *Wider den falsch*

[90] Douglas H. Parker (ed.), *A Critical Edition of Robert Barnes's A Supplication Vnto the Most Gracyous Prince Kynge Henry the. VIIJ. 1534* (Toronto, 2008), 18–19; Maas, *The Reformation and Robert Barnes*, 27. On the differences between Barnes's 1531 and 1534 texts, and his reasons for altering the text, see Parker (ed.), *A Critical Edition*, 16–20.

[91] Compare STC 1470 [1531], 3v with STC 1471 [1534], b1v. Given Barnes's friendship with Luther and Melanchthon, it is also worth noting the contemporaneous claims of both that they would not attack the bishops if they ceased opposing the gospel and fulfilled their offices properly; see Avis, *The Church in the Theology of the Reformers*, 113–114.

[92] Maas, *The Reformation and Robert Barnes*, 21–32; Wabuda, "Archbishop Cranmer's Early Patronage of Preachers," 82.

[93] For these passages in the 1534 edition, see Robert Barnes, *A supplicacion unto the most gracyous prynce H. the. viii* (London, 1534; STC 1471), f4r-v.

genantten geystlichen stand des Babst und der bischoffen by William Marshall, a prolific translator of Protestant theological literature in the mid-1530s.[94] The original text – which was being read in Latin translation by evangelicals at Oxford in the late 1520s[95] – was composed by Luther in 1522 as a denunciation of the Archbishop of Mainz, the figure at the heart of Luther's attack on the indulgence trade. It was so abusive and politically inflammatory, however, that it "shocked the Saxon government," and Luther was prevailed upon to reframe the text as an attack on bishops in general.[96] While Marshall attempted to obscure Luther's authorship in his 1536 translation, the book's contents proved so controversial that its publication in England seems to have ended Marshall's literary career, though his friendship with Cromwell and Cranmer spared him from any serious danger.[97]

What made this text so volatile? The book launched a scathing attack on bishops, repeatedly arguing that there ought to be at least one bishop in every city and that this bishop ought to be equal in authority to every other bishop. As in Tyndale's writings on the subject, this form of church polity was treated as a matter of Christian doctrine, not as an indifferent or political matter. Luther argued at length that this was the model of church government that "god and the holy ghoste hath constytuted and ordeyned" and that it was therefore inescapably binding:

> [T]he sentence of Paule, or rather the wordes of the holy ghoste dothe contynue fyrme, stable, and not able to be moved or stered of the gates of hel, & doth stande as styffe, as a brasen wall, whiche saythe playnly and evydently, that in every cytie there ought to be constytuted and ordayned one bysshop, and these then shall be every one of them of egall power with the other. For Paule speaketh playnly of every cytie, and he gyveth to every bysshop full power & auctorytie in his owne cytie.[98]

The popish bishops had "taken quyte away al true bysshops out of all cyties" so that they themselves could be "made bysshops or over seers of many cyties, and also of many provynces," and in so doing they were resisting the Word of God and forsaking the example of the apostles and

---

[94] William Underwood, "Thomas Cromwell and William Marshall's Protestant Books," *The Historical Journal* 47:3 (September 2004), 519.

[95] Underwood, "Thomas Cromwell," 529.

[96] John M. Headley (ed.), *The Complete Works of St. Thomas More*, vol. 5, pt. 2 (New Haven, CT, and London, 1969), 722–723.

[97] Underwood, "Thomas Cromwell," 529, 532–533.

[98] Martin Luther, *The images of a verye Chrysten bysshop, and of a couterfayte bysshop* (London, 1536?; STC 16983.5), o1r, m5r-m5v. Cf. *LW* 39, 282, 278.

church fathers like Cyprian, Hilary, Ambrose, Augustine and Irenaeus who were not "the bysshops of many cyties."[99] This argument about the scope of a bishop's ministry was closely tied to the view of the nature of the bishop's proper ministry that Luther developed in this text. Paul "doth cal these onely bysshops, whiche doo preache the gospell unto the people, and do mynystre unto them the sacramentes, as nowe in our tyme be the parysshe preestes and the preachers," which led to the conclusion that even the faithful preachers in "very lytle vyllages and graunges . . . have by good ryght the tytle and name of a bysshope."[100] According to Luther, therefore, the true bishops in sixteenth-century Europe were not necessarily those who currently held that title – a group that he viciously denounced – but rather "the chrysten curates or parysshe preestes" that preached, cared for the poor, and administered the sacraments.[101] (Hugh Latimer had claimed as much in 1531 when he, as a parish priest, referred to "my little bishopric of West Kingston."[102]) For Luther, the requirements of the job made it impossible to be the bishop of a larger unit, because the word meant "overseer" or, in Hebrew, "vysytoure, that is to saye, one which vysyteth men at theyr owne house, & doth dylygently enquyre and searche the condycyon of theym, and the state of theyr lyfe."[103] How could the bishop of an entire diocese do this?

This was radical enough in its implications for the structure of the church. Luther argued not only that every city or village ought to have its own bishop, however, but that the bishop also ought to have "full power & auctorytie in his owne cytie," a claim that led to a defense of the equality of all bishops. Basing his claim on 1 Peter 5:1–5,[104] Luther

[99] Luther, *The images of a verye Chrysten bysshop*, m5r, n4v-n5r. Cf. *LW* 39, 278, 281. Noting that the Church of Rome claimed that Paul used the word "cytie" to refer to "an hole provynce or kyngdome," Luther launched into a diatribe about how the papists distorted "the true sense of scripture," claiming that they would eventually go so far as to claim that "yf it lyke them well, from hensforthe this worde garden shall betoken a cytie, and a starre, a stabule, and an asse, a man." Luther, *The images of a verye Chrysten bysshop*, m8v-n1r.

[100] Luther, *The images of a verye Chrysten bysshop*, n7r. Cf. *LW* 39, 281–282.

[101] Luther, *The images of a verye Chrysten bysshop*, o1r. Cf. *LW* 39, 282.

[102] Quoted in Patrick Collinson, "Episcopacy and Quasi-Episcopacy in the Elizabethan Church," in Bernard Vogler (ed.), *L'institution et les pouvoirs dans les églises de l'antiquité à nos jours* (Miscellanea Historiae Ecclesiasticae, viii, Louvain, 1987), 232.

[103] Luther, *The images of a verye Chrysten bysshop*, o1v. Cf. *LW* 39, 282.

[104] "The seniours which are amonge you I exhorte, which am also a senioure, and a witnes of the afflictions of Christ, and also a part taker off the glory thatt shalbe opened: se thatt ye fede Christes flocke, which is amonge you, takynge the oversyght off them, nott as though ye were compelled thereto: butt willyngly: Nott for the desyre of filthy lucre: but of a good mynde. Nott as though ye were lordes over the parisshes: but that ye be an insample to the flocke. and when the chefe shepheerde shall apere, ye shall receave an incorruptible croune of glorye. Lykewyse ye yonger submit yourselves unto the elder. Submit yourselves every man, one to another. Knet youreselves

noted (in a passage that Marshall amplified in translation) that Peter was writing to priests and calling himself a "felowe preest" and therefore "he maketh theym all of egall power one with another, and he for byddeth theym to behave theym selves so, as yf they were lordes, or hadde domynyons over those whom they have charge of," showing "that all parysshe preestes & bysshops of cyties are of egall power amonge them selves, and as touchyng to the auctorytie of a bysshop, that one is nothynge superyor to an other, and that he [Peter] hym selfe also is felowe preest with theym, and hath nomore power and auctorytie in his owne cytie then have the other or every one of theym in theyr owne congregacion."[105] In contrast to Peter's example, the current bishops "do never cease with excedynge madde braulynges and suytes to contende & stryve amonge them selves about the dyfference, & degrees of power & auctoryte."[106] In light of Peter's words, and Christ's words in Luke 22:25–26 that while the princes of the pagans were "lordes over theym . . . it shall not be so amonge you," Luther concluded that "here undoubtedlye is rebuked your kyngdome, and your condycyon and state. For this ought not to be suche a one as it is, yf it were a Chrysten state."[107]

Shortly after Marshall's translation of Luther was published in early 1536, a far more elaborate proposal for ministerial parity and reformation of the church's government was published in London by a Cambridge evangelical named Tristram Revel. The book was *The summe of christianitie*, a translation of the French reformer François Lambert's *Farrago omnium fere rerum theologicarum* (1525).[108] Lambert was a Franciscan who converted to the evangelical cause after meeting Zwingli and Luther in 1522 and would go on to become the official theologian of the early Hessian Reformation.[109] Lambert wrote the *Farrago* in 1525 for

togedder in lowlines of mynde. For god resisteth the proude and geveth grace to the humble" (1 Peter 5 in William Tyndale (trans.), *The New Testament: The text of the Worms edition of 1526 in original spelling*, ed. W. R. Cooper (London, 2000), 467–468).

[105] Luther, *The images of a verye Chrysten bysshop*, m5v, o6r-v. Cf. *WA* 10[ii], 144–145 ("Nennet sich selb ein Mittelstiften, wil alle pfarrer unnd prediger ihm gleich unnd sich den sellbigen widderumb gleich haben"), which Luther's modern translators render as "He calls himself a fellow elder and wants all pastors and preachers to be his equals and to be equals among themselves." *LW* 39, 284.

[106] Luther, *The images of a verye Chrysten bysshop*, o6v-o7r. Cf. *LW* 39, 284.

[107] Luther, *The images of a verye Chrysten bysshop*, o7r-o8r. Cf. *LW* 39, 284.

[108] François Lambert (trans. Tristram Revel), *The summe of christianitie gatheryd out almoste of al placis of scripture, by that noble and famouse clerke Francis Lambert of Avynyon* (London, 1536; STC 15179); François Lambert, *Farrago Omnium Fere Rerum Theologicarum* (Strassburg, 1525). Lambert's influence in England has been previously noted. His commentary on Revelation was cited by John Bale in *The Image of bothe churches* more than any other text: see Richard Bauckham, *Tudor Apocalypse* (Appleford, 1978), 23. The text discussed here, however, has not received adequate attention.

[109] For biographical information on Lambert, see Roy Lutz Winters, *Francis Lambert of Avignon (1487–1530): A Study in Reformation Origins* (Philadelphia, 1938).

Sebastian of Mountfaulcone, prince-bishop of Lausanne, and offered a very specific plan in the form of 385 "paradoxes" or conclusions about the reform of church government, discipline, and doctrine. Like Luther's *Wider den falsch genantten geystlichen stand des Babst und der bischoffen*, Lambert's *Farrago* had been circulating within the English evangelical community since the late 1520s, being sold in London and found in the possession of Oxford evangelicals during the raid on Cardinal College in 1528.[110] Tristram Revel was clearly enamored with Lambert's plan, as he not only translated it into English but attempted at Easter 1535 to get his translation into the hands of England's most influential evangelical, Queen Anne Boleyn. The book was vetted by Anne's advisors, including Archbishop Thomas Cranmer, Archdeacon Edmund Cranmer, and Bishop Hugh Latimer, who unanimously rejected it.[111] While *The summe* did present a controversial sacramentarian view of the Eucharist – a position that both Cranmer and Latimer rejected in the 1530s – it seems more likely that the evangelical bishops' hostility toward the text was based on its proposals for revolutionary reforms to the structure and discipline of the Church of England. Given the highly negative reaction it elicited from England's leading evangelicals, Revel's decision to publish his translation of *The summe* in London the following year – with a dedication to the Queen – was a bold decision to bypass official approval and present this vision of a reformed church directly to the reading public.[112]

The summe contained a comprehensive and detailed plan for the establishment of a reformed church, all of which Revel depicted in his preface to Anne Boleyn as a matter of strict fidelity to Scripture, which was Christ's "laste wyll, and testamente" and to which his "lawyers, byshopes over the

[110] *The Acts and monuments of John Foxe*, vol. 5 (New York, 1965), appendix 6; Underwood, "Thomas Cromwell," 529.

[111] MacCulloch, *Thomas Cranmer*, 147. MacCulloch suggests that the text was rejected because of its "sceptical comments on the physical presence of Christ in the eucharist" (147), while Eric Ives has also argued that Anne rejected the text because it "denied the sacrifice of the mass," although he remarks in an endnote that it "must always have been unacceptable because of its full-blooded advocacy of the priesthood of all believers and its exposition in detail of the socially disruptive implications." Eric Ives, *The Life and Death of Anne Boleyn* (Malden, MA, 2004), 283, 409n39. Maria Dowling has described the translation as "extremely radical," but only mentions the text in passing: Maria Dowling, "The Gospel and the Court: Reformation under Henry VIII," in Lake and Dowling (eds.), *Protestantism and the National Church*, 47.

[112] This dedication enables us to date *The summe of christianitie* to March or April 1536. Anne's fall publicly began with the arrest of Mark Smeton on 30 April 1536, and she was executed three weeks later. It is extremely unlikely that a book dedicated to the queen would have been published during or after this period.

congregation" were "nether to adde or dymynyshe one Jote."[113] Most fundamentally, *The summe* demanded the abolition of the existing ecclesiastical hierarchy of archbishops, bishops, priests, and deacons. Ecclesiastical hierarchy was denounced as contrary to Scripture, which prescribed only two offices: bishop and deacon. There was to be complete parity among the bishops: "No byshop hathe aucthoryte, upon hys felowe, but to teache hym, if he knowe the truthe better, for the feynynge of archbyshoppes is nat of the worde of god."[114] This was a revolutionary claim and hardly one likely to appeal to Archbishop Cranmer. *The summe* drew the qualifications for bishops directly from the New Testament books of 1 Timothy and Titus, which it read quite literally: because Paul wrote that bishops should be the husband of only one wife, for example, Lambert claimed not only that bishops *could* be married but that "there ought none to be chosen byshoppe of the congregacyon, excepte he be maryed or have bene or wyll be."[115] A bishop was defined as a "minister of the worde of god" whose primary activity was preaching. In places where there was no preacher, there was by definition no bishop. Preaching was so important, in fact, that Lambert defined the administration of the sacraments as accidental to the bishop's ministry and a task that could be delegated to others so that the bishop could concentrate more fully on declaring God's Word.[116]

Given this fairly restricted view of the bishop's functions, therefore, it is perhaps unsurprising that *The summe* also called for the abolition of ecclesiastical courts and the body of officials that administered them. Bishops should not have vicars, officials, secretaries, chancellors, or "courtes of stryfe," and "there is no processe, that maye lawfully be determyned, before him, or hys offycyalles, for this doth belonge to prynces and rulers."[117] Wills and other contracts were to be removed from "the notaryes of Antychryst, and his

---

[113] Lambert, *The summe of christianitie*, +3v.

[114] Lambert, *The summe of christianitie*, d7r[ii]. There was no need for human hands to consecrate a bishop, since the calling of the Lord and the consecration of the Holy Ghost was sufficient.

[115] Lambert, *The summe of christianitie*, c6v[ii]. In the next paradox, Lambert acknowledged that there had been some unmarried "prophetes, apostles, and byshopes," but insisted that these were exceptions that proved the rule (c6v[ii]). There were other evangelicals in London during 1535 who were preaching that priests must marry (see Susan Brigden, *London and the Reformation* (Oxford, 1989), 268), and Tyndale had also argued that priests must be married men (*The obedience*, 71v-72r).

[116] Lambert, *The summe of christianitie*, +8r-v. "Thys mynysterye of sacramentes whiche is but accydent to them, and not pryncypall, they may commyt to other, when they be let with ministery of the worde. they be nat sende to baptyze, but to preache" (d7v[ii]).

[117] Lambert, *The summe of christianitie*, e1r[ii]. Revel/Lambert also rejected the system of mandatory tithes and first fruits as "thefte, and tyrannye of the apostate kyngedome" (e3v[ii]). Tithes were ordained for the Levitical priesthood, which came to an end with Christ, so requiring tithes would place Christians under the bondage of the old law. While congregations *should* support their bishops voluntarily, they could not be compelled to under evangelical law.

tyrannes" and placed under the authority of city councils or princes.[118] Here
The summe was not simply calling for an end to the church's independent legal
jurisdiction, but rather for an end to its legal functions entirely. Any exercise of
judicial power by the clergy was defined in *The summe* as contrary to God's
Word and inappropriate in a properly reformed commonwealth.

The summe depicted the bishop in a parochial rather than diocesan
context. Lambert insisted not only that every city ought to have a bishop
but that "In every cety, towne, & village there ought to be many
byshoppes," and that "Yf many peryshes be so great, that one byshope is
not suffycient for them, let them be devyded, and to every parte a byshoppe
assygned."[119] When it came to the assignment of bishops, parishioners were
to be given control. Rather than being appointed by the king or by a patron
who owned the advowson, bishops would be elected by each parish,
"chosen of the people, and confyrmed by the cominaltie of the churche of
every place, and to do this thing they have no nede of letters, rynges, sealles,
tokens, and suche other of this kynde very muche usyd clene contrary to the
worde of god."[120] Magistrates played a supervisory role in this system,
however, and the "counsell of every place" and "prynces" were instructed
to monitor elections to ensure that godly candidates were elected.[121] If the
congregation was unable to reach a consensus, or if the prince and the
congregation disagreed about whether their choice was fit, they should cast
lots after the example of the apostles.[122] *The summe* placed extraordinary
importance on these elections, calling it "the most grevous cryme" that
Christians had been deprived of "theyr ryght, and juste tytle, that is to chose
them a pastor."[123] Indeed, the election of ministers was so important that if
princes refused to permit it, they were "to be put downe and other to be
chosen for prynces."[124] This was truly shocking: full-blown Protestant
resistance theory, tied to the popular election of ministers, two decades
before the Marian exiles would demand the deposition of Mary Tudor and
Mary Stuart.[125] However staggering these claims might have seemed at the

---

[118] Lambert, *The summe of christianitie*, e1v[ii].   [119] Lambert, *The summe of christianitie*, c4v[ii].

[120] Lambert, *The summe of christianitie*, a1v[i]. Princes and nobles were to choose "very many lerned men
in the worde of god, whiche shulde be byshoppes in theyr courtes, and shulde teache theyr courtyers
oft the most pure worde of god" c6r[ii].

[121] Lambert, *The summe of christianitie*, c5r[ii].   [122] Lambert, *The summe of christianitie*, c5v[ii].

[123] Lambert, *The summe of christianitie*, c5r[ii].

[124] Lambert, *The summe of christianitie*, e1r[ii]. On Lambert's resistance theory, see William J. Wright,
"The Homberg Synod and Philip of Hesse's Plan for a New Church-State Settlement," *Sixteenth
Century Journal* 4:2 (October 1973), 29.

[125] This was not the only place where Lambert permitted subjects to rise up against their rulers in
defense of God's Word. Also see Lambert, *The summe of christianitie*, b6r-v[i].

time, *The summe* depicted the election of ministers and the provision of vernacular Scriptures as matters of such grave importance that their denial justified revolution.

The congregational exercise of discipline was also an important part of the church order articulated in *The summe*. An entire chapter was devoted to the "punyshment and puttynge out [of] false byshoppes and false apostles from the congregacion of the faytheful."[126] Because a bishop's only purpose was to preach the pure gospel, "if they swarve one jote, and teache straunge doctryne, they ought to be deposyd, and put out, of them by whom they were electe and chosen, that is to say of the comynaltie of the churche afore namyd, and other more apte to be electe."[127] Bishops could also be deposed "yf they myxte lawes, decrees, and tradycyons of men, with goddes ordynaunce," as well as for offensive behavior or conversation, either committed by themselves or their family.[128] *The summe* entrusted congregations with the primary duty of removing an errant bishop, for "They that have chosen byshopes, where as cause is, maye lawefully depose them."[129] Bishops who taught heresy or who were guilty of ungodly living were to be admonished three times and then "flede as a banyshed man," neither received into people's homes nor greeted on the street.[130] Princes were also to be involved in the discipline of errant bishops, even to the point of inflicting the death penalty.[131] If this system broke down, however, and neither the congregation nor the prince were willing to remove a false bishop, *The summe* provided an escape clause for faithful Christians: "Yf one, or two, or mo houses of the faythfull perceyve that they have not faythful byshoppes suffred to them, or the people of the peryshe wyl not chose evaungelycall men, they maye pryvatlye take them selves aproper byshope or pastor."[132] This was another shocking instruction, licensing the creation of separatist congregations as the proper response of parishioners forced to live under an ungodly clergyman.

The Summe also insisted on sharp discipline of the laity. The enemies of "the gospel" and notorious sinners were to be separated from "the outwarde company of the faythful" so that "they shall nat dwell with them or otherwyse kepe company."[133] Unsurprisingly, given the text's willingness to envisage the deposition of ungodly rulers, this discipline was also to extend to princes and magistrates. Bishops were required "to correcte with

---

[126] Lambert, *The summe of christianitie*, c7v[ii].   [127] Lambert, *The summe of christianitie*, a2r[i].

[128] Lambert, *The summe of christianitie*, c7r[ii], d7r-v[ii].

[129] Lambert, *The summe of christianitie*, c7r [ii].   [130] Lambert, *The summe of christianitie*, c8r[ii].

[131] Lambert, *The summe of christianitie*, c8v[ii], d1v[ii].

[132] Lambert, *The summe of christianitie*, c6r[ii].   [133] Lambert, *The summe of christianitie*, b6v[ii].

the worde of god, ye kynges and prynces and rulers, and with the church to gyther to seperate apostates, and slanderers of the worde from the comunion of the faythfull, and they so amending to receyve them agayne."[134] Christians should not be "conversant with bretherne that be [a] reproche to the churche, and falseprophets," and they should flee from all those who remain in the kingdom of the pope, especially those who claimed to be evangelicals.[135] Indeed, Christians were to be zealously hostile toward the wicked.[136]

While Revel's text provided a particularly comprehensive account of parochial ecclesiastical discipline, he was not the only Henrician evangelical advocating the vigorous exercise of congregational discipline as a crucial component of a reformed church. Indeed, discipline was identified as a necessary component of congregational life in one of the earliest printed evangelical texts in England, William Roy's 1527 translation of a catechism by the Strassburg reformer Wolfgang Capito, transformed by Roy into a dialogue between father and son.[137] Capito's view of discipline was similar to his fellow Strassburg reformer, Martin Bucer, who stressed the independence of the church from civil magistrates when exercising ecclesiastical discipline and also identified discipline as an essential "mark" of a true church (stances that departed, respectively, from the views of Zwingli and Luther).[138] When asked by his son, "Is this excomunicacion nedfull unto the churche of Christ?" the father responded "Ye surely/ that christen men cannot be without it. For herby prove they all thynges/ and kepe that gode is/ and beleve not every sprete/ but prove theym whether they are off god or nott. And herby syngulerly beware of faulce learnynges. and so exchewe all faulce and disceatfull delusions of the wicked."[139] While the father emphasized that excommunication was the public task of the congregation, he also stressed the independent responsibility of every Christian to treat an open and unrepentant sinner as excommunicate, regardless of what the congregation had done. In Matthew 18, Christ commanded "his churche" that "yf there be amonge theym eny that will not heare the right admonicion of the congregacion/ he which knoweth it/ ought to take hym as an hethen / and as a

---

[134] Lambert, *The summe of christianitie*, d5r[ii].   [135] Lambert, *The summe of christianitie*, d2r[ii].

[136] Lambert, *The summe of christianitie*, d8r-v[ii].

[137] *ODNB*. The first scholar to identify Capito as Roy's source was Anthea Hume, "William Roye's 'Brefe Dialoge' (1527) an English Version of a Strassburg Catechism," *Harvard Theological Review* 60:3 (July 1967), 307–321. Hume identified a variety of ways in which Roy altered Capito's catechism, though not with any substantial change to Capito's theology.

[138] MacCulloch, *The Reformation*, 176.

[139] William Roy, *A Brefe Dialoge bitwene a Christen Father and his stobborne Sonne*, eds. Douglas H. Parker and Bruce Krajewski (Toronto, 1999), 135–136.

publican. and therfore Christ sayth/ let hym be unto the as an open synner. He sayth not/ unto the hole churche. Flye thou hym with compassion/ and lett the congregacion do that thynge whiche accordynge to love and charite/ is conformable unto the doctryn of their hed."[140]

Tyndale had also stressed the necessity of discipline and its necessarily local character. In his 1531 commentary on 1 John, Tyndale wrote that in the early church the imposition of (and eventual release from) penance on "fraile parsones, that coulde not rule them selves was under thauctoritie of the curate, and the sad and discrete men of the parish."[141] As he had explained in the *Obedience* (following the models laid out in Matthew 18, 1 Corinthians 5, and 2 Corinthians 2), an unrepentant sinner should be "rebuked openly" by the curate, who would then exhort the parish "to avoyde the companye of all soch, and to take them as hethen people," in the hopes that this would drive him or her to repentance and then reincorporation into the parish community.[142] Tyndale lamented the fact that the exercise of church discipline was currently limited to diocesan officials: "se what oure busshopes officers doo, and where thauctoritie of the curate and of the Parishe is become. If in x. parishes rounde ther be not one lerned and discrete to healpe thother, then the devell hath a great swynge amonge us: that the busshopes officers that dwell so ferre of, must abuse us as they doo. And if within a diocese or an hole lande, we can fynde no shyft, but that the pope that dwellyth at the devell in hell, must thus mocke us, what a stroke thinke ye hath Sathan amonge us?"[143] This was by no means a minor problem in Tyndale's view, who treated the exercise of ecclesiastical discipline as a crucial element of congregational life. Indeed, congregations must move quickly to discipline sinners: "if an open synner be founde amonge us, we must immediatlie amende hym or cast hym out of the congregation with defiaunce and detestation of his synne, as thou seist howe quyckly Paule cast out the Corinthian, that kept his fathers wife, and when he was warned wold not amende."[144] The failure to cast out open sinners would be

---

[140] Roy, *A Brefe Dialoge*, 137.

[141] William Tyndale, *The exposition of the fyrste Epistle of seynt Jhon with a Prologge before it* (Antwerp, 1531; STC 24443), h4r.

[142] Tyndale, *The obedience*, 104v–105r.

[143] Tyndale, *The exposition of the fyrste Epistle*, h4r. George Joye likewise unfavorably contrasted the exercise of church discipline in the "congregacion," seen in Matthew 18 and 1 Corinthians 5 with "our bishops lighteningis & thondringis of theyr excommunicacions & kursingis, & loke how they agre with Christis worde & Paulis forme in al circumstancis." George Joye, *The letters which Johan Ashwel Priour of Newnham Abbey besids Bedforde, sente secretely to the Bishope of Lyncolne* (Antwerp, 1531?; STC 845), a7v–a8r.

[144] Tyndale, *The exposition of the fyrste Epistle*, h3v.

disastrous for the congregation, for "if we soffre soch to be amonge us unrebuked, we can not but attonce fall from the constancie of oure profession, and laughe and have delectation and consent unto their synne, as it is come to passe thorowe out all Christendome."[145] This was a danger for even "the best man in the world" and it was 10,000 times worse than sinning yourself.[146] Laughing and tolerating an open sinner in the congregation was "a sure token that the spirit of Christe is not in us," even if "we oure selves absteyne for shame or feare of hell."[147] The absence of proper discipline was so serious that it had corrupted the Eucharist itself:

> We never reconcyle oure selfes unto oure brethern which we have offendid: we receave un to oure masse the open synners, the covetouse, thextorcioners, the adulter, the bacbiter, the comen whore, and the whore keper, which have no parte in Christe by the scripture, ye suche are soffred to say the masse, as the use is nowe to speake, ye suche are we compellyd with the swerde to take for oure pastores and curates of oure soules and not so hardy to rebuke them.[148]

To summarize thus far, in the earliest years of the English Reformation there were evangelicals who were calling in print for an end to diocesan episcopacy, clerical hierarchy, ecclesiastical courts, and the clergy's civil occupations. The reformed church envisioned by these evangelicals would have potentially thousands of bishops, all possessing equal authority, and devoting themselves wholly to preaching, administering the sacraments, and exercising discipline within their parishes. What these evangelicals were proposing, in other words, was the creation of a fundamentally new sort of church in England, one that would have wreaked havoc on established patterns of authority, all in the name of fidelity to Scripture.

This was very much *not* the sort of reformation that Henry VIII had in mind. Rather than ushering in a radical transformation of the church's offices and internal governance, the institutional impact of the Henrician reformation in these areas was primarily jurisdictional.[149] Under Henry

---

[145] Tyndale, *The exposition of the fyrste Epistle*, h3v.
[146] Tyndale, *The exposition of the fyrste Epistle*, h3v.
[147] Tyndale, *The exposition of the fyrste Epistle*, h3v.
[148] Tyndale, *The exposition of the fyrste Epistle*, h4r. Some Edwardian Protestants would also link calls for the exercise of ecclesiastical discipline and excommunication with "the integrity of the Lord's Supper": Davies, "'Poor Persecuted Little Flock,'" 91–92.
[149] On the various forms of church government established in Protestant territories after the Reformation, see Robert Kingdon's excellent overview, "The episcopal function in Protestant Churches in the sixteenth and seventeenth centuries," in Vogler (ed.), *L'Institution et les pouvoirs dans les églises de l'antiquité à nos jours*, 207–220.

VIII, the church was "removed from the spiritual and jurisdictional supremacy of the pope, and subjected to a similar dominion exercised by the Crown," with the king receiving "all those powers over the Church in England which the pope had exercised: he controlled its laws, its courts, its appointments, its revenues, and also its doctrine."[150] These aspects of the late medieval church were not abolished, but rather re-founded on a new basis of royal authority. Bishops, for instance, found their jurisdictional powers suspended by the royal visitation of 1535, leaving them essentially powerless. By royal command, "not only could bishops not visit, ordain, or transact any of their usual judicial activity, most particularly correction and probate, they could not admit to benefices, consecrate churches, bless altars or even confirm children."[151] In a sort of episcopal surrender-and-regrant policy, the bishops were forced under threat of *praemunire* to surrender the papal bulls that appointed them to their sees and to sue for new commissions from the king.[152] Virtually all of their powers were returned, but their jurisdictional independence was gone: "their powers had, during this period, been demonstrated as emanating from the king alone to be given or taken away according to his pleasure."[153] Likewise, canon law and the existing system of ecclesiastical courts continued to function in England. The "Act for the Submission of the Clergy and Restraint of Appeals" (1534) prohibited Convocation from creating new canons on their own authority and established a commission to review and annul canons deemed prejudicial to royal authority or statute law, but concluded by proclaiming that all canons not considered prejudicial should "still be used and executed as they were afore the making of this Act" until the commission could review them further.[154] In practice, the "courts of the archbishops, bishops and archdeacons were left in place, unchanged to outward appearance," and when Henry established five new dioceses in the 1540s, "courts virtually identical with those of the medieval establishment were set up."[155] The post-Reformation Church of England would therefore possess an "administrative structure typical of the later Middle Ages which stood on altered

[150] G. R. Elton, *The Tudor Constitution: Documents and Commentary*, 2nd edn. (Cambridge, 1982), 327, 341–342.

[151] Margaret Bowker, "The Supremacy and the Episcopate: The Struggle for Control, 1534–1540," *The Historical Journal* 18:2 (June 1975), 236.

[152] Kenneth Carleton, *Bishops and Reform in the English Church, 1520–1559* (Woodbridge, 2001), 14.

[153] Bowker, "The Supremacy and the Episcopate," 242–243; also see Carleton, *Bishops and Reform*, 23.

[154] Gerald Bray (ed.), *Documents of the English Reformation* (Cambridge, 2004), 87.

[155] Richard H. Helmholz, "Canon Law in Post-Reformation England," in Richard H. Helmholz (ed.), *Canon Law in Protestant Lands* (Berlin, 1992), 204–205.

foundations but was otherwise remarkably undisturbed by recent events."[156]

Henry's jurisdictional reforms in the Church of England were supported with arguments that were superficially similar to many of the evangelical arguments we have just examined, but which proceeded under profoundly different assumptions regarding the authority of Scripture and the nature of popery. In rejecting the pope's claim to be the divinely appointed head of the Church, for example, propaganda and policy statements by the regime argued that a hierarchy of clerical authority had not existed in the early church, nor had it been authorized by Christ. William Marshall's translation of Marsilius of Padua's *Defensor Pacis*, which had been commissioned by Thomas Cromwell in the early 1530s and was finally published in 1535, stressed the equality of the apostles and gave examples to prove that Peter "chalengeth to hym selfe, or taketh upon hym, none excellence or prehemynence above other, but maketh hym selfe felowe lyke with theym."[157] The development of a hierarchy of clerical authority was not of divine origin: in Ephesus, for instance, the office of priest and bishop was identical, and only later were individual priests "instytuted & made cheyfe or hyghest of all the preests, of that cytie or place."[158] Likewise, the Bishops' Book (1537), which was produced by the bishops at the regime's instruction but never received official approval from Henry VIII, stressed that there was no mention in Scripture or in the writings of the earliest church fathers of the notion that "Christe dyd ever make or institute any distinction or difference to be in the preeminence of power, ordre, or jurisdiction betwene thapostles them selfe, or betwene the bishoppes them selfe, but that they were all equall in power, order, auctoritie, and jurisdiction."[159] The King's Book (1543), the official doctrinal statement of the Henrician Church of England at this point, also emphasized the equality of the apostles, since "Christe never gave unto saint Peter, or to any of the apostles, or their successours, any suche universall authoritie over all the other. But he set theim all indifferently, and in lyke power, dignitie, and auctoritie," with even the

[156] Collinson, "Episcopacy and Reform," 166.

[157] Marsilius of Padua (trans. William Marshall), *The defence of peace: lately translated out of laten in to englysshe* (London, 1535; STC 17817), 6r. On Cromwell's intentions for this text, see Underwood, "Thomas Cromwell and William Marshall's Protestant Books," 522. Marshall's translation of Marsilius for Cromwell took a rather different view of church polity than did his translation of Luther several years later.

[158] *The defence of peace*, 83r. The origins of clerical hierarchy and "preemynence" were "not made immedyatly by god but by the wyll and mynde of men, lykewyse as other offyces of a commune weale be" (41v).

[159] *The Institution of a Christen Man* (London, 1537; STC 5163), 48v.

great apostle Paul describing himself as "equall in authoritie with" apostles like James, Peter, and John.[160]

Arguments like these were intended to undercut papal claims to possess divinely ordained supremacy, but they did not necessarily lead – as they had for the evangelical authors discussed earlier in this chapter – to an attack on the idea of clerical hierarchy itself. In a June 1535 sermon published by the royal printer Thomas Berthelet, a conservative London cleric named Simon Matthew offered a range of arguments against Petrine supremacy and in favor of the equality of the apostles, but for him these claims did not imply the continuing equality of all clergy, but rather the jurisdictional independence of every bishop in his diocese from *Roman* interference.[161] Richard Taverner's 1536 translation of the Augsburg Confession, a text produced at "the commaundement of his Master the ryght honorable Mayster Thomas Cromwel," also criticized the lordship of bishops but insisted that this had no implications for the present-day structure of the church.[162] After stating that "Peter forbiddeth bysshops to be lordes, and emperours over the churche," the Confession immediately asserted that "it is nat entended by us to take away jurisdiction from the bysshops, but this one thinge is required of them, that they wolde suffre the gospell to be purely taught, and that they wolde release a fewe certeyne observations, whiche can not be observed without synne."[163]

Moreover, while the Henrician regime denied that clerical hierarchy existed among the apostles or the early church, it explicitly defended the later development of hierarchy within the church as legitimate and beneficial. According to *The defence of peace*, clerical hierarchy had been created to deal with practical problems that arose from the growth of the Christian Church.[164] After the death of the apostles, the numbers of Christian clergy were "notablye augmented and increased," so "to avoyde sclaundre and occasyon of offendynge any man, and to avoyde scisme and dyvysyon, the

---

[160] *A Necessary Doctrine and erudicion for any chrysten man, set furth by the kynges majestye of Englande* (London, 1543; STC 5176), h7v-h8r.

[161] Simon Matthew, *A Sermon made in the cathedrall churche of saynt Paule at London, the XXVII day of June, Anno. 1535 by Symon Matthewe* (London, 1535; STC 17656), c1r-c7v. Ethan Shagan has suggested that Matthew's views "might serve as a model for the ideal of a Henrician *via media*": Ethan H. Shagan, *Popular Politics and the English Reformation* (Cambridge, 2003), 46.

[162] Richard Taverner (trans.), *The confessyon of the fayth of the Germaynes exhibited to the most victorious Emperour Charles the v* (London, 1536; STC 908), a1r. On this text, see James H. Pragman, "The Augsburg Confession in the English Reformation: Richard Taverner's Contribution," *Sixteenth Century Journal* 11:3 (1980), 75–85.

[163] *The confessyon of the fayth of the Germaynes*, 34r.

[164] On this point, Marshall's translation of *Defensor Pacis* for Cromwell stood at odds with his 1536 translation of Luther, which vehemently denounced this development.

preestes chose one amonge them selves, whiche shulde dyrecte and ordre
the other, as touchynge to thee xercysynge of the ecclesiasticall offyce, or
servyce, and the dystrybutynge of the oblacyons, & the dysposynge &
orderynge of other thyngs in the most convenyent maner."[165] If these
matters were left up to every individual clergyman, "the good ordre &
servyce of the churches myght be troubled, by the reason of the dyverse
affeccions of men."[166] Hence, the clergy decided to elect one of their fellows
"to ordre and rule the other preests."[167] He alone took the title "bishop,"
since he "had the oversyght of the other preests," and the rest of the clergy
voluntarily took the name of "preest."[168] A similar process occurred among
the deacons, who elected an archdeacon "to ordre & rule the other deacons."[169] The text repeatedly stressed that those elected as archpriests and
archdeacons were thereby given no greater *priestly* or *diaconal* power, but
only "a certayne powre of a canonycall ordynacyon . . . to ordre & dyrecte or
rule other preests and deacons, and other offycers and mynystres."[170]

This positive account of the origins of clerical hierarchy in *The defence of
peace* was repeated almost verbatim in a 1534 defense of the Royal
Supremacy by Edward Fox, an evangelical closely involved in the king's
quest for an annulment, and the same sorts of claims were subsequently
made by the Bishops' Book in 1537 and the King's Book in 1543.[171] The
Bishop's Book claimed that there had been "diversitie, or difference amonge
the bishops" which "was devysed by the aunciente fathers of the prymitive
churche, for the conservation of good order, and unitie of the catholique
churche," a development that was – crucially – either authorized or permitted by princes.[172] Why had they altered the original equality of bishops?
Taking into account the expansion of early Christianity, by which a "great
and infinite multitude of christen menne so largely encreased throughe the
worlde," and looking to Old Testament models, the church fathers

> thought it expedient to make an ordre of degrees, to be amonge bysshops,
> and spiritual governours of the church, and so ordeined some to be
> patriarkes, some to be primates, some to be metropolitanes, some to be
> archbishops, some to be bishops. And to them dyd limite severally, not
> only their certayn dioceses or provinces, wherin they shuld exercise their
> power, & not excede the same: but also certayn boundes & limittes of their
> jurisdiction & power.[173]

---

[165] *The defence of peace*, 83r.   [166] *The defence of peace*, 83r.   [167] *The defence of peace*, 83r.
[168] *The defence of peace*, 83v.   [169] *The defence of peace*, 83v.   [170] *The defence of peace*, 83v.
[171] Edward Fox (trans. Henry Stafford), *The true dyfferens betwen the regall power and the Ecclesiasticall
power* (London, 1548; STC 11220), 26v-27r.
[172] *The Institution of a Christen Man*, 48v.   [173] *The Institution of a Christen Man*, 48v.

In the earliest church, for instance, groups of bishops would appoint and consecrate new bishops, but "the said fathers restrayned the said power" and granted it only to Metropolitans and Archbishops.[174] This hierarchy of offices and powers was not *iure divino* – it was not "prescribed or established in the gospel, or mencioned in any canonicall writings of thapostles, or testified by any ecclesiastical writer within thapostles tyme" – but it was a praiseworthy human development "to thentent that therby contencion, strife, variance, and scismes or division, shulde be avoyded, and the churche shulde be preserved in good order and concorde."[175]

If the polity of the church had human rather than divine origins, the argument went, then civil authorities like Henry VIII had the power to alter the government of the church to fit contemporary circumstances. While bishops and archdeacons had been elected by their fellow priests in the early church, *The defence of peace* went on to explain that this procedure was no longer appropriate at the present day.[176] The source of authority within the church evolved and changed over time. At first, Christ directly ruled and ordered the activities of the apostles, and continued to do so even after his ascension through direct revelations to the apostle Paul.[177] Later the apostles made decisions about the church "amonge them selves," appointing bishops and directing them to minister in particular places, and in some circumstances the "hole congregacion and multytude of the chrysten people" elected bishops.[178] But all of these loci of authority were predicated on the fact that kings and emperors at that time were not Christian.[179] The church became "perfyte" with the advent of Christian magistrates and the authority to appoint, deprive, and instruct bishops fell to the "cheyfe hyghest governour."[180] In case there were any confusion about who this might be in Tudor England, a marginal note explained that this meant "it is graunted to our most gracyous sorayne lorde the kynge by acte of parlyament," but since it would be "to[o] moche & tedyous for the kyngs grace to be troubled his owne persone with the eleccion of every symple preeste," the king could entrust this to his officers, while still retaining full authority in this area.[181] The King's Book likewise depicted clerical hierarchy as lawful and just, but only if it had been authorized by the Christian prince. It was the king's duty to appoint the officers of the church, to ensure that they did their jobs properly, to chastise them if they failed, and to remove them if necessary.[182]

---

[174] *The Institution of a Christen Man*, 49r.   [175] *The Institution of a Christen Man*, 49r.

[176] For one thing, as Marshall explained in a marginal gloss, there was "a great doubte" that the contemporary clergy were "all of the apostles complexcion." *The defence of peace*, 91v.

[177] *The defence of peace*, 90r.   [178] *The defence of peace*, 90v.   [179] *The defence of peace*, 92r.

[180] *The defence of peace*, 92r.   [181] *The defence of peace*, 91v.   [182] *A necessary doctrine*, d7v, i3v-i4v.

The problem with papal supremacy was not the existence of an ecclesiastical hierarchy of offices, but the *iure divino* claims that underwrote that hierarchy's authority. If a bishop exercised authority over another bishop that was *not* "gyven to hym by suche consente and ordynaunce of men," then it was unlawful and "playne usurpacion and tyrannye."[183] While previously the Bishop of Rome had exercised jurisdiction in England "by princis sufferance onely," he could have this jurisdiction taken away from him by the king, just like the king could remove one of his officers "from his rome and office, and committe it to an other."[184]

In arguing against the papacy's spiritual jurisdiction, these official and quasi-official texts wielded Scripture to undercut the pope's claim to possess authority *iure divino*, but turned to history and grants of human authority to establish clerical hierarchy as a legitimate human development. The authority of diocesans and archdiocesans was thus salvaged by placing it on a new footing of royal authority. A similar sort of move can be seen in the regime's attack on the papacy's claim to possess temporal jurisdiction in the world, which again was superficially similar to the radical evangelical arguments considered above regarding the civil engagements of the clergy, but predicated on very different assumptions. *The defence of peace*, for instance, vehemently argued that Christ forbade "his apostles and dyscyples, & consequently the successours of them, bysshoppes or preestes, from all domynyon, or worldly governaunce of this sorte, that is to wytte coactyve [i.e., coercive]."[185] The same claim was made in the Bishops' Book, which pronounced that Christ "dyd by expresse wordes prohybite, that none of his apostels, or any of their successours, shulde under the pretense of the auctoritie gyven unto theym by Christe, take upon them thauctoritie of the swerde, that is to say, the auctoritie of kynges, or of any civyle power in this worlde. yea or any auctoritie to make lawes or ordynances, in causes appertainynge unto civile powers."[186] While arguments like this undercut papal claims to exercise temporal authority, they were – as we have seen – potentially revolutionary, given that the upper clergy were deeply enmeshed in the temporal governance of Tudor England. Bishops were Lords, sat in Parliament, served in high royal office and on the Privy Council, and participated in local governance as magnates in their dioceses. To deny that clergy could participate in "worldly governaunce" entirely – as Tyndale, Barnes, and Revel had done – was revolutionary, and neither *The defence of peace* nor the Bishops' Book pushed the argument to this conclusion.

---

[183] *A necessary doctrine*, h7v. [184] *A necessary doctrine*, i5v. [185] *The defence of peace*, 50r.
[186] *The Institution of a Christen Man*, 49r.

The source of the clergy's powers was again the crucial issue. According to *The defence of peace*, clergy had no divinely ordained right to coercive or civil powers, but they could be properly *given* such powers by the king. Bishops possessed "Powre I say not coactyve of any man but onely so farforth as shalbe graunted concernynge this poynt, by the auctoryte of the kynge, to the person so elected."[187] Royal authority was the means "howe & by which meane coactyve jurysdyccions hath come to them [bishops] or to certayne of them."[188] This was very much the view advanced by Taverner's 1536 translation of the Augsburg Confession. The Confession decried the meddling of bishops in civil affairs and defined the power granted to bishops in terms of preaching, binding and loosing sin, and administering the sacraments. But while on one page it would proclaim that "the power of the churche & the civile power may not be mixed and confounded together," on the next it would qualify this claim by stating that "If byshops have any power of the swerde, that power have they nat as bysshoppes by the commaundement of the gospel, but by mannes lawe gyven to them of kynges, and emperours, to the civile ministration of theyr owne goodes."[189] Later the confession would claim that "If byshops have any other power or jurisdiction as in cognisauns of plee or in determinynge of certayne causes, as of matrimony or of tythes: they have it by mans lawe," and these civil powers could be reclaimed by the prince if or "when the ordinaries fayle to do theyr dueties."[190] In these Cromwellian texts, then, bishops could not claim to possess inherent civil jurisdiction, but they could legitimately exercise civil jurisdiction at the grant of the prince.

The Bishops' Book made this claim at greater length, defending the traditional role played by bishops in English politics and society. While the episcopal office had not been granted any inherent civil authority by Christ, "Trouthe hit is, that priestis and bishops may execute all suche temporal power and jurisdiction, as is committed unto them, by the ordinance and auctoritie of kinges or other civile powers, and by the consent of the people (as officers and minysters under the said kynges & powers) so longe as it shall please the said kinges and people to permitte and suffre them so to use and execute the same."[191] So while Christ "dyd never seke nor exercise any worldly kyngedome or domynion in this worlde, but rather refusynge and fleinge from the same," it was nevertheless legitimate for a bishop to exercise worldly dominion, just so long as

---

[187] *The defence of peace*, 83v.   [188] *The defence of peace*, 89v.
[189] *The confessyon of the fayth of the Germaynes*, 29r-v.
[190] *The confessyon of the fayth of the Germaynes*, 30v.   [191] *The Institution of a Christen Man*, 49r.

he did not "arrogate or presume upon hym any suche auctoritie, and woll pretende the auctoritie of the gospell for his defense therin."[192] Princes had given civil authority to the clergy from the early days of the church, when they gave "unto priestes and byshops further power and jurisdiction in certayne other temporall and civile matters, lyke as by the lawes, statutes, immunyties, privyledges, and grauntes of princis made in that behalfe, and by the uses also and customes of sondry realmes and regions, it dothe manyfestly appere."[193] Since this was merely a human grant, and not a divine right, princes could always "revoke and calle agayne into theyr owne handes, or other wyse to restrayne al the power and jurisdiction" that they or their forebears had given to the clergy.[194]

An expansive understanding of the prince's power to define the church's external forms underwrote these arguments about the legitimacy of clerical hierarchy and the clergy's social and political role. Indeed, from this perspective, there was virtually nothing about the church that the prince was not free to order as he saw fit. The Bishops' Book emphasized the extensive power that princes possessed to define and control the activities of the bishops, even their divinely appointed duties. In addition to their duties of preaching and administering the sacraments, Scripture granted bishops jurisdiction over three areas of the Church's public life: the excommunication of obstinate and unrepentant sinners, the admission or rejection of candidates for the ministry, and the creation of "rules or canons" for "the preservation of quietnes and decent order" in matters

> concernynge holydayes, fastynge dayes, the maner and ceremonies to be used in the mynystration of the sacramentis, the maner of syngynge the Psalmes and spyrytualle hymnes, as (saynte Paule calleth theym) the diversitie of degrees amonge the ministers, and the forme and maner of their ornamentes, and fynally concernyng suche other rites ceremonies and observaunces . . . used amonge the people, whan they shall be assembled together in the temple.[195]

But while Scripture granted priests and bishops these powers in "general wordes" the

> particular maner & forme is not expressely declared, determyned, or prescribed in scripture: but was, and is lefte to be declared frome tyme to tyme, and from age to age by certayne positive rules and ordynances, to be made by the ministers of the churche, with the consent of the people, before suche

[192] The Institution of a Christen Man, 49v.   [193] The Institution of a Christen Man, 46r.
[194] The Institution of a Christen Man, 46r.   [195] The Institution of a Christen Man, 44r.

tyme as prynces were christened. and after they were christened, with thauctoritie and consent of the said princis and their people.[196]

Just like the specific details of how, when, and where to preach or administer the sacraments were not spelled out in the New Testament, neither were the procedures and processes for excommunication, appointing clergy, or ordering public worship. These details were left to the determination of the church during the early period when they lived under "infidel princis, and before any pryncis were chrystened."[197] In this model, passages in the New Testament laying out rules in these areas were not perpetually binding. The apostle Paul, for instance, laid out rules for excommunication and worship to the Corinthians, and other canons were made by bishops and early church councils.[198] But things changed with the advent of Christian princes, who examined these rules and "consyderynge the same to tende to the furtherance of Christis religion, dyd not onely approve the sayde canons, then made by the churche: but dyd also enacte and make newe lawes of their owne, concernyng the good order of the churche."[199] So while bishops retained these powers in general outline, the specific ways in which they exercised them were now fully at the discretion of the prince, who might change them to best suit his realm. In this model, the New Testament was mute on most details and when it did speak, it contained temporary and localized rules.

In crucial respects, then, these central texts of the Henrician Reformation adopted a very different approach to ecclesiastical reform than did the evangelicals considered earlier in this chapter. The regime wielded a surgical knife – rather than a sledgehammer – against the late medieval English Church, cutting away papal authority but leaving its institutions and structures intact. Papal supremacy was denounced, but episcopal hierarchy was validated as a means of maintaining order and peace when authorized by the monarch. Papal claims to exercise temporal power were repudiated, but the role played by bishops in politics and civil society was reestablished with royal authorization. This was not only the position taken in the propaganda produced under Cromwell's direction and in official and quasi-official documents like the King's Book and the Bishops' Book. It was also, quite significantly, the view taken by England's most powerful evangelical: Thomas Cranmer. Archbishop Cranmer clearly did not reject the principle of clerical hierarchy, nor did he – as a former ambassador,

---

[196] *The Institution of a Christen Man*, 45r.   [197] *The Institution of a Christen Man*, 45v.
[198] *The Institution of a Christen Man*, 45v.   [199] *The Institution of a Christen Man*, 46r.

Privy Councilor, and active politician – reject the possibility of clergy serving in these civil capacities. Bishops, "beeyng called to the name of Lordes," could still be godly pastors of Christ's flock in Cranmer's estimation.[200] Befitting his archiepiscopal status, and surely with an eye to the possibilities inherent in his office for enacting reform in England, Cranmer was "the one Edwardian bishop to live in the style of the other noblemen on the Council, maintaining his four palaces and his military resources as the equal of any other magnate."[201] There was much about the traditional clerical estate that Cranmer rejected, not least celibacy, but he retained the threefold apostolic orders of bishops, priests, and deacons in his reformed *Ordinal* (1549), with each office differentiated by a different age requirement and distinct services of ordination.[202] His attempt to reform canon law under Edward VI culminated in the unsuccessful *Reformatio Legum Ecclesiasticarum*, a text that aimed to improve the pastoral ministry while retaining large swathes of existing canon law, diocesan episcopacy and the traditional diocesan hierarchy (though with the addition of parish elders), ecclesiastical courts and their traditional jurisdictions, and traditional forms of clerical patronage.[203] This churchmanship reflected a fundamental difference between Cranmer's thought and the radical evangelical views discussed in this chapter. As Diarmaid MacCulloch has discussed, Cranmer thought that the "apostolic Church was imperfect, incomplete" because it lacked a Christian magistrate to govern it.[204] When the earliest Christians created clergy, they were "casting round to create makeshift structures of authority," a flaw "which had only been remedied when the

---

[200] Thomas Cranmer, *An answer . . . unto a crafty and sophisticall cavillation devised by Stephen Gardiner* (London, 1551; STC 5991), 329. Indeed, Cranmer claimed that he and Gardiner were "so commonly . . . called byshoppes (you of Winchester, and I of Canterbury) that the moste parte of the people knowe not that your name is Gardyner, and myne Cranmer" (329).

[201] MacCulloch, *The Boy King*, 102–104. Felicity Heal, while noting Cranmer's conservative views, also highlights the political concerns influencing Cranmer's archepiscopal style: "it is hardly surprising to find that even convinced Protestants such as Cranmer and Ridley felt it necessary to provide as large a household as possible and to retain the trappings of wealth and power. The enforcement of the Reformation was a complex task, and the prelates needed all the strength they could command to undertake it. In Tudor society strength and authority sprang partly from the display of wealth; since the bishops had had much of their natural spiritual authority undermined by the actions of the crown, they needed to husband their surviving image of power more carefully than even before." Felicity Heal, *Of Prelates and Princes: A Study of the Economic and Social Position of the Tudor Episcopate* (Cambridge, 1980), 167.

[202] Bray (ed.), *Documents of the English Reformation*, 277–278; MacCulloch, *Thomas Cranmer*, 460–461.

[203] See Gerald Bray (trans. and ed.), *Tudor Church Reform: The Henrician Canons of 1535 and the Reformatio Legum Ecclesiasticarum* (Woodbridge, 2000); James C. Spalding, "The Reformatio Legum Ecclesiasticarum of 1552 and the Furthering of Discipline in England," *Church History* 39:2 (June 1970), 162–171; MacCulloch, *Thomas Cranmer*, 500–501, 533–534.

[204] MacCulloch, *Thomas Cranmer*, 280.

first Christian rulers appeared."[205] It was the authority of the Christian magistrate, rather than Scripture or apostolic practice, that was to determine the external forms of the church.

When these views are placed alongside the radical evangelical arguments discussed in the first part of this chapter, therefore, we see at least two extremely significant ideological disagreements forming in the earliest years of the English Reformation. First, there was a basic disagreement about who or what ought to define the church's external order. "English Reformers" did *not* agree "that a definitive form of polity could not have been laid down in the New Testament for all time because the Church's circumstances change from age to age."[206] Repeatedly treating Scripture as providing normative rules for the church's structure, Tyndale treated the polity of the apostolic church as a matter of "folowing & obeying the rule doctrine & commaundment of oure saviour Jesus Christ their master," while Barnes described the bishop of more than one city as violating the "lawe off God." Marshall's translation of Luther presented its arguments for the equal authority of all bishops as the teaching of the Holy Ghost that will "contynue fyrme, stable, and not able to be moved or stered of the gates of hel," while Revel's translation of Lambert consistently presented its church order as a matter of zealously executing the "Word of God," a document that Christians should treat like Christ's last will and testament. By contrast, the officially sponsored texts we have examined did not treat the New Testament as providing binding rules for the governance and practice of the Christian Churches. These were not matters of doctrine or divine command, but indifferent matters that pertained purely to external order, which God had left up to the best judgment of *human* authorities – first the apostles, then the church, and finally (and most perfectly) to Christian magistrates and princes. These were dramatically different ways of approaching the issue of the church's external order, and they would be the source of enormous conflict between English Protestants in the sixteenth and seventeenth centuries. Second, and following from this first disagreement, there were significantly different perceptions in the 1520s and 1530s of what exactly had been wrong with the pre-Reformation English church. To put it another way, we can see very different sorts of anti-popery in the early years of the English Reformation. To the Henrician regime and to evangelicals like Cranmer, it was specifically the pope and papal authority that had corrupted the institutional church. Once papal authority was

---

[205] MacCulloch, *Thomas Cranmer*, 278–279.
[206] Avis, *The Church in the Theology of the Reformers*, 116.

abolished and the church was properly subjected to royal authority, its existing institutions and structures could begin to function properly again. Bishops would govern their dioceses as royal agents, not agents of a foreign ruler; church courts would regulate English life in ways that were congruent with English law, not contrary to it. This was not the view of the late medieval church taken by evangelicals like Tyndale or Revel, for whom the malignancy of popery was not limited to the pope himself or the authority that the papacy had wielded over the English church and people. To these evangelicals, the very laws, offices, ceremonies, and structures of the church were perverted, in some cases even before the rise of the papacy. If there was to be a true break with Rome – indeed, if there was to be a reformation at all – a clean sweep was necessary.

With the passage of the conservative Six Articles in 1539 and the fall of Cromwell in 1540, the prospects for evangelical reform in England dimmed. They were not entirely extinguished, however, as Alec Ryrie has reminded us, and many evangelicals in England continued to pursue reform in non-confrontational, conciliatory ways during the early 1540s.[207] But other evangelicals chose to confront the regime openly, typically from the relative safety of continental exile, by exhaustively cataloging and denouncing a host of "popish" ceremonies, doctrines, practices, and laws that remained within the Henrician Church.[208] Anticipating Anthony Gilby's later lament that there was "no reformation, but a deformation in the tyme of that tyrant and lecherous monster," these evangelicals were convinced that the Henrician reformation was a sham.[209] In their writings, the ideological tensions we have seen forming in the late 1520s and 1530s over authority and the nature of popery erupted into open disagreement, as militant evangelicals like Henry Brinkelow, John Bale, and William Turner criticized not only the popish elements remaining within the Church of England but also the *way* that these popish practices, laws, and institutions had been legitimated as matters of royal "policy." In doing so, they were attacking not only the principle that was at the heart of Henry VIII's religious policy, but also a principle that many of their fellow evangelicals accepted: the power of the prince to determine the use of "things indifferent."[210]

---

[207] Ryrie, *The Gospel and Henry VIII*.

[208] For a particularly exhaustive list of the "Popes doctrine & traditiones" remaining in the Church of England, see William Turner, *The huntyng & fyndyng out of the Romishe fox* (Bonn, 1543; STC 24353), a6v-b5r.

[209] For Gilby's denunciation of the Henrician reformation, see his admonition in John Knox, *The Appellation of John Knox* (Geneva, 1558; STC 15063), 69v.

[210] On the centrality of this principle for the religious politics of the early 1540s, see especially Shagan, *The Rule of Moderation*, 73–110.

In *The complaynt of Roderyck Mors* (1542), for instance, the London evangelical Henry Brinkelow argued that "the pope remayneth wholly styll in Ingland," because although the pope's name had been banished, his body (bishops) and his tail ("his filthy tradicyons, wicked lawys, and beggarly ceremonyes . . . yea and the whole body of his pestiferos canon lawe") remained.[211] Probably referring to the 1539 proclamation "concernynge rites and ceremonies to be used in due fourme in the Churche of Englande," in which the king had authorized the continued usage of a variety of traditional ceremonies and customs, Brinkelow explained that the bishops had managed to maintain this "popedome" by causing "a proclamacyon to be set out in the kyngs name, that from hense forth the ceremonyes of the church, that were of the popys makyng, shuld no more be taken for the popys ceremonys, but the kyngs, and so thei made the kyng father to the popys childern."[212] According to Brinkelow, this was utterly ineffectual, since redescribing or reauthorizing these ceremonies as the king's did nothing to transform their inherently popish nature. Indeed, Brinkelow argued that England's bondage to false religion had actually *increased* over the past decade, because although the name of the pope had been banned, with laws like these "the popes condicyon is not put away, but it is ii. partes gretter than ever it was."[213]

John Bale expressed similar complaints in his vituperative and bitter writings from exile during the 1540s. In *Yet a course at the Romyshe foxe* (1543), Bale claimed that the pope had been "admytted ageyne unto hys olde seate" through the craft of papists, since the English continued to use the pope's laws: "what other is it to be sworne to hys pilde lawes, but to acknowlege him inwardlye for ther master and lorde? Non canne ryghtlye allowe hys wares, unlesse they allowe hym also. He and hys creaturs must nedes go togyther, as the worke manne with his worke toles."[214] Like Brinkelow, Bale complained about how the pope's law had been retained through creative yet ineffectual redescription. Writing against the Six Articles in 1544, Bale complained that the bishops had ensured that the pope's ceremonies, traditions, and laws were being treated as "laudable, convenient, and comelye, precyouse, fyt, and necessary to by styll admitted for the spirituall lawes of the churche of Englande and for the true

---

[211] Henry Brinkelow, *The complaynt of Roderyck Mors, somtyme a gray fryre, unto the parliament howse of Ingland his natural cuntry* (Strassburg, 1542; STC 3759.5), f7r.

[212] Henry VIII, *A proclamation, concernynge rites and ceremonies* (London, 1539; STC 7791); Brinkelow, *The complaynt of Roderyck Mors*, d6r-v.

[213] Brinkelow, *The complaynt of Roderyck Mors*, e1r.

[214] John Bale, *Yet a course at the Romyshe foxe* (Antwerp, 1543; STC 1309), 10r-v.

worshyppynges of God therin."[215] By convincing the king to keep these things, they caused him "to honoure your Pope a fresshe, what though his name be abolysshed with a fewe yearlye pollages besydes."[216] In his influential commentary on Revelation, *The Image Of bothe churches*, Bale discussed more directly the method the papists had used to retain popery within the Church of England, in spite of the king's seeming abolition of papal authority. While

> some notable governours hath gotten victoryouslye of them, the primacye of their owne realmes, to be the supreme, hyghest, and immediate heades of there clergye here in earth under God (which is awondre) yet are they scarse able to put asyde one corrupt custome or dyrtye ceremonye of theirs. But all their devylyshnesse must nedes stande styll under the couloure of laudable rites, decent usages, and politique orders.[217]

As a result, Bale made the ironic claim that England had indeed experienced a successful reformation – that is to say, popery had been re-formed under the guise of politic laws: "have they not now a newe refourmed church, in whom the beastes wounded head is newly restored? So longe as it is lyke the popes churche, it must folowe his rewles, and cleave to his ordinaunces."[218]

Interestingly, Bale identified several features of Henrician episcopacy as ways in which popery remained untouched in the Church of England. In his *Epistle exhortatorye* of 1544, Bale lashed out against the bishops, but stressed that he was not aiming to condemn "godlye" bishops who preached, cared for the poor, and administered the sacraments "ryghte."[219] While this presumably exempted Archbishop Cranmer, Bale nevertheless denounced central elements of episcopacy as practiced in Henrician England. The apostles never had the "hygh auctoritie as you be in now," nor did they have "anye soche prehemynence of prelacye as to be called my lorde busshopp, my lorde deane, master doctour, or mastre persone with cappe and knee."[220] In the *Image Of both churches*, Bale identified the titles of the papal Church's officers as blasphemies against God: "What other els is Pope, Cardinal, Patriarke, Legate, Metropolytane, Primate, Archbysshoppe, Diocesane, Prothonotarye, Archedeakon, Offycial, Chaunceller, Commissarie, Deane, Prebende, Person, vicar, my Lorde Abbot, master doctor, & such lyke, but very names of

[215] John Bale, *The epistle exhortatorye of an Englyshe Christyane unto his derelye beloved contreye of Englande against the pompouse popyshe Bysshoppes therof* (Antwerp, 1544?; STC 1291a), 7r.
[216] Bale, *The epistle exhortatorye*, 7v.   [217] Bale, *The Image Of bothe churches*, r8v; also see Oo4r-v.
[218] Bale, *The Image*, i[1]4v.
[219] Bale, *The epistle exhortatorye*, 27r; elsewhere in the text, Bale denounced the bishops "a verye fewe excepted" as blood thirsty tyrants (9r).
[220] Bale, *The epistle exhortatorye*, 22r-v.

blasphemie?"[221] While Bale praised a handful of English bishops for rejecting the Beast, he did not hope for more evangelicals on the episcopal bench, at least as the office was currently defined.[222] Indeed, Bale praised Hugh Latimer and Nicholas Shaxton for resigning their bishoprics in the wake of the Six Articles and hoped that others would join them. God had moved "Godlye men … to rendre up her blasphemouse kingdome (whom somtyme of ignoraunce they usurped) unto the malygnaunt beast againe, as the hornes of his pestylent heades. After this sorth dyd good Latimer and Shaxton geve over their bishopryckes, and so hath diverse other godlye men their promocions and lyvynges, as manye more yet here after wyll do."[223]

While Brinklow and Bale expressed criticism of specific aspects of the Church of England that had been retained under the auspices of "politic laws," the evangelical botanist and exile William Turner went even further to denounce the entire *concept* of "politic laws" within the church. In *The huntyng & fyndyng out of the Romishe fox* (1543), a text that bears numerous similarities to Brinkelow's earlier book, Turner argued that all papal ceremonies and canon law must be abolished. Turner's book – which together with *The Rescuynge of the Romishe Fox* (1545) and *The Huntyng of the Romyshe Wolfe* (1555) formed a sort of zoological anti-papal trilogy – was predicated on the notion that the pope had remained in England despite Henry VIII's best efforts to banish him. The Romish fox had achieved this trick by hiding underneath the "tame bestes skinnes" of canon law and religious ceremonies, which had been redefined in England as "the law of the chirche of Englond" and as "the kynges ceremonies."[224] Like Brinkelow, Turner complained about how the clergy insisted that Henry's subjects refer to canon law and ceremonies as "the kynges ceremonies & ordinances." Turner thought that this was a useless subterfuge: canon law and traditional ceremonies would *always* be popish, no matter what they were called or by whom they were authorized. Turner deployed a series of analogies to make this point: if the king of France proclaimed that the acts of Alexander the Conqueror were henceforth to be called Francis's acts, would such a proclamation make it so? "I thynk no." Could the king of Portugal make the works of Plato and Aristotle his own by proclaiming them such? "I thynk nay." More to the point, Turner asked whether the king of Denmark could declare that Moses's ceremonies and burned offerings were his own and no longer Moses's. "[S]huld not Moses ceremonies

---

[221] Bale, *The Image*, g[1]1v-2r.
[222] Bale named Cranmer, Goodrick, Barlow, Bird, Thirlby, Latimer, and Shaxton.
[223] Bale, *The Image*, t[1]1r.   [224] Turner, *The huntyng and fynding out of the Romishe fox*, b5r-b6r.

continue Moses ceremonies still for all the proclamation? I think so." In sum, Turner claimed, "Then is theyr no proclamation that can disposses the the [sic] pope of hys ceremonies and constitutiones but the ceremonies & ordinances whiche was hys xii yere ago shall be hys ceremonies and ordinances still thoge a thousand proclamationes shuld command the contrari."[225]

Given this state of affairs, Turner demanded that Henry VIII purge England completely of anything tainted by popery, restoring the church to its primitive state. Henry VIII should completely abolish the canon law, since "Christen men nede no other law (as touchyng theyr soules) but the law of the gospel."[226] This was a striking proposition, made all the more striking in Turner's writings by his explicit insistence that even *profitable* elements within the canon law must be abandoned. This was a biblical approach, according to Turner, since God commanded the Israelites to abandon even the good customs of Egypt and Canaan: even "in theyr most lawful wayes shall ye not walk."[227] To Turner, all of this proved that "thoge the ordinances of the pope had ben lawful, that ye ought not to have holden them."[228] The king and his deputies "ought to have sweped the chirch & dryven quite out of it all that ever any pope had made."[229] Turner elaborated this position in *The Rescuynge of the Romishe Fox* (1545), in which portions of Bishop Stephen Gardiner's critique of Turner's 1543 text were reprinted alongside a refutation.[230] Gardiner had ridiculed Turner's arguments, rejecting the notion that association with the papacy irrevocably tainted doctrine, customs, or laws when he wrote that "the fundacion of thys mannis resonyng to reprove or reject any ordinance becaus our enemy ether made it or used it, is very slender and folishe . . . that, that is good is good who soever hathe abused it."[231] One had to evaluate how far a thing

---

[225] Turner, *The huntyng and fynding out of the Romishe fox*, b8r.

[226] Turner, *The huntyng and fynding out of the Romishe fox*, c2v.

[227] Turner, *The huntyng and fynding out of the Romishe fox*, c2v.

[228] Turner, *The huntyng and fynding out of the Romishe fox*, c3r. Compare with the position outlined in Richard Taverner's translation of Erasmus Sarcerius' *Commonplaces*, which argued that it was erroneous "To cast forth of the church al humane tracicions [sic], yea & those also whiche be not repungnaunt to the word": Erasmus Sarcerius (trans. Richard Taverner), *Commonplaces of scripture* (London, 1538; STC 21752.5), 176r-v.

[229] Turner, *The huntyng and fynding out of the Romishe fox*, c2v. Statements like these call into question Bernard Verkamp's insistence that Turner's strong emphasis on the sufficiency of Scripture did not make him a "biblical reductionist." Bernard Verkamp, *The Indifferent Mean: Adiaphorism in the English Reformation to 1554* (Athens, OH, 1977), 68.

[230] Gardiner's response to Turner was *The examination of a prowd praesumptuous hunter*, but this text has not survived. See Rainer Pineas, "William Turner's Polemical Use of Ecclesiastical History and His Controversy with Stephen Gardiner," *Renaissance Quarterly* 33:4 (Winter 1980), 605.

[231] William Turner, *The Rescuynge of the Romishe Fox* (Bonn, 1545; STC 24355), c7v-8r.

departed from the truth in order to accept or reject it; guilt by association was out of bounds. Turner's position, according to Gardiner, would unnecessarily "destroy withe the bad the good also" and throw away "that whiche was good and that whiche was evel also."[232] While this was absurd to Gardiner, it was exactly what Turner envisioned. When God sent the people of Israel into Canaan, he instructed them to depose the Canaanite kings and "to dryve and put away with them, all theyr lawes ceremonies and traditiones even them that were laufull, were they never so profitable or pleasant for the comon welth."[233] The Canaanites surely had "sum good politike lawes, and sum profitable and pleasant for a comon welthe," but God nevertheless demanded that they be rejected, and God's law alone followed.[234] The ultimate example of this was King Saul, who was commanded by God to kill all of the Amalekites and their animals, including women and children. All of God's creation is good, especially animals, women, and young children, "and yit god commanded them not only to be expelled withe the tyran[t] [A]gag, but also to be destroyed and kylled withe hyme."[235] Saul intended to honor God by saving the best animals for sacrifices, but good intentions were far less important than obedience, and God rejected Saul as king for his disobedience.

What lay at the heart of Turner's reform agenda was the idea that *nothing* apart from the gospel could provide the order for the Church. Turner again accused Gardiner of attempting to cloak papal laws and ceremonies under the title of "the kyngis polytike lawes."[236] Politic laws – "an ordinance devised by wise men for the profit of a citie or a cuntre" – were good and necessary in the commonwealth, but not in the church, which needs "the worde of god alone."[237] When Gardiner contemptuously accused Turner of wanting "no law but the gospel" – a stance Gardiner considered "so far out of reson, that i will not reson withe hym in it" – Turner agreed that this was precisely what he wanted.[238] If Moses' law was sufficient for the people of Israel, "then is the law of the gospel miche more sufficient by it self for all them that ar under it, and miche less nedethe any mannis ordinances to be added unto it to ordre them that ar under the new Testament."[239] Bringing together two words that

[232] Turner, *The Rescuynge of the Romishe Fox*, d8r, e2v.
[233] Turner, *The Rescuynge of the Romishe Fox*, e3v.
[234] Turner, *The Rescuynge of the Romishe Fox*, e3v.
[235] Turner, *The Rescuynge of the Romishe Fox*, e4r.
[236] Turner, *The Rescuynge of the Romishe Fox*, b2r.
[237] Turner, *The Rescuynge of the Romishe Fox*, b2v, b4v.
[238] Turner, *The Rescuynge of the Romishe Fox*, e5v.
[239] Turner, *The Rescuynge of the Romishe Fox*, e7r-v.

Protestants tended to separate – law and gospel – Turner claimed that the gospel was the perfect law made by the perfect lawmaker, and it "alone is sufficiend bi it self to order the chirche," "conteneth all thyng in it that is necessari for the chirche of Christe," and therefore "only the law of the gospell shuld be in the chirche."[240] Ultimately, then, Turner's critique of popery-turned-policy went further than either Brinkelow's or Bale's. Turner was not simply criticizing the way in which certain popish elements had been retained under the guise of royal policy, but arguing that royal policy should play no role in ordering the structures, institutions, and practices of the true church. Scripture was so complete in its instructions that it left nothing to the discretion of princes.

The radical views of church government discussed in this chapter would not be a constant throughout the subsequent history of the English Reformation. In 1547, the Henrician exiles returned to England to lend their hands to the reformation unleashed by the accession of Edward VI and orchestrated by Archbishop Cranmer. Former exiles like John Hooper – "whose radicalism," Catharine Davies has noted, "might have led him to attack episcopacy" – instead accepted preferment to the church's highest offices and sought to use episcopal office to further the cause of reformation.[241] John Bale provides a perfect example of this dynamic. A fierce and pessimistic critic of the English Reformation from exile in the 1540s, Bale accepted the Bishopric of Ossory in the very different circumstances of 1552 and embarked on an energetic, if short-lived, episcopal reign in Ireland. Political context – and varying evangelical perceptions of that context and its possibilities – played an important role in shaping reformers' attitudes toward the church's structure and government.

Edwardian evangelicals remained troubled by many aspects of traditional diocesan episcopacy, yet rather than proposing its abolition or radical transformation, they sought to revivify it with the spirit of the "apostolic bishop." As Patrick Collinson has shown, there "was wide agreement in the mid-sixteenth century, not merely among Protestants, but on both sides of the great divide" between Protestants and Catholics about the qualities of the good bishop.[242] The true bishop was to be primarily a preacher and a pastor. Bale explained in an autobiographical

---

[240] Turner, *The Rescuynge of the Romishe Fox*, e7v-8r. For a similar view, see Tristram Revel's preface to *The summe of christianitie*, +3v-+4v.
[241] Davies, *A religion of the Word*, 104.   [242] Collinson, "Episcopacy and Reform," 162.

account of his time as Bishop of Ossory that "the office of a Christen byshop, is not to loyter in blasphemouse papistrie, but purely to preache the Gospell of God, to his christened flocke," a theme that can be found throughout Edwardian evangelical writings on episcopacy.[243] The bishop was also, however, an administrator and a superintendent of other clergy. He was to carry himself "as a true father in God, not like a lord or a secular judge," an ideal expressed by Bale when he explained that he assumed episcopal office "against my wille" and that he did not "rejoyce so muche in the dignite therof, as in doinge for the time, the office therunto belonginge."[244] While evangelicals might declare that the true bishop had no time for political affairs, Catharine Davies has shown how even the most radical Edwardian evangelicals saw godly bishops as potent political actors. Robert Crowley "did not appear to disapprove of bishops serving as royal advisors so long as they remained uncorrupted by the desire for worldly advancement and power," and Bishop Hooper played an active role in the House of Lords and as a preacher at court.[245] With the Edwardian regime "engaged in a revolution on the march," former exiles like Bale, Hooper, and Miles Coverdale accepted episcopal office and aimed to infuse the largely unreformed structures of the Church with evangelical vigor, although, as Felicity Heal has noted, "Coverdale and Hooper still remained exceptions among the Edwardian prelates in adopting a way of life fundamentally different from that of their Catholic predecessors."[246]

After the wilderness years of Mary's reign, the ideal of the apostolic bishop or godly superintendent would again inspire another group of Protestant exiles to assume episcopal office at Elizabeth's accession. Thwarted by the queen, however, the "progressive bishops" would fail to achieve further reformation in the 1560s and the role that the bishops were forced to play in enforcing conformity to the Elizabethan Settlement would result in a new round of calls to abolish episcopacy in the 1570s. The presbyterian platform is well known.[247] Inspired by the teachings of Theodore Beza and the example of the Genevan church, the

---

[243] John Bale, *The vocacyon of Johan Bale to the bishoprick of Ossorie in Irelande* (Wesel?, 1553; STC 1307), 2r; Davies, *A religion of the Word*, 103–104.

[244] Collinson, "Episcopacy and Reform," 163; Bale, *The vocacyon*, 4r.

[245] Davies, *A religion of the Word*, 105–106.

[246] MacCulloch, *The Boy King*, 196; Heal, *Of Prelates and Princes*, 167. On Hooper and Coverdale's efforts "to live the life of a reformed supervisor," see Heal, *Of Prelates and Princes*, 166.

[247] Key presbyterian texts include John Field and Thomas Wilcox, *An Admonition to the Parliament* (Hemel Hempstead?, 1572; STC 10848); Anon., *A Second Admonition to the Parliament* (Hemel Hempstead?, 1572; STC 4713); Travers, *A full and plaine declaration*. On presbyterianism, see

English presbyterians denounced clerical hierarchy and lordship, diocesan episcopacy, the clergy's civil occupations, and the continuance of canon law and medieval ecclesiastical courts. They proposed instead the creation of a fourfold ministry of congregationally elected pastors, doctors, lay elders, and deacons; ministerial parity and congregational autonomy; the sharp exercise of discipline in the congregation by the pastor and elders; and the government of the church through an ascending series of synods and elected assemblies. In all of this, they insisted that the polity and discipline of the church were matters of doctrine and scriptural prescription, rather than things left to the magistrate's discretion. This was an extraordinarily radical plan for reformation and one that was rejected even by many of the hotter sort of Elizabethan Protestants, for whom the ideal of the apostolic bishop remained powerful. Especially with the accession of Grindal to Canterbury in 1575 – "an archbishop for thoroughgoing protestants" – the godly hoped that bishops could again serve as agents of progressive reform in the Elizabethan Church, but Grindal's fall and the accession of John Whitgift to Canterbury would again spur presbyterian activism.[248]

The radical reforms sought by the presbyterians from the 1570s onward are typically seen as part of "a new dogma," one that was not only the product of foreign influences but also "foreign to earlier protestant teaching."[249] The presbyterian platform did have limited appeal in Elizabethan England and there was much about it that was new and unprecedented in the history of English Protestantism. There was neither a straight nor an inevitable line connecting the ecclesiology of Henrician radicals in the 1530s with Elizabethan radicals in the 1570s: political context and perceptions of the Reformation's fortunes played a major role in bringing certain concerns to the fore and in shaping Protestant thought about the church. But the revolutionary visions of a reformed church that this chapter reveals within early English evangelicalism force us to see the presbyterians of Elizabeth's reign in a new light. The presbyterians were not the first English Protestants to call for an end to diocesan episcopacy and ecclesiastical courts, or to demand the equality of ministers and the complete withdrawal of the clergy from secular affairs. Nor were they the first to reject the notion that these

---

Donald Joseph McGinn, *The Admonition Controversy* (New Brunswick, NJ, 1949); Collinson, *Elizabethan Puritan Movement*; Lake, *Anglicans and Puritans?*; Polly Ha, *English Presbyterianism, 1590–1640* (Stanford, CA, 2011).
[248] Collinson, *Elizabethan Puritan Movement*, 159.
[249] Collinson, *Elizabethan Puritan Movement*, 101; Collinson, "Episcopacy and Reform," 161.

issues were "things indifferent" or to argue that the church's government was a matter of strict Scriptural prescription. Walter Travers and other presbyterians seem to have been unaware of this in 1574, but – as we will see in this book's concluding chapter – they would soon discover it to their great delight.

CHAPTER 2

Not peace but a sword

From the very beginning, the Reformation produced division and conflict among the English people. As Geoffrey Elton summed it up, "it is plain that the first decade of the English Reformation produced enough matter 'to set men by the ears' – enough arguments, accusations, scurrility, conviction, abuse and unsettlement to guarantee every possibility of unrest and disturbance in a country always hard to control and impossible to police efficiently."[1] The coming of the Reformation did not, of course, disturb a kingdom that was hitherto peaceful and merry. As Eamon Duffy has pointed out, the important place of peacemaking rituals in late medieval liturgies was "as much a testimony to the fragility of those blessings in the communities of late medieval England as they are to their presence."[2] Yet the theological conflicts produced by the Reformation added to and became intertwined with the existing conflicts that divided the people of early modern England. Not limited to the rarefied air of the university faculties or sniping among the religious orders, religious division and debate quickly became a feature of daily life in towns and villages across Henrician England, where the grand theological controversies of the day took on flesh in interpersonal conflicts between clergy and laity alike.[3] As two leading scholars of the English Reformation have written, English Protestantism "could not convert the nation; but it could, and did, permanently divide it."[4]

---

[1] G. R. Elton, *Policy and Police: The Enforcement of the Reformation in the Age of Thomas Cromwell* (Cambridge, 1972), 44.

[2] Duffy, *The Stripping of the Altars*, 126. Also see David Aers's pointed comments on this subject in "Altars of Power: Reflections on Eamon Duffy's *The Stripping of the Altars: Traditional Religion in England, 1400–1580*," *Literature and History* 3 (1994), 101–102.

[3] Elton, *Policy and Police*, chs. 1, 3; Duffy, *The Stripping of the Altars*, chs. 11–13; Haigh, *English Reformations*, ch. 8; Shagan, *Popular Politics*, esp. ch. 6.

[4] Peter Marshall and Alec Ryrie, "Protestantisms and their beginnings," in Marshall and Ryrie (eds.), *The Beginnings of English Protestantism*, 13. Also see Ryrie, "Counting sheep, counting shepherds: the problem of allegiance in the English Reformation," in Marshall and Ryrie (eds.), *The Beginnings of English Protestantism*, 109–110.

The divisions engendered by the English Reformation had painful consequences for families and communities across England, as people lamented the fact that kin and friends were mired in damnable heresy, but to the men and women of Tudor England, religious division was *in itself* a distressing and dangerous state of affairs. Religious unity was widely seen as absolutely essential, not only for the maintenance of political unity and social peace, but because religious division was an affront to God that would bring judgment upon the realm and its people.[5] Conrad Russell noted that commitment to religious unity was such an important component of Tudor-Stuart thought that people rarely felt the need to explain or defend its importance: it was simply "too automatic to be easily made matter for debate." It was obvious to contemporaries that "devotion to Christianity must necessarily involve a devotion to unity" and that "[c]ontention was one of the fruits of the flesh, not of the Spirit."[6] Making the same point in a different way, John Bossy has paraphrased Richard Baxter, writing that "the trouble with talking about peace and unity is that it is hard to find anybody who is against it."[7] For opponents of the reformation, therefore, the fact that it had produced such division and strife was especially damning proof of its demonic origins. How could a movement that claimed to be from God have such divisive effects? As William Barlow put it in *A dyaloge descrybyng the orygynall ground of these Lutheran faccyons* (1531), Christ "noryssheth no suche contencyous dyversyte: for he is the god of peace & not of dyssencion."[8]

Henry VIII wholeheartedly agreed, and his reformation aimed to eradicate religious division. As the king broke with Rome and began to exercise his supremacy over the new national church, the regime argued that the papacy was to blame for contention and strife in England and that the king's reformation would restore peace and unity to the realm. In *A Litel Treatise ageynst the mutterynge of some papistis in corners* (1534), published by the king's printer, the evangelical Thomas Swinnerton explained that before the

---

[5] On the deep commitment to religious unity across early modern Europe, see especially Brad S. Gregory, *Salvation at Stake: Christian Martyrdom in Early Modern Europe* (Cambridge, MA, 1999), ch. 3; Alexandra Walsham, *Charitable hatred: Tolerance and intolerance in England, 1500–1700* (Manchester, 2006), ch. 2. For powerful contemporary statements of the dangers of division, see John Lydgate, *This lyttell treatyse compendiously declareth the damage and Destruction in Realmes caused by the Serpente of Division* (London, 1535; STC 17027.5); Richard Morison, *A Remedy for Sedition* (London, 1536; STC 18113.7).

[6] Conrad Russell, "Arguments for Religious Unity in England, 1530–1650," *Journal of Ecclesiastical History* 18:2 (1967), 202.

[7] John Bossy, *Peace in the Post-Reformation* (Cambridge, 1998), 74.

[8] William Barlow, *A dyaloge descrybyng the orygynall ground of these Lutheran faccyons* (London, 1531; STC 1461), g2r.

papacy had become corrupted by wealth, "there was peace and unitie, that causedde great plentie in every place." After the papacy's corruption, this peace and unity was shattered as the popes sought to maintain their wealth and power: "Who be the occasion and styrrers uppe of warre and stryffe in Christendome, but the pope and papistis?"[9] The papacy was portrayed as a grand manipulator, dividing nations against each other and setting the clergy against the laity. As Swinnerton argued in another pamphlet, the papacy fomented divisions not only within and between the kingdoms of Europe but also within the church, as "there hath ben xxiii scismes in the churche, amonge the popes them selves."[10] By destroying the power of the papacy in England and restoring royal sovereignty, therefore, the Henrician reformation would restore peace and unity.[11] As a remedy to popish divi-siveness, Swinnerton promised that the break with Rome would bring the realm "from trowble and grevous vexacion to quietnesse and reste, and so finally to al the former welthy state," while Cromwell's evangelical agent Francis Bigod would praise Henry in 1535 for seeking the "quietnesse and unyte of this youre christen comen welth" and for pursuing religious reforms that had been "so hyghly to the gret peace, unyte, & welth of this most noble empyre of Englande."[12] The purportedly peaceful nature of the Henrician Reformation was even anthropomorphized in a fascinating 1538 pamphlet in which "Peace" recounted how he refused to dwell at the papal court and instead fled to England, where he gladly accepted Henry VIII's invitation to reside at the English court.[13]

The goal of establishing peace and unity was repeatedly proclaimed in the legislation creating and then regularly redefining the Henrician Church of England.[14] The Act of Supremacy (1534) made Henry head of the Church of England for "the conservation of the peace, unity and tranquility of this realm," while the Act of Ten Articles (1536), the first doctrinal statement of the Church of England, sought to produce "charitable unity and loving

---

[9] Thomas Swinnerton, *A Litel Treatise ageynste the mutterynge of some papistis in corners* (London, 1534; STC 23551.5), b6v–b7v; on this pamphlet, see Elton, *Policy and Police*, 183–185. Also see Lancelot Ridley, *An exposition in the epistell of Jude the apostel of Christ* (London, 1538; STC 21042), g8v.

[10] Thomas Swinnerton, *A mustre of scismatyke bysshoppes of Rome* (London, 1534; STC 23552), a6v.

[11] On Henry's attitude toward unity, see G. W. Bernard, *The King's Reformation: Henry VIII and the Remaking of the English Church* (New Haven, CT, and London, 2005), 475–476.

[12] Swinnerton, *A Litel Treatise*, b8v; Francis Bigod, *A treatise concernynge impropriations of benefices* (London, 1535?; STC 4240), a2v–a3r. On Bigod's career before he turned rebel in 1537, see *ODNB*.

[13] *A pretye complaynt of Peace that was banyshed out of dyvers countreys & brought by Welth in to England* (London, 1538; STC 5611), a3v–a4r, c2r.

[14] For an extensive theoretical statement of this position, see Thomas Starkey, *A preface to the Kynges hyghnes* (London, 1536; STC 23236). On the affinities between Starkey's vision and Henrician religious policy, see Shagan, *The Rule of Moderation*, 76, 84–85.

concord" and explained that it was the king's duty to see "that unity and concord in opinion, namely in such things as doth concern our religion, may increase and go forthward, and all occasion of dissent and discord touching the same be repressed and utterly extinguished."[15] The *Bishops' Book* (1537) aimed at "the perfite establyshyng of your said subjectes in good unitie and concord, and perfyte quietenes bothe in theyr sowles and bodyes," while the "Act Abolishing Diversity in Opinons" (1539) praised God as "the very author and fountain of all true unity and sincere concord," and laid out the Church of England's doctrinal stance for "the common quiet, unity and concord to be had in the whole body of this realm for ever."[16] It was the failure of his reformation to achieve these goals that fueled Henry VIII's tearful lament to Parliament on Christmas Eve 1545 that "charitie and concord is not amongest you, but discord and dissencion, beareth rule in every place . . . the one calleth the other, Hereticke and Anabaptist, and he calleth hym again Papist, Ypocrite, and Pharisey."[17]

While evangelicals hoped that Henry would be a powerful ally of the gospel in England, this chapter argues that they did not all necessarily share this view of the reformation and its proper consequences. For some evangelicals, the notion of a national church in which the English people would be peacefully united was not only an impossibility; it was antithetical to the way they envisioned life in a post-reformation world. Viewing the world as fundamentally divided into a godly minority and an anti-godly majority, and insisting that the proclamation of the gospel (in word and deed) would inevitably bring these groups into conflict with each other, these evangelicals articulated highly agonistic visions of the reformation and godly life. In the wake of the "rediscovery of the gospel," the creation of the national church would not enable religious peace, nor would a godly king bring about true religious unity. Instead, the church would be a battleground where godly ministers and laypeople would face ceaseless opposition from the ungodly, and the godly king would be a partisan figure in constant conflict with his ungodly subjects – possibly violent conflict. By tracing the various ways in which early English evangelicals expected that the English Reformation would bring not "peace, but a swearde," this chapter sheds light on highly militant ways in which early English evangelicals were envisioning the reformation, the national church, the monarch, and godly

---

[15] Bray (ed.), *Documents of the English Reformation*, 114, 163–164.
[16] *The Institution of a Christen Man*, a2r; Bray (ed.), *Documents*, 223–224.
[17] Edward Hall, *The union of the two noble and illustre famelies of Lancastre & Yorke* (London, 1548; STC 12722), 261r-v.

life. It also helps us understand better the early history of one of the most important tensions produced by the English Reformation: the problematic relationship between the self-styled "godly minority" and the kingdom as a whole.

In investigating evangelical attitudes regarding peace and unity, we must begin with a theme that runs throughout the history of Christianity, but one that was of particular significance for early English Protestants: the belief that persecution was inevitable. As we saw in the preceding chapter, persecution loomed large in the experience and thought of the earliest English evangelicals, "both for reasons of historical circumstance and of theology."[18] The earliest evangelicals faced the prospect of prosecution for heresy, imprisonment, humiliating public recantations, execution, and exile for their commitment to what they viewed as the "pure gospel." As they sought to make sense of all this, they embraced the doctrine of "the two churches," which depicted history as an ongoing battle between the fol-lowers of Christ and Antichrist and rendered persecution an inevitable part of life for true Christians. This was a constant theme in the writings of the earliest evangelical exiles like John Frith, William Tyndale, and Robert Barnes.[19] Immediately after he had fled prosecution for heresy at Oxford, for instance, Frith wrote in 1529 that Christ was persecuted by Herod from the very moment that he was born, that the apostles "were all persequuted, beten, presoned, and at the lengthe kild," and that therefore "impossible it is that the worde of the crosse shuld be with out affliction."[20] Persecution was the air that Christians breathed, and Frith argued that the apostles' succes-sors were only good Christians "when they were persequuted and mar-tyred, & no lenger."[21] Frith's friend Tyndale had argued in 1528 that persecution was not only inescapable, since "ther is no nother waye in to the kyngedome of lyfe, then thorow persecucion & soferinge of payne and of very deeth, after the ensample of Christe," but that it was therefore desirable as a confirmation that one was following the truth.[22] If you were persecuted for reading the Scripture, this was "an evidente token" that you were encountering "the true worde of God," since God's Word could never

[18] Bauckham, *Tudor Apocalypse*, 62.

[19] See Tyndale, *The obedience*, ff. 2–10; Barnes, *A supplicatyon*, 57r-v; Tyndale, *An answere unto Sir Thomas Mores dialogue*, 63r-67r; Tyndale, *The exposition of the fyrst epistle of seynt Jhon*, f4v; Frith, *A boke made by John Frith prisoner in the tower of London* (Antwerp, 1533; STC 11381), b3r-v; Tyndale, *An exposicion uppon the v. vi. vii. chapters of Mathew*, 22r-v; Frith, *A mirroure to know thyselfe* (Antwerp, 1536?; STC 11390), a5r.

[20] Frith, *A pistle*, 10r.   [21] Frith, *A pistle*, 10r.   [22] Tyndale, *The obedience*, 9v.

escape persecution, "no moare then the sonne can be without his lyghte."[23] This persecution would not only arise from distant enemies or malevolent officials, but from the godly's closest acquaintances, since "brother shall betraye or delyver the brother to deeth and the father the sonne. And the childerne shall rise agenst father and mother, and put them to deeth."[24]

As many evangelicals pointed out in this regard, Simeon had prophesied to Mary in Luke 2:34 that Christ would bring about "the resurrection of many of Israel," but that he would also be "the signe which shalbe resisted and spoken against."[25] Proclaiming the evangelical gospel, with its promise of salvation through faith in Christ and its call to godliness, therefore could not and would not be "good news" to everyone. Commenting on Matthew 5:13, where Christ called his apostles the "salt of the erthe," Tyndale argued that godly preachers were called "to salt, not onlye the corrupt maners and conversacion of erthie people," but also to apply salt to "their fayth and beleffe and all that they have imagened without Gods worde, concernynge righteousnes justifienge, satisfaccion and servinge of god."[26] According to Tyndale, therefore, "true preachinge is saltynge, and all that is corrupt must be salted."[27] This was not going to be pleasant for anyone involved, since "the nature of salt is to byte, frete and make smarte," and the "erthie people" would become infuriated when they heard "their righteousness their holinesse and servynge of God and his sayntes, disalowed, improved and condempned for damnable and develyshe."[28] The salty Christian would in turn find him- or herself "called a rayler, sedicious, a maker of discord and a troubeler of the comen peace, ye a scismatick and an hereticke also" and be forced to either "synge a new songe and forswere saltynge, or else to be sent after thy felowes that are gone before, and the waye thy master went."[29] While only those who were properly called should preach from the pulpit, Tyndale viewed salting as the duty of all Christians.[30] Kings ought to "be salt and lyght not onlye in exsample of lyvynge, but also in teachynge of doctryne unto theyr subjectes," and "every pryvate man ought to be in

---

[23] Tyndale, *The obedience*, 2r.   [24] Tyndale, *The obedience*, 6v.
[25] Frith, *A pistle*, 10r; also see *The summe of christianitie*, a[i]4r.
[26] Tyndale, *An exposicion upon the v. vi. vii. chapters of Mathew*, 25r-v.
[27] Tyndale, *An exposicion upon the v. vi. vii. chapters of Mathew*, 26r.
[28] Tyndale, *An exposicion upon the v. vi. vii. chapters of Mathew*, 25v. Tyndale argued in *The obedience of a Christen man* that if the godly preached only against "pryde covetousnes, lechery, extorcion, usary, symony and agenst the evell lyvinge both of the spiritualte as well as of the temporalte and agenst inclosynges, of parkes, resynge of rente & fynes, and of the caryenge out of wolle out of the realme, we myghte endure longe ynowe." It was instead their preaching against "false doctrine" that led to persecution from the ungodly (88r).
[29] Tyndale, *An exposicion upon the v. vi. vii. chapters of Mathew*, 25v.
[30] Tyndale, *An exposicion upon the v. vi. vii. chapters of Mathew*, 29r.

verteouse lyvynge both lyght and salt to his neyboure" and to "preache in worde and deade unto his housholde and to them that are under his governaunce."[31]

According to Tyndale, therefore, the true Christian would – indeed, should – act in ways that offended and scandalized many friends, neighbors, and family members.[32] As he put it elsewhere, "The nature of Gods worde is to fyght agenst ypocrites."[33] While the Pauline epistles contained many prohibitions on giving "offense," and Christ sternly warned against offending "lytell wons, which beleve in me" (Matt. 18), early evangelical theologians identified a range of situations in which Christians should offend others.[34] It was widely agreed, for example, that it was acceptable for Christians to cause offense by proclaiming biblical doctrine or performing necessary good works.[35] Quoting Christ's words in Matt. 10:34 that "I have not come to bring peace, but a sword," Philip Melanchthon argued in his *Loci Communes* that Christians need not be concerned about offense with regard to "that which is demanded by divine law," since "what is so demanded must be obeyed, done, and taught without respect to offense. For faith must always be preferred to love."[36] Erasmus Sarcerius's *Common places*, translated into English by Richard Taverner and printed in 1538, likewise argued that when Christians offended hypocrites and pharisees with "right doctrine or necessary workes commaunded in the word," they did so "without synne."[37] Indeed, Sarcerius went so far as to claim that the divine plan *required* the godly to offend hypocrites in this manner so "that they shold perish which by the just judgement of god ought to perish, it must nedes be that sclaunders be gyven, which be as it were meanes wherby the ungodlye hypocrites be called away, & frayd from the trouthe."[38] When hypocrites were offended, their hearts were hardened against the truth and "the hypocrites be confounded & destroyed whiche by the just judgement

---

[31] Tyndale, *An exposicion uppon the v. vi. vii. chapters of Mathew*, 29r-v.
[32] See Tyndale, *An exposicion uppon the v. vi. vii. chapters of Mathew*, 22r: when the Christian "goest forth and testefiest that fayth and lawe of righteousnes openlie unto the worlde in worde and deade. Then will Sathan stere up his membres agaynst the, and thou shalt be persecuted on every side."
[33] Tyndale, *The obedience*, 3r.   [34] Tyndale (trans.), *The New Testament*, p. 42.
[35] In these cases, offense was not "given" (as it was when weaker brethren were offended) but rather (wrongly) "taken."
[36] Philip Melanchthon, *Loci Communes* in Wilhelm Pauck (ed.), *Melanchthon and Bucer* (Philadelphia, 1969), 150; also see Richard Lant, *A compendyous treatyse of sclaundre* (London, 1545; STC 24216a), a2r-a3r; Johann Spangenberg (trans. Robert Hutten), *The sum of divinitie drawen out of the holy scripture* (London, 1548; STC 23004.5), n1v-n2v.
[37] Sarcerius, *Common places* 187r.   [38] Sarcerius, *Common places*, 186v.

of god ought to perysh."[39] The operative text here was again Luke 2:34 and Simeon's prophecy that "Christ is put unto suche for a fall. &c."[40] Offending the hypocrites in this way would stir up "cruel tyranny" against those who proclaimed the truth of Christ's gospel, but the godly must continue to obey God and proclaim his word, "though the guttes of the hypocrites sholde brust, & of the hole worlde."[41]

Not only would godly doctrine have this provocative effect, but so too would the proper exercise of Christian liberty in "things indifferent." Luther's *Freedom of a Christian* (1520), the urtext of Christian liberty for evangelicals, differentiated between how a Christian ought to behave toward the "weak in the faith" and toward the "unyielding, stubborn ceremonialists" when it came to the use of *adiaphora*.[42] The Christian must take care not to offend the weak when exercising Christian liberty with regard to "things indifferent," but when he encountered a stubborn ceremonialist, "he must resist, do the very opposite, and offend them boldly lest by their impious views they drag many with them into error. In the presence of such men it is good to eat meat, break the fasts, and for the sake of liberty of faith do other things which they regard as the greatest of sins."[43] According to Luther, therefore, Christians were called to avoid offending the weak when exercising Christian liberty, but they must intentionally offend or scandalize those who stubbornly insisted that "things indifferent" contributed to one's salvation. In the same vein, Robert Barnes – the most Lutheran of all early English evangelicals – noted that St. Paul only counseled charity toward "weke brethren (and not of obstinate and induratyd persons, agenst whome thow shalte alle ways withstond an defend thy liberte as he dyd)."[44] John Frith reminded his readers that "we have oure conversacion with men in this world of the which the moste parte knowe not God," and likewise argued that when Christians encountered the "selfe willed and obstinate which put confidence in such indifferent thynges … Them ought we to resist in the face & not to yelde an yenche unto them as Paule giveth us ensample which wold not for theyr pleasure circumcyse

---

[39] Sarcerius, *Common places*, 189r.   [40] Sarcerius, *Common places*, 189r.

[41] Sarcerius, *Common places*, 189r-v.

[42] Martin Luther, "The Freedom of a Christian," in *Martin Luther's Basic Theological Writings*, ed. Timothy F. Lull (Minneapolis, 1989), 625. Copies of Luther's text were being circulated in London during the 1520s by Lutheran merchants and hand-copied in the Protestant underground; see Brigden, *London and the Reformation*, 110, 192; *The Complete Works of St. Thomas More*, vol. 8, pt. 1, p. 22. Ethan Shagan has discovered a manuscript translation of *The Freedom of a Christian* by the prominent Henrician polemicist Richard Morison (British Library (BL) Harley MS 423), and I would like to thank him for bringing it to my attention.

[43] Luther, "The Freedom of a Christian," 625.   [44] Barnes, *A supplicatyon* 122v.

Titum but utterlye resisted theyr obdurate ignoraunce."[45] Indeed, we have already seen the provocative lengths to which Frith thought the English should go in order to ensure that Christian liberty with regard to the Sabbath was publicly proclaimed.

As long as Christians remained "salty," in short, they would inevitably and righteously offend many of their neighbors, producing hostility and opposition from those who they stung. Crucially, however, evangelicals like Tyndale insisted that it was not only rank-and-file Christians who would have this effect but also a godly king. Tyndale numbered godly kings among the ranks of the inevitably persecuted "salters" and argued that if a "kynge or Emperour" was a disciple of Christ and intended "to walke in the sight of God, and to mynistre thyne office trulye," he would experience great trouble. Were the godly king to "folowe the right waye, and nether turne on the right hande ner on the lefte, thou shalt have immediatlye thine awne subjectes, thyne awne servantes, thyne awne lordes, thyne awne councellours and thyne awne prophetes therto agaynst the[e]," demanding all manner of things against the king's godly conscience.[46] This was the experience of many godly English kings throughout history, not least King John, who was "forsaken of his awne lordes, when he woolde have put a good and godlye reformacion in his awne lande," and Henry II who was "compased in like maner of his awne prelates whome he had promoted of nought, with the secrete conspiracie of some of his awne temporall lordes with them."[47] Hugh Latimer had promised as much to Henry VIII in an open letter of 1530 when he urged the king to support the publication of a vernacular Bible.[48] Rather than promising that the Scripture would unify and pacify the land, Latimer told the king that he sought his support *not* because

> I think the word of God should go forth without persecution, if your grace had command that every man within your realm should have it in his mother's tongue. For the gospel must needs have persecution unto the time that it be preached throughout all the world, which is the last sign that Christ shewed to his disciples should come before the day of judgment: so that if your grace had once commanded that the scripture should be put forth, the devil would set forth some wile or other to persecute the truth.[49]

[45] Frith, *A myrroure or lokynge glasse*, b8v, c1v-c2r.
[46] Tyndale, *An exposicion uppon the v. vi. vii. chapters of Mathew*, 14v.
[47] Tyndale, *An exposicion uppon the v. vi. vii. chapters of Mathew*, 15r.
[48] On this letter, see Clebsch, *England's Earliest Protestants*, 273.
[49] Hugh Latimer, *Sermons and Remains of Hugh Latimer*, ed. George Corrie (Cambridge, 1845), 307.

The persecution of the godly would mutate in accordance with the times, in other words, but it would not stop simply because the king was supporting the gospel.

From this perspective, the godly king would not – *could not* – be the guarantor of religious peace or unity. Rather, he would be a partisan figure who would rule over a divided kingdom, standing with his godly subjects and facing opposition and persecution from the ungodly. Indeed, evangelical exiles like George Joye, John Bale, and John Hooper would argue in the 1540s that this was precisely what had happened to Henry VIII when he had supported reform in the mid-1530s. The popish clergy and their lay henchmen had persecuted Henry by stirring up the Pilgrimage of Grace, an act of persecution that Bale rather dubiously equated with the martyrdoms of Jan Hus and Jerome of Prague at the Council of Constance.[50] Hooper acknowledged the logical corollary that a peaceful realm must have an ungodly ruler, but he drew back from it, writing that he did not "condemne all princes and Kynges as Ennymies of the gospell because they peaceable enyoi there kingdomes," but he nevertheless then pushed ahead, stressing that the more "syncere" a king was in the cause of the gospel, "the more shalbe his crosse" and denouncing those who claimed otherwise as "flaterers."[51]

What these evangelicals were arguing, therefore, was that the king ought to expect that supporting the reformation would produce strife and division, and that a realm where religion had been reformed would be home to division and conflict.[52] This was the message proclaimed in two translations published by evangelicals in the heady middle years of the 1530s. The first was William Marshall's 1534 translation of Joachim Vadian's *Vom Alten und Neuen Gott* (1521), a text that had also heavily influenced William Tyndale.[53] Marshall's translation promised on the title page to show readers "what to beleve in this so greate dyssencion of all chrystendome, and in this so unquiet & troblous estate of comen weales."[54] It not only told people what to believe, however, but also put a positive gloss on these "greate

---

[50] Bale, *The Image Of bothe churches*, m1v-m2r; also see Joye, *A present consolation*, a7v; Hooper, *A declaration of Christe* (Zurich, 1547; STC 13745), k4v-k5r.

[51] Hooper, *A declaration of Christe*, k4v-k5r. On this point, also see Davies, "'Poor Persecuted Little Flock,'" 87.

[52] Also see Jean Calvin's advice along these lines to Protector Somerset in his letter of October 1549: *An epistle both of Godly Consolacion and also of advertisement* (London, 1550; STC 4407), a8v-b4r.

[53] Joachim Vadian (trans. William Marshall), *A worke entytled of the olde god and the newe* (London, 1534; STC 25127). On the original text by Vadian, see Carlos M. N. Eire, *War Against the Idols: The Reformation of Worship from Erasmus to Calvin* (Cambridge, 1986), 75–76. On Marshall's translation, see Underwood, "Thomas Cromwell and Protestant Books," 525–526. On Tyndale's use of *Vom Alten und Neuen Gott*, see Clebsch, *England's Earliest Protestants*, 169–170, 254, 312.

[54] Vadian, *A worke entytled of the olde god and the newe*, a1r.

discordes and debates" that had arisen.[55] The book began by describing how
the "swerd" that Christ promised to bring in Matthew 10 was newly drawn
from its scabbard and placed into the hands of Christ's "electe Captaynes &
mynesters."[56] This sword, which had been coated with dust and rust after
many years of disuse, was being freshly wielded against sinners, idolaters, and
the devil himself. Satan longed for "the olde wycked and ungracyous peace,
the quyete and peaceable seate of his power in hypocrisye" and attempted to
bribe princes with the Church's wealth in order to "get our olde peace" once
again.[57] Peace could not be restored in the wake of the gospel's rediscovery,
however, because "the glyttrynge bryghtnes of the fyery swerde, hathe so
perced & entred in to the eyes of many mens hertes, that stryfe is spronge &
rysen well neare in all the erthe the sone rysynge agaynst his father, and the
doughter agaynste her mother, & all the hole house beynge in a styrre & grete
unquietnes, & every one in others top, throughe dyscorde and debate."[58]
Religious "devysion" had existed even before Cain and Abel, dating back to
the conflict between the righteous and the fallen angels, and would continue
"even to the world ende" between "theyr posterite."[59]

Tristram Revel's 1536 English translation of François Lambert's *Farrago
Rerum Theologicarum*, which he had sent and dedicated to Anne Boleyn,
told a similarly positive story about the conflict the reformation was
producing. Lambert had embraced and transformed the accusation that
evangelicals were divisive sectarians, proclaiming that "we be adherentes
and defenders of thys eternall, hevenly, and devyne secte, & it is necessary,
that we be tumultuous or bryngers up of rumoures for it, agaynst the
execrable, cursid, and abhomynable secte of antichriste."[60] Making the
unusual choice to own rather than repudiate the word "sect," Lambert
depicted a world of tumult and conflict that was the unavoidable consequence of true religion's opposition to Antichrist.[61] In making this claim, he

[55] Vadian, *A worke entytled of the olde god and the newe*, a7v.
[56] Vadian, *A worke entytled of the olde god and the newe*, b1v. Tyndale developed a similar metaphor for
    Scripture, writing that in Christ's time, "The scribes and phariseyes had thrust up the swearde of the
    worde of God into a scabarde or shethe of gloses, and therin had knitte it fast, that it coulde nether
    sticke ner cutt." Christ drew the sword from its scabbard and used it to divide men against themselves,
    "The fleshe halinge one waye, and the spirite drawinge a nother." Tyndale, *An exposicion uppon the v.
    vi. vii. chapters of Mathew*, 114v-115r.
[57] Vadian, *A worke entytled of the olde god and the newe*, b2r-3r.
[58] Vadian, *A worke entytled of the olde god and the newe*, b3r.
[59] Vadian, *A worke entytled of the olde god and the newe*, b6r.
[60] Lambert, *The summe of christianitie*, a3v[i].
[61] The term "sect" did not have a positive connotation, and evangelicals typically contrasted "sects" with
    "Christ's most holy religion": Miles Coverdale (trans.), *The original & sprynge of all sectes & orders by
    whome, whan or were they beganne* (Southwark, 1537; STC 18849), +1v. On Cranmer's derisive use of

did not deny the desirability of peace and unity per se, but he relocated them purely within the fellowship of true Christians. While true Christians *internally* possessed the Holy Spirit, which was the "spirit of unyon and peace" and "loveth true peace, and is enemy of contencyon," this was unfortunately not their lot when they confronted the world.[62] When Christ was preached, it "dothe burst up carnal pease, & dothe rayse up the sworde very ofte in hym selfe, accordynge to the saying of the lorde, I dyd nat come to sende pease, but a sworde. Math. x."[63] Going on to cite Luke 2:34 and the prophecy that Christ would be "a sygne that shalbe resysted and spoken agaynste (of those unfaythful)," Lambert explained that "bycause we preache things contrary to the worlde, the worlde hatyth us, and callyth us tumultuous, and sedecyous felowes," just as they had accused Christ.[64]

These sorts of claims, which evangelicals in central Europe had been making throughout the 1520s, turned accusations of causing disorder and conflict on their heads, but they did so at a cost.[65] By so closely linking persecution, conflict, and the gospel, this way of thinking practically demanded that Christians behave in ways that produced opposition. If preaching did not produce any offense or resistance from its hearers, for example, was it truly gospel preaching? Had it lost its savor? Did a peaceful realm, as Hooper had been forced to wonder, really have a godly king? We can see this line of reasoning in the writings of the idiosyncratic but influential Cambridge evangelical Thomas Bilney.[66] Facing trial for heresy in 1527, Bilney had been accused of claiming that "the gospel hath not of long time ben sincerely preched."[67] In a letter to Bishop Tunstall, Bilney claimed not to remember

the term to refer to both papists and evangelical "radicals," see Diarmaid MacCulloch, "Archbishop Cranmer: concord and tolerance in a changing Church," in Ole Peter Grell and Bob Scribner (eds.), *Tolerance and intolerance in the European Reformation* (Cambridge, 1996), 203.

[62] Lambert, *The summe of christianitie*, a4v[ii]. In this regard, the Antichristian papal church was the perfect inversion of the true Christian Church: internally it was full of "discencyon never ceasyng," but externally it lived in "abhomynable peace of the fleshe" and "execrable pease" (a4v-a5r[ii]).

[63] Lambert, *The summe of christianitie*, a3v[i].   [64] Lambert, *The summe of christianitie*, a4r [i].

[65] On these arguments in a central European context, see Beat Hodler, "Protestant Self-Perception and the Problem of *Scandalum*: a Sketch," in Bruce Gordon (ed.), *Protestant History and Identity in Sixteenth-Century Europe*, vol. 1 (Aldershot, 1996), 23–30. Also see Luther's arguments along these lines in *On the Bondage of the Will* in *Luther and Erasmus: Free Will and Salvation*, ed. E. Gordon Rupp and Philip S. Watson (Louisville, 1969), 128–129.

[66] On Bilney's place on the reformist spectrum, see John F. Davis, "The Trials of Thomas Bylney and the English Reformation," *The Historical Journal* 24:4 (December 1981), 775–790; Greg Walker, "Saint or Schemer? The 1527 Heresy Trial of Thomas Bilney Reconsidered," *Journal of Ecclesiastical History* 40:2 (April 1989), 219–238.

[67] John Foxe, *The Unabridged Acts and Monuments Online* (1563 edition) (HRI Online Publications, Sheffield, 2011). Available from: http://www.johnfoxe.org [Accessed: 02.06.14]

whether he had ever said or written that, but admitted that "I have often ben afraid that Christ hath not ben purely preched now a long time. For who hath ben now a long ceason offended through him? who hath now this many yeares suffred any persecution for the gospels sake? wher is the sword which he came to send upon the earth?"[68] These "frutes" of the gospel had been conspicuously absent for many years, which led Bilney to ask whether "the tre whyche bryngeth forth those frutes, hath now a long time bene wanting in our region or country? much les is it to be beleved, that it hath ben nouryshed amongs us. Have we not sene al things quiet & peaceable a long time?"[69] While peace and quiet were precisely what Henry VIII would aim to achieve with his reformation in the decades to come, these were very bad things from Bilney's perspective. Bilney's disciple Hugh Latimer took the same line three years later in his aforementioned open letter to Henry VIII, when he attempted to discredit the opponents of Bible translation. Latimer proposed to teach the king how to discern "who be the true followers of Christ and teachers of his gospel, and who be not."[70] Persecution was the crucial index, because

> where the word of God is truly preached, there is persecution, as well of the hearers, as of the teachers: and *where as is quietness and rest in worldly pleasure, there is not the truth*. For the world loveth all that are of the world, and hateth all things that are contrary to it. And, to be short, St Paul calleth the gospel the word of the cross, the word of punishment. And the holy Scripture doth promise nothing to the favourers and followers of it in this world, but trouble, vexation, and persecution, which these worldly men cannot suffer, nor away withal.[71]

To borrow a phrase from Michael Walzer, this was to suggest that "[o]ne could almost test the divinity of the Word by the violence of Satan's opposition."[72]

These attempts by evangelicals to link division, conflict, and persecution with true religion did not go unchallenged. In his *Dialogue Concerning Heretics*, Thomas More complained about how one of the "new kynde of prechers" denounced contemporary preachers because "he saw not the prechers persecutyd / nor no stryfe nor business aryse upon theyr

---

[68] Foxe, *The Unabridged Acts and Monuments Online* (1563 edition) [Accessed: 02.06.14]

[69] Foxe, *The Unabridged Acts and Monuments Online* (1563 edition) [Accessed: 02.06.14]

[70] *Sermons and Remains of Hugh Latimer*, 300.

[71] *Sermons and Remains of Hugh Latimer*, 303; emphasis added.

[72] Michael Walzer, *The Revolution of the Saints: A Study in the Origins of Radical Politics* (New York, 1972), 65.

prechyng."[73] According to More, this was a grotesque misunderstanding of Christ's statement that "I am not come to sende peace into the world but the sworde."[74] When Christ uttered these cryptic words, he meant that he would bring "a devysyon amonge infydels," not that he or his apostles would "sowe some cocle of dyssensyon amonge the crysten peple."[75] If preaching among Christians produced "the frute of stryfe . . . and persecucyon of the precher," these were not signs of truth or the going forth of Christ's gospel, but rather signs that the preacher was introducing "some straunge neweltyes, and bryngynge up of some new fangell heresyes."[76] According to More, the proclamation of the gospel would bring a sword among the Turk, but it would instead produce peace in a Christian kingdom like England. Latimer was personally confronted with a version of this argument in 1531 when he received a letter from Sir Edward Baynton, a courtier with evangelical sympathies and links to Cromwell and the Boleyns, who lived only a few miles away from Latimer's parish in West Kingston.[77] Latimer had already developed a well-deserved reputation for controversial preaching – he was, as Alec Ryrie has aptly put it, "a man able to start a religious riot merely by opening his mouth" – and Baynton wrote to him about certain friends who wished Latimer's "reformation" because his preaching "geveth occasion of sclaunder & trouble in let of your good purposes."[78] Baynton tended to agree with Latimer's critics that "an opinion or maner of teachyng, whiche causeth dissension in a Christen congregation, is not of God."[79] The gospel would produce dissension and persecution among the "unchristened," but preaching that produced "contention" in a Christian congregation "is not to be taken as of God."[80]

Latimer's response to Baynton reveals not only his assumptions about the proper consequences of godly preaching but also his radical view of the nature and life of the church. Utterly unrepentant, Latimer told Baynton

---

[73] Quoted in Eamon Duffy, "Continuity and Divergence in Tudor Religion," in R. N. Swanson (ed.), *Unity and Diversity in the Church* (Oxford, 1996), 178.

[74] Thomas M. C. Lawler, Germain Marc'Hadour, and Richard C. Marius (eds.), *The Complete Works of St. Thomas More*, vol. 6, pt. 1 (New Haven and London, 1981), 124.

[75] *The Complete Works of St. Thomas More*, 6.1.124.

[76] *The Complete Works of St. Thomas More*, 6.1.125.

[77] *ODNB*; Maria Dowling, "The Gospel and the Court: Reformation Under Henry VIII," in Lake and Dowling (eds.), *Protestantism and the National Church*, 49–50.

[78] Ryrie, *The Age of Reformation*, 124; Foxe, *The Unabridged Acts and Monuments Online* (1563 edition) [Accessed: 02.06.14]

[79] Foxe, *The Unabridged Acts and Monuments Online* (1563 edition) [Accessed: 02.06.14]

[80] Foxe, *The Unabridged Acts and Monuments Online* (1563 edition) [Accessed: 02.06.14]

that he and his friends seriously misunderstood the nature of "a Christian congregation." Christian churches were full of people who were baptized and professed Christ as lord, but who were in fact hypocrites and "antichrists."[81] The most fundamental distinction to be drawn between people was "not betwene christened and unchristened, but betwene Christians and Antichristians," a division that ran straight through the heart of the so-called "Christian congregation."[82] As such, Baynton was being naive if he thought the gospel could be preached in a Christian congregation without causing dissension, and Latimer insisted that it would be better "to have a deformitie in preaching" if God's truth were proclaimed "then to have such a uniformitye, that the sely people shoulde bee thereby occasioned to continue still in their lamentable ignoraunce, corrupt judgement, superstition and idolatry, and esteme thynges as they doe al, preposterously."[83] Where More and Baynton envisioned the church as a body characterized by its peace and unity, Latimer was insisting that the inevitably mixed membership of the church meant that it was not a place where the gospel would ever be peaceably embraced by all. This was very much the view of life in the church laid out by Tyndale that same year in *An answere unto Sir Thomas Mores dialoge* (1531). Responding to More's claim that the church could not fall into error, Tyndale stressed that the church would always contain a combination of elect and false brethren, with the latter always forming the majority and persecuting the former.[84] Within the "dowble" church, the elect would proclaim the true gospel and reject the idolatry of "the greate multitude," only to be labeled heretics, excommunicated, and threatened with death.[85] "Thus hath it ever bene and shall ever be," Tyndale proclaimed, "lett noman therfore disceave him selfe."[86] For Latimer and

---

[81] Foxe, *The Unabridged Acts and Monuments Online* (1563 edition) [Accessed: 02.06.14]

[82] Foxe, *The Unabridged Acts and Monuments Online* (1563 edition) [Accessed: 02.06.14]. Latimer returned to this point in his notorious 1537 sermon to Convocation, which Eamon Duffy has characterized as "a *tour de force* of offensiveness, a manifesto calculated to outrage the overwhelming majority of his hearers" (Duffy, *The Stripping of the Altars*, 390). To their faces, Latimer told the assembled clerics that "as light hath many her children here, so the world hath sent some of his whelps hither: amongst the which I know there can be no concord nor unity, albeit they be in one place, in one congregation." *Sermons by Hugh Latimer*, ed. George Corrie (Cambridge, 1844), 44–45.

[83] Foxe, *The Unabridged Acts and Monuments Online* (1563 edition) [Accessed: 02.06.14]

[84] Tyndale, *An answere unto Sir Thomas Mores dialoge*, 63r.

[85] Tyndale, *An answere unto Sir Thomas Mores dialoge*, 65v.

[86] Tyndale, *An answere unto Sir Thomas Mores dialoge*, 67v. Two years later, returning to this theme in his exposition of the Sermon on the Mount, Tyndale continued to stress the endless nature of this "fight above all fightes." In the course of this "warre fare and a perpetuall batayle" against the false prophets, if the elect were to "get the victorye of the falsse prophetes, and plucke a multitude out of their handes, there shal immediatlye ryse of the same and set upp a new falsse secte agaynst the." Tyndale, *An exposicion uppon the v. vi. vii. chapters of Mathew*, 101r.

Tyndale, the church was a battleground where true Christians would contend against Antichrist and his followers in their midst.

The clear implication of this argument, again, was that the absence of conflict signaled the absence of the gospel. This conclusion was expressed most forcibly by George Joye, a quarrelsome evangelical whose personal history and keen sense of persecution certainly inclined him to embrace such a view. Joye had known Bilney and Latimer at Cambridge during the 1520s and had been an extraordinarily fractious member of the first generation of evangelical exiles in the late 1520s and early 1530s, working with Tyndale on biblical translation until the two had an acrimonious falling-out in 1534–1535.[87] When Joye was driven into exile again after the passage of the Six Articles because he was a married priest, he reprised and sharpened many of the arguments that his former friends had made regarding the gospel and conflict. In *A present consolation for the sufferers of persecucion for ryghtwysenes* (1544), Joye addressed those in England who opposed the reformation because "where this newe lerninge is preached, there foloweth myche trouble, inquietnes tumult sondri sectes diverse opinions."[88] "Truth it is," Joye replied, "For never was the sead of gods worde sowne & begane to aryse, Satan beinge a sleape."[89] Joye claimed that "all things are in peace" wherever Satan reigned because the Devil, like any good prince, worked to subdue strife and tumult so that "those thinges whiche he yet possedith myght continewe in peace."[90] Satan would foster peace and unity on earth unless he was challenged by those who had "forsaken his Satanike fraternite and synagoge, and casten of his dampnable yoke, and sayd him adiew."[91] Peace reigned and "there semed to be a good quiete" in the Pope's church until Wyclif, Hus, Erasmus, and Luther challenged Rome, but "Then beginneth Satan to rustle when a stronger armed invadeth his realme. Or els what shuld he do but ly dowun & laugh or sleape to se his realme in tranquilyte and in a paceable possession?"[92] The only way to achieve peace on earth, therefore, was to make peace with Satan. If Christians failed to

---

[87] Charles C. Butterworth and Allan G. Chester, *George Joye, 1495?–1553* (Philadelphia, 1962). For Joye's account of his controversy with Tyndale, see *An Apologye made by George Joye to satisfye (if it maye be) w. Tindale* (London, 1535; STC 14820).

[88] George Joye, *A present consolation for the sufferers of persecucion for ryghtwysenes* (Antwerp, 1544; STC 14828), a3v. Brad Gregory has suggested that Joye used Urbanus Rhegius's *Consolatory Letter to all the Christians of Hildesheim* (1531) as a model for *A present consolation*: Gregory, *Salvation at Stake*, 155. Joye's text was found in the possession of a separatist conventicle in London during 1545: see Brigden, *London and the Reformation*, 358; Ryrie, *The Gospel and Henry VIII*, 107.

[89] Joye, *A present consolation*, a3v. [90] Joye, *A present consolation*, b1v.

[91] Joye, *A present consolation*, c6v. [92] Joye, *A present consolation*, b1v, a4v.

proclaim the gospel and confront popery, then they would find themselves "at peace with them and Satan with his serpentyne seade wolde favour exalt & defend us."[93] Following the gospel, however, would "incense and provoke the worlde ageynst us" and produce the persecution and dissension that Joye described as "a perpetuall inseperable companion of the gospell."[94] It was these premises, then, that enabled Joye to reach the jarring conclusion that "there is no certayner argument and more evident token of the gospell to be utterly oppressed, & of Satan to raigne in peace, as to se the publike concorde of, and in the religion. And there is no token so certayn manifest and evident of the worde of god arysing and cominge forth into lyght, as when ye se a comon publike discorde in, and of the religion."[95]

Unsurprisingly, then, Joye demanded militant action on behalf of the gospel. As Alec Ryrie has discussed, Joye was sharply critical of fellow evangelicals who were "playing down controversial doctrines and presenting reformist ideas in traditional terms" as they attempted to convert conservatives and "to avoid unnecessary provocation."[96] From Joye's perspective, attempts to proclaim the gospel peacefully and without offense were fundamentally misguided, and he treated the efforts of moderate evangelicals with "scorn and contempt."[97] Because Joye insisted that the gospel would always be inflammatory and offensive to some, Christians should not wait to proclaim the gospel until "it bringeth with it fayer wether in a worldly peace" or until "it may be beter borne of your commons and lordis," because then it would never be preached at all.[98] Confessing Christ was an aggressive act of violence against the devil, who did not turn the other cheek. When the Jews rebuilt the temple after the Babylonian exile, "they wrought with one hande, holding their swerdis in the tother hande, nether made they their morter nor did other labours aboute it, but were gyrte with swerdis havinge weapons redy by them, which difficultye techeth us that the chirche of cryst with the gospell cannot be edifyed withoute lyke difficultye and perell to the buylders and prechers."[99] Christians were called "unto the most hardeste sharpe and jeoperdest batails" as they sought to reform the church and proclaim the gospel.[100]

---

[93] Joye, *A present consolation*, c6r-v.   [94] Joye, *A present consolation*, d1r, b5r.

[95] Joye, *A present consolation*, b2r. Joye did envision one other scenario in which peace might exist. God sometimes granted a short victory to the godly, so "that peace might reigne upon the erthe and the godly to have a breathinge tyme to reste them," but this was only a respite until the next wave of raging persecution. George Joye, *The exposicion of Daniel the Prophete* (Antwerp, 1545; STC 14823), 175r. For another example of this argument, also see Bale, *The Image Of bothe churches*, f4r.

[96] Ryrie, *The Gospel and Henry VIII*, 128–129.   [97] Ryrie, *The Gospel and Henry VIII*, 132.

[98] Joye, *A present consolation*, b2v; Joye, *The exposicion of Daniel*, 91r.

[99] Joye, *The exposicion of Daniel*, 159v.   [100] Joye, *The exposicion of Daniel*, 215r.

In a brilliant essay on Edwardian evangelicalism, Catharine Davies has shown how evangelicals' view of themselves as a persecuted minority became "an integral part of the self image of English protestants, and one which they were unwilling to give up even when it no longer really fitted with their objective situation."[101] The accession of Edward VI transformed the fortunes of persecuted evangelicals like Joye, but it did not change many evangelicals' expectation that reformation – and the godly preaching and godly living that would come with it – would continue to bring not "peace, but a sword." Miles Coverdale, for example, had written from his second exile in 1541 that the gospel would always be resisted and persecuted in this world. This opposition would not always take the same form – it might come from tyrannical rulers, from foreign enemies, from false prophets and heretics, or from "multitudes, that pretending a love toward Christes word, did but folow him for their own belies sake" – but it would always be present.[102] Sure enough, Coverdale continued to sound the same theme after the accession of Edward VI when he published two editions of *A faythfull and true pronosti-cation*, a scripturally based alternative to astrological forecasts that predicted that the Sun (Christ), Mars (the gospel), and Mercury (the devil) would govern the coming year.[103] Noting that his readers might wonder why he called the gospel "Mars," Coverdale pointed to Christ's promise in Matthew 10 to bring not peace but a sword, explaining that "where it [the gospel] is preached there is the swerde, there is trouble and persecucyon, there wyll the enemyes sometyme draw theyr daggers at the preachers therof."[104] The source of this strife and trouble was the fact that Christ and the world "shall never be at one." On the one hand, the "chyldren of this worlde are scornefull, and therfore are they not contente to be refourmed by the gospel," while on the other hand the followers of Christ "wyll not consent to the workes of darknesse, nether wyll the belevers have parte with infidels. ii. Cor. vi. Thus can there be no agremente, for they be of contrarye natures."[105] Coverdale therefore predicted that "strife (I saye) & debate shall happen this yeare because of the worde of god, for the enemyes therof had rather draw theyr daggers at it, then to be refourmed."[106]

---

[101] Davies, "'Poor Persecuted Little Flock,'" 84.

[102] Miles Coverdale, *A confutacion of that treatise, which one John Standish made agaynst the protestacion of D. Barnes* (Zurich, 1541?; STC 5888), n6r.

[103] Miles Coverdale, *A faythfull and true pronostication upon the yere. M. CCCCC .xlviii* (London, 1547; STC 20423); *A faythful & true pronostoication upon the yeare. M.CCCCC .xlix* (London?, 1548?; STC 20424). All subsequent quotations from the 1547 edition.

[104] Coverdale, *A faythfull and true pronostication*, a4v.

[105] Coverdale, *A faythfull and true pronostication*, b5v-b6r.

[106] Coverdale, *A faythfull and true pronostication*, b7r.

While Coverdale urged the godly to "mayntayne peace" and expressed hope that many people would turn to the gospel in the coming year, at the same time he demanded that Christians behave in ways that would only exacerbate this strife – ways that Coverdale's old friend Tyndale would have called "salty." The almanac attached to Coverdale's prognostications assigned several daily tasks: learn and believe God's Word, keep the Ten Commandments, do good works, and rebuke your neighbors' faults. Readers were told that "This daye is it good one of us to tell another his faute," motivated not by malice but by love, in the hope that the ignorant would be made aware of their errors and that the fallen would turn from their sin.[107] Following Christ's instructions for how to deal with sinners in Matthew 18, this rebuke might just be the first step on a path that would lead to informing the church of your neighbor's sin and then resolving to "not eat, nor kepe company with soch."[108] The daily life of the faithful Christian who in love rebuked his neighbors for their sins would unfortunately (but inevitably) lead to conflict and division, for "a scornefull bodye (as Salomon sayeth) loveth not one that rebuketh hym. Pro. xv."[109]

Hugh Latimer likewise continued to predict – and encourage – conflict between the godly and the worldly during Edward VI's reign. After resigning his bishopric in 1540 and remaining largely silent during the last decade of Henry VIII's reign, Latimer returned to the pulpit with a vengeance under Edward VI, becoming the most prominent evangelical preacher of the era. He had not lost his knack for offensive preaching and was denounced as "a sedicious felow" after a 1549 Lenten sermon at court for sharply criticizing the bishops, royal chaplains, the Lord Protector, and royal judges. Defending himself from the pulpit the following week, Latimer boldly proclaimed that preaching that did *not* produce opposition was ipso facto popish:

> [I]n the popish masse time, ther was no gaynsaiynge, al thynges semed to be in peace, in a concorde, in a quiet agrement. So longe as we had in adoration, in admiration, the popyshe masse, we were then withoute gaynsaying ... When Sathan the devyl hath the guydynge of the house, he kepeth all in peace that is in his possessyon: whan Sathan ruleth, and bereth domynion in open Religyon, as he dyd with us when we preched pardon matters, purgatory matters & pylgremage matters, al was quiet. He is ware inough, he is wily, and circumspect for stiryng up any sedition. When he kepeth his

---

[107] Coverdale, *A faythfull and true pronostication*, d2v.
[108] Coverdale, *A faythfull and true pronostication*, d3v.
[109] Coverdale, *A faythfull and true pronostication*, b6r.

terrytory al is in peace … When he hath the religyon in possessyon he sturreth uppe no sedytyon, I warrent yow.[110]

When Christ and the gospel were openly proclaimed, "then the Devyll roareth, then he bestyrreth hym, then he rayseth diversitie of opinions to slaunder Gods word."[111] The fact that Latimer's preaching was producing hostility and opposition was therefore not only not a problem; it was a positive sign that the gospel was going forth. Much like he had told the young king's father two decades before, he informed Edward that religious dissension was a "sure argumente and an evident demonstration, that the lyght of Gods worde is a brode, and that this is a true doctrine that we are taught now, else he [Satan] would not rore and stirre a boute as he doeth whan he hath the upper hande."[112]

We can also see a willingness to encourage "offensive" preaching in the Edwardian writings of Anthony Gilby, an evangelical with close ties to Latimer, specifically with regard to the controversial doctrine of predestination. While the majority of sixteenth-century Protestant reformers adhered to some form of predestinarian theology, they were divided about whether it was a doctrine fit for public consumption.[113] In his preface to the English Bible of 1540, Archbishop Cranmer had cited Gregory Nazianzen to argue that it was not appropriate "for every man to dispute the high questions of divinity, neither is it to be done at all times, neither in every audience must we discuss every doubt; but we must know when, to whom, and how far we ought to enter into such matters."[114] Despite Cranmer's own belief in predestination, therefore, it "remained the doctrine that dared not speak its name" in the Edwardian homilies, as Cranmer feared the confusion and danger that the doctrine might create if preached to the general population.[115] According to Gilby, however, the doctrine of predestination must be preached, despite – or rather *because of* – the offense it would cause. Gilby's 1553 commentary on Malachi contained a digression "Of Eleccion and Reprobacyon," which defended the teaching of these doctrines to all people, even "thoughe the matter seameth to manye learned men mooste daungerous of all other to be entreated and taughte amonge

---

[110] Latimer, *The seconde Sermon* (London, 1549; STC 15274) e6r-v.
[111] Latimer, *The seconde Sermon*, e7r.   [112] Latimer, *The seconde Sermon*, k1r-v.
[113] Euan Cameron, *The European Reformation* (Oxford, 1991), 131.
[114] *The Work of Thomas Cranmer*, ed. G. E. Duffield (Philadelphia, 1965), 39.
[115] MacCulloch, *Thomas Cranmer*, 375.

the unlearned."[116] Not preaching on election and reprobation, Gilby argued, would be to hide a comforting doctrine and to imitate the papists by hiding the full teaching of the Scriptures from the people. The fact that "some poysoned spythars, hadde gathered poyson" from these doctrines did not warrant keeping silent about them, "[f]or by the same reason, Christe shoulde not be preached at all, Because he is a stomblynge stone unto some and the savour of death unto deathe."[117] Indeed, Gilby fully expected that teaching predestination to "the wycked" would lead them to embrace "lasciviousnes and wantonnes" – an accusation evangelical preaching had faced from the very start – but in so doing it would serve as a "testemonye towards condempnacion" and a doctrine that would drive them "towarde theyr Jornayes end, to the pytte of hell."[118] Gilby had no qualms about this and even seemed to revel in it: "I do feare nothing at al to offend you with my wryting," even though the wicked would "swere, stampe, & stare for a litle space in a furious rage, when you heare & feele thynges contrarye to your poyson."[119]

It was not only godly preaching that was supposed to produce dissension, however, but also godly living. In a 1552 sermon, Latimer argued that the "professors of Christ" and "the world" could never be in agreement "for they love godlines, and the other love wickednes which two can never be set together."[120] He lamented that so many people chose to pursue earthly peace rather than godly conflict, since "every man wil rather apply him selfe after the world and have quietnes and a mery lyfe, then to forsake the same, and to have trouble with Christ and his flocke."[121] What sort of trouble would the godly experience by forsaking the world? Latimer offered a practical example in the following week's sermon when he advised his audience what to do "if thou dwellest in a towne where are some wicked men that will not be reformed, nor in any wise wil amend their lives, as there are commonly in every town some."[122] One should not flee the town and withdraw into some sort of holy commune – this was

[116] Anthony Gilby, *A Commentarye upon the prophet Malachy* (London?, 1553; STC 11885.5), c1r. The contents of Gilby's *A Briefe Treatice of Election and Reprobation*, published in 1556 and 1575, were almost entirely drawn from the Malachi commentary.

[117] Gilby, *A Commentarye*, c1v-c2r.   [118] Gilby, *A Commentarye*, c2r-v.

[119] Gilby, *A Commentarye*, d3v. On this point, also see Bernardino Ochino, *Certayne Sermons of the ryghte famous and excellente Clerk Master Barnardine Ochine* (London, 1551; STC 18766), f7r, where Ochino argued that offence was no reason to stop preaching predestination: "The truth is dyspleasaunt to the false christians, they fynde offence of the gospell, and Justificacion by Christ, should it then be kepte in silence?"

[120] Latimer, *Frutefull Sermons* (London, 1575; STC 15278), 203r.

[121] Latimer, *Frutefull Sermons*, 203r.   [122] Latimer, *Frutefull Sermons*, 209r.

what monks and Anabaptists did – but instead "exercise thy patience amongest them exhortyng them whensoever occasion serveth to amendement."[123] Latimer urged his audience to model their lives on Lot living among the Sodomites: they should "not flatter them in their evill doings and naughty livinges, but rebuke their sinnes & wickednes, and in no wise consent unto them," a course of action that had, of course, brought great suffering to Lot and his family.[124] Latimer was even more explicit about this conflict in another 1552 sermon on the Lord's Prayer. Those who sought "to lyve after Gods will and commaundementes" would find themselves living "amongest the wicked even as it were amongst the rebels ... that dwelled in Northfolke or Devonshier at the tyme of rebellion," attacked on all sides just as those who "were faithfull to their king and prince" had been attacked in 1549. It was this reality that Christ was addressing when he promised that "I am not come (sayth he) to sende peace, but the sword."[125] This was a "straunge saying," Latimer admitted, given that "God is a God of peace and concord he loveth unitie and concorde: but when hee can not have peace, by the reason of the devill, than he will have the sword."[126]

Latimer's ringing endorsement of "the sworde" perfectly encapsulates the militant view of godly life that this chapter has thus far examined within early English evangelicalism. Viewing conflict and division as normative features of godly life not only enabled evangelicals to defend themselves effectively against accusations that they were destroying peace and unity – and were therefore agents of Satan rather than Christ – but it also demanded that the godly engage in a variety of provocative behaviors as they proclaimed the gospel and certainly required that they not shrink from conflict. All of this had important implications for how some evangelicals understood their place in a post-Reformation England, but it was not the only way in which early English evangelicals could envision the reformation as bringing "a sword."

In his notorious *Sermon to the Princes* (1524), Thomas Müntzer argued that Christ's promise to bring a sword in Matthew 10:34 was a literal command to slaughter the enemies of the gospel without mercy.[127] Müntzer's graphic call to the princes for holy violence seems to be a world apart from the thinking of early English evangelicals, who commonly

---

[123] Latimer, *Frutefull Sermons*, 209r.   [124] Latimer, *Frutefull Sermons*, 209v.
[125] Latimer, *Frutefull Sermons*, 26r[ii].   [126] Latimer, *Frutefull Sermons*, 26r[ii].
[127] Thomas Müntzer, "Sermon to the Princes," in Baylor (ed.), *The Radical Reformation*, 27–32.

argued that they *suffered* violence, while anti-Christians *inflicted* it.[128] Yet when evangelicals described themselves as a persecuted minority, there was a sting in the tail. When he discussed the persecution that Christians would inevitably face in *The obedience of a Christen man* (1528), for instance, Tyndale reminded his readers that "tyrauntes and persecuters are but Gods scourge and his rodde to chastise us," and that when they had served their purpose, "then the rodde is taken awaye."[129] Scripture was full of examples of how "God destroyed them [persecutors] utterly and toke them cleane from the erthe," and Tyndale pointed to the great flood in Genesis 6–8, the destruction of the Sodomites and the Egyptians, and especially the "wrath & cruell vengeaunce" that God visited on the Jews for crucifying Christ.[130] When George Joye wrote about the persecution that married priests faced in 1531, he proclaimed that "As verely as the bloude of Abel cryed and obtained vengeaunce, shal the bloude of other good men vexed & slayne, obtayne the same to fall upon these persuers & sheders of like innocent bloude for kepinge of goddis commaundements."[131] Unless the persecutors repented quickly, they should "loke for no nother but the vengeaunce and wrath of god now hanging over your headis, shortly to be powerd downe upon you," a prospect in which Joye would elsewhere urge evangelicals to take comfort.[132] Even John Frith, who argued for a sort of religious toleration, begged God to "avenge thyne awne cawse" against the enemies of his people and to make them "feall thy scourge and be compelled (as Pharao was) to dimitte thy chosen children, and to knowlege thy power & omnipotencye."[133]

While evangelicals regularly proclaimed that they would taste the sword of persecution, therefore, they were equally certain that they would be avenged. It was *especially* when they depicted themselves as a persecuted minority that evangelicals could easily envision future violence against their persecutors. When Tyndale talked about the vengeance that would befall persecutors, he was decidedly vague about how it would come about,

---

[128] As John Frith put it, Christ "did never presone nor persequute eny," while the Pope and his followers "persequute, punishe, presonne, and put to death, them that are disobedient to their voluptuous pleasurs." Frith, *A pistle*, 92r. On this contrast, see Bauckham, *Tudor Apocalypse*, 61.

[129] Tyndale, *The obedience*, 9v.   [130] Tyndale, *The obedience*, 11r.

[131] Joye, *The letters*, c4r. Addressing prayer to saints, John Hooper argued that the saints in heaven only prayed the prayer found in Revelation 6: "Moost holy and trew god when wolt thow revenge our blud upon them that be in the Erthe." Hooper, *An Answer unto my lord of wynchesters booke* (Zurich, 1547; STC 13741), r2r.

[132] Joye, *The letters*, c7v; Joye, *The exposicion of Daniel*, 95r.

[133] Frith, *A pistle*, 11v-12r. On Frith's commitment to toleration, see Karl Gunther and Ethan H. Shagan, "Protestant Radicalism and Political Thought in the Reign of Henry VIII," *Past and Present* 194 (Feb. 2007), 63–69.

stressing only that God would achieve it "sodenlye agenst all possibilyte of mans witte."[134] Similarly, a published 1534 proclamation from "the hyghe Emperoure Jesu Christe" briefed its readers about the impending "Christen batell (agaynste the devell and his courte of perdicion)" in which the true Christians would retake the castle that the papists had captured.[135] Christ promised his English followers that he would "fyght for you," but while he claimed that they would achieve victory "without yron, swerde or any other bodelye weapen onely thorow your beleve & prayer," he proceeded to offer a variety of historical examples of both divine and human violence against the "enemies unto my people of Israel." God had personally killed Pharaoh and his army in the Red Sea, but he had empowered human agents to be his avengers in the case of Judas Maccabeus, who "went out agaynst hys enemies and slewe .xxx.M. men thorow my [Christ's] assistence."[136] While the exact means were not entirely clear, what was clear was that the persecutors would soon become the persecuted, a point not lost on one reader who wrote in the margin next to the passage quoted above that "god persecutyd phar. & meny mo for the love of hys Electe specially when they callyd on hym in fayth."[137]

Evangelicals often had reason to view Henry VIII as another persecuting Pharaoh, but when the king turned against the pope and began wielding his sword against "persecutors" like Thomas More in the early 1530s, some clearly began to envision him as an agent of divine vengeance against their enemies. Several of Thomas Cromwell's correspondents in the mid-1530s hoped that the king would shortly take up arms against papists, both at home and abroad. One anonymous manuscript in Cromwell's papers stridently demanded a holy war against the papists, claiming that Scripture required all princes "to make war" against "the said forsaken Antecriste & his, Orells yf they omitt or refuse so to do, they shewe and declare them selfs, to be of his damnable Sinogoge, And so disobedient unto god and his word."[138] That this would not merely be some sort of spiritual war was immediately made clear when the author explained that all of the possessions of Antichrist "in what land or cuntrey soever they be thorugh the universall world" belonged to the king and that he was commanded by Scripture to reclaim them "with the sword or otherwise."[139] While this

---

[134] Tyndale, *The obedience*, IIr.
[135] *A proclamacyon of the hyghe Emperoure Jesu Christe, unto all his faythfull Christen* (London, 1534; STC 14561a), aIv.
[136] *A proclamacyon of the hyghe Emperoure*, bIv-b2r.
[137] Marginalia from the Folger Shakespeare Library copy of STC 14561a, b2r.
[138] SP 6/3, 47r. I owe this reference to Ethan Shagan.   [139] SP 6/3, 47r.

anonymous author was apparently calling for Henry VIII to lead something like a worldwide crusade against Antichrist and to establish a godly empire, the London evangelical printer Thomas Gibson called for a campaign of royal vengeance against papists in England when he sent a series of prophecies to Cromwell in the mid-1530s.[140] Gibson's cover letter to Cromwell chillingly described how Henry – champion of "the worde of god" and the "mynyster" of the "kyngdome of Christ" – was now miraculously empowered by God to slaughter the papists in England.[141] God would "delyver his electe and delyver in to oure kyngs hands his enymies," just as he had done for the people of Israel.[142] The godly's persecutors would now taste the sword themselves, just as Pharaoh and the Egyptians had been destroyed when they pursued the Israelites in their attempt to "persecute godes electe . . . so shall the papistes seke there owne confucion and sodenly shall fynde it . . . and be drowned in there owne bloode by swerde."[143] Through his instrument Henry VIII, God would "fulfyll his promyse agenst them and that we shall rewarde the papystes as they rewarded us, as is saide in the apocalypes the 18 chapter rewarde her as she rewardyd yow, which reward shalbe wyth swerde and so dryven out of this lande for ever as is saide in the proverbes, the ryghtwyse shall never be over thrown, but the ungodly shall not remaine in the lande."[144] The time for payback had come.

Even for a monarch as bloodthirsty as Henry VIII and a minister as ruthless as Cromwell, this surely would have been beyond the pale: writing to one of the most powerful men in England, Gibson was recommending a sweeping campaign of retributive violence in which Henry VIII would purge England of papists with the sword, a call to arms that has its closest Reformation-era parallel in Müntzer's equally unsuccessful efforts to persuade the Saxon princes to annihilate the "godless" and rid the land of "evildoers who obstruct the gospel."[145] Gibson's suggestion that the reformation in England should be accompanied by a royal campaign of terror is all the more significant given that he was not a man on the fringes of either English society or the evangelical community, but rather a respectable figure

---

[140] BL Cotton MS Cleopatra E vi, ff. 401–406. For a brief discussion of the way in which Gibson reworked earlier prophetic collections, see Sharon L. Jansen, *Political Protest and Prophecy under Henry VIII* (Woodbridge, 1991), 59, 112; also see Alistair Fox, "Prophecies and Politics in the Reign of Henry VIII," in Alistair Fox and John Guy (eds.), *Reassessing the Henrician Age: Humanism, Politics and Reform, 1500–1550* (Oxford, 1986), 92–93. Elton dismissed Gibson and his prophecies as "all fairly mad." G. R. Elton, *Reform and Renewal: Thomas Cromwell and the Common Weal* (Cambridge, 1973), 21.

[141] Cotton MS Cleopatra E vi, f. 402r.   [142] Cotton MS Cleopatra E vi, f. 401v.

[143] Cotton MS Cleopatra E vi, f. 401v.   [144] Cotton MS Cleopatra E vi, f. 402r.

[145] Müntzer, "Sermon to the Princes," in Baylor (ed.), *The Radical Reformation*, 27–28; on Müntzer and the sword, also see James M. Stayer, *Anabaptists and the Sword* (Eugene, OR, 1976), 73–90.

in the London printing community. Edward Crome recommended Gibson to Hugh Latimer, who then recommended him to Cromwell as "an honest, poor man" in 1537.[146] His brutal call for the king to visit apocalyptic violence on English papists reveals, therefore, the extent to which mainstream evangelicals not only could imagine the English Reformation as a moment of revolutionary violence, but were also attempting to convey this vision to those at the center of power.

Indeed, it is striking how casually evangelicals suggested that Henry VIII take up the bloody example of Old Testament kings. In *The Lordis flayle* (1540), the former Augustinian canon Thomas Solme – an evangelical convert with close ties to both William Turner and Hugh Latimer – matter-of-factly wrote that "owre supreme hed" Henry VIII would not only use God's word to destroy the idol Baal, but that "his grace shal sle[y]" the priests of Baal in England "which do devowere dayly innumerabyl, mell, and wyne, and shepe."[147] John Bale flirted with advocating mass violence against the clergy in the conclusion of a 1544 pamphlet when he praised Henry VIII for utterly destroying the shrine of Thomas Becket.[148] Bale noted that Henry was following the godly example of Josiah, recorded in 2 Kings 23, but went on to add that "If he had upon that and soche other abhomynable shrynes brent those ydolatrouse prestes which were (& are yet) theyr chefe maynteners, he had fulfylled that godlye historye through out."[149] Perhaps Henry refrained from slaughtering the priests on their altars because he hoped the clergy would repent, but Bale ominously hoped that "that which was not than perfourmed in hope of theyr amende-ment, maye by chaunce lyght upon them herafter, whan no gentyll war-nynge will seme to be regarded."[150] Bale took up the theme again in *The apology of Johan Bale agaynste a ranke papyst* (1550). In his preface to Edward VI, Bale discussed biblical reforming kings, praising the "revengemente" taken by Jehu for the blood of those slain by Jezebel and returning again to the example of Josiah, who "slew al the ydolatrouse priests & brent their

---

[146] *Sermons and Remains of Hugh Latimer*, 381; *ODNB*. Calls for violence against the enemies of the gospel were also coming from figures who *were* very much on the fringes of the evangelical community. See John Champneys's extraordinarily violent *The Harvest is at Hand, wherin the tares shall be bound and cast into the fyre and brent* (London, 1548; STC 4956). An extensive analysis of this text can be found in Pearse, *Between Known Men and Visible Saints*, 99–111; on Champneys's trial, see Horst, *The Radical Brethren*, 112–115; Davis, *Heresy and Reformation*, 103–104.

[147] Solme, *Here begynnyth a traetys callyde the Lordis flayle* (Antwerp, 1540; STC 22897), c3v-c4r.

[148] Bale, *A brefe Chronycle concernynge the Examincacyon and death of the blessed martyr of Christ syr Johan Oldecastell* (Antwerp, 1544; STC 1276), 55v.

[149] Bale, *A brefe chronycle*, 55v.

[150] Bale, *A brefe chronycle*, 55v. Henry, Bale optimistically claimed, "perseyveth moche more in that wycked generacyon of the Popes norryshynge up . . . than he ever in his lyfe yet uttered" (55v-56r).

bones in places of their wicked sacryfyces."[151] In case the king or other readers missed the contemporary significance of this reference, the margin helpfully reminded them that England's idolatrous priests were the popish "Masmongers."[152]

The ease with which evangelicals could imagine and openly talk about this sort of anticlerical carnage is strikingly illustrated by a fleeting aside in an unusual place, a lengthy and highly technical 1547 treatise on the Eucharist by John Hooper. Writing from Zurich, where he had lived in exile at the end of Henry VIII's reign and where he remained for several years after the accession of Edward VI, Hooper had received a letter from a friend in England recounting how royal commissioners visiting a parish church had discovered "the leffte arme of one of those chartechouse Monkes that died in the defense of the byshope of Rome Reverently hyd in the hygh aulter of the church, with a wryting conteyning the day and cause of his deathe."[153] This hidden relic was clear evidence that the parish's priest and people "be hypocrites and desemblers, and not perswadyd of the truith in there hartes," a fact that led Hooper to remark that "I trust to hyre that the Kynges majestie, never put his officers to great payne to bring them to Tiburn, But put them to death in the churche upon the same aulter wherin this relique was hyd, and burnt there the bones of the treterous ydolatraes, with the relique, as Josijahu did all the false pristes 4. Reg. 23."[154] Hooper continued to spin out this grisly fantasy by explaining that "the doyng therof shuld not have suspendid the churche at all, but have byn, a better blissing therof then all the blissins of the byshopes of the worold, for god lovithe those that be zealous for his glorie."[155] Rather than desacralizing the church, the shedding of idolaters' blood within its precincts would provide a fitting consecration for a place devoted to godly zeal. Hooper did not proceed to detect and then murder "idolatrous" priests on their own altars when he became Bishop of Gloucester several years later, but his playful musing about such actions in print is a potent illustration of the violent fantasies lurking within the thought of evangelical leaders like Hooper.

While Bale and Hooper fantasized about papists being slaughtered on their altars, other evangelicals were urging large-scale prophylactic violence, claiming that the spread of the gospel itself required the king to wield his sword proactively against its enemies. The most remarkable proposal along

[151] Bale, *The Apology of Johan Bale agaynste a ranke Papyst* (London, 1550; STC 1275), 3r-v.
[152] Bale, *The Apology*, 3r.   [153] Hooper, *An Answer unto my lord of wynchesters booke*, q2v.
[154] Hooper, *An Answer unto my lord of wynchesters booke*, q2v.
[155] Hooper, *An Answer unto my lord of wynchesters booke*, q2v.

these lines can be found in a detailed plan for reform sent to Henry VIII in the mid-1540s.[156] In his discussion of this manuscript, Alec Ryrie has noted that one of the most striking reforms proposed was "a campaign of mass deprivation of the clergy, with the wilfully ignorant to be pensioned on a pittance and the well-meaning to be restored once they had acquired sufficient education."[157] This, however, was only half of it. As the manuscript's evangelical author explained at length, the coming of reformation had been a disaster for the clergy, depriving them of jurisdiction, "princely power," and wealth. Now that the English people could compare "the lyves and dooings of their pastors" with the model provided by Scripture, the clergy lived in "ffeare of a greater ffawle" and anxiety over the "sherpe reformation" to come that would restore "apostolike povertie and pure simplicite of the primityve church."[158] They resisted reformation through crafty maneuvering at court and by attacking godly preachers in the countryside, but above all by using their influence over the common people to turn their hearts against "the gospell."[159] The author painted a vivid picture for the king of how exactly this happened. On the Sabbath day, the village parson would wait until his parishioners were "at the hottest in their aele" and then join them at the alehouse.[160] He would be warmly received, as "One biddeth mr parsone *welcoom*, of[f] goeth every mans cap, *coome hither Sir Jhon to me* saith a nother, and well is he that can soonest get A chaire and a koosshen to the highest end of the table for the preest to sytt yn."[161] Presiding over this convivial group, the priest would casually turn the conversation to England's increasingly dire economy, asking about current market prices and scarcity. While his simple parishioners would be eager to share stories, none would be able to explain why any of this was happening, and the priest would then jump in and explain that the dearth and high prices were all due to the suppression of the abbeys and the break with Rome. Not knowing any better, the "poore innocent men by and by perswaded with this evill false and apparunt reason crie owt *I pray god save your lif good mr parsone*," and were turned against both the gospel and their king.[162]

It was to prevent this alehouse subversion, supposedly happening on a weekly basis in every village in the kingdom, that the author proposed not

---

[156] BL Royal MS 17 B xxxv. This manuscript was discovered by Ethan Shagan, who I would like to thank for bringing it to my attention. Diarmaid MacCulloch dates the text between 1544 and 1545: MacCulloch, *The Boy King*, 123n45.
[157] Ryrie, *The Gospel and Henry VIII*, 154. [158] Royal MS 18 xxxv, ff. 6r-7r.
[159] Royal MS 18 xxxv, ff. 7v-8v. [160] Royal MS 18 xxxv, f. 9r.
[161] Royal MS 18 xxxv, f. 9r emphasis added. [162] Royal MS 18 xxxv, f. 9v emphasis added.

only the mass deprivation of clergy deemed incorrigible but also their internment. To make sure that the deprived clergy would "be brydled from making lawes in ale howses and do good or els no hurt," the author proposed that every deprived cleric "immediately withowt excuse or delay goe too and remeyne in soom one or twoo places in every diocese to be appointed," where they would occupy themselves in prayer for the king and the realm.[163] These deprived clergymen would of course be banned from visiting alehouses, but they would also be prohibited from leaving these "places" for more than a month at a time, receiving wages for performing any clerical duties, or doing anything else "prejudiciall to the welth of other poore preests lyving of their stipnds and good peoples devotion" upon pain of forfeiting their pensions.[164] In sum, this scheme would not only require the deprivation of the majority of the English clergy – a scenario the author was fully content to envision, because "it seemeth unto me much more commodioose necessarie and profitable for the realme to have no preests at all, than ignorant and unlearned vicioose and of evyll conversation"[165] – but also the creation of a new penal system, anchored by dozens of centers across the realm that would function like a cross between a sort of clerical concentration camp and a monastery. England's incorrigible clergy would not be slaughtered on their altars, but if this evangelical had his way, they would die out under the crown's enforced hospitality.

A virtually identical set of concerns animated the French émigré Jean Véron, but mass executions rather than internment were his preferred solution. Véron had been living in England since the mid-1530s and would become a priest in the Church of England in 1551. In the preface to *The ymage of bothe Pastoures* (1550), an English translation that Véron made of Zwingli's *Der Hirt* (1525) and dedicated to Protector Somerset, he blamed the failure of the English people to embrace the gospel on the papist clergy, who were "blynde guydes . . . ravenynge wolves, and false Prophetes."[166] Like the crowds that welcomed Christ on Palm Sunday, only to be turned

[163] Royal MS 18 xxxv, f. 13r.
[164] Royal MS 18 xxxv, f. 13v. A similar visitation was proposed by William Turner in *The Huntyng of the Romyshe Wolfe* (Emden, 1555; STC 24356). In this text, "Hunter" urges "Foster" to put forward a bill in Parliament "for the destroiyng of the excedinge nombre of wolves." This would be achieved through a visitation that would "assaye if al these that are now wolves, both bishoppes & other, myght be brought to be right shepherdes." Those who would convert should have their livings increased, but those "that will not parte frome their wolvishnesse" should either be banished or "all their tethe should be pulled out, and put out of office, and casten into the tower, lest they should do any more harme abrode" (e6r-v).
[165] Royal MS 18 xxxv, f. 11v.
[166] *ODNB.* Huldrych Zwingli, *The ymage of bothe Pastoures, sette forth by that mooste famouse Clerck, Huldrych zwinglius, & now translated out of Latin into Englishe. By John Veron, Sinonoys* (London,

against him in a few short days by the "hyghe pryestes, scrybes, and Pharyses," so too the people of England embraced the gospel when preached by itinerant "honeste and godlye menne," only to be made "a thousande tymes worse" by the wolves and false prophets after the peripatetic godly preachers departed "into soome other place."[167] The popish wolves convinced the simple people that the gospellers were preaching heresy and destroying the true Catholic religion, which they insisted would surely be restored in only a few years. The papists were so persuasive and skillful that it was "impossyble" for the "poore symple folkes of thee contreye" to escape being deceived by their arguments and even "manye witted and learned persons that are not yet stronge, stedfast, fyrme, & sound in the fayth, ar oftentymes by them overthrowen and clene subverted."[168] Given this set of facts, Véron proceeded to argue that the best course of action was to put the popish clergy to death.[169] Citing texts like 2 Kings 23, Véron wrote that "it was not for nought (as I have often sayd, and now I say it againe) that those godly kinges, which in times past dyd put down al ydolatry, & superstition, setting up again, with al godly studye & dylygence, the true worshipping of the living god, did slaye & kyl up al Baalles priestes, & false prophetes of groves, & hille altars. Whyche thing truly they did, because that they shoulde not brynge the people agayne into errour."[170] Véron went on to describe "What moderation must be used in rooting out of the papistes" – by which he meant that their conversion should be sought and that magistrates should not proceed out of a desire for the clergy's wealth – but it was clear that Véron expected that these efforts would nevertheless result in widespread executions.[171] Estimating that only one in forty parishes "hathe a true pastoure or minister," he asked "Is it not (I praye you) moch more expedyente, that viii hundrethe and L. false prophetes, shoulde bee kylled uppe, by some Helyas, than that al the whole Israell shoulde perysshe. Judge ye all, that have anye wytte in youre heads."[172]

1550; STC 26142) a2v-a3v. A separate edition was printed the same year by William Seres and Richard Kele, STC 26143. On Veron, see Carrie E. Euler, "Bringing Reformed theology to England's 'rude and symple people': Jean Véron, minister and author outside the stranger church community," in Randolph Vigne and Charles Littleton (eds.), *From Strangers to Citizens: The Integration of Immigrant Communities in Britain, Ireland, and Colonial America, 1550–1750* (Brighton and Portland, OR, 2001), 17–24. On Véron's approach to translation in this text, see Euler, *Couriers of the Gospel*, 126, 148–154.

[167] *The ymage of bothe Pastoures*, a4v-a5r.   [168] *The ymage of bothe Pastoures*, a5r-v.

[169] The violent aims of Veron's preface and translation are absent from Euler's discussion of the text in *Couriers of the Gospel*, which notes only that Zwingli's original text had called for the deposition of false ministers (150).

[170] *The ymage of bothe Pastoures*, a5v-a6r.   [171] *The ymage of bothe Pastoures*, a6r.

[172] *The ymage of bothe Pastoures*, a8v, a6r.

Veron's plea to Protector Somerset in the preface was a preview of what
Zwingli would advise in the translated text regarding the treatment of "false
Pastours." Quoting Deuteronomy 13 and its command to put false prophets
to death, Zwingli wrote that false prophets "ought to be roted out of the
earth" because of the great danger they posed, not merely to the "weake" but
also to "the elect."[173] Zwingli – who had written in the heady days of the
early reformation in Zurich – wrote as if mob violence against popish priests
was an imminent threat, finding it necessary to stress that God had
empowered magistrates to wield the sword against false pastors, since
there were some Christians "that are desyrous to kyll them, where soever
they fynd them," and these "hote and fierce Christians, do greatly erre,
whyche, as sone as thei se a false prophet, do thinke that any man may kyl
him."[174] If magistrates refused to put false pastors to death, Zwingli advised
people to "patiently beare thys yoke, layde upon us, as yf it were another
captivitie of Babylon," but he then undercut this insistence by promising
that God would then ordain extraordinary means to punish the false
prophets.[175] If the "ravening wolves can not peasibly, or without tumulte,
and insurrection be expelled & put awaye, he wyl wythout fayl rayse up
some Helias, which shall at one clappe kyll up. iiii. hundreth and [muti-
lated] priests of Baal and. iiii. hundreth prelates of groves & hyll aulters."[176]
Elijah was an example of a non-magistrate who killed legitimately with "a
speciall commandement of god," a precedent that Zwingli suggested might
be repeated and even expanded to the people at large. If the "ravenynge
wolves" could not be expelled from "the rowmes of Pastours," then Zwingli
advised his readers that "the dreadeful judge Christ, wyll come, whyche wyl
arme eyther the Prynces or the people theym selves to vengeaunce."[177]

While we are well aware that sixteenth-century Christians possessed a
"willingness to kill" in defense of true religion, we generally do not associate
calls for violence like these with early English Protestantism, with its martyrs
like Tyndale and cautious politicians like Cranmer.[178] Although Cranmer
was willing to see heretics executed, including fellow evangelicals like John

[173] *The ymage of bothe Pastoures*, L3r-v.
[174] *The ymage of bothe Pastoures*, L6v-L7r. Private persons should try to expel these clergy from their
     congregations, or flee from their ministry if they could not be removed.
[175] *The ymage of bothe Pastoures*, L8r.   [176] *The ymage of bothe Pastoures*, L8v.
[177] *The ymage of bothe Pastoures*, L6v, L8v-M1r.
[178] Gregory, *Salvation at Stake*; Walsham, *Charitable Hatred*, ch. 2. James Simpson's *Burning to Read:
     English Fundamentalism and its Reformation Opponents* (Cambridge, MA, 2007) is keenly attuned to
     the violent tendencies of early English Protestantism, but focuses on the psychological and cultural
     violence within evangelicalism.

Frith and John Lambert, he was not an eager persecutor and inclined to sheath the sword in most circumstances, especially when it came to papists who "might well be part of the elect" and "were simply awaiting the call of God in faithful preaching of the word."[179] Indeed, as a number of scholars have stressed, executing heretics was seen as a pastoral and political failure and something that ecclesiastical authorities went to great lengths to avoid.[180] The calls for violence discussed in this chapter however, went much further than simply defending or urging the execution of obstinate heretics: they were eager calls for the king to wield his sword on a massive scale, enacting revenge against persecutors, punishing idolaters, and eliminating huge numbers of priests deemed enemies of the gospel. All of this is a potent reminder of the violence that lurked within English Protestant thought from its very beginnings, even – or perhaps especially – among those who depicted themselves as a suffering, persecuted minority.

When evangelicals urged their king to wield his sword against the enemies of reformation, they were envisioning an often shockingly violent reformation, but they were not suggesting anything that was in principle incompatible with the Tudors' willingness to enforce their reformations at the point of the sword. By contrast, when evangelicals proclaimed that the coming of the gospel would "burst up carnal pease," or argued that religious concord was a sign of the gospel's utter suppression, they were charting a very different course. Henry VIII envisioned his reformation and his new Church of England as an institution that would restore peace and unify the English people, a program that Ethan Shagan has described as "a Sisyphean task of reconciliation put to a rancorous and divided nation."[181] Many early English evangelicals saw themselves engaged in an equally Sisyphean task, but of a very different sort: a war against Antichrist that would come to an end only when Christ returned in glory.

At the heart of this vision was the notion that religious division was an ineradicable feature of reality. This division, as Hugh Latimer had explained to Sir Edward Baynton, was not between the christened people of the world and the non-christened, but between Christians and Antichristians coexisting within the boundaries of the Christian Church. Antichrist could not be cleanly assimilated to the Turk, the Jews, or the Pope and the papists: Antichrist was within, in "Christian" families, neighborhoods, parishes,

---

[179] MacCulloch, "Archbishop Cranmer," 210. As MacCulloch notes, Cranmer was far harsher toward errant evangelicals than he was toward unconverted papists.
[180] D'Alton, "The Suppression of Lutheran Heretics in England, 1526–1529."
[181] Shagan, *Popular Politics*, 232.

cities, and kingdoms.[182] As Tyndale put it, "there are ever ii. maner people that wil cleave unto god a fleshli, & a spiritual," a "carnall Israel and a spirituall."[183] This was not an abstract theological distinction, but the defining divide in human life, because the carnal Antichristians would endlessly persecute the Christians.[184] It was in experiencing this conflict, in being wrongly labeled as divisive hypocrites, that Christians knew themselves. According to John Bale, "By non other token is the trewe churche of Christ knowne from the false and cownterfett synagoge, but by persecucyon for ryghtousnesse sake. For hys churche ys evermore as he was, hated, blasphemed, vexed, trobled, scorned, dysdayned, accused, lyed upon, and cruellye afflicted unto deathe, els is it not of hys marke."[185] Christ brought peace to the conscience and unity to the body of true believers, but this would not be their lot in the world.

All of this had important implications for how these evangelicals viewed the church, and it sat uncomfortably with the vision of the Church of England as an inclusive institution that could peacefully unify the entire English population. But rather than embracing a sectarian vision of the Christian community – becoming "a light set upon a hill to influence the world by example rather than by participation" – the English evangelicals examined in this chapter were committing themselves to a different path.[186] Rather than advocating withdrawal from the world or the national church, they demanded that the godly thrust themselves into conflict *within it*, envisioning the mixed membership of the church as a battleground and the monarch as a powerful ally in the "warre fare" and "perpetuall batayle" against Antichrist.[187] Sowing salt from the pulpit and among their neighbors, they expected to be hated and persecuted for their godly activism, and they purposed to endure the strife that they expected to be the constant companion of the gospel. The result was a militant vision of reformation without end. Peace and unity were godly things, but they would be unattainable on earth. As Hugh Latimer put it in 1552, "God loveth unitie, he would have us all agree togither: but because of the wicked we cannot. Therefore he will rather have us to chuse the sworde, that is, to strive and withstand theyr wickednes, then to agree unto them."[188]

---

[182] John Frith argued that Antichrist was even within the true Christian, in the form of the lusts of the flesh that ran contrary to the spirit; Frith, *A pistle*, 6r.

[183] Tyndale, *An answere unto Sir Thomas Mores dialogue*, 89v, 32r.   [184] Frith, *A pistle*, 9v-10r.

[185] Bale, *Yet a course at the Romyshe foxe*, 16r.

[186] Roland Bainton, "The Left Wing of the Reformation," 122.

[187] Tyndale, *An exposicion uppon the v. vi. vii. chapters of Mathew*, 101r.

[188] Latimer, *Frutefull sermons*, 26r[ii].

CHAPTER 3

Anti-Nicodemism as a way of life

English Protestants faced a serious dilemma when Mary Tudor succeeded Edward VI in 1553 and restored Catholicism. Thomas Hancock, a Protestant minister in Dorset, came up with an interesting solution: denial. Hancock dutifully read to his parish the royal proclamation of 18 August 1553 in which Mary "dyd declare what religion she dyd profes in her yowthe, thatt she dyd continew in the same, and thatt she mynded too end her lyf in the same religion; wylling all her loving subjects too embrace the same." The proclamation excited Hancock's Catholic parishioners, who expected to have the Mass restored "post haste," but Hancock quickly quashed their hopes when he "declare[d] the meaning of hytt" to the parish. Mary was not changing the religion of the realm, Hancock explained, but simply commanding her subjects "nott too rebell agaynst her, being there princes, but to lett her alone with her religion." According to Hancock's gloss, the English should accept Mary's personal choice, but Protestantism was going to remain the law of the land. Unsurprisingly, Hancock's Catholic parishioners were unconvinced and immediately set up an altar, only to find it quickly torn down by Protestants under Hancock's direction. The result was a split parish: the "papistes" abandoned the parish church to hear the Mass in a private house, while the "Christians" heard "the gospel preched openly in the churche" by Hancock. Hancock was not able to maintain this brash gambit for long. The Catholics of the parish presented a wide range of articles against Hancock, deemed so offensive that the minister's crimes were not covered by Mary's initial pardon, and Hancock fled into a peripatetic exile.[1]

Few Marian Protestants would have the luxury of attending Prayer Book services in their parish church, at least not for very long. The restoration of Catholicism and the prospect of persecution forced English Protestants to

---

[1] John Gough Nichols (ed.), *Narratives of the Days of the Reformation* (London, 1859), 81–82. For the original, see Harley MS 425, ff. 128r-129v.

make a series of difficult decisions. While exiles and martyrs have traditionally received the lion's share of historical attention, recent scholarship has
given us a much richer understanding of the various ways in which evangelicals responded to persecution in the early decades of the English
Reformation. Alec Ryrie has shown how many Henrician evangelicals,
when faced with pressure to affirm doctrines or religious practices that
they considered contrary to Christ and his gospel, attempted "to negotiate
their way out of such demands."[2] Given the "ambiguity of English religious
policy" under Henry VIII and the biblical obligation to obey civil authorities, "was obeying Henry VIII tantamount to a denial of Christ?"[3] If exile
was a legitimate response to persecution, as it was widely – if not universally – considered to be, were equivocation and dissimulation also acceptable ways to avoid persecution while remaining at home?[4] Many
evangelicals in the 1530s and 1540s embraced cautious forms of godly
activism, not only seeking to spread the gospel in ways that avoided
provocation but also adopting "a low-key, pragmatic attitude to the issues
of recantation and dissembling" when faced with persecution.[5]
"Nicodemism," the term used by Jean Calvin to characterize those who
outwardly conformed to Catholicism while inwardly holding Protestant
convictions, was a significant feature of English evangelicalism during the
ambiguous years of Henry VIII's reign and it would be widely practiced by
Protestants during Mary's reign.[6] Andrew Pettegree has stressed that
Nicodemism was a "widespread phenomenon" among Marian
Protestants, with the numbers of Protestant Nicodemites dwarfing the
more visible but relatively small numbers of exiles and martyrs.[7] While

---

[2] Ryrie, *The Gospel and Henry VIII*, 70.   [3] Ryrie, *The Gospel and Henry VIII*, 71.
[4] On evangelical attitudes toward exile, see Jonathan Wright, "Marian Exiles and the Legitimacy of
Flight from Persecution," *Journal of Ecclesiastical History* 52:2 (April 2001), 220–243.
[5] Ryrie, *The Gospel and Henry VIII*, 86. On this subject, also see Wabuda, "Equivocation and Recantation";
Ranson, "Sincere Lies and Creative Truth"; Gray, *Oaths and the English Reformation*, ch. 6.
[6] On Nicodemism, see Carlos M. N. Eire, "Calvin and Nicodemism: A Reappraisal," *Sixteenth Century
Journal* 10:1 (Spring 1979): 44–69; Eire, *War Against the Idols*, chap. 7; Perez Zagorin, *Ways of Lying:
Dissimulation, Persecution, and Conformity in Early Modern Europe* (Cambridge, MA, 1990). While the
figure of Nicodemus was allegedly first invoked by dissemblers to justify their actions, Calvin and
others pitted Nicodemus against the Nicodemites by pointing out that Nicodemus eventually made
an open (and dangerous) confession of allegiance to Christ (John 19:39–42). See Calvin (trans.
Eric Kayayan), "Apology of John Calvin, to Messrs the Nicodemites upon the Complaint that they
make of his too great rigour (1544)," *Calvin Theological Journal* 29 (1994), 358; Pierre Viret (trans. F. H.
[Francis Hastings?]), *An Epistle to the Faithfull, necessary for all the children of God: especially in these
dangerous dayes* (London, 1582; STC 24779), g5r-v; Johan Wigand, *De Neutralibus et Mediis, Grosly
Inglyshed, Jacke of both Sydes* (London, 1562; STC 25612, 25612.5), L5v.
[7] Pettegree, *Marian Protestantism*, 89. As Thomas Freeman has argued, however, it is also important to
note that the numbers of Marian Protestants who refused "to save themselves by denying, or even
concealing, their beliefs was unprecedented" in English history: Thomas S. Freeman, "Over their

many surely dissembled out of fear, Pettegree has emphasized that there were a variety of principled arguments available to justify Nicodemism. Nicodemites "could often continue to perform signal service to the cause of the Gospel" while outwardly conforming during Mary's reign, but more importantly, they would prove "vital to the emergence during Elizabeth's reign of a Protestant society in England."[8] As Pettegree puts it, the Elizabethan Settlement – overseen by the Nicodemite triumvirate of Parker, Cecil, and Elizabeth and implemented on the ground by thousands of laymen and clerics who had conformed during Mary's reign – was "[t]o a very large extent . . . a Nicodemite Reformation."[9]

Nicodemism was an important aspect of sixteenth-century English Protestantism, but so too was anti-Nicodemism. Reformed Protestants across Europe – particularly Calvin – denounced dissimulation in the most vehement terms imaginable, depicting it as a heinous sin against God and against one's neighbors, and many vocal English evangelicals shared this view. For the anti-Nicodemites, Christ's call to acknowledge him "before men" was crystal clear and brooked no compromise, requiring that Christians openly proclaim their allegiance to Christ and his gospel in words and deeds. Thomas Freeman has pointed to an "increasing intolerance of compromise" among English evangelicals during the last decade of Henry VIII's reign, and anti-Nicodemism would arguably be the central concern of the Marian exiles.[10] Pettegree notes that the majority of the exiles' publications addressed the problem of Nicodemism in one way or another, "calling brethren in England to a more faithful witness and defending their own conduct in going abroad."[11] The issue of Nicodemism produced a significant debate within early English Protestantism, therefore, albeit a largely one-sided debate, given that dissemblers understandably did not broadcast their reasons, defend themselves publicly, or even necessarily think of themselves as "Nicodemites."

This chapter examines the anti-Nicodemite ethos in Reformation England. It argues that anti-Nicodemism and demands to make an open and unambiguous confession of Christ played a central role in shaping the activism of the hotter sort of Protestants, not only when they faced overt persecution during Henry and Mary's reigns but also throughout the reign

---

Dead Bodies: Concepts of Martyrdom in Late Medieval and Early Modern England," in Thomas S. Freeman and Thomas F. Mayer (eds.), *Martyrs and Martyrdom in England, c. 1400–1700* (Woodbridge, 2007), 19.

[8] Pettegree, *Marian Protestantism*, 101, 117. [9] Pettegree, *Marian Protestantism*, 106.

[10] Freeman, "Over their Dead Bodies," 17fn74. On anti-Nicodemism in the early years of the Reformation, see Gregory, *Salvation at Stake*, 150–162.

[11] Pettegree, *Marian Protestantism*, 88.

of Elizabeth. On its face, this argument seems counterintuitive: why would Nicodemism be a concern for Protestants under a Protestant regime? As one of the leading scholars of the subject has put it, "[t]he correlation between periods of persecution and Nicodemite activity clearly shows that dissembling behavior becomes a concern only when free worship is denied."[12] When we think of Nicodemism and anti-Nicodemism in Elizabeth's reign, we typically think of "church papistry" and debates among Catholics over the legitimacy of conformity.[13] Yet as we will see, explicitly anti-Nicodemite literature continued to be produced by Protestants for Protestants throughout Elizabeth's reign, criticizing Nicodemites for their previous failures and preparing readers to remain steadfast when persecution returned. In sometimes conflicting ways, moreover, the hotter sorts of Elizabethan Protestants would continue to perceive dissembling as a major *current* problem and a perilous ongoing temptation for Protestants in the church, at court, and in society at large. As we will see in this and in subsequent chapters, the anti-Nicodemite ethos that developed within early English Protestantism would not die with Mary Tudor and the restoration of a Protestant national church. A deep anxiety about "denying Christ before men" would remain at the heart of the ecclesiastical and social activism of "the godly" as they sought further reformation in Elizabethan England and sought to maintain a godly witness in the midst of the ungodly multitude.

While historians have convincingly demonstrated the willingness of early English evangelicals to dissimulate, equivocate, recant, and lie, there were also many voices rejecting dissimulation and insisting on a "constant confession" of Christ and his gospel. Unsurprisingly, many of these voices belonged to Protestant exiles who – like Jean Calvin, Reformation Europe's fiercest anti-Nicodemite – had fled persecution for friendlier religious confines. Tyndale wrote in 1533 that the light of the gospel "will not be hid" and where it was "trulye received" it led a person "to consent to the lawes of God and to begynne a new and a godlye lyvynge, facioned after

[12] Eire, "Calvin and Nicodemism: A Reappraisal," 69. Eire further notes that "English treatises dealing with dissembling behavior correspond with the era of Marian persecution," a claim that is certainly true but does not explain the substantial amount anti-Nicodemite writing during the reigns of Henry VIII, Edward VI, and Elizabeth (69). For Edwardian anti-Nicodemite texts, see the 1548 translation of Calvin's *Petit traicté*: Jean Calvin, *The Mynde of the Godly and excellent lerned man M. Jhon Calvyne, what a faithfull man, whiche is instructe in the Worde of God, ought to do, dwellinge amongest the Papistes* (Ipswich, 1548; STC 4435, 4435.3, 4435.5, 4435.7). Also see Bullinger and Calvin, *Two Epystles* (London, 1548; STC 4080).
[13] See Alexandra Walsham, *Church Papists: Catholicism, Conformity and Confessional Polemic in Early Modern England* (Woodbridge, 1999).

Gods lawes and without all dissimulacion."[14] Miles Coverdale urged his readers in 1541 to be sure "that in confessing the true faith and beleve of Christ, thy hart mouth and dede go together, and that thou consent to none opinon contrary to the same, That god maye have the prayse, and thy neghboure be edified in all thy conversacion."[15] John Bale claimed in 1543 that England was experiencing an epidemic of dissimulation: many in England erroneously believed that they could outwardly dissemble or even deny their evangelical convictions and yet "avoyde the daunger of gods indygnacion" by maintaining their internal profession of the gospel.[16] William Turner and George Joye each insisted during the 1540s that inner convictions and external actions must coincide, a view that was also expressed in an anonymous English translation of anti-Nicodemite letters by Heinrich Bullinger and Jean Calvin in 1544.[17] Bullinger wrote that it was not "sufficient for us to beleve in the herte and secretlye to confesse God. The syncerefull & playne confession of the tonge must goe wyth all," while Calvin argued that a Christian "is bounde not only to worshyppe god spirituallye in his hart, but also to testefye the same outwardlye."[18]

To understand the power and lasting significance of anti-Nicodemite anxieties within English Protestantism, we must first grasp why dissimulation was perceived as such a dangerous course of action. Why was dissimulation wrong? First, a person's salvation was literally at stake. For Tyndale, the key biblical passage was Christ's promise to reject those who were ashamed of him or who denied him on earth.[19] These passages showed "how Christe threatneth them that forsake hym for what so ever cause it be: Whether for feare, eyther for shame, eyther for losse of honoure, frendes, lyfe or goodes?"[20] It was a recurring theme in early English Protestant literature that true Christians would willingly suffer for God's Word, while hypocritical Christians would flee from persecution and thereby

<hr />

[14] Tyndale, *An exposicion uppon the v. vi. vii. chapters of Mathew*, 28v. It has been argued that Tyndale's statement that "to lie also and dissemble is not allwaye synne" (Tyndale, *An exposicion*, 48v) reflected early English Protestants' willingness to dissemble (Pettegree, *Marian Protestantism*, 97; Ryrie, *The Gospel and Henry VIII*, 74–75). Tyndale was not entirely consistent on this point – his purpose in this statement was to qualify his previous claim that "to lye for the entent to begile, is dampnable of it selfe" by pointing out situations where the demands of charity might trump the prohibition on lying (Tyndale, *An exposicion*, 48r) – and the present chapter highlights many instances where Tyndale denounced dissimulation in the context of religious persecution.

[15] Coverdale, *A confutacion of that treatise*, n6v.   [16] Bale, *Yet a course*, 4r.

[17] Joye, *The exposicion of Daniel*, 34v, 36v; Turner, *The Rescuynge of the Romishe Fox*, g6v.

[18] *Two Epystles One of Henry Bullynger . . . another of Jhon Calvyn . . . whether it be lawfull for a Chrysten man to communycate or be pertaker of the Masse of the Papystes, wythout offendyng God and hys neyghboure, or not* (Antwerp, 1544; STC 4079.5), a4v, a5v.

[19] Matthew 10:32–33, Mark 8:38, and Luke 9:62.   [20] Tyndale, *The obedience*, 11v.

reveal themselves to be children of the devil.[21] A person's response to persecution for the sake of the gospel, then, was a key signal of their eternal destiny. According to Tyndale, if a person found that they had "power to confesse" when opposed by antichristian tyrants, then "arte thou sure that thou arte saffe" and have God's spirit. By contrast, "if when it cometh unto the poynte, thou have no lust to worke nor power to confesse, how coudest thou presume to thinke that Gods sprite were in the[e]?"[22] In fact, according to John Bale, antichristian tyrants knew full well the eternal consequences of recantation and they forced people to publicly renounce Christ so "that they myght lose that crowne and be dampned."[23]

The underlying notion here was that a person could (at least in part) gauge his or her eternal destiny by observing how he or she responded in the face of persecution.[24] In the last year of Edward VI's life, Anthony Gilby had written that the elect "fele" their election especially in times of temptation and affliction, and many Marian authors expounded on this theme.[25] Throughout Mary's reign, Protestants identified perseverance in the face of persecution as an assurance of salvation: John Bradford, imprisoned at King's Bench in 1554, wrote a letter to an unknown lady that praised God for giving her "so bold a spret that yow are not ashamed of hys gospell, which is a playne token that yow be the very elect child of god, If yow hold fast to the end this godly confession. But this you cannot do onles you be content to sufre suche persecutions as commenly do folow the same for as S. peter teachethe us it is not onely geven us to beleve but allso to suffer for the same."[26] Robert Glover wrote to a fellow Protestant that suffering for his beliefs was "a sure sygne and a infaullable token that you be one of them that be sygned and shealed up to his everlastynge kyngdome, and of that nomber whose names be written in the booke of lyffe."[27] Stephen Gratwyke praised God for his correspondent's bold and constant profession of Christ, which confirmed "the moste sartayne assurans of your etternall sallvation in Jhesus Chryste acordinge as he hath chossen you in him before the fowndation of the worlde was layde."[28] This linkage between election and a constant profession in the face of suffering was not simply comfort given to brethren in the heat of persecution, but it persisted into Elizabeth's reign. In June

---

[21] Tyndale, *The obedience*, 8v-9r; Tyndale, *An exposicion uppon the v. vi. vii. chapters of Mathew*, 23v-24v, 91v.

[22] Tyndale, *The obedience*, 96r-v.   [23] Bale, *Yet a course*, 5r.

[24] On this point, see Gregory, *Salvation at Stake*, 162.

[25] Gilby, *A Commentarye upon the prophet Malachy*, e8v. This was a common view within Edwardian Protestantism: see Davies, "'Poor Persecuted Little Flock,'" 87.

[26] Harley MS 416, f. 35r.   [27] BL Add. MS 19400, f. 80v.   [28] Add. MS 19400, f. 82r.

1559, Robert Wisdom explained that the Marian persecution had been sent by God "to make manyfeste the incomperable riches of Grace that God had with his worde and gospell bestowed upon his holie and electe people of England." Wisdom was not equating the elect with the nation of England, however, but with Protestants who had refused to compromise under Mary and instead suffered for their steadfastness: "[W]ho wolde have thoughte so perfecte constant and trewe faith cowlde have bene found in manye one yea in all that cam to the tryall as was? What contempt of the world was this to lose faire howses, goodlie landes, riches possessions, large revenuewes, deare frendes, their beloved childern and wives, yea to give their bodies to the fire, rather then to defille them selfs with popishe Idolatrye."[29] John Foxe would write to former Marian exiles during Elizabeth's reign that

> [t]o forsake your countrey to despice your commodyties at home, to con-tempne rycheis and to set naught by honors which the whole woorld hath in gret veneracyon for the love of the sacred gospell of christ are not workes of the flesshe but the most assured frutes of the holye goost and undeseveable argumentes of your regeneracyon or new birth. Whereby god certyfyeth yow that ye are justyfyed in hym and sealed to eternall liff.[30]

If evangelicals could identify steadfast confession as a mark of election, they could far more ominously identify dissimulation and recantation with damnation. As Bale put it, the Christian under persecution had two choices: profess Christ and suffer death, or "openlye denye Christes verite which is moche worse than the death," which would place a person "whollye undre Antichristes yoke agayne."[31] A decade later, an anonymous Marian Protestant wrote to his brethren that if they proved to be unfaithful Christians, they would "meryte to be expulssyd" from Christ's fellowship and "to be Racyde owt of the bocke of lyfe and to be reprobatyd and a cowrsyd for ever trely we do desserv nothung else and even so shall yt hapen unto us harken."[32] John Hullier, a Cambridgeshire minister, violently condemned dissembling in a letter to his congregation, telling them that backsliding would prove that they were not among the "nomber of them" destined for heaven.[33] Other evangelicals put the matter a slightly different way, arguing that dissimulation was actually impossible for a true Christian, who would never outwardly deny Christ by countenancing idolatry. John Bradford doubted that "masse gospellers & popyshe protestantes" could

---

[29] Robert Wisdom, preface to "A Sermon of the knowledge of the trewe God," 1559, Emmanuel College Library (ECL) MS 261, f. 70r.
[30] Harley MS 416, f. 144r. [31] Bale, *The epistle exhortatorye*, 25r. [32] Harley MS 416, f. 93v.
[33] Harley MS 416, ff. 17v-18r.

really have true faith, because it is "impossyble [for] trewe fayth of goddes gospell to be in the hart of that man which commynge to masse uttereth it not by some thing, wherbye men maye perceyve the lyghte of fayth inwardlye in the bosome."[34] If a person were truly a Christian, their faith could not be hidden. Likewise, John Hooper wrote that "christianitie and true religion cannot be in him that is afraide to confesse Christe and hys gospel in the time of persecution" and Thomas Sampson argued that "if ye thinke that ye can bothe embrace Popery and the Gospel, ye do disceave your selfes . . . This can ye not do bothe, they are so contrarie."[35]

Indeed, dissimulation and recantation were often identified as the "unforgivable sin," or blasphemy against the Holy Spirit. George Joye wrote in 1545 that men should "beware how they dissemble with the trewth in this worlde, lest in soche an ungodly securitie they pluke the synne of the holy ghost into theyr bosoms."[36] John Bale wrote in 1547 that Nicholas Shaxton had been damned by his recantation, since "them (sayth S. Paule) whych voluntarylye blaspheme the truthe, after they have receyved the Gospell in faythe and in the holye Ghost, remayneth no expyacyon of synne. but the fearfull judgement of hell fyre. For a mocke have they made of the sonne of God, Hebreo. 6. and 10."[37] According to these terrifying admonitions, dissembling one's faith to avoid persecution was literally the worst thing a person could do.

The second problem with dissimulation was that it was not only a grievous sin against God but also a sin against one's neighbors. Nicodemites purportedly justified their actions by claiming that they attended Mass and other "popish" ceremonies in order to serve their neighbors and further the prospects of the gospel. Calvin claimed that some Nicodemites justified their actions as a way of preserving a godly remnant for the future: if zealous Christians fled idolatrous ceremonies, "all landes where Antichrist reygneth, shulde be destitute of faithfull people" and "how can the doctrine of the gospel be multiplied, yf the sede be taken awaye?"[38] The eponymous protagonist in Robert Pownall's 1555 translation of Musculus's The Temporysour defended his Nicodemism in missionary terms, claiming that if true Christians refused to attend church, then the "simple" would think evil of them and the gospel they professed. The "Temporysour" also claimed that Protestants could not rush the simple

[34] Bradford, The Hurte of Hering Masse (London, 1561; STC 3494), civ, d3v.
[35] Hooper, Whether Christian faith maye be kepte secret in the heart (London?, 1553; STC 5160.3), a3r; Sampson, A letter to the trew professors of Christes Gospell (Wesel?, 1554; STC 21683), b4r.
[36] Joye, The exposicion of Daniel, 33r.
[37] Bale, The lattre examinacyon of Anne Askewe (Wesel, 1547; STC 850), 40r.
[38] Jean Calvin, The Mynde of the Godly and excellent lerned M. Jhon Calvyne (STC 4435), h8v-i1r, i2r.

into rejecting idolatry: people must follow their consciences and the simple might be "provoked by oure example to leave theyr publyke servyces, whiche they as yet exteme to be holy and lawefull, and in so doyng sinne agaynst theyr consciences." To avoid offense, therefore, Protestants should attend Mass until the simple "are more playnelye instructed in the trueth of Gods worde, and doe abandon the same by theyr owne proper consent, as we have done."[39] Above all, "Temporysour" insisted that no one misunderstood his dissembling as approval for popish services or a denial of his Protestant convictions. His neighbors, who knew he had been a Protestant for twenty years, realized "that I owe no good wyll unto theyr relygion."[40]

Anti-Nicodemites rejected these lines of reasoning and insisted that attending the Mass could never help one's neighbors or country. Instead, refusing all compromise with idolatry would best edify one's neighbor. Miles Coverdale argued that refusing to dissemble would "not onely stoppe the mouth of evell speakers," but it would provide a powerful witness that would "allure and provoke other men to be frutefully geven to faith and good workes, and to helpe (with such their unfained faith and godly livinge) that the tabernacle of god maye be set up againe."[41] This point was reiterated in 1544 by the anonymous English evangelical who translated Bullinger and Calvin's anti-Nicodemite letters. In the preface, the translator insisted that Christians must "fle from the worshippinge of ydoles, least by thyne evell example thou confirme the weake brother in his erroure, & so thy weake brother peryshe for whom Christ dyed and so will God requier his bloude of thy hande."[42] This claim was based on the notion that the ceremonies a person attended were a proclamation of their allegiances.[43] Bullinger claimed that the person who attended Mass "doth openlye testifye, that he doth acknowledge the masse, and the masses relygyon to be the true servyce of God. Therfore bi his presence, he establysseth all the erroures of the masse."[44] Conversely, if a person refused to attend the Mass,

---

[39] Wolfgang Musculus, *The Temporysour* (Wesel?, 1555, STC 18312), e5v.

[40] Musculus, *The Temporysour*, e2v. This was allegedly a common Nicodemite rationale, one that Catholics would employ in defense of attendance at Church of England services under Elizabeth. See Walsham, *Church Papists*; Walsham, "'Yielding to the Extremity of the Time': Conformity, Orthodoxy and the Post-Reformation Catholic Community," in Peter Lake and Michael Questier (eds.), *Conformity and Orthodoxy in the English Church, c. 1560–1660* (Woodbridge, 2000), 211–236.

[41] Coverdale, *A confutacion of that treatise*, n6v.   [42] *Two Epystles*, a2v.

[43] As George Joye wrote, "Every utwarde reverent behaviour is a token of an inwarde worship & reverence of the same thing where unto thou knelest, as is the prostracion before thy parents or kynga signe of thy inwarde love obedience and worship to them or els thou art but a dissembler, wherfore when thou gevest any utwarde reverence to an image, thou shewest thy self, with inwarde worship to reverence the same." Joye, *The exposicion of Daniel*, 36r.

[44] *Two Epystles*, a4v.

"hym take the adversaryes for a contemner of ther servyce, & all the whole papistrye."[45] Calvin proclaimed in his letter that since the Mass was an idol, when "thou therfore art at it, thou stondest before the symple, and gevest very evyll ensample, for they thynke, thou worshyppest whatsoever abhomynacyon is in the masse."[46] The apostle Paul taught that the Christian who partook of the cup of devils "although he do it without conscience of superstycyon, only by outwarde ensample, medleth with prophane usages: and moreover that he is gyltye of bloude, because he confirmeth the erroure of the ignoraunt by his ensample."[47]

Attending idolatrous rites and/or dissembling one's evangelical convictions, in other words, fell under the well-known Pauline prohibition of causing "offense" to weaker brethren. Calvin hammered this point home in another anti-Nicodemite work, translated into English and published four times in 1548, in which he explained that the apostle Paul used the word "offense" to signify "the troublyng of a conscience wherby it is letted to come unto Jesus Christ or caused to fall or drawe backe from hym."[48] According to Calvin, when a weak Christian saw a Nicodemite attend idolatrous worship, "thinketh he not that you have the Idol in some estimation?"[49] The Nicodemite corrupted the weaker brethren who initially "wolde make conscience to defile them selves with Idolatry," but who were then encouraged to violate their consciences by the Nicodemite's wicked example.[50] Perhaps even more dangerously, dissembling in the presence of weaker brethren created "doubte & scrupulosite that they wote not what to beleve."[51]

Dissimulation was seen not only as damaging weaker brethren but also hindering the possible conversion of papists. As Calvin put it, dissemblers "confyrme the unbelevers and harden them in their errours."[52] In Musculus's *The Temporysour*, the godly interlocutor "Eusebius" explained that when a Catholic saw a Protestant dissembler attend Catholic services, the Catholic would believe that "thou doest likewyse reverence & worship those services, as I do," thinking moreover that the Protestant had realized how he had been "seduced & abused by the new gospel whiche he lately professed, & now knoweth certainly that we have the trew gospel, & that we are the trew church."[53] According to anti-Nicodemites, the attendance of

---

[45] *Two Epystles*, a4v.   [46] *Two Epystles*, a7r.   [47] *Two Epystles*, a7r.
[48] Calvin, *The Mynde of the Godly and excellent lerned M. Jhon Calvyne*, f8r.
[49] Calvin, *The Mynde of the Godly and excellent lerned M. Jhon Calvyne*, c5r.
[50] Calvin, *The Mynde of the Godly and excellent lerned M. Jhon Calvyne*, g2r.
[51] Calvin, *The Mynde of the Godly and excellent lerned M. Jhon Calvyne*, h3v.
[52] Calvin, *The Mynde of the Godly and excellent lerned M. Jhon Calvyne*, g2r.
[53] Musuclus, *The Temporysour*, e4r.

known Protestants at Mass would only strengthen Catholics in their heretical beliefs and give them hope that all Protestants would soon return to Rome. As Peter Martyr Vermigli put it concisely in his *Treatise of the Cohabitacyon of the faithfull with the unfaithfull*, translated into English and published in 1555, the papists would say to themselves "these gospellers do comme to our masses, which they wold not do yf our masses wer so evell as thei call them: wherfor we may persevere and continue in our old purpose."[54] According to John Bradford, this made the dissembler guilty of murdering his neighbor's soul.[55]

If Nicodemism was a sin against both God and one's neighbor, how were Christians to maintain a constant confession of Christ when they encountered idolatry and heresy? One of the earliest evangelical texts to take up this question was William Roy's *A Brefe Dialoge*, a translation of a catechism by the Strassbourg reformer Wolfgang Capito. *A Brefe Dialoge* demanded that Christians refuse to worship idols "nott inwardly in the herte alone / but also in every exteriall thynge."[56] When a Christian stood "Be fore stockes and stakes / stones and pillars se that ye once putt no honde to youre cappe / nor yet bowe ye youre kne / butt morne in youre hert / for the blyndnes of theym which thus abuse the honoure due unto god."[57] While insisting on open signs of disapproval, Capito's approach permitted Christians to be present at idolatrous worship, but other evangelicals suggested that a better course of action was for the godly to absent themselves entirely. Tyndale argued in 1531 that the Mass was so deeply seductive that it would inevitably damage a person's soul, since when a priest "leadith me by the darkenesse of sacramentes with out significacion, I can not but ketch harme and put mi trust and confidence in that which is nether god ner his worde."[58] George Joye urged his readers in 1534 to "hear the exhortacion of Jeremye crying upon us sayng. Fle from oute of the middes of Babylon & let every man save himself, let no man dissemble nor holde his tongue at hir wikednes," advice that he would repeat during his second exile in the mid-1540s when he urged the godly to flee from "images, altars, misses, menis sacraments, rytes, cerem. tradicions, yea and menis actis and articles stande in the chirches, red and preched out of the pulpits in stede of the gospell."[59] Henry Brinkelow targeted the Mass specifically in 1542, writing that it was impossible to

---

[54] Peter Martyr Vermigli, *A Treatise of the Cohabitacyon of the faithfull with the unfaithfull* (Strassburg, 1555; STC 24673.5), e4r.

[55] Bradford, *The Hurte of Hering Masse*, c6r, e1v. [56] Roy, *A Brefe Dialoge*, 114.

[57] Roy, *A Brefe Dialoge*, 115. [58] Tyndale, *An answere unto Sir Thomas Mores dialoge*, 93r.

[59] George Joye, *Jeremy the prophete, translated into Englisshe* (Antwerp, 1534; STC 2778), a5v; Joye, *The exposicion of Daniel*, 169v.

attend Mass without being guilty of idolatry, for "surely ye can not remaine as ye do, but ye muste be partakers of ther Idolatrye."[60] The only course of action was to "forsake thys whore," and Brinkelow urged "all prestes that wylbe of Christes congregacion, to fle and geve over that abhominable massinge, which is a blasphemy to Christes bloude, in that they make of it a sacryfice."[61] Evangelicals also directed their co-religionists to flee from false preaching and popish clergy. In 1531, Tyndale wrote that "for as moche as we may have no felowship with them that kepe not Gods commaundmentes. i. Cor. v. and in as moche as al such ar falseprophetes voyde of al truthe, it foloweth that we owght to geve our doctors none audience, thoughe their defenders stoode by them with their swerdes drawne, but rather to laydowne oure hedes & stretch forth our neckes, to be slayn."[62] The same advice was being given in 1541 by Miles Coverdale, who instructed his readers that if Scripture showed a preacher or author's words to be "false, sedicious or abhominable, then hold them accursed, avoyde them utterly, eschue them in anye wise, and geve over thy selfe to the wholsome hearing and reading of the scripture."[63]

Tyndale, Joye, Coverdale, and Bale were themselves exiles when they demanded that Christians boldly repudiate idolatry, but even evangelicals who remained in England could counsel their co-religionists to absent themselves from idolatrous worship. The former Augustinian canon turned-evangelical-polemicist Thomas Solme suggested in a 1540 pamphlet that it would be better for evangelicals to stay home from church than to dignify idolatry with their presence. Commenting on the Fourth Commandment, Solme argued that after Christ's coming, the Sabbath day existed "that the cherche myght com togethere in that day to prayers and lawdis of God, to here the worde of God, & to use the Sacramentis in ryght order."[64] But if God's word were

> not towght men were better to kepe theyre bysynes at home accordinge to theyre vocacions ... then for to cum to the persons barne, and there commyt ydolitre in mayntenynge his ambision, pride, and bestly lyvinge. Nobyl statis were better to hunte the bull here, hert or ony othere thynge lyke intendinge to suckure the powre with the mette, then to here sere Jhon singyl sowle stombel a payer of mattens in laten, flynge holy water, curse holy brede, and to play a caste kyke yack an napes in a foles cotte ... this day ordinyd for a

---

[60] Henry Brinkelow, *The lamentacyon of a Christen against the Citye of London* (Bonn, 1542; STC 3764), d7r.

[61] Brinkelow, *The lamentacyon*, d6r-v.

[62] Tyndale, *The exposition of the fyrste Epistle of seynt Jhon*, d2r.

[63] Coverdale, *A confutacion of that treatise*, n6v.   [64] Solme, *Here begynnyth*, d4r.

godly polysy, is nowe usyd to the grett dishonore of God, so that it were better to be usyd never a dell, ye not to be had in remembraunce, wherby men myght worke, then to use it as they do for the most parte.[65]

Anti-Nicodemites encouraged the godly not only to separate themselves from idolatrous services but to avoid idolaters themselves. During Mary's reign, Joyce Hales promised John Careless that she would follow his counsel "not to have much to do wyth them" that she perceived "to be obstenat Agaynst the truth."[66] The Marian Protestant Robert Glover counseled his wife to "have no fellowshipp with them ['the children of the devill'] therfore my dear wife, with their doctrine & traditions, lest ye be partakers of there synnes."[67] The best policy concerning papists, according to John Knox, was "to flee and avoid the society and company of the proud contemners of God."[68] Peter Martyr's *Treatise of the Cohabitacyon of the faithfull with the unfaithfull* aggressively denounced Nicodemism and analyzed the proper relations between the godly and ungodly in exhaustive detail. According to Martyr, weak Christians should have no fellowship at all with the "unfaithful" because they would inevitably be corrupted by their false opinions. "Strong" Christians could have contact with the unfaithful "only in respect of wynnynge them to the gospell of christe."[69] This contact must not take place at Catholic services, which no Christian should attend, and the "strong" must not enjoy their contact with Catholics. The strong should only communicate with the unfaithful to proselytize them, not for "pleasure and recreacion," and all companying with the ungodly should feel "heavy and bitter" to the strong Christian.[70] There was an evangelistic reason for this: just as Nicodemism confirmed papists in their idolatry, the conversion of the ungodly would also be hindered by friendly communication,

> for whilest the unbelevers do se that the faithful do lyve so frendly, and familiarly with them, they do judge forthewith that their supersticion, and unbeleif, is not so wicked a thinge, nor yet a thinge so to be abhorred and condemned, as it is reported, yea thus maye they be brought to imagin, that they maye be saved though they do persevere, and contynue in their unbeleif. For if it wer otherwise (shall they thincke) theise goode and godly men, wold not be thus familiar and frendly with us.[71]

---

[65] Solme, *Here begynnyth*, d4v–d5r. [66] Add. MS 19400, f. 78v. [67] Harley MS 416, f. 9r.
[68] John Knox, "Letter to the Commonalty," in *On Rebellion*, ed. Roger A. Mason (Cambridge, 1994), 125.
[69] Martyr, *A Treatise of the Cohabitacyon*, a4v.
[70] Martyr, *A Treatise of the Cohabitacyon*, a4r-v, b6v. [71] Martyr, *A Treatise of the Cohabitacyon*, b4v.

Finally, Vermigli taught that the strong should only keep company with the unfaithful "so long as ther is goode hoope of wynninge, and converting them to the gospell of christe. For yf the unbeleavers shall shew themselves so obstinate in their evell, that they gyve juste cause to despaire of ther amendement, then are they utterly to be forsaken, and no conversacion or companie is to be hadd with them, farther then the necessitie of lyfe enforcith either partie."[72]

In his extensive anti-Nicodemite writings, Calvin did not necessarily insist that Christians openly confront idolatry or idolaters. Calvin wrote that "we do not requyre of every one, an open confessyon of his fayth," insisting that the need for an open confession was conditioned by circumstances like "the measure of his understonding, facultye, & as occasion is offryd hym."[73] While "outward profession" was necessary, it was neither "expedient nor convenient" for every Christian to "publysh it in the stretes as the blowing of a trompet: but that everye one after their vocation in the which he is called to take hede that he geve god his glory."[74] But there were English evangelicals who, unlike Calvin, demanded that the true Christian must openly confront the idolatry in their midst. When Tyndale described the Christian's duty to "salt" sin and evil doctrine, he emphasized that "anye man" could rebuke a preacher/bishop privately for preaching false doctrine, but if that failed to bring about a change, "then we must come forthe openlye and rebuke theyr wyckednes in the face of the worlde and jeoparde life and all theron."[75] John Bale argued that God demanded extreme hostility toward idolatry: the Jews "tare ther outwarde vesturs whan they harde ther God blasphemed," so Christians ought likewise to feel their hearts torn and face death rather than "leave those Antichristes untowched, that so depelye blasphemeth hys wholsome wayes and withstandeth hys godlye testymonyes."[76] Again criticizing "Gentyll and soft wyttes" in 1546 who were "offended, that we are now a dayes so vehement in rebukes," Bale demanded that the elect assail hypocrites and insisted that "Necessarye is it that the elect flocke of God, do hate the uncleane fowles, whych yet holde their habytacyon in Babylon, Apoca. 18."[77] George Joye was, if anything, more extreme than Bale was on this point. According to Joye, "it is all one thynge, not to defende the trewth and to denye the trewth."[78] It was not enough for true Christians to refuse to deny Christ, then; they must also be

[72] Martyr, *A Treatise of the Cohabitacyon*, a4v.   [73] *Two Epystles*, a5v.
[74] Calvin, *The Mynde of the Godly and excellent lerned M. Jhon Calvyne*, b6r-b7r.
[75] Tyndale, *Exposicion*, 29v-30v.   [76] Bale, *Yet a course*, 97r.
[77] John Bale, *The first examinacyon of Anne Askewe* (Wesel, 1546; STC 848), 44r-45r.
[78] Joye, *The exposicion of Daniel*, 33r.

actively confessing Christ and his gospel against its enemies. Joye pointed to the example of Daniel who made a "constant confession" when he not only refused to obey Darius's law prohibiting prayer to God but provocatively chose to pray before an open window. Joye asked why Daniel did this: "Why daniel? What nedest thou thus openly to have put thyself in perell? thou mighst have worshipt god in spirit or secretely and not by these externe gestures have declared it: or for that space not to have praid at all. No, not so did daniel, for he knewe that the trewe religion and worship must be farre from all colourable dissembling without any lying shyftis of hypocricie especially in siche an archebisshop."[79] Writing in the first year of Edward VI's reign, Anthony Gilby glossed the very fact that he was writing against the "Idolatrie" and "supersticion" advocated by Stephen Gardiner as a rejection of dissimulation, since "I judge it my parte to publishe my faith, rather then by my silence to seame to consent to suche divillishe doctrine."[80] This sort of active profession was necessary, "leste bi our silence for sakinge hys cause here upon erth, we be forsaken in his heavenly palace."[81] Indeed, it was not only necessary to speak against idolatry but to do so in extreme terms. Gilby explained to his readers that any "bitter worde" or "sharpe sentence againste the mainteiners of thys Idole" was utterly necessary, since more moderate language would make him worthy "to be vometted up againe, being nether hote nor colde."[82]

This was, in broad outlines, the anti-Nicodemite stance that developed among the hotter sort of early English Protestants and that would dominate the thought of the Marian exiles. Anti-Nicodemism was an intellectually powerful, highly elaborated, and increasingly influential ethic within English Protestantism by the 1550s. Anti-Nicodemites not only insisted that Christians must do nothing that could be construed as "denying Christ" before men, but the most aggressive argued that Christians must "acknowledge Christ" provocatively in the face of idolaters and heretics. Failure to fulfill these duties was depicted as a monstrous sin: the person who dissembled was possibly revealing himself to be among the reprobate and persistent dissimulation was literally described as unforgivable. The dissembler also did immeasurable harm to others by grieving the godly,

[79] Joye, *The exposicion of Daniel*, 84v.
[80] Anthony Gilby, *An answer to the devillish detection of Stephane Gardiner* (London?, 1547/8; STC 11884), 2v-3r.
[81] Gilby, *An answer*, 3r.   [82] Gilby, *An answer*, 10v.

drawing weaker consciences into damnable sin, and confirming papists in their error.

Despite the obsession with anti-Nicodemism among the Marian exiles, one might expect that this ethos would have lost its raison d'être for English Protestants when Mary died in 1558 and Catholic worship was abolished in England. It did not. The anti-Nicodemite message itself, if measured only by the production of explicitly anti-Nicodemite texts, was alive and well among Protestants in Elizabethan England. In part, this was a by-product of the hagiographical project that valorized the Marian martyrs and reproduced their writings for an Elizabethan reading public. As Brad Gregory has noted, "martyrologies functioned like anti-Nicodemite exhortations" by showing that the extreme behavior demanded by the anti-Nicodemites was indeed possible.[83] More directly, martyrological writings also reproduced broad swathes of anti-Nicodemite argument and admonition. Bull and Coverdale's 1564 anthology of the martyrs' writings, alongside the successive editions of Foxe's *Acts and Monuments*, ensured that the Marian martyrs' incessant denunciations of Nicodemism remained front and center in the Elizabethan Protestant consciousness. Anti-Nicodemite pamphlets like John Hooper's *Whether Christian faith maye be kepte secret in the heart, without confession thereof openly to the worlde*, which was first published at the start of Mary's reign in 1553, found new readers when it was republished in Bull and Coverdale's 1564 anthology.[84] Other anti-Nicodemite texts by Marian martyrs were printed for the first time during Elizabeth's reign, such as John Bradford's *The Hurte of Hering Masse*, which was written before his martyrdom in 1555 but not printed until 1561 (and then again in 1580).[85]

Arguments against Nicodemism did not appear only in hagiographical literature, however, and anti-Nicodemite works by foreign divines continued to be freshly translated and printed throughout Elizabeth's reign. The list of anti-Nicodemite works printed during Elizabeth's reign is extensive. Calvin's anti-Nicodemite *Quatre sermons*, partially translated and printed by Robert Horne at the beginning of Mary's reign in 1553, were reprinted in

[83] Gregory, *Salvation at Stake*, 174.

[84] Hooper, *Whether Christian faith maye be kepte secret in the heart*; Hooper, "A letter sente to the Christian congregation, wherin he proveth that true faith cannot be kepte secrete in the heart without confession therof openly to the world when occasion serveth," in Henry Bull and Miles Coverdale (ed.), *Certain most godly, fruitful, and comfortable letters of such true Saintes and holy Martyrs of God* (London, 1564; STC 5886), 157–163.

[85] John Bradford, *The Hurte of Hering Masse* (London, 1561; STC 3494); Bradford, *The hurt of hearyng Masse* (London, 1580; STC 3495). A manuscript of this text is among John Foxe's papers: Harley MS 422, ff. 104–132.

full in English for the first time in 1561, with a new translation of the third and fourth sermons.[86] In 1562, an English translation of the Gnesio-Lutheran Johann Wigand's *De Neutralibus et Mediis, Grosly Inglyshed, Jacke of both Sydes* was printed for the first time in London, containing an extensive denunciation of Nicodemism and dissembling.[87] In the 1570s and 1580s, anti-Nicodemite texts were being reproduced by figures at the heart of the Elizabethan puritan movement. Anthony Gilby translated an abridgment of Calvin's commentary on Daniel in 1570, which contained extensive anti-Nicodemite passages.[88] Calvin's complete *Quatre sermons* were newly translated and reprinted by John Field in 1579, while Horne's Marian translation of the second of the *Quatre sermons* was reprinted by the puritan printer Robert Waldegrave as a standalone pamphlet in 1581 (the same year in which Waldgrave registered, but did not print, Knox's anti-Nicodemite *An admonition or warning that the faithful Christians in London, Newcastle, Barwycke, and others, may avoide God's vengeance* [1554]).[89] In the following year, an anti-Nicodemite letter by Calvin's friend and colleague Pierre Viret was translated and printed as *An epistle to the faithfull necessary for all the children of God* (1582) and Calvin's *Quatre sermons* appeared again in 1584, when Anthony Munday claimed to respond to "the daily request of zelous persons" who were "very desirous of them" by publishing Horne's translation of Calvin's first two sermons (which purportedly "have long lyen hidden in silence").[90] Wolfgang Musculus's anti-Nicodemite dialogue, *The Temporisour*, originally translated and printed in 1555 by Robert Pownall, was also reprinted in Edinburgh in 1584. Finally, Wigand's *De Neutralibus & Mediis, Grosly Englished* was republished in 1591.[91]

The production of so much Protestant anti-Nicodemite literature in Elizabethan England is curious and raises the obvious question of why it

---

[86] Jean Calvin, *Foure Godlye sermons agaynst the pollution of idolatries* (London, 1561; STC 4438, 4438.5).

[87] Wigand, *De Neutralibus et Mediis*.

[88] Jean Calvin, *Commentaries of that divine John Calvine, upon the Prophet Daniell* (London, 1570; STC 4397).

[89] Jean Calvin, *Foure Sermons of Maister John Calvin, Entreating of matters very profitable for our time . . . Translated out of Frenche into Englishe by John Fielde* (London, 1579; STC 4439); Jean Calvin, *A Sermon of the famous and Godly learned man, master John Calvine, chiefe Minister and Pastour of Christs church at Geneva, conteining an exhortation to suffer persecution for followinge Jesus Christe and his Gospell* (London, 1581; STC 4439.5). On the Knox pamphlet, see Susannah Brietz Monta, "Martyrdom in Print in Early Modern England: The Case of Robert Waldegrave," in Johan Leemans (ed.), *More than a memory: the discourse of martyrdom and the construction of Christian identity in the history of Christianity* (Leuven, 2005), 276.

[90] Viret, *An Epistle to the Faithfull*; Jean Calvin, *Two godly and learned Sermons* (London, 1584; STC 4461), a3r, a1r.

[91] *De Neutralibus & Mediis, Grosly Englished, Jacke of both sides* (London, 1591; STC 25613).

was being published at all. With the Mass abolished, why would Protestants continue to translate and print books that urged Protestants not to dissemble their faith by attending Mass? The producers of this literature themselves recognized that their readers might think that these texts were irrelevant. In dedicating his 1579 translation of Calvin's *Quatre sermons* to the Earl of Huntingdon, John Field opened by acknowledging that "men will marvayle, whye I shoulde publishe these ... excellente Sermons of Maister John Calvines, the Argumentes whereof bee not so fitte and agreeable (as they thinke) to these times: seeing GOD in mercy hath geven us peace, and set us at libertie from that Romish yoke, suffering the beames of his glorious Gospel to spread far and wide, to the great comfort of many, and his owne everlasting glory."[92] Here Field was echoing his source material, as Calvin began the first of the *Quatre sermons* by noting that "some may thinke that this is a superfluous argument in respect of us, who have by the grace of God, our churches purged from the infections and the Idolatryes of the Papacie."[93]

There were several reasons, however, why Field, Calvin, and others thought that such skeptics were "foulely deceived" and that the anti-Nicodemite message remained "very profitable, for these our times" in a Protestant land like Elizabethan England.[94] On one level, the ongoing publication of anti-Nicodemite literature was quite provocatively presented as a way to remind former Nicodemites of their previous compromises with idolatry. Calvin argued in the first of the *Quatre sermons* that people living in a reformed church still needed to hear "what an offence it is too defile our selves with Idolatries, faigning to consent or to cleave too their impieties," because it would prick the conscience of those who had formerly sinned in these ways.[95] This touched on a rather sensitive subject for an Elizabethan Protestant readership, not only because the majority of Edwardian Protestants had conformed under Mary but because the Elizabethan Church and state were headed by a trio of former Nicodemites: Archbishop Parker, Secretary Cecil, and the Queen herself. While few Protestants were willing to remind figures like Elizabeth or Cecil of this fact, some did find it necessary to make a point of it. John Knox urged Elizabeth in a 1559 letter to "consider depely how for feare of your life yow did decline from God and bowe to idolatrie" and to "Let it not appere a small offense in your eyes that yow have declined from Christ Jesus in the

[92] Calvin (trans. Field), *Foure Sermons*, 2r.   [93] Calvin, (trans. Field), *Foure Sermons*, iv.
[94] Calvin (trans. Field), *Foure Sermons*, iv; Viret, *An Epistle*, ¶2r.
[95] Calvin (trans. Field), *Foure Sermons*, iv.

day of the battaile."[96] Even decades later, some former exiles reminded the queen and her councillors of their compromises with idolatry, expressing dismay at their persistent refusal to repent. William Fuller, who had been an elder in Knox's exile congregation at Geneva, sent an astonishingly brazen admonition to Elizabeth in July 1585, in which he directed the queen to remember that God had preserved her life during her sister's reign, even though she was "unworthie by reason of your yielding to that Idolatrie."[97] Fuller told the queen that he had been so troubled by her apostasy and failure to repent publicly at the outset of her reign that he had initially intended to remain in Geneva after Mary's death. Calvin had convinced him to return to England, but even so, Fuller had journeyed home with a French Bible, a New Testament, and the Genevan service book as a gift for Elizabeth "to move you to repentance."[98] Upon arriving home, however, he decided against confronting her – a sinful act of dissimulation that he was now remedying? – because he knew that if he had begun "as I durst not do otherwise" with "telling your Majesty of your faults," there would have been no hope that his advice about religious reform would have been heeded.[99] Twenty-five years later, he had apparently decided that the state of the Church of England was so dire that he could no longer withhold his rebuke.

William Cecil's Marian Nicodemism was also criticized in an extraordinarily bold 1579 letter from Richard Prowde that was intended to "to let you to undrstand what is sayd of you."[100] Prowde, a former Marian exile, was currently the parson of Burton upon Dunmore in Buckinghamshire and the husband of Rose Nottingham, who had been noted in Foxe's *Acts and Monuments* for her support of the martyrs and commitment to true religion.[101] Prowde's letter began by criticizing Cecil for dissembling under Mary. After noting Cecil's "brynginge up in trewe relygyon," Prowde

---

[96] Copy of letter from Knox to Elizabeth, c. 1559, Add. MS 32091, f. 168r. As Thomas Freeman has shown, even John Foxe's portrayal of Elizabeth in the *Acts and Monuments* was tinged with criticism of her Marian conformity. Rather than attempting "to conceal his Queen's conformity during a time of persecution, Foxe conducted detailed, accurate research but manipulated his sources to criticize Elizabeth." Thomas S. Freeman, "'As True a Subiect being Prysoner': John Foxe's Notes on the Imprisonment of Princess Elizabeth, 1554–5," *English Historical Review* 117, no. 470 (February 2002), 116.

[97] Dr Williams's Library Morrice MS B, p. 297.

[98] Dr Williams's Library Morrice MS B, pp. 305–306.

[99] Dr Williams's Library Morrice MS B, pp. 307–308. There were also other circumstances that Fuller claimed had led him to avoid an audience with the queen, including the possible impact it would have had on his relationship with Knox, Goodman, and the other Genevan exiles.

[100] Lansdowne MS 28, f. 214r.

[101] On Prowde, see Garrett, *Marian Exiles*, 262; Pearse, *Between known men and visible saints*, ch. 1. On Rose Nottingham, see Foxe, *The Unabridged Acts and Monuments Online* (1576 edition) [Accessed: 02.06.14].

reminded him how he "dyd openly revolt from your relygyon & fell to goo to idolatrus sarvys" during Mary's reign and how, by doing so, he had "consented to all the blude of the profetes & marters that was shed unryghtously in manasses dayes" (a claim that Knox had made about dissemblers).[102] Cecil had not penitently come to the London underground church after Mary's death, as others had done "that were in your faute, as ye ought to have done . . . and then there to have showed your sorowfull hart for your faute, confessyng ther your open falles & syning in idolatry, axing mercy of god for it & purposyng by his grace never here after to fall into that synne agayne; and so to have entred into a new lege & covenaunt with hym."[103] Instead, Cecil had moved on with life as if nothing had happened.

While most were too savvy or too fearful to say it publicly, therefore, it is clear that Marian Nicodemism – and a failure to repent of it – had not been forgotten by some Elizabethan Protestants. The continued publication of anti-Nicodemite literature stood not only as an explicit rebuke to these dissemblers but also hopefully (in Calvin's words) as a spur "to mourne for our former faultes, and to aske pardon of God for them with all humilitie" and to thank God for "pulling us out from such filth wherein wee were plunged."[104]

Elizabethan anti-Nicodemite literature was aimed not only at the past, however, but also at the future and the dangers that were feared ahead. Elizabethan Protestants were all too aware of the potentially fleeting nature of the gospel's restoration in England. As James Calfhill noted with concern in 1565, idolatry had been destroyed during Edward's reign, but the human heart was so prone to idolatry that pilgrimages and other idolatries were "straight erected" almost immediately after Edward's death.[105] If the queen were to die suddenly – hardly an unlikely scenario – why expect anything different? Indeed, Catholic restoration and renewed persecution were depicted not only as a distinct possibility but as an inevitability by puritans like John Field. Hence, English Protestants needed to remain on something like anti-Nicodemite high alert, constantly preparing to resist the impending temptation to dissemble and submit to popery. In his 1579 introduction to the *Quatre Sermons*, Field explained that he had translated these sermons because "I thought they coulde not but be very profitable, at the leaste too prepare us against the time to come."[106] God had given England a long

[102] Lansdowne MS 28, f. 214r.   [103] Lansdowne MS 28, f. 214r.
[104] Calvin (trans. Field), *Foure Sermons*, IV.
[105] James Calfhill, *An aunswere to the Treatise of the Crosse* (London, 1565; STC 4368), 5v.
[106] Calvin (trans. Field), *Foure Sermons*, 3r.

period of peace, but they had misused it and shown "contempt of his graces," provoking God to punish England "with the fire of adversitie, that we may be purged from our foule corruption."[107] Persecution and the temptation to dissemble were coming again, so English Christians needed to read and internalize anti-Nicodemite literature like "wise Marriners" preparing for the impending storm.[108] Here Field was again echoing Calvin's own advice in the text, where Calvin told those who had liberty to profess the gospel to "take the time wherin we be in rest, not as though it should alwaies last us: but as a truce in which god giveth us leasure to fortifie our selves" and to prepare for future bouts of persecution when steadfast and costly confession would be necessary.[109]

The temptation to dissemble was not only seen as a future possibility, however; it was also perceived as a present-day lure for the godly and one to which many were already succumbing. The world of the courtier, where dissimulation was a way of life, provided one source of temptation. Writing in the wake of the Northern Rebellion of 1569, Thomas Drant accused high-status Elizabethan Protestants of refusing to make a full and complete confession of Christ, because doing so would clash with the demands of civility and politeness:

> There be many Gospellers at these dayes that will be content to take that name, and as they say beleve so: but they will not make their talke of Christ, or of divinitie, for that is no gentlemanly talke, no fellowlike talke, no courtlike talke. But the truth is, the truth must be beleved, & *the truth must be talked*. If they be ashamed to talke of Christ before men, Christ will be ashamed to talke of them before his heavenly father.[110]

While these courtly Protestants "have taken on them a profession of the truth, and have not denied any part of the Scripture," they did not speak the fullness of Christian truth that they knew in their hearts and were "in Gods cause so faint and couragelesse, that they will not open their lippes to speake for Christ."[111] A decade later, Richard Prowde would accuse Cecil of

---

[107] Calvin (trans. Field), *Foure Sermons*, 3r.

[108] Calvin (trans. Field), *Foure Sermons*, 3v.

[109] Calvin (trans. Field), *Foure Sermons*, 1v-2r. Calvin also noted that this subject matter was relevant for Christians who might have to "travell into the countries of Papistes" and needed to be "armed aforehand" for the "combate" (1v). Thinking about anti-Nicodemism would also instill "pittie" in the hearts of the godly for "our pore brethren, which are kept under the tyranny of Antichrist" elsewhere (2r).

[110] Thomas Drant, *Two Sermons preached* (London, 1570; STC 7171), L2v; emphasis added.

[111] Drant, *Two Sermons*, L3r-v. Drant equated this with committing treason against God, quoting "*Basil* in a certaine Epistle doth say: *They be traytors to the truth whosoever do not aunswere readily & truely of religion, and matters of divinitie*" (L2v). This treason against God had brought down the "rebels sworde, and whatsoever mischiefe is els to come." (L3r).

precisely this kind of ongoing Nicodemism in his bold letter to the Secretary, for "also it [is] sayd, that you from tyme to tyme ferynge to exasperate the prynce & to mack har worse in relygyon, hath spared your playnenes, and hathe not delt with har so playnely from tyme to tyme as your knowledge hathe requyred, both towchinge gods churche, har owne presarvacyon & the safytie, profyt of the common welthe, to the increase of gods gospell to us and our posterytie for evr more."[112] Cecil erred in so doing, and Prowde astonishingly called Cecil to embrace martyrdom when he wrote that it was his duty to "be bolde & cowragyous" in advancing the gospel at the Elizabethan court, "althoughe it shuld coste you your lyfe."[113]

Keenly aware that they continued to live amid a multitude of "papists," moreover, Elizabethan Protestants also identified a host of social and even economic motives that continued to drive Protestants to dissemble their beliefs. James Pilkington warned about the social pressure to dissemble in his 1560 commentary on Haggai, asking his readers "When thou shalt syt among Papystes and heare them blaspheme thy God and prayse theyr Idolatry, howe canst thou escape with a safe conscience undefyled, yf thou holde thy peace?"[114] It was much safer simply to avoid all contact with papists, since "If thou syt by, heare the truth spoken agaynst, and wyll not defende it to thy power: thou art gylty to thy Lorde God, for Christ sayth: he that is not with me is against me. If thou speak in Gods cause thou shalt be in daunger of thy lyfe and goodes, or both."[115] A decade later, Thomas Norton claimed that Protestants were dissembling in order to attain professional advancement. Papists remained in positions of power in "Colleges, houses of studie, offices in the greatest houshold, in Courtes, in Cathedrall churches, worshipfull roomes in the countrey, and such like," so for Protestants who sought to make a career in these settings, "many times it is more safe, or at least more commodious and avantageable to be taken for a Papist, than for a Christian."[116] Thus "unconstant Gospellers for necessitie or profites sake, become yelders, and dissemblers," the first step on a slippery slope that led "by degrees from hypocrites to playne apostataes, which are in deede the most desperate kinde of Papistes."[117]

[112] Lansdowne MS 28, f. 214r.   [113] Lansdowne MS 28, f. 214r.

[114] James Pilkington, *Aggeus the Prophete declared by a large commentarye* (London, 1560; STC 19926.3), Bb2v-Bb3r.

[115] Pilkington, *Aggeus*, Bb3r.

[116] Thomas Norton, *A warning agaynst the dangerous practises of Papistes* (London, 1569; STC 18685.7), h1r-v.

[117] Norton, *A warning agaynst*, h1v.

Nicodemism was seen not only as a present temptation for Protestants in social settings but also potentially within the confines of the Church of England. It would beg one of the central questions of the day to assume that popish "idolatry" had been banished from the Church of England. Puritans like Field enumerated dozens and even hundreds of ways in which popery continued to defile the Elizabethan Church of England. Some claimed that conservative clergy were simulating popish worship in their parishes: as one preacher claimed at Paul's Cross in January 1566, there were three or four thousand churches in England that "even now a dayes" continued to worship "according to the purification of the Jewes," where clergy and laity alike used the surviving remnants of the Catholic past to continue in their popery – a substantial estimate given England's ten thousand parishes.[118] It was not just crypto-papists in the Church of England who were to be feared, however, but the crypto-popery of the Church of England itself. When leading puritans like Field could refer to the communion service in the Book of Common Prayer as "your masse," then the immediate relevance of anti-Nicodemite literature to the lives of Elizabethan Protestants would have been quite obvious to those who had serious qualms about the "remnants of popery" remaining within the Church of England.[119] Could the godly remain in this church?

The answer was clear to Elizabethan Protestants like Robert Browne, Robert Harrison, John Greenwood, Henry Barrow, and their followers. The situation in Elizabethan England was identical to the situation in Marian England: the godly must separate from the Church of England because its worship, ministry, government, and discipline were Antichristian abominations.[120] Having discovered this fact, they could not remain within the church's communion and fellowship without denying Christ. But many of the most vehement Protestant critics of the Church of England disagreed with this course of action, and when pressed to separate from the national church by their more radical brethren, they offered a variety of private and public defenses of their continuing

---

[118] Bodleian Tanner MS 50, f. 37r. Also see Patrick McGrath and Joy Rowe, "The Marian Priests Under Elizabeth I," *Recusant History* 17 (1984), 103–120; Christopher Haigh, *Reformation and Resistance in Tudor Lancashire* (Cambridge, 1975), ch. 14.

[119] John Field, *Certaine Articles, collected and taken (as it is thought) by the Byshops out of a litle boke entituled an Admonition to the Parliament, wyth an Answere to the same* (Hemel Hempstead?, 1572; STC 10850), a4r.

[120] See Henry Barrow's "Four Causes of Separation," in Leland H. Carlson (ed.), *The Writings of Henry Barrow 1587–1590* (London, 2003), 49–66.

membership in it.[121] When George Gifford published responses to the separatists in 1590, for instance, he argued that "where the worship is Idolatrous and blasphemous, a man is to separate himselfe," but there were degrees of error and "there are many and great corruptions before it come to that."[122] The errors that existed within the Church of England were "not to bee approved," but these errors did not constitute idolatry, destroy the true worship of God, or fatally compromise the exercise of discipline.[123] The Church of England was an imperfect church but a true church nonetheless, and separation was therefore not necessary. The godly must also consider the peace and unity of the church, Gifford argued, as well as remember that private individuals lacked the necessary authority to reform the church or establish new congregations.[124]

To the Separatists, this was self-justifying Nicodemism, pure and simple. Henry Barrow warned his flock from prison in 1587 against these "dubell minded . . . haltyng hipocrits which will seek to quench your spirit, zeall, and love unto the Lord, advisyng you to bear those burdens with them for a season, till God's good plesuer be otherwyse; in the mean tym to use prayer and such libertye as you may."[125] Men like Gifford knew full well that the Church of England possessed an antichristian form of government, Barrow claimed, but "they will not suffer for the truthe," refusing to leave the Church of England out of fear, greed, pride, or a misplaced hope of achieving good from within.[126] Barrow responded to Gifford in 1591, accusing him directly of dissimulation. Gifford purportedly knew that the Church of England was antichristian, but "dissembling with God and your owne conscience to avoyde open shame, [you] care not what wrong you doe

[121] On the special difficulties that the separatist position posed for non-separating puritans and Thomas Cartwright's private responses, see Lake, *Moderate puritans*, ch. 5.

[122] George Gifford, *A Plaine Declaration that our Brownists be full Donatists* (London, 1590; STC 11862), 37. Space does not permit discussion of Gifford's elaborate and more theologically sophisticated analysis of this issue in *A Short Treatise against the Donatists of England* (1590), where he argued that just as the regenerate Christian would always have to fight against sin, so too was it the Church's lot on earth to remain "in some bondage to sinne" and yet strive against it and towards perfection (p. 46).

[123] Gifford, *A Plaine Declaration*, 37.   [124] Gifford, *A Plaine Declaration*, 19–35.

[125] Henry Barrow, "A Pastoral Letter from Prison" (1587) in Carlson (ed.), *The Writings of Henry Barrow 1587–1590*, 111.

[126] Barrow, "A Pastoral Letter," 111–112; also see Barrow, "Four Causes of Separation" (1587) in Carlson (ed.), *The Writings of Henry Barrow 1587–1590*, where he insisted with regard to implementing godly discipline and church government that "Inward intents will not excuse outward, yea, obstinat, transgressions" (65). This is a critique found throughout Elizabethan separatist literature from the early 1580s onward. See Albert Peel and Leland H. Carlson (eds.), *The Writings of Robert Harrison and Robert Browne* (London, 2003), 39–40, 48, 201, 408; Carlson (ed.), *The Writings of Henry Barrow 1587–1590*, 141; Leland H. Carlson (ed.), *The Writings of John Greenwood 1587–1590* (London, 2003), 216–220; Leland H. Carlson (ed.), *The Writings of Henry Barrow 1590–1591* (London, 2003), 243–244.

others, or what judgments you heape upon your self against the daye of wrath."[127] It was hardly coincidence, in Barrow's view, that Gifford's attempts to explain why puritan ministers could remain within the Church of England could equally be used by people to "stande sworne to the masse-booke, joyne to such idolatrous priests and people as use it, yet if in their owne conscience or secretly they dislike some faultes therof, be as cleare as these ministers you speake of are of the corruptions they condeme."[128] In his 1595 response to the puritan minister Arthur Hildersham, Barrow's successor Francis Johnson likewise claimed that Hildersham's arguments for remaining within the Church of England "may with like colour be alledged for abiding in any the most popish assemblyes wheresoever."[129]

To the Separatists, therefore, non-separating puritans were as guilty of Nicodemism as those Protestants who had conformed in the Marian Church. This accusation was surely particularly galling to non-separating puritans like Gifford, because, while rejecting separation in principle, they took a variety of (often very costly) measures to ensure that their continued membership in the national church would never be misinterpreted or confused with whole-hearted acceptance of the popish elements remaining in the Elizabethan Church of England. When Gifford said that abuses were not to be "approved," he did not merely mean withholding active assent. He insisted that with regard to the "abuses and corruptions in the Churche, everie private godlie man is to keepe a good conscience," and that "it is the dutie of every private man, in all humble and peaceable manner, to keepe himselfe unpolluted, from those corruptions and abuses that creep in."[130]

---

[127] Henry Barrow, *A Plaine Refutation* (1591) in Carlson (ed.), *The Writings of Henry Barrow 1590–1591*, 96.

[128] Barrow, *A Plaine Refuation* in Carlson (ed.), *The Writings of Henry Barrow 1590–1591*, 97. Without insinuating that Gifford actually *was* a Nicodemite (a designation that was always polemical and contested), it is worth noting that Gifford's arguments for remaining in the Church of England *were* structurally similar to purported Nicodemite rationales for remaining within the Roman Catholic Church. According to Calvin, for instance, Nicodemites purportedly justified their attendance at Mass by arguing that it was not idolatry, but "remayneth the supper for the faythfull," despite the fact that it was "defyled, deformed . . . corrupt and poluted with wicked opinions." The Nicodemite also purportedly justified himself by claiming that "he him selfe may not reforme the abhominacions that ther appeare," but only pray to God for "a reformacion therof," and also that "he doth his diligence that he seme not to consent unto ydolatrye, nor to such rytes or usages as do robbe God of his honoure, but that he may be perceaved to seke God and his pure worshepe, and utterly to refuse all such thinges as are contrary to his Gospell" (Calvin, *Two epystles*, a8r). The need to maintain peace and unity, moreover, were purported to be the constant refrain of the self-justifying dissembler (Wigand, *De Neutralibus*, a8r, h8v, k6v-L8v).

[129] Francis Johnson, *A Treatise Of the Ministery of the Church of England. Wherein is handled this question, Whether it be to be separated from, or joyned unto* (n.p., 1595; STC 14663.5), 70.

[130] Gifford, *A Short Treatise*, 105, 96.

Puritan nonconformity was produced by a commitment to remaining within the Church of England, but – as we will see in Chapter 6 – was often driven by an anti-Nicodemite insistence that the godly must never appear to be publicly dignifying the "popish trash" that remained within it as well. For Gifford, who had himself been deprived for refusing to affirm the Book of Common Prayer in its entirety in 1584 and then suspended for vestiarian nonconformity in 1586, it was the godly's duty to remain within the national church, but to remain there uncomfortably – maintaining a faithful witness against its corruptions, working for its further reformation, and willingly suffering the consequences for their faithful confession.[131]

While separatists would persistently accuse non-separatists of Nicodemism throughout the 1580s and 1590s, therefore, anti-Nicodemite imperatives were central to the ecclesiastical vision and activism of both separating and non-separating puritans. Their true disagreement lay in what they thought a "constant confession" of Christ required and what "denying Christ" entailed in the circumstances of Elizabethan England. This disagreement extended beyond the realm of ecclesiastical activism into the realm of everyday life. As Patrick Collinson argued, the differing ecclesiological choices of separating and non-separating puritans had important consequences for their social behavior.[132] The separatists would "insist that in church matters the saints (themselves) were to have no communion with the wicked (all the rest). But outside religion and in all secular affairs it was permitted to them to live and deal normally with those living around them." By contrast, non-separating puritans insisted that while "they had no choice but to gather with the wicked and promiscuous multitude in the public exercise of religion ... in all other non-public respects, 'familiar accompanying in private conversation', they must separate severely, or 'as lawfully and conveniently as we may'."[133] Forced to worship alongside the visibly "ungodly" in a church that lacked the sort of rigorous church discipline that they believed to be necessary, non-separating puritans responded to the stresses this situation created through "a constantly maintained witness of social and cultural distinctiveness practised against neighbours with whom

[131] ODNB.
[132] See especially Collinson, Birthpangs, 144–145; also see Collinson, "The Cohabitation of the Faithful with the Unfaithful," in Ole Peter Grell, Jonathan I. Israel, and Nicholas Tyacke (eds.), From Persecution to Toleration: The Glorious Revolution and Religion in England (Oxford, 1991), 51–76; Collinson, "Separation In and Out of the Church: The Consistency of Barrow and Greenwood," The Journal of the United Reformed Church History Society 5:5 (November 1994), 239–258.
[133] Collinson, Birthpangs, 145.

the godly were in daily face-to-face contact and with whom they met in church communion."[134]

This ostentatious social behavior was also clearly motivated by deep anxieties about boldly "acknowledging Christ" before sinful men and women. Protestant anti-Nicodemite literature typically focused on avoiding idolatry in the context of the church, but Reformed Protestants across Europe had an expansive conception of idolatry. Catharine Davies has noted that for Edwardian Protestants, "The Mass was but one form of idolatry; another, more insidious, form was the worship of worldly power and wealth," where "[t]he only difference between the idolatry found in popery and that in covetousness was that the former was found openly in worship."[135] This view was commonplace among the most radical Edwardian Protestants, who argued that idolatry had not been eradicated by the Edwardian Reformation, but that it had survived in a new form. Anthony Gilby claimed in a 1551 commentary on Micah, for instance, that even "thoughe our governours here in Englande through the mighty hand of God have for the comforte of hys electe banyshed the outwarde shewe therof ... Idolatrye is not banyshed, but raigneth more clokedly among us."[136] Some people committed idolatry through their avarice, changing "the kinde of Idolatri, making the muck which they found heaped about those idols, to be their god," while others harbored love for the Mass and the saints in their hearts, and still others called themselves gospellers but worshipped their lusts or wit.[137] This view was echoed by Thomas Lever, who repeatedly equated idolatry with covetousness in a series of high-profile sermons during 1550: "every covetouse manne is an Idolator" because he worships riches instead of God.[138] Men flattered the king when they told him "that thinges in thys realme for the most parte be honourablye, godlye, or charytably reformed ... Ffor papistry is not banyshed out of Englande by pure religion, but overrunne, suppressed and kepte under within thys realme by covetous ambicion."[139] In fact, Lever argued that England was

---

[134] Collinson, "The Cohabitation of the Faithful with the Unfaithful," 62.

[135] Davies, *A Religion of the Word*, 52, 206. Elsewhere Davies has described this Edwardian "description of covetousness as the 'new idolatry'" as "a conscious adaptation of the language of anti-popery to the description and criticism of a supposedly reformed commonwealth": "'Poor Persecuted Little Flock'" in Lake and Dowling (eds.), *Protestantism and the National Church*, 86.

[136] Anthony Gilby, *A Commentarye upon the Prophet Mycha* (London, 1551; STC 11886), a6v-a7r.

[137] Gilby, *A Commentarye*, a6v.

[138] Thomas Lever, *A fruitfull Sermon made in Poules churche at London in the shroudes the seconde daye of February* (London, 1550; STC 15543), a5r. Also see Thomas Lever, *A Sermon preached at Pauls Crosse, the xiiii day of December* (London, 1550; STC 15546.3), b2r-b3r.

[139] Lever, *A Sermon preached at Pauls Crosse*, a3v.

more idolatrous during Edward's reign than it had been when it was out-wardly popish, because while "Papistrye abused many thyngs, covetousnes hath distroyed more: papistry is supersticion, covetousnes is Idolatry."[140] Popery had been banished, but this merely meant that the front line of reformation had now shifted to the battle against greed and covetousness, against the idolatrous behavior and attitudes of "carnall gospellers" who were Christians in name but not deed, and whose behavior grieved godly consciences, slandered true religion, and damned themselves to hell.[141]

While radical Edwardian preachers equated carnal sins with idolatry for polemical effect, anti-Nicodemites in the very different circumstances of Mary's reign reversed the formula, equating idolatry with carnal sins. In Musculus's *The Temporysour*, godly Eusebius attempted to get his Nicodemite friend Temporysour to see the folly of his ways by forcing him to admit that "in the societe and felowship of adulterers and theves, I cannot outwardly joyne my self thereunto without sinne."[142] As Eusebius attempted to explain to Temporysour, dignifying these sins and sinners with his presence was no different from attending Mass. Idolatry was equated with adultery in a letter from a "godly Matrone, which is in exile, unto certain Sisters of hyrs abiding in England," printed in 1554 by John Knox.[143] Since Christ was their "spyritual husband," attending Mass was no different from "geving the use of her body to another man," "spyritual whordom," or "keping company with brothels & dronkerds."[144] Pierre Viret's anti-Nicodemite *Epistle*, translated into English and first published in 1582, also equated sexual sin with idolatry when it discussed the ways in which Christians ought to behave around "whoredome, because it is most like unto idolatrie."[145] Viret argued that if a person frequented dances, or was willing to be present in "brothell houses" and "passe the time with baudes, whores, and harlots," then it was inevitable that he or she would

---

[140] Lever, *A Sermon preached at Pauls Crosse*, a3v.

[141] Lever, *A Sermon preached at Pauls Crosse*, b6r. Invoking the prophet Isaiah in a sermon before Edward VI, Lever claimed that God would not be pleased by the Prayer Book or the English Bible if covetousness were not also abolished. Paraphrasing Isaiah 1, Lever preached that God would say, "What pleasure have I, yea what care I for al your Englishe Bibles, Homilies, and all youre other bookes: set furthe no more godly servyce to honor me with: I hate them all with my herte, they are grevous unto me, I am wery of them: Yea, it is a great payne for me to suffer them." The fault was not in these things, but "in you that have set them furthe." Thomas Lever, *A Sermon preached the thyrd Sonday in Lent before the Kynges Majestie and his honorable Counsell* (London, 1550; STC 15547), c1r.

[142] Musculus, *The Temporysour*, d2r.

[143] Found in John Knox, *A Percel of the vi Psalme expounded* (London?, 1554; STC 15074.4), d8v-e4v. Also see J.T., *An apologie or defence agaynst the calumnacion of certayne men* (Wesel?, 1555; STC 23619), a5v.

[144] Knox, *A Percel*, e1v-e3v. [145] Viret, *An Epistle*, a5v.

succumb to sexual depravity. Likewise, "to enter into idoles temples, to bee conversant and communicate with Idolaters, and to beholde their juglings, and to be there assistant with them, & to daunce the same daunce that they doe, what is it else, then to enter into the brothel houses of Sathan & to be acquainted with Baudes and Harlots: whiche committe fornication with straunge Gods."[146]

For these Protestants, therefore, the duty to repudiate public idolatry was equivalent to (and reinforced by) the duty to repudiate public sins. The godly were to flee idolatry like they fled sin, and vice versa. With the abolition of the Mass and Catholic worship in 1559, Protestant authors immediately began to warn their readers again about the slippery and transformative nature of idolatry. Laurence Humphrey wrote in *De Religionis Conservatione et Reformatione Vera* (1559) that "If the idols are removed from the churches but steal into the mind and statues are erected in the heart, that is deformation not reformation; a change of place not a driving away of the thing, and so much the more dangerous because it is interior and personal. When we confess the simplicity and nakedness of Christ, will lightness in morals, extravagence in clothes, pleasures, freedom from care and indolence, I do not say remain but be increased?"[147] According to radical puritans like John Udall, it was obvious that this sort of transformed idolatry was everywhere in Elizabethan England. In a series of sermons on Christ's temptation in the wilderness, published in 1588, Udall claimed that the gospel and godly Christians were constantly mocked, while wickedness was "advaunced and extolled" almost everywhere.[148] All of this might not have looked like idolatry, but that was precisely what it was, despite Satan's crafty efforts to hide this fact. Since the true worship of God was to fear him and "bring forth the fruites of the same which is obedience," when people "give themselves over unto sinne, in neglecting of the worde of God, blaspheming of his holie name, profaining of hys Saboath, disobedience, whoredome, drunkennes, unlawfull gettyng & slaundering," then "how soever they pretend the contrarie," such people "doe obey Sathan in this poynt to fall down and worship him."[149] Idolatry had mutated once again.

---

[146] Viret, *An Epistle*, a5v-a6r.

[147] Laurence Humphrey, *De Religionis Conservatione et Reformatione Vera* (Basle, 1559) trans. in Janet Karen Kemp, "Laurence Humphrey, Elizabethan Puritan: His Life and Political Theories" (West Virginia University, Ph.D. Dissertation, 1978), pp. 178–179.

[148] John Udall, *The Combate betwixt Christ and the Devill* (London, 1588; STC 24492), g8v.

[149] Udall, *The Combate*, i3v-i4r.

Udall's writings from the 1580s nicely illustrate how classic anti-Nicodemite arguments and themes underwrote the confrontational approach toward sin and sinners that defined "puritans" in the eyes of many Elizabethans. Udall published two sermons in 1584 on Peter's denial of Christ (Matthew 25 and Luke 22), a text that was an obvious staple in anti-Nicodemite literature and that Udall claimed was unparalleled in importance for teaching Christians how to live. Udall's dedication to the Earl of Beford announced that England was full of Peters who were denying Christ, or rather Nicodemites who "desire to come to Christ by night with Nicodemus, for feare of worldly losses."[150] England's Nicodemites were not publicly denying Christ by "revolting in time of persecution" as they had done under Mary, since at the present time "all men may freelye professe the Gospell," but rather by refusing to allow their profession of Christ to manifest itself in their daily behavior.[151] In part, this Nicodemizing manifested itself in insufficient zeal for the gospel and reformation. This dissimulation was partly designed, Udall claimed, to escape the possibility of future persecution were England's religion to change once again. Just like Peter "durst not come neare [to Christ] for feare of troubles, so dare they come no faster on, for feare of after clappes: they thinke that keeping themselves a loofe, they maye bee safe at all seasons, if a change come: (for which they gape) then they thynke they may with honestye change."[152] Even those in positions of authority were denying Christ by pursuing an incomplete reformation, for "if they shoulde be desirous to pull downe Papistrie (if they bee in any authoritie) and earnestlye establishe the preachyng of the Gospell, they shoulde be ashamed in those d[a]ies, whyche I truste shall never bee."[153] While it might have been thought that the pressures that had produced Nicodemism under Mary had disappeared, then, Udall claimed that the temptation to "deny Christ before men" remained exceedingly powerful and was producing a generation of preemptive Nicodemites.

Elizabethans were denying Christ with Peter not only by failing to enact a complete reformation, Udall claimed, but also by being complacent in the face of sinful Elizabethan society. Udall isolated Peter's decision to sit with Christ's persecutors as a crucial factor in his subsequent denial of Christ: "marke how fitly *Peter* applieth himselfe to the time, and companie: with the professors of Christ he professeth, but with persecutors he denieth."[154]

---

[150] John Udall, *Peters Fall. Two Sermons upon the Historie of Peters denying Christ* (London, 1584; STC 24503), a3v.
[151] Udall, *Peters Fall*, c4r.   [152] Udall, *Peters Fall*, c4v.   [153] Udall, *Peters Fall*, c4v.
[154] Udall, *Peters Fall*, c6v.

The wicked company that Elizabethan Protestants kept was likewise leading them to deny Christ, as they gladly married their daughters to wealthy papists, chose to do business in Spain where they could not but defile themselves with "daily service unto *Baal*," and generally "careth not whether it be *Turke* or *Jewe*, Gods servant or Satans, that beare him company."[155] Spending time in "wicked companie" would inevitably "pervert even the godly," and Udall insisted that "the worde of God alloweth no such dealing, but commaundeth the contrarie."[156] Evil company tempted Christians not only to commit outward sins but also to dissemble their Christian confession by remaining silent about the sinful behavior that surrounded them. In his series of sermons on the temptation of Christ, published as *The Combate betwixte Christ and the Devill* (1588), Udall wrote that a Christian "shall scarse come into that company, but either he shall heare the Gospell of Jesus Christ, and the professors thereof evill spoken of, or the name of god (in common talke) blasphemed and taken in vayne."[157] When Christians found themselves in the presence of these sins and sinners, they immediately faced the same dilemma that the godly faced when they encountered idolatry in a church: they could "consent by scilence, or sooth them up in theyr sinnes and wickednes . . . or els boldly (according to his duety) reprove the offenders."[158] Rebuke was the only legitimate response, but since it would provoke "outrage" among the sinners, Udall suggested that it would be better to flee such company entirely.[159]

With reference to sinners, then, Udall urged his readers to practice the sort of social segregation that was commonplace in anti-Nicodemite exhortations. If a person intended "unfeynedly to take that course which becommeth a true christian," then he or she should "beware of places of wickednes, and ungodly companie: and learne to frequent those places and that company where godlines, is exercised."[160] Udall praised separation from the wicked as the best way to avoid denying Christ, but noted that it was impossible for Christians to fully separate themselves since "we be mingled so with Antichristians, prophane persons, Papists, and others of Satans broode, that we can not utterly avoide them."[161] Semi-separation had to be achieved, therefore, through ostentatious, confrontational, godly behavior in which "we ought to beare them aloofe, to use no familiaritie with them, but seeke to adjoine our selves to them that feare God."[162] The examples that Udall offered were remarkable for their aggression: St John

---

[155] Udall, *Peters Fall*, c8v. [156] Udall, *Peters Fall*, c6v-c7r, d1r. [157] Udall, *The Combate*, g8v-h1r.
[158] Udall, *The Combate*, h1r. [159] Udall, *The Combate*, h1r. [160] Udall, *The Combate*, h1v-h2r.
[161] Udall, *Peters Fall*, d1v. [162] Udall, *Peters Fall*, d1v.

came across the heretic Cirinthus at a bath and "leaped backe suddenly," while Policarpus refused to speak to the heretic Marcion and, when asked if he knew who Marcion was, answered "Yes, I knowe thee to be the first begotten of Sathan."[163]

Remaining aloof from the wicked was not only a way of protecting oneself from sin, however; it was also an evangelistic tactic that "may be the beginning of their conversion."[164] In phrases that could have been taken directly from anti-Nicodemite pamphlets, Udall claimed that "if we observe this order, we knowe not what great good we may do even to the wicked, for he may by occasion thereof thinke thus with himselfe: why do these men shun my companie? what am I? what foule enormitie is in me, that they detest: and I know, I am a drunkard, or I am a whoremonger, or I am a swearer: if men will not come neare me, because of my sinne, sure God will reject me much rather, therefore it is best for me to amend."[165] Where dissembling would only confirm the sinner in their sin, this sort of ostentatious public rejection by the godly would drive the sinner to recognize the enormity of his sin and lead him to repentance. Maintaining outward friendship with the wicked did them no favors, for "if we keepe them companie, if we banquet, eate & drinke with them, and shew them a familiar countenance, we keepe them secretly in their sinnes, and so we being hinderers of their repentance, by this meanes are partakers of their sinnes."[166] Udall was not necessarily being unrealistic about the consequences of this sort of aggressive social shunning, but he subordinated earthly peace with the wicked to his duty to obey God: "I knowe what this worketh in the reprobate, and how they account of the godlie for so doing: they say, they be proude, straunge, and disdainefull persons, but I had rather they should thinke and speake so of me falsely, then (being familiar with the wicked) to provoke the Lord my God unto anger wilfully."[167]

Despite this note of pessimism, Udall and other puritans remain committed to the notion that this sort of confrontational behavior would produce good effects in the wicked. Job Throckmorton dramatized the hoped-for consequences of such a confrontational confession of Christ in his widely read dialogue *Diotrephes* (1588), which depicted an encounter at an inn between a bishop, a papist, a usurer, and a "preacher of the worde of God" named Paul (or, as the bishop called him, "one of these peevish

[163] Udall, *Peters Fall*, c7v-c8r.   [164] Udall, *Peters Fall*, d2r.   [165] Udall, *Peters Fall*, d1v.
[166] Udall, *Peters Fall*, d2r.   [167] Udall, *Peters Fall*, d2r.

Puritanes").[168] The dialogue opened with the innkeeper complaining to the bishop about Paul's behavior: he had rebuked a servant for swearing, inconvenienced fellow diners by insisting on prayers before and after dinner, preached against drunkenness and gambling in the town, and in general "setteth men together by the eares."[169] The innkeeper was concerned about his business – his policy was to "bee friendly to all, least I leese my custom, and drive away some of my guests" – but others had been touched more directly.[170] Demetrius the usurer complained that Paul had rebuked him as soon as he learned his business: he "tooke me up as if I had bin but a kitchin boye, and all because I saide I lived by my moneye, and was of no other trade, calling me caterpiller, thief, and murtherer, and saide plainely, that he that robbed in Stran-gate hole, was an honester man then I."[171] Demetrius hated Paul for this and much preferred the bishop – who had told him merely to "not oppresse your brother too muche" – but by the end of the dialogue, Demetrius had experienced a change of heart.[172] Demetrius explained to the innkeeper that when he had surreptitiously overheard the bishop speaking about him, "the bishop disallowed my course, and yet tooke my parte. And why? Because I might defend him in his unlawfull calling. But I see their jugling wel inough, and if the manne, with whome I was so offended [Paul] be not gone, I will talke further with him, for I perceive that hee meant better unto me than they did."[173] While Paul's salty rebuke had smarted, Demetrius eventually realized that it was the confrontational puritan, not the feigning bishop, who truly cared about his soul. Throckmorton's hopes for this policy shone through in the innkeeper's concluding words to Demetrius: "I perceive we shall have a Puritan of you, if you would so faine speake with him."[174]

In Throckmorton's *Diotrephes* and in Udall's sermons we have perfect examples of the ongoing centrality of anti-Nicodemite habits of thought for puritans as they aspired to maintain a constant and unambiguous confession of Christ in Elizabethan England. Encountering heinous sins as they walked down the street and living among a population that seemed willfully inured to wickedness, puritans were convinced that a pernicious form of idolatry continued to flourish, despite the successes of the reformation (such

---

[168] Job Throckmorton, *The state of the Church of Englande, laide open in a conference betweene Diotrephes a Byshop, Tertullus a Papist, Demetrius an usurer, Pandochem an Inne-keeper, and Paule a preacher of the worde of God* (London, 1588; STC 24505), b1r. This dialogue has also been attributed to Udall; see Antoinina Bevan Zlatar, *Reformation Fictions: Polemical Protestant Dialogues in Elizabethan England* (Oxford, 2011), 161.

[169] Throckmorton, *The state*, b1r, h3r.   [170] Throckmorton, *The state*, b2v.

[171] Throckmorton, *The state*, c2r-v.   [172] Throckmorton, *The state*, c2v.

[173] Throckmorton, *The state*, h3v.   [174] Throckmorton, *The state*, h3v.

as they were) in purifying the church. The puritans feared the consequences for themselves and for their neighbors if they were tacitly to condone this idolatrous sinfulness by dissembling their disapproval and silencing their godly witness, in precisely the same ways that their predecessors had feared the consequences of quietly attending Mass. Refusing to enter the neighborhood "temples" of sin was the best course of action, but if full social separation from the ungodly was impossible – as most puritans acknowledged it was – then their sin must be boldly rebuked, not only to protect one's own soul but to edify weaker brethren and potentially convert the wicked. When Christ told his disciples that "whosoever shall denye me before men, him will I also denye before my father which ys in heven," it was a fearsome warning. Anxiety about avoiding this sin and its dire consequences motivated an outpouring of anti-Nicodemite sentiment throughout the English Reformation, and as this chapter has shown, Protestant hostility to dissimulation went far beyond forbidding attendance at Mass. There were many ways in which Christians would be tempted to "deny Christ before men," and the anti-Nicodemite ethos would play a central role in shaping the activism of the hotter sorts of Elizabeth Protestants as they sought to make a constant confession of Christ in every aspect of their lives.

CHAPTER 4

Reformation without tarrying

Mary's accession forced English Protestants not only to make difficult choices regarding conformity but also to reassess their views regarding royal authority and the role of the monarch in establishing true religion. As Mary reversed the English Reformation by returning England to papal authority, restoring the Mass, and imprisoning and burning "the godly," English Protestants had to face more squarely than ever before what the biblical injunction to "obey God before man" actually meant in practice. Some of the Marian exiles famously began to demand active resistance to the Marian regime, arguing that those who "supported Mary's tyrannous regime, whether actively or passively, rendered themselves partners in her guilt."[1] John Ponet, John Knox, and Christopher Goodman argued that open resistance to royal actions and even regicide were necessary responses to the Antichristian rule of Mary Tudor in England and Mary Stuart in Scotland.[2]

The development of resistance theory, however, was only the most controversial and spectacular way in which the hotter sort of Marian Protestants were redefining their relationship to political authority. Even

---

[1] Joy Shakespeare, "Plague and Punishment," in Lake and Dowling (eds.), *Protestantism and the National Church*, 117.

[2] John Ponet, *A Shorte Treatise of politike power* (Strassburg, 1556; STC 20178); Knox, *On Rebellion*; Christopher Goodman, *How Superior Power Oght to be Obeyd* (Geneva, 1558; STC 12020). Also see Martin Luther, *A faythful admonycion* (Strassburg, 1554; STC 16980); Luther, *A faithful admonition* (London, 1554; STC 16981). There is a vast literature on the Marian resistance theorists, but see especially Quentin Skinner, *The Foundations of Modern Political Thought*, vol. 2, *The Age of Reformation* (Cambridge, 1978); Gerald Bowler, "English Protestants and Resistance Theory, 1553–1603," (London Ph.D. dissertation, 1981); Bowler, "Marian Protestants and the Idea of Violent Resistance to Tyranny," in Lake and Dowling (eds.), *Protestantism and the National Church*, 124–143; Jane Dawson, "Revolutionary Conclusions: The Case of the Marian Exiles," *History of Political Thought* 11:2 (Summer 1990), 257–272; Dawson, "Resistance and Revolution in Sixteenth-Century Thought: The Case of Christopher Goodman," in J. van den Berg and P. G. Hoftijzer (eds.), *Church, Change and Revolution: Transactions of the Fourth Anglo-Dutch Church History Colloquium* (Leiden, 1991), 69–79; Dawson, "Trumpeting Resistance: Christopher Goodman and John Knox," in Roger A. Mason (ed.), *John Knox and the British Reformations* (Aldershot, 1998), 131–153.

Protestants who refused to countenance acts of resistance against the queen found themselves adopting a new posture toward royal authority during Mary's reign. Since the 1530s and the creation of the Royal Supremacy, Protestants had accepted – some more enthusiastically than others – that ecclesiastical policy was the prerogative of the king and parliament. The theology and liturgy of the Church of England were determined through royal proclamations and parliamentary legislation, and "private" people could not reform the church any more than they could choose to start or join a different one. As the 1552 *Book of Common Prayer* proclaimed, "no man ought to take in hand, nor presume to appoynct or alter any publique or common order in Christes churche, except he be lawfully called and aucthorized thereunto."[3] All of this changed during Mary's reign for the Protestant vanguard that refused to conform to the Marian Church and set about establishing churches in exile or secretly at home. During this desperate time for "the gospel," the hottest Protestants took matters into their own hands, dramatically decoupling the advancement of true religion from both royal authority and the institution of the national church.[4]

The fact that Mary was a papist, however, had made it "relatively simple for the Protestants to push the Royal Supremacy into the background without having to reject it outright."[5] With the accession of Elizabeth, Protestants would once again profess their allegiance to the Royal Supremacy, and the Church of England would again be governed by act of parliament and through royal injunctions. Elizabeth was regularly portrayed by Protestants as a new Josiah, Deborah, Esther, or a second Constantine who would abolish idolatry and restore true religion in England.[6] As Patrick Collinson put it, after five years in which "many of the habits and attitudes that belonged to life in an established Church – the habits of centuries – were temporarily discarded ... the accession of protestant Elizabeth at once revived deeply-rooted notions of the Church

---

[3] *The boke of common praier* (London, 1552; STC 16284.5), a3v.

[4] For the church order established by the Wesel exiles, see Lambeth Palace Library (LPL) MS 2523, ff. 3–4; on the development of new forms of church government, see "The historie of that sturre and strife which was in in [sic] the Englishe church at Franckford from the 13. daie off Jan. Anno Domini 1557. forwarde," in Wood, *A Brieff discours*, 62–186. Also see J. W. Martin, "The Protestant Underground Congregations of Mary's Reign," in *Religious Radicals in Tudor England* (London, 1989), 125–146.

[5] Dawson, "Revolutionary Conclusions," 261.

[6] Recent research has stressed the highly qualified and prescriptive nature of these biblical comparisons: Thomas S. Freeman, "Providence and Prescription: The Account of Elizabeth in Foxe's 'Book of Martyrs'" and Alexandra Walsham "'A very Deborah?': the myth of Elizabeth I as a providential monarch," in Susan Doran and Thomas S. Freeman (eds.), *The myth of Elizabeth* (Basingstoke, 2003), 27–36, 143–168.

as a great public corporation, one with the Commonwealth, and presided over by royal governors."[7]

While English Protestants certainly welcomed Elizabeth's accession, this chapter will argue that the accession of a Protestant queen did not necessarily lead to the abandonment of the more expansive conceptions of religious authority and godly activism that had taken hold during Mary's reign. An older historiographical tradition assumed that these radical views became irrelevant after Mary's death.[8] In recent decades, however, a growing body of scholarship has shown that the political thought of the resistance theorists "survived beyond the Marian exile" and profoundly shaped the outlook of Elizabethan Protestants.[9] Elizabethan Protestants were intimately acquainted with the arguments for resistance to wicked rulers that had been articulated under Mary and continued to be developed by French Protestants. As Gerald Bowler and others have shown, "resistance theory was now often openly discussed in a way that it had not been before the accession of Elizabeth," finding expression in sermons, in the margins of the Geneva Bible and Bishops' Bible, in academic debates at Oxford before the queen, in parliamentary debate urging the death of Mary Stuart, and in widely read works like *A Mirror for Magistrates*.[10] Indeed, the ongoing purchase of resistance theory has come to play an important role in our understanding of Elizabethan politics and the various manifestations of "monarchical republicanism." In his path-breaking 1987 essay on the subject, Patrick Collinson argued that "what is vulgarly called 'resistance theory'" might be "better described as the polemical critique of monarchy," a critique that involved a series of principles asserting limits on monarchy and the monarch's accountability to God and their subjects.[11] These

---

[7] Collinson, *Elizabethan Puritan Movement*, 24.

[8] See, for example, A. F. Scott Pearson, *Church & State: Political Aspects of Sixteenth Century Puritanism* (Cambridge, 1928), 90–93. On this historiographical tradition, see Patrick Collinson, "The Monarchical Republic of Queen Elizabeth I," in *Elizabethan Essays* (London, 1994), 43; Gerald Bowler, "'An Axe or an Acte': The Parliament of 1572 and Resistance Theory in Early Elizabethan England," *Canadian Journal of History* 19:3 (December 1984), 349. For more recent and more qualified scepticism about the importance of resistance theory for Elizabethan puritans, see Glenn Burgess, *British Political Thought, 1500–1660: The Politics of the Post-Reformation* (Basingstoke, 2009), 114–117.

[9] Stephen Alford, *Kingship and Politics in the Reign of Edward VI* (Cambridge, 2002), 184.

[10] Bowler, "English Protestants and Resistance Writings 1553–1603," esp. ch. 4; Bowler, "'An Axe or an Acte'"; Dawson, "Revolutionary Conclusions," 272; Scott Lucas, "'Let none such office take, save he that can for right his prince forsake': *A Mirror for Magistrates*, Resistance Theory and the Elizabethan Monarchical Republic," in John F. McDiarmid (ed.), *The Monarchical Republic of Early Modern England* (Aldershot, 2007), 91–108; Rosamund Oates, "Puritans and the 'Monarchical Republic': Conformity and Conflict in the Elizabethan Church," *English Historical Review* 127:527 (2012), 819–843.

[11] Collinson, "The Monarchical Republic of Queen Elizabeth I," 43.

principles – which Stephen Alford has shown to be themselves the legacy of
earlier Edwardian views of kingship – would be taken up by figures at the
heart of the Elizabethan political establishment as they sought to defend
the kingdom and true religion "with or without the active participation of
the queen."[12]

This chapter argues that resistance theory not only informed Protestant
responses to the Elizabethan succession crisis but also continued to shape
Protestant thought about religious reform in the early years of Elizabeth's
reign. It makes this argument through a close reading of one of the earliest
printed manifestos calling for further reformation in the Elizabethan Church
of England: James Pilkington's *Aggeus the Prophete declared by a large commentarye* (1560).[13] Pilkington, who we briefly encountered in the preceding
chapter, was an influential figure within mid-Tudor Protestantism. He had
been Lady Margaret Professor of Divinity at Cambridge from 1550 until the
death of Edward VI and after spending Mary's reign in peripatetic exile
(including time in John Knox's congregation at Geneva), he returned to
Cambridge in February 1559 where he quickly became Master of St. John's
and Regius Professor of Divinity.[14] By November of that year, Pilkington had
been offered the bishopric of Winchester, but his episcopal promotion was
halted due to his renewed opposition to the 1559 Act of Exchange and the
crown's efforts to appropriate episcopal lands. While he would accept the
Bishopric of Durham on more favorable terms in November 1560, it was as
Master of St. John's in 1559–1560 that Pilkington likely had his most lasting
influence on the Elizabethan Church through the education of a group of
young fellows at St John's that he referred to as his "halfe a score," a number

---

[12] Stephen Alford, "A Politics of Emergency in the Reign of Elizabeth I," in Burgess and Festenstein
(eds.), *English Radicalism, 1550–1850*, 18; also see Alford, *Kingship and Politics*, ch. 6.

[13] James Pilkington, *Aggeus the prophete declared by a large commentarye* (London, 1560; STC 19926.3),
hereafter *Aggeus* ("Aggeus" being the Greek form of the word rendered "Haggai" in modern English
Bibles). A second edition was printed in 1560 and then a slightly emended edition was published in
1562 alongside a new commentary on Abdias, or Obadiah: *Aggeus and Abdias Prophetes* (London, 1562;
STC 19927). All quotations in this chapter from *Aggeus* are taken from STC 19926.3. Pilkington's
works were edited in 1842 by James Scholefield for the Parker Society, for whom Pilkington "possessed
in an eminent degree that rare judgment and moderation, which are the characteristics of our early
English reformers," (xiii) but this volume can be unreliable. Scholefield conflated editions of *Aggeus*,
frequently without note, and he sometimes sanitized Pilkington's language to suit Victorian sensi-
bilities. For example, Scholefield altered Pilkington's condemnation of papists' "buggerye" to read
"unnatural lust," remarking in a footnote only that "This expression is altered from the original."
James Scholefield (ed.), *The Works of James Pilkington, B.D.* (Cambridge, 1842), 614. Compare on this
point with James Pilkington, *The burnynge of Paules church* (London, 1563; STC 19931), P2r.

[14] Patrick Collinson, Richard Rex, and Graham Stanton, *Lady Margaret Beaufort and her Professors of
Divinity at Cambridge: 1502–1649* (Cambridge, 2003), 49; Garrett, *The Marian Exiles*;
Richard Bauckham, "Marian Exiles and Cambridge Puritanism: James Pilkington's 'Halfe a
Score,'" *Journal of Ecclesiastical History* 26:2 (April 1975), 137–148.

that included future puritan leaders like Ralph Lever, Percival Wiburne, Roger Kelke, and Thomas Cartwright.[15]

Pilkington's commentary on Haggai, which Richard Bauckham suggests "probably originated in sermons delivered at Cambridge,"[16] provides a fascinating view into an influential individual's thought regarding the task of further reformation in the Elizabethan Church. Pilkington selected Haggai because "[t]he state of religion in these oure miserable dayes, is muche lyke to the troublesom time that this Prophet lived in."[17] The prophet Haggai prophesied to the Jews some forty years after their return to Jerusalem from the Babylonian exile.[18] After seventy years in exile, the Persian king Cyrus had given the Jews permission and funds to return to Jerusalem and rebuild the Temple. The Jews returned, laid a foundation for the Temple, and built an altar upon which to make sacrifices to God. Within two years of their return, however, the inhabitants of Israel had accused the Jews of rebellion against the new king in Babylon, Assuerus. Assuerus forbade the Jews to rebuild the Temple and they ceased work for forty years until God sent Haggai to rebuke them for their inactivity and demand that work begin again on the Temple.

When Pilkington read this story, he saw the history of the English Reformation. Just as the Temple remained unbuilt in Jerusalem for forty years, so had forty years passed in England since the beginning of the Reformation and the church still remained unbuilt. In fact, "under pretence of receyvyng the Gospell, and buylding Gods house" the English people had actually "pulled it downe."[19] Monasteries had been abolished, but this was "to enriche our selves," and the English had not "destroyed Gods enemies, nor provyded for the poore, and furthered learning nor placed preachynge Ministers in place of dumme Dogges, after the rule of his woord as we should have done, and buylded hys house."[20] Even now, having been delivered from "the late dayes of bloudy persecucion & cruel popery" and

---

[15] Brett Usher, "Durham and Winchester Episcopal Estates and the Elizabethan Settlement: A Reappraisal," *Journal of Ecclesiastical History* 49:3 (July 1998), 395–396; Felicity Heal, "The Bishops and the Act of Exchange of 1559," *The Historical Journal* 17:2 (June 1974), 237–238; Bauckham, "Marian Exiles", 142–143, 148.

[16] Bauckham, "Marian Exiles," 139. [17] *Aggeus*, a2v-a3r. Also see e4v-e6v.

[18] As we will see later in the chapter, Pilkington's chronology of Israel's early post-exilic history differed from that of most other commentators, a seemingly minor point which had important consequences for the dating of Haggai's prophecy and its significance. This paragraph recounts Pilkington's version of the chronology at *Aggeus*, b2r-b5v and q6r.

[19] *Aggeus*, c8r.

[20] *Aggeus*, c8r. Pilkington repeatedly complained about impropriations and continuing attempts to exploit the wealth of the church: *Aggeus*, a7r-v, iir, pir.

living "under our myld Ester," the English showed only "cold slacknes in gods religion."[21] Sin was rampant and the "whip of gods discipline is not shaken in gods house," nor was it used to drive the papists into the parish churches.[22] "We have all synned from the hyghest to the lowest, in not earnestly professing thy holye woorde and religion. Both the Princes, rulers, and Magistrates, Bishops, ministers of al sortes, and al the people no state nor condicion of men hath done their duty herein unto the[e] our onely Lord and God."[23]

In writing *Aggeus*, therefore, Pilkington took on the prophetic mantle himself, criticizing the failures of the English Reformation to date and attempting "to bringe some of every sort (for all is not possible) to an earneste fortheringe of gods true relygyon, of late moste mercifullye restored unto us."[24] In the process of urging the English people to be "hote" in the cause of true religion, Pilkington made a series of interesting claims about the nature of religious authority, the role of magistrates in establishing true religion, and the responsibility of all people to build God's house.[25] These claims unfolded as he denounced the excuses made by the Jews – and some that he simply invented – for not building the Temple after their return from Babylon. The Jews had claimed that there was too much work to be done, that the king had forbidden them to build, that work needed to be done on their own homes, that they were too poor, that they were not capable of building the temple, that the work was too costly, that they had to go slowly because of the weak, and finally that the task "belonged not to them."[26] These, according to Pilkington, were exactly the excuses that the English had made, and his demolition of each excuse became a ringing indictment of England's failure to complete the reformation begun under Henry VIII.[27] Like Haggai before him, Pilkington insisted that no excuse was legitimate: "Why, wyll no excuse serve, but that every man must lay hys helping hand to the building of Gods house?" His answer was adamant: "God alowes none at all."[28]

It is particularly interesting that Pilkington repeatedly chose to discuss Assuerus's royal prohibition on temple building and the failure of the Jewish civil and ecclesiastical leaders to begin the work themselves. Pilkington speculated that some of the Jews "would say we are forbidden

---

[21] *Aggeus*, Bb8v, a3v. [22] *Aggeus*, a4r. [23] *Aggeus*, r3v-r4r. [24] *Aggeus*, a2v.
[25] *Aggeus*, a5v. "I feare rather that christe, of whom we more talke, than diligentlye folowe, or earnestly love, for this colde slacknes that he sees in us, will say unto us. Bycause ye be nether hote nor colde, I wil spue you out of my mouthe [Rev. iii]" (a5r-v).
[26] *Aggeus*, d7r-d8r. [27] *Aggeus*, f3v-f4r. [28] *Aggeus*, f1r-v.

by the kyng & hys officers (and so they were in dede, as apperes in Esdras [1 Esdras 4]."[29] They thought that this would excuse their inaction, saying, "let the Rulers begyn and we wyl helpe. Other, we shall loose our lyfe & goodes if we disobey the Kinges commaundement."[30] They might claim that "we dyd not thys faulte, but our Rulers, or we were not able ta take it in hand, or if they had begon we would have folowed."[31] None of these excuses were legitimate to Pilkington. The entire Jewish people were rebuked "for theyr disobedience that they builded not Gods house, althoughe they were forbydden by thy kyng, or coulde make lyke excuses."[32] Pilkington's decision to highlight these excuses regarding authority is significant because they were not excuses that the prophet had specifically identified: Haggai had rebuked the Jews for saying that "the tyme is not yet come to buyld the house of God" and for building their own houses rather than the house of the Lord.[33] As he called the English people to complete the reformation after Elizabeth's accession, therefore, Pilkington was *choosing* to address one of the most problematic and volatile political problems created by the Reformation. What did it mean, in practice, to obey God before man?

Bauckham has noted that Pilkington showed "no patience with the excuse of obedience to authority" and treated reform as a duty "which no man should neglect even by royal command."[34] Pilkington's rejection of excuses regarding royal authority began with his insistence that God had laid the duty of building the temple on *all* of his people. Pilkington did not dedicate his commentary to any one person, but to "al degrees of menne . . . to the rulers, the ministers & comminalty," in imitation of Haggai who had called the entire Jewish people to the task of rebuilding.[35] This was not to say that everyone had the same role to play. While none were excused from the task of building, "He that hath received greater gyftes, hathe a greater charge, and more worke shal be looked for of hym."[36] God "hath appoynted rulers in the comon wealth to minister justice, punyshe synne, defend the ryght, & cause men to do their duties. And in his church he hathe placed Preachers to teache hys law, to pull downe supersticion and idolatrye, and to styrre uppe the slouthfull and negligent, to serve and feare hym."[37] Men who "be not a ruler or a preacher" still had families to "see lyve in the feare of God" and their own souls, which were a "temple of the holy ghost whych we should buyld."[38] Yet while delineating different roles, Pilkington's repeated and overwhelming message was the collective guilt of the English people:

---

[29] *Aggeus*, d7r. [30] *Aggeus*, d7r. [31] *Aggeus*, n3r. [32] *Aggeus*, f7r. [33] *Aggeus*, c6v-c7r.
[34] Bauckham, "Marian Exiles," 139–140. [35] *Aggeus*, a2r-v. [36] *Aggeus*, d8v. [37] *Aggeus*, e1v.
[38] *Aggeus*, d8v.

"in England, al be gilty, al have bene punished, because every sort of men should have laid his helpynge hande to the buyldinge of Gods house, refourmynge his religion, restoringe and maintayning hys gospel, which none or very few have earnestly done."[39]

Because God himself had assigned this task, moreover, Pilkington was adamant that the Temple must be built, regardless of whether earthly rulers approved:

> God wold not spare the simplest and basest man lyvynge, but as they had synned in not buyldyng hys house, so shoulde they perishe, least they should thinke or saye: we dyd not thys faulte, but our Rulers, or we were not able ta take it in hand, or if they had begon we would have folowed, or such like fonde excuses. God requires hys house to be buylded, hys woord and religion to be kept and maintayned as well of the lowest as the hyghest, and they whych do not, shall not escape unpunished.[40]

Pilkington was well aware that people who reformed the church without the authority of their rulers or against the direct commands of their rulers would be considered disobedient rebels and traitors. Pilkington resolved this problem by redefining terms. According to Pilkington, "treason" and "rebellion" were terms that most meaningfully applied to people's response to *divine* commands. If people were obeying God's commands, their actions could be neither treason nor rebellion, no matter what earthly princes might wrongly claim. "Why, they were forbydden by the Kyng to buylde anye more, as appeares in Esdras: and must they not obey? they should have runne into the Kynges dyspleasure, bene in jeopardye to have lost lyfe, lande and goodes: Shoulde they have bene Rebelles and Traytours to the Kyng? No surelye, thys is not treason to Kinges to do that whych God commaundes."[41] When Daniel prayed three times a day and when the apostles chose to obey God and preach the gospel "contrarye to the Kynges commaundement" in Acts 4, "it was neyther treason nor rebellion. So muste we doo always that whych God commaundes, and if the rage of the Rulers go so farre as to kyll or cast us into Lions dens as Daniel was, or whipt & scourged as the Apostles were, we muste suffer wyth Daniell, and say wyth the Apostles: we must rather obey God in doyng our dutye, than man forbyddyng the same."[42] In relation to God, kings were merely sheriffs, and "If the Shiriffe shoulde byd thee one thyng, and the Kynge commaunde thee an other, wylt thou obey the lower officer afore the hygher? So is the Kyng Gods under Officer, and not to be obeyed before hym."[43]

---

[39] *Aggeus*, h5v.   [40] *Aggeus*, n3r.   [41] *Aggeus*, f1v.   [42] *Aggeus*, f2r.   [43] *Aggeus*, f2r.

Pilkington stressed that when the Jews finally heeded Haggai's stinging rebuke and began to rebuild the temple, they did so without regard for the royal prohibition on building and, indeed, without even attempting to gain royal support. After

> manye yeares not regardyng the buyldynge of Gods house, for feare of the Kynges dyspleasure, who had commaunded the rulers in the countrye to stoppe the buyldyng of that house ... they were so styrred up that thei regarded not now, their owne gayne and pleasure, nor they feared not the Kynges officers dyspleasure whych had forbidden them to buylde anye more: but strayghte wythout suyng for a new commission, or lycence of the Kyng, or speakyng wyth the kinges officers, they set up their worke, knowing that he [God] whych promysed woulde bee wyth them, and that they shoulde prosper well in it, for he was able and wold perfourme it.[44]

Pilkington chose to underline the fact that they did not wait for royal permission, reiterating that the Jews "went forwarde in their buyldynge, askynge no lycence at all of anye man, before they were complayned on."[45] As a result, the Jews were immediately confronted by royal officers who "asked them by what authoritye they beganne to renue their olde woorke" and who then sent a letter to King Darius inquiring "whether they shoulde be suffered to go forward in their buildyng or not."[46] As promised, however, God blessed his people's obedience and "so moved the Kynges hart, that he gave them not onely libertye to buylde, but money also to doo it wyth all."[47] This royal blessing lay in the future, however, and Pilkington repeatedly emphasized that the task of building went forward in the face of stiff official opposition. "The kinges officers asked them often tymes who gave them leave to renue thys buylding, & what commission they had," and many of the Jews were discouraged and in "feare of the Kynges dyspleasure whyche hadde forbydden them, to buylde anye more."[48] To strengthen the Jews in their work, "least the feare of the Kynge or the Rulers should discourage them, they had nede to be comforted, and therefore Aggeus is sent unto them againe to encourage them, leaste they shoulde have faynted or left of working."[49] Since they had been "forbidden to buylde" and the royal officers "were as dilygent to stoppe them," Haggai's message reminded the Jews that "God sets hym selfe agaynst the kyng, as though he should say: though the kings power be great, yet I am greater: thoughe he forbyd, yet I byd, though he be agaynst you, yet am I wyth you, saith the Lord of hostes."[50]

---

[44] *Aggeus*, q7v.   [45] *Aggeus*, q8r.   [46] *Aggeus*, q7v-q8r.   [47] *Aggeus*, q8r.   [48] *Aggeus*, s5r, r8r.
[49] *Aggeus*, r5r.   [50] *Aggeus*, x3r.

While the duty to "obey God before man" was a biblical imperative, this was an unusual way of talking about reformation for a leading Protestant living under a Protestant monarch. It was generally assumed – and a matter of law – that neither the people, the clergy, nor inferior magistrates could reform the church any more than they could decide to start or join a different one. This view of the monarch's supreme authority over the church had recently been reiterated by Sir Nicholas Bacon, who warned parliament after the passage of the Acts of Supremacy and Uniformity in 1559 about

> those that be too swift as those that be too slow; those I say, that go before the laws, or beyond the laws, as those that will not follow; for good government cannot be where obedience faileth, and both these alike break the rule of obedience; and these to be those, who in likelihood should be beginners, and maintainers, and upholders of all factions and sects, the very mothers and nurses of all seditions and tumults, which necessarily bring forth destruction and depopulation.[51]

Pilkington was taking a very different view of "obedience" and "sedition," however, when he wrote *Aggeus* in 1560. The Jews' decision to heed the prophet and build the Temple, despite royal forbidding, "was neyther treason nor rebellion agaynste the Kinge to do that which God by his prophet so straitly commaunded as was declared and noted before but they were rather traytours to God that had not of so many yeares gone more ernestly about that buildinge of Goddes howse as God willed them to doo."[52] In Pilkington's version of post-exilic Israel – a place that was always explicitly or implicitly contemporary England – those who built God's temple might be wrongly accused of rebellion and treason, but they were doing God's work and he would reward them.

We can see the distinctiveness of Pilkington's claims even more clearly when we recognize that they were based on a contentious reading of Haggai that differed in important ways from the accounts offered by other contemporary Protestant commentators.[53] Calvin lectured on the minor prophets at

---

[51] Quoted in Norman Jones, *The Birth of the Elizabethan Age: England in the 1560s* (Oxford, 1993), 13.
[52] *Aggeus*, q8v.
[53] It should also be noted that English Catholics, unsurprisingly, also read Haggai's lessons regarding civil magistrates very differently from Pilkington. While Pilkington interpreted Haggai's form of address – to Zerubabel first and Joshua second – as teaching the supremacy of secular magistrates over priests, Thomas Dorman argued the opposite in 1564. Prophets like Malachi and Haggai taught Christians to seek the "law of God" from priests, rather than civil magistrates, "which had they [kings] bene the chiefe governours in those matters without faile they [the prophets] would have doen": *A Proufe of Certeyne Articles in Religion, Denied by M. Juell sett furth in defence of the Catholyke beleef* (Antwerp, 1564; STC 7062), f2v.

the end of the 1550s, and these lectures were first published in 1559 with a dedication to the reformist king of Sweden, Gustavus Vasa. Calvin's dating of Haggai's prophecy differed slightly from Pilkington's, a seemingly minor point that nevertheless had major implications for how the two commentators understood the lessons of Haggai regarding authority and reformation. As we have seen, Pilkington argued that (1) Assuerus forbade further rebuilding and the Jews ceased work on the Temple; (2) Haggai rebuked the Jews' inactivity; (3) the Jews began to rebuild the temple; and (4) Darius then granted them royal authorization and funds to complete the work *after* the work had begun and his officials had reported the Jews' presumptive action. By contrast, Calvin argued that Haggai prophesied to the Jews *after* King Darius had given them liberty and funds to build the temple.[54] Unlike Pilkington, then, who chose to interpret Haggai's prophecy as a rebuke for fearing to disobey a royal command, Calvin interpreted it as a rebuke for failing to obey a godly king. Calvin wrote that since "Darius had so kindly permitted them to build the Temple, they had no excuse for delay."[55] In Calvin's interpretation, moreover, the blame for failing to build the Temple lay entirely with the people, not their civil magistrate or high priest, for "if a probable conjecture be entertained, neither Zerubabel nor Joshua were at fault . . . Zerubabel was a wise prince, and that Joshua faithfully discharged his office as priest."[56] For Calvin, therefore, Haggai was a text that urged people to obey God *with* their princes.

This was also how the text had been interpreted by English evangelicals in the reign of Henry VIII. Nicholas Wyse used this episode to praise Henry VIII in *A consolacyon for chrysten people to repayre agayn the lordes temple* (1538).[57] Wyse recounted how the Jews had been authorized by King Cyrus to return and rebuild, then ceased building after facing opposition, and then began to build again *after* King Darius "gyveth them lycence to buyld the temple with all thynges necessary ther unto belongynge."[58] For Wyse,

<hr>

[54] For details on this publication, see Wulfert de Greef (trans. Lyle D. Bierma), *The Writings of John Calvin: an Introductory Guide* (Grand Rapids, MI, 1993), 60. The lectures appeared first in Latin as *Ioannis Calvini praelectiones in duodecim prophetas (quos vocant) minores* (Geneva, 1559).

[55] John Calvin (trans. John Owen), *Commentaries on the Twelve Minor Prophets by John Calvin* (Grand Rapids, MI, 1950), 324.

[56] Calvin, *Commentaries on the Twelve Minor Prophets*, 322. Calvin later qualified this claim by admitting that Zerubabel and Joshua "were not wholly free from blame," although he provided no details, and then suggested that Haggai presented his prophecies to Zerubabel and Joshua so that they might together form a united front against the sloth of the people.

[57] Nicholas Wyse, *A consolacyon for chrysten people to repayre agayn the lordes temple* (London, 1538; STC 26063). Pilkington was a student at Cambridge when this text was published, though there is no evidence that he read it.

[58] Wyse, *A consolacyon*, c4r.

writing at a high point of the Henrician reformation for evangelicals, Henry VIII was playing the role of Darius, as "our godly kyng beynge inspired with the spirite of grace, renueth the commaundemente of our savyour Christ, gevyng fre lybertye to buylde up the lordes temples agayne."[59] George Joye was much less sanguine about Henry as a reformer, but he offered a similar chronology of post-exilic Jewish history in his massive commentary on *Daniel* (1545), noting that the rebuilding of the temple "ceassed and was letted nothing in a maner done, tyll the 2 yeare of this Darius and then begane they a fresshe *at his commandement and licence to buylde*."[60]

The same chronology and interpretation was offered in Elizabethan England by Bishop John Jewel in a sermon on Haggai 1:2–4 preached at Paul's Cross sometime during the 1560s.[61] Jewel preached that Haggai prophesied after Darius gave the Jews license to rebuild the Temple and he also contrasted the sloth of the people with the enthusiasm of their rulers for building the Temple. "God had mollified the Kings hearte to bee gracious towards them, he had delivered them, he had restored them home to their countrie, hee gave them Prophetes to call uppon them, and a godly Prince to rule over them: but the people cried out, The time is not yet come that the Lordes house shoulde be buylded.'"[62] Zerubabel was the hero of Jewel's sermon. While the building of the Temple entailed real hardship, "all this discouraged not the good Prince Zorobabel, hee armed himselfe with Gods promise against all impossibilities, and so called the people to the buylding of the temple . . . that man of GOD despayred not, though hee sawe all the worlde against him."[63]

According to these Protestant commentators, therefore, the prophet Haggai joined forces with godly civil and religious leaders to rouse a slothful people to build God's Temple. These interpretations emphasized the central place of the godly ruler in God's providential design for Temple-building and the necessity of civil and ecclesiastical authorities for its success. Calvin noted, for example, that when the rebuilding of the Temple finally began, the prophet "names both Zerubabel and Joshua; for it behoved them to lead the way, and, as it were, to extend a hand to others. For, had there been no leaders, no one of the common people would

---

[59] Wyse, *A consolacyon*, c4v.   [60] Joye, *The exposicion of Daniel*, 156r; emphasis added.

[61] Millar MacLure includes Jewel's sermon among the undateable Paul's Cross sermons of the 1560s. Millar MacLure, *The Paul's Cross Sermons, 1534–1642* (Toronto, 1958). For another Elizabethan account that placed Haggai's prophecy after Darius's decree, see Henoch Clapham, *A Briefe of the Bible Drawne First into English Poësy* (Edingburgh, 1596; STC 5332), 99–100.

[62] John Jewel, *Certaine Sermons preached before the Queenes Majestie, and at Paules crosse* (London, 1583; STC 14596), f3r-v.

[63] Jewel, *Certaine Sermons*, f4r.

have pointed out the way to [the] rest. We know what usually happens when a word is addressed indiscriminately to all the people: they wait for one another."[64] Jewel's emphasis was even more strictly on the civil magistrate: the Temple "was restored, not by the Bishoppes, but by Zorobabel the Prince of Juda."[65] Wyse's Henrician reading of this episode was a paean to royal reformation, praising the godly monarch and his reformist efforts as he "wypeth awaye Idolatry" and distributed the "lawe of the lorde" to his people "in theyr maternall tonge."[66]

It is highly unlikely that Pilkington was unfamiliar with this way of reading Haggai and he could have easily adopted it, using the text as a springboard to call the English people to follow the lead of their godly queen in rebuilding the Church of England after their babylonical exile under Mary. Indeed, he was aware that the sequence of Persian kings and the chronology of post-exilic Israel was a vexed academic question and that his chronology was not universally accepted. Pilkington defended his interpretation by invoking the principle of *sola scriptura* and implicitly criticizing other commentators for relying overmuch on pagan histories, writing that "although the countinge of these yeares be harde to count, and are dyverslye reckened of dyvers men, because they woulde make the Greeke histories to agre with the scriptures, I shall let al other histories passe, because they be to[o] troublesome, and folow that onelye whiche the scripture teacheth."[67] Whatever the reason, Pilkington's chronological choice enabled him to develop a distinctive interpretation of the passage. All of the Jews – not just the "people" – had failed to build the Temple and faced Haggai's rebuke.[68] When he did assign blame to particular persons, Pilkington's stance was the opposite of Calvin's, arguing that Zerubbabel and Joshua were most to blame because they not only failed to build themselves but also failed to lead the people in building. Zerubbabel (who was importantly for Pilkington not the Jews' king, but rather something like a duke, governor, mayor, or one of the "hed men" among the Jews[69]) and the high priest Joshua "had offended moste," since they ought to have taken the lead and "should have bene better then the rest" in the work of building.[70]

[64] Calvin, *Commentaries on the Twelve Minor Prophets*, 339–340.   [65] Jewel, *Certaine Sermons*, f6v.
[66] Wyse, *A consolacyon*, c4v-c5v.   [67] *Aggeus*, b3r-v.   [68] *Aggeus*, n8v.
[69] *Aggeus*, c5v. Zerubabel "had not a Kyngly Majesty, crowne & power" and his inferior status become a crucial point for Pilkington when he wanted to argue that the prophet's address to Zerubabel before Joshua taught that even lesser magistrates like Zerubbabel were "preferred" over the high priest: *Aggeus*, c5v.
[70] *Aggeus*, s5r-v.

Rather than using this text as an opportunity at the beginning of Elizabeth's reign to praise royal reformation, therefore, or even to highlight the godly leadership of inferior magistrates like Zerubabel or priests like Joshua, Pilkington chose to portray the Jews' building as a *collective* act of obedience to God and disobedience (although it was really no such thing) to their earthly king. In doing so, he was hardly denying that the monarch *should* play a central role in building the temple. Pilkington depicted Darius' assistance as desirable and welcome and, while it is worth noting that Elizabeth was very rarely mentioned in the text (perhaps due to his anger over the Act of Exchange), he elsewhere praised God "for restoring religion through the Quenes travaile."[71] Pilkington was entirely in favor of a sort of "royal reformation," in other words, but the story he told about the rebuilding of the temple ultimately made the monarch an *optional* part of the process of reformation rather than its necessary wellspring. The only other Elizabethan Protestant that I have discovered who interpreted Haggai in this fashion was none other than the early separatist leader Robert Browne. In *A Treatise of reformation without tarying for anie, and of the wickednesse of those Preachers which will not reforme till the Magistrate commaunde or compell them* (1582), Browne pointed to the prophets Haggai and Zachariah as example of reformers who refused to "tarie for the Magistrates," because "when the King (whose subjectes they were) commaunded them to cease, they refused to give over the building ... And before also, because they [the Jews] ceased and lingered the building, for that the Magistrates were against them, they were sharpelie reproved of Haggai, and it was a most grievous curse unto them."[72]

While Pilkington's interpretation of Haggai diverged from most contemporary Protestant interpretations of the text, the view of authority and reformation he advanced had a great deal in common with arguments made in recent years by John Knox (Pilkington's minister at Geneva for part of the Marian exile) and Christopher Goodman. Knox and Goodman were notorious for advocating the violent overthrow of Mary Tudor and Mary Stuart,

---

[71] Pilkington, *The burnynge of Paules church*, p1r.

[72] Robert Browne, *A Treatise of reformation without tarying for anie* (Middelburgh, 1582; STC 3910.3), b3r-v. This is the only sixteenth-century English Protestant text I have found that shared Pilkington's chronology of Haggai's prophecy, alongside Robert Aylett's *A Briefe Chronologie of the Holie Scriptures* (London, 1600; STC 14), 27. This chronology was also employed by Martin Luther, who wrote that the Jews faced "a mad and inflated king who didn't want them to rebuild the temple," but that "it is the Word of God which commands such things, and to it we must listen even though the whole world resists it." Martin Luther, *Lectures on Haggai*, trans. Richard J. Dinda, in *Luther's works*, ed. H. C. Oswald (St. Louis, 1975), 18:369.

but their "revolutionary conclusions" followed from the less flashy premise that God directly commanded *all* people to obey his commands, even if their rulers refused to obey them. In *How Superior Powers Oght to be Obeyd* (1558), for example, Goodman laid out a theory of "true obedience" where concepts like obedience, disobedience, rebellion, and treason "must not be measured by the will of man, but by the juste Lawes and ordinances of the livinge Lorde."[73] All people "high and lowe, riche and poore, man and woman" owed God "first and principall obedience: and secondly unto men for him, and in him onlie."[74] Earthly kings could not limit people's obedience to God, let alone command them to disobey God, for "after God hathe once pronounced anie thinge that he would have done, either in his Lawe or otherwise: there is no man that may or can dispence therwith."[75] The person who acted in obedience to God could never be considered a rebel, therefore, "how so ever the worlde judgeth."[76] Instead, it was the person who issued or obeyed ungodly commands who was "a rebell agaynst thy Lorde and God."[77]

All of God's commands must be obeyed, therefore, whether the earthly authorities approved or not. Goodman knew this was controversial and rehearsed a variety of "excuses" that people gave for refusing to "obey God before man." Commoners might try to shirk their responsibilities to God by asking, "[i]f the Magistrates and other officers contemne their duetie in defending Gods glorie and the Lawes committed to their charge, lieth it in our power to remedie it?"[78] The "comen and symple people, they thinke them selves utterly discharged" of the responsibility to obey God since they think that "they muste be obedient, because they are ignorant, and muste be led them selves, not meete to leade others."[79] Since the actions of commoners "are counted tumultes and rebellion (except they be agreable to the commandmentes, decrees, and proceadinges of their superior powers and Magistrates, and shal in doing the contrary be as rebells punished)," the people presume that "we have least to do, yea nothing at all withe the doinges of our Rulers."[80] Goodman thought all of this was nonsense and completely rejected these sorts of arguments as "vaine excuses of the people."[81] It was certainly "discouraging to the people when they are not stirred up to godlynesse by the good example of all sortes of Superiors, Magistrates and officers

---

[73] Goodman, *How Superior Powers*, 44.   [74] Goodman, *How Superior Powers*, 44–45.
[75] Goodman, *How Superior Powers*, 44.   [76] Goodman, *How Superior Powers*, 60–61.
[77] Goodman, *How Superior Powers*, 62. For additional treatments of rebellion in these terms, also see 44, 47, 86, and ch. 14.
[78] Goodman, *How Superior Powers*, 179.   [79] Goodman, *How Superior Powers*, 145.
[80] Goodman, *How Superior Powers*, 145–146.   [81] Goodman, *How Superior Powers*, 179.

in the faithefull executing of their office," and it was even worse when these rulers "inforce them to wicked impietie."[82] But "all this can be no excuse for you," for even "thoghe you had no man of power upon your parte: yet, it is a sufficient assurance for you, to have the warrant of Godds worde upon your side, and God him self to be your Capitayne who willeth not onely the Magistrates and officers to roote out evil from amongest them, beit, idolatrie, blasphemie or open injurie, but the whole multitude are therwith charged also."[83] In other words, magistrates and monarchs were very *helpful* in implementing God's commandments, and it was their duty to do so, but their assistance was not necessary for the work to go forward, nor was their opposition an excuse for common people not to obey God actively. It was this theory of obedience that underwrote Goodman's notorious call for even a commoner to obey God's command to punish idolaters by wielding the sword against Mary "as an open idolatres in the sight of God, and a cruel murtherer of his Saints before men, and merciles traytoresse to her owne native countrie."[84]

John Knox similarly argued that religious reform was a duty laid upon all people by God and that this duty was not obviated by the failure of civil or religious leaders to act. In his *Appellation* (1558), for instance, Knox repeatedly attempted to disabuse the Scottish nobility of the notion that "the reformation of religion and defence of the afflicted doth not appertain to you because you are no kings but nobles and estates of a realm."[85] In his *Letter to the Commonalty* (1558), Knox stressed that even common people were duty-bound to establish a preaching ministry and the pure administration of the sacraments in their churches. Knox told the people that "to you it doth no less appertain than to your king or princes to provide that Christ Jesus be truly preached amongst you."[86] Christ was present among his people through "the true preaching of His Word and right administration of His sacraments. To the maintenance whereof is no less bound the subject than the prince, the poor than the rich."[87] If the people's "superiors" failed to provide true preachers, the people should withhold their tithes and "ye may provide true teachers for yourselves, be it in your cities, towns or villages; them ye may maintain and defend against all that shall persecute

---

[82] Goodman, *How Superior Powers*, 179–180.   [83] Goodman, *How Superior Powers*, 180.

[84] Goodman, *How Superior Powers*, 99. On Goodman's notion of obedience to God as entailing the active implementation of divine commands – rather than simply the refusal to obey ungodly commands – see Dawson, "Resistance and Revolution," 70–72.

[85] Knox, "The Appellation of John Knox," in Mason (ed.), *On Rebellion*, 94.

[86] Knox, "The Letter to the Commonalty," in Mason (ed.), *On Rebellion*, 119.

[87] Knox, "The Letter to the Commonalty," 121.

them."[88] The fact that they were commoners and not rulers did not excuse inaction:

> It will not excuse you (dear Brethren) in the presence of God, neither yet will it avail you in the day of His visitation to say: 'We were but simple subjects; we could not redress the faults and crimes of our rulers, bishops and clergy. We called for reformation, and wished for the same, but lords' brethren were bishops, their sons were abbots, and the friends of great men had the possession of the church, and so were we compelled to give obedience to all that they demanded.' These vain excuses, I say, will nothing avail you in the presence of God who requireth no less of the subjects than of the rulers.[89]

While these texts were addressed to the Scots, Knox saw them as relevant to the English as well.[90] In a letter to his former congregants at Newcastle and Barwick, dated 10 November 1558 (only a week before Mary's death), Knox wrote that if his English readers wished to understand "[f]arther of my mynde concerning your dueties in these most dolorous dayes," they should consult "my appellation and by myne admonition to the nobilitie and communaltie of Scotlande."[91] According to Knox, however, his readers already understood his advice and had already put these principles into practice during the reign of Edward VI when they had reformed their churches without tarrying for the magistrate. In those days, "Ye feared not to go before statutes and lawes, yea openly and solemnedly you dyd professe by reciving the sacramentes not as man had appointed, but as Christ Jesus the wisdome of God the father had institute."[92] Baptism and the Lord's Supper had been "used & ministred in all simplicitie, not as man had devised, nether as the kinges procedinges dyd alowe, but as Christ Jesus dyd institute, and as it is evident, that Sainct Paule dyd practise."[93] Knox wrote these words with Mary Tudor still on the English throne, but he continued to urge this course of action to the English after the accession of Elizabeth. In his January 1559 exhortation to England, printed alongside this November 1558 letter to Newcastle and Barwick, Knox urged the people of Elizabethan England to reform immediately, with or without

---

[88] Knox, "The Letter to the Commonalty," 123.   [89] Knox, "The Letter to the Commonalty," 124.

[90] Jane Dawson has emphasized the differences between Knox's English and Scottish writings: Dawson, "The Two John Knoxes: England, Scotland and the 1558 Tracts," *Journal of Ecclesiastical History* 42:4 (October 1991), 555–576. For further analysis of these differences, see Scott Dolff, "The Two John Knoxes and the Justification of Non-Revolution: A Response to Dawson's Argument from Covenant," *Journal of Ecclesiastical History* 55:1 (January 2004), 58–74.

[91] John Knox, *The Copie of an Epistle Sent by John Knox one of the Ministers of the Englishe Church at Geneva unto the inhabitants of Newcastle, & Barwike. In the end wherof is added a briefe exhortation to England for the spedie imbrasing of Christes Gospel hertofore suppressed & banished* (Geneva, 1559; STC 15064), 53.

[92] Knox, *The Copie of an Epistle*, 10.   [93] Knox, *The Copie of an Epistle*, 16.

the approval and assistance of the crown. God's religion must be established and defended and the English must "Let not the King and his proceadinges (what soever they be) not agreable to his worde be a snare to thy conscience."[94] This advice, which Roger Mason notes was "hardly compatible with the doctrine of the royal supremacy," was entirely compatible with what the Marian exiles and the members of underground congregations in England had been doing for the past five years.[95]

While Pilkington rejected the legitimacy of violent rebellion against an ungodly ruler in *Aggeus*, the continuities between Knox and Goodman's theories of obedience and Pilkington's arguments about authority and reform in *Aggeus* are striking.[96] They shared the notion that all people were directly charged by God with the fulfillment of his commandments, as well as the insistence that true religion must be established whether or not the ruler approved. The similarities even extended to their choice of topics in 1560: Knox preached a "vehement" series of sermons on Haggai to the Scottish parliament in the summer of 1560, remarking that the "doctrine was proper for the time."[97] Unfortunately, the content of these sermons has not survived, but – given Knox's arguments in his *Appellation, Letter to the Commonalty*, and published exhortations to the English in 1559 – one would strongly suspect that it had much in common with Pilkington's published interpretation of Haggai that same year.

It is also significant that Pilkington shared with the resistance theorists a common fondness for the Old Testament figure of Phineas. As the story is recounted in Numbers 25, an Israelite nobleman married a Midianite woman – a mixed marriage directly prohibited by God – and when Moses and the authorities failed to punish them for violating the law, the priest Phineas burned with zeal for God's law and took matters into his own hands by entering their tent and killing both with a single thrust of his spear. God was highly pleased by Phineas's act, ended the plague he had sent among Israel as punishment for their sin, and made an eternal covenant of

[94] Knox, *The Copie of an Epistle*, 89.
[95] Roger A. Mason, "Knox, Resistance and the Royal Supremacy," in Mason (ed.), *John Knox and the British Reformations*, 171.
[96] *Aggeus*, c6v. In his later commentary on Nehemiah, left unfinished at his death in 1576, Pilkington wrote that "to rebell and draw the sword against thy lawfull Prince for religion, I have not yet learned, nor cannot alow off it," and he proceeded to justify this position with many of the traditional arguments *against* resistance that Goodman had explicitly rejected in 1558. Pilkington, *A Godlie Exposition Upon Certeine Chapters of Nehemiah* (Cambridge, 1585; STC 19929), 63v. It is worth noting that Pilkington's arguments on this count were somewhat ambiguous, as he simultaneously accepted private-law arguments that permitted defensive action against religious enemies (64v).
[97] John Knox, *History of the Reformation in Scotland*, ed. William Croft Dickinson (Edinburgh, 1950), 1:335.

priesthood with Phineas and his descendants. For resistance theorists, Phineas was a perfect example of a godly individual who actively obeyed God's law (in this case by violently punishing open sin) when the magistrates were disobeying it.[98] Knox prayed in a 1554 pamphlet that "God for his great mercies sake stirre up some Phinees, Helias, or Jehu, that the bloude of abhominable Idolaters maye pacifie goddes wrath, that it consume not the hole multitude."[99] Knox might have considered his prayer answered the following year when a former monk named William Flower entered St Margaret's church in Westminster on Easter morning and stabbed a priest in the midst of celebrating mass. Awaiting trial in Newgate, Flower explained to his fellow prisoner Robert Smith that when he had entered the church and seen "the people falling down before a most shameful & detestable Idole," he was "moved with extreme zealez for my god" and became a direct minister of God's will like "Moses Aaron, Phinees, Josua, Zimrie, Thobie, [and] Judith Mathathiah" had been in the pages of Scripture, "plantng zeales to his honor, against all order and respect of flesh and bloud."[100] Phineas's example would again inspire violence in 1573 when Peter Byrchet attempted to assassinate Christopher Hatton, insisting that he was "a wylfull papyst and hindereth the glory of god so moche as in him lyethe."[101] Byrchet had "a history of progressive mental derangement of a paranoiac nature, unconnected with religious mania,"[102] but when asked whether he believed his actions to be warranted by Scripture, Byrchet responded that he had become "perswaded in conscien[ce]" that he was appointed to be divine avenger like Joab, Ehud, or Phineas.[103] He had not, therefore, acted "of his owne authoryty," and his attempt to murder Hatton was "lawfull by gods lawe yf not by mans lawe."[104]

---

[98] See the invocations of Phineas in Lambert, *The summe of christianitie*, d8r-e1r; Ponet, *A Shorte Treatise*, g8r-v; Goodman, *How Superior Powers*, 196. Phineas had been invoked (alongside other Old Testament avengers) by fifteenth-century French resistance theorists and then again by Huguenot resistance theorists: Paul Saenger, "The Earliest French Resistance Theories: The Role of the Burgundian Court," *The Journal of Modern History* 51:4, On Demand Supplement (December 1979), pp. D-1245–1246.

[99] John Knox, *A Faythfull admonition made by John Knox* (Emden, 1554; STC 15069), 80.

[100] Foxe, *The Unabridged Acts and Monuments Online* (1563 edition) [Accessed 2.6.2014].

[101] Lansdowne MS 17, f. 192r.

[102] Collinson, *Elizabethan Puritan Movement*, 150; also see Alexandra Walsham, "'Frantick Hacket': Prophecy, Sorcery, Insanity, and the Elizabethan Puritan Movement," *The Historical Journal* 41:1 (March 1998), 52n119.

[103] Lansdowne MS 17, f. 192r; Byrchet's actions and his rationale were specifically invoked as an example of bad biblical interpretation by Thomas Wilson in *Theologicall Rules, to Guide Us in the Understanding and practise of holy Scriptures* (London, 1615; STC 25798), 67.

[104] Lansdowne MS 17, f. 192r.

Phineas was, in short, a potentially explosive biblical figure and while regularly invoked by resistance theorists and assassins, he was a troubling figure to more conservative thinkers.[105] As Bishop Cooper noted in 1573, if Phineas were "taken as an example," it would prove to be a recipe for "very greate disorder," and Tudor commentators and preachers regularly sought to marginalize Phineas's example and render it irrelevant as a model for action.[106] The "Homily of Contention" (1547) praised Phineas's zeal but stressed that his actions were not an example "to be folowed of every body but as men be called to office and set in aucthoritie."[107] Hugh Latimer argued that Phineas was not an example for everyone to follow because he had received "a special callyng, a secrete inspiration of god to do such a thing," and "we which have no such calling may not folowe hym, for we ought to kyl no body, the magistrates shall redresse all matters," but unlike the Homily of Contention, Latimer left open the possibility that other people might also receive such an extraordinary calling.[108] Calvin was likewise not keen on identifying Phineas as a possible model for action, but in a sermon on Deuteronomy he was not willing to rule out the possibility: Phineas had performed a "peculiar deede which wee may not follow, without a special moving of the holy Ghost."[109] But these commentators were very careful to hedge their discussions of Phineas with thickets of disqualifications and even Laurence Humphrey, whose *De Religionis Conservatione et Reformatione Vera* (1559) defended the legitimacy of resistance to a wicked and ungodly ruler, called the example of Phineas "extraordinary," and claimed that it did not "achieve anything."[110] "Everyone is not Phinehas,"

---

[105] On Foxe's discomfort with Flower's example, see David Loewenstein, *Treacherous Faith: The Specter of Heresy in Early Modern English Literature & Culture* (Oxford, 2013), 128–131.

[106] Thomas Cooper, *A briefe exposition of such Chapters of the olde testament as usually are redde in the Church at common praier* (London, 1573; STC 5684), 203r-v.

[107] Thomas Cranmer, *Certayne Sermons, or Homelies, appoynted by the kynges Majestie* (London, 1547; STC 13640), z3r.

[108] Hugh Latimer, *Certayn Godly Sermons* (London, 1562; STC 15276), 126r; this was also the line taken by Cooper, for whom Phineas had received "a peculiar instinction of God in this one cause" and "is not to be taken as an example commonly of all persons to be folowed": Cooper, *A briefe exposition*, 203r-v.

[109] Jean Calvin, *The Sermons of M. John Calvin Upon the Fifth Booke of Moses called Deuteronomie* (London, 1583; STC 4442), 400. This potentially rebellious loophole was ingeniously closed by Thomas Bilson in 1585 by arguing that Phineas was really only carrying out the commands of his magistrate. "*Phinees* had for his warrant afore he did the deede the voice both of God and the Magistrate," Bilson explained, because "*Moses* had charged the Judges of Israell before *Zimri* came with the woman of Midian into the tentes: *Every one slaie his men that joyned unto Baal Peor*. And the Magistrate commaunding, as in this case you see he did, it was lawfull for *Phinees* or any other private person to execute that sentence." Thomas Bilson, *The True Difference Betweene Christian Subjection and Unchristian Rebellion* (Oxford, 1585; STC 3071), 385–386.

[110] Humphrey, *De Religionis* in Kemp, "Laurence Humphrey," 222.

Humphrey stressed, but more importantly, Phineas was not "truly acting as an individual," but rather as a sort of magistrate or leader who had been directly commissioned by the divine voice.[111]

Given the radical use to which Phineas had been put during Mary's reign, as well as the extreme care (and outright dismissal) with which his example was treated by commentators throughout the century, it is therefore striking that Pilkington chose to offer completely unqualified praise of Phineas in his commentary on Haggai. Indeed, Pilkington put Phineas on the *title page* of his commentary: "Phinees hath turned away my anger because he was moved with love of me. Numer. 25."[112] Rather than beginning his call to build the temple in England by invoking a godly king like Solomon or a queen like Esther, Pilkington chose to start by reminding his readers on the very first page of a priest whose zeal for God led him to take bold action when the authorities refused to obey God's law. This was, as we have seen, a fitting introduction to Pilkington's argument throughout the text that (as he put it on the next page) "al degrees of menne, doe owe a duetye to the buildinge, of this gods house," a duty that he then repeatedly argued was not obviated by royal forbidding or the failure of the authorities to build.[113] Pilkington returned to Phineas a few pages later as he lamented the fact that the "rulers and officers" who hold "the whippe of correction in their hand" had not followed Christ's example of cleansing the Temple, having instead "so coldly behaved them selves, in setting up the kingdome of Christ."[114] Pilkington prayed for hot zeal lest Christ spew England's lukewarm Christians ought of his mouth, and he proceeded to list a series of unqualified exemplars that would have been familiar to readers of Knox, Goodman, or Ponet: "Phinees turned awaye gods anger from his people, bycause so zelouslye hee avenged gods quarell and punished, that wickednesse which other wincked at ... Though Jehu was a evill man otherwaies, yet god gave him a worldelye blessinge, & commaunded him for his earnest zele in rooting out the posterite of Achab, pulling downe Baall, & his sacrificinge priestes, makinge a common jakes of the house, w[h]ere they worshipped him."[115] Indeed, when Pilkington described the moment when the Jews awoke from their sloth and began to build, he depicted it in much the same terms that Phineas's actions were described. The Israelites were "so styrred up" that they immediately chose to obey God, even though it involved disobedience to their earthly rulers, and God was so pleased with their zeal that he rewarded their obedience and blessed their work.[116] For

---

[111] Humphrey, *De Religionis* in Kemp, "Laurence Humphrey," 222. [112] *Aggeus*, a1r.
[113] *Aggeus*, a2r. [114] *Aggeus*, a5r. [115] *Aggeus*, a5v. [116] *Aggeus*, q7v.

Pilkington, as for the resistance theorists, Phineas was not a problem to be explained away, but a godly example to be followed.[117]

When Pilkington set out "to bringe some of every sort . . . to an earneste fortheringe of gods true relygyon" in 1560, therefore, he was employing ideas and biblical topoi that had been central to radical Marian Protestant thought about obedience, authority, and reformation. To be clear, Pilkington does not seem to have envisioned "resistance" as something that was necessary in 1560. He was certainly angered by the crown's efforts to seize episcopal lands in 1559, but he seems to have viewed Elizabeth as a godly prince and he hoped that she would lead her people in rebuilding God's temple in England.[118] Yet the experience of Mary's reign had left a lasting impression on Pilkington and his view of authority. During Mary's short time on the throne, the mass submission of commoners, clergy, and political elites to the will of their popish monarch had led to the rapid reestablishment of idolatry and national apostasy.[119] It was surely to avoid a repetition of this scenario that Pilkington so vehemently emphasized the need to "obey God before man" in his commentary on Haggai. Pilkington certainly hoped that the English people would be able to build the temple *with* their godly ruler Elizabeth – obeying God while obeying man – but the time might come very shortly when they would have to pursue this task without royal support. After recounting with disgust the ease with which idolatry had been restored under Mary, for example, Pilkington sarcastically urged his readers "to pray unto God that he would geve thee good Rulers, for thou must beleve as thei doo, and if they love not God, thou shalt not heare hym speake unto thee by hys woorde, and if they wyll not woorshyppe God aryght, thou shalt not be suffered to do it if thou wold. Can anye people escape unpunished, that thus mockes God?"[120] If the queen proved cold in building the temple, died prematurely, married a papist, or was replaced by another Mary from the north – all distressingly real possibilities for Protestants in 1560 – God's people must not cease building the temple. Indeed, he concluded the commentary with a lengthy passage praising the fortitude of the Marian martyrs and exiles and praying for similar courage: "God for his mercye sake graunt all his lyke boldnes to withstande their crueltye, whan so ever God shall trye us."[121]

---

[117] Pilkington would continue to appeal to Phineas as a godly example in his posthumously published commentary on Nehemiah: see Pilkington, *A Godlie Exposition*, 26r-v.

[118] On Pilkington's comments regarding Elizabeth, see *Aggeus*, a7v, b3r, Ff5r; *The burnynge of Paules church*, o8v-p1v.

[119] *Aggeus*, L5r-v.   [120] *Aggeus*, L6r.   [121] *Aggeus*, Ff4v.

Pilkington's commentary reveals how aspects of Marian resistance theory could continue to shape Protestant thought about reform at the outset of Elizabeth's reign, but we can also see different ways (and different degrees) in which many early Elizabethan Protestants were proceeding to "build the temple" without waiting for the queen's authorization or heeding the limits she had established. As Patrick Collinson wrote, "the puritans were not disposed to 'tarry for the magistrate' in all respects and for ever. In fact they were already fulfilling the further reformation within their own brotherhood, and in those parishes, households and other communities where their influence was not resisted."[122] Godly magistrates were establishing lectureships and prophesyings in the early 1560s and providing opportunities to hear daily sermons and participate in communal psalm singing. None of this "owed much to the initiative of the ecclesiastical authorities," nor was it "part of the official programme of the established Church" in the Queen's eyes, but the lack of royal authorization was of little concern to those responsible for establishing these activities.[123] When a group of ministers in Leicestershire defended themselves against the charge of holding illegal exercises during the 1570s, they claimed that they had warrant from the Bible and from the authorities, but insisted that "let it be that we had no commaundement of man, yet that the necessitie of our tyme doth requyre suche publique exercises there is no man can denye that hath any conscience of synne, or any consyderacon of gods plagues imminent, or any care for the furtherance of Christs holy gospell among us."[124] None of these godly activists would have seen themselves as "resisting" Elizabeth, but as the furor over prophesyings in the 1570s would reveal, the queen certainly saw these initiatives as a shocking arrogation of her authority. So too did other Protestants, like the Bocking minister who complained to Archbishop Parker about these innovators, writing that "I depend upon them that have authority to alter ceremonies, not upon the lewd brethren that seem and would be thought to have authority, and have none . . . Sir, truly, I write as other men talk."[125]

The most radical Protestant clergymen were also taking reformation into their own hands during the early 1560s when they chose not to wear the uniform mandated by the crown, as were bishops (Pilkington perhaps chief among them) who colluded in their nonconformity.[126] The nonconformists

---

[122] Collinson, *Elizabethan Puritan Movement*, 14; on these activities in the early years of the reign, see especially pp. 50–68.

[123] Collinson, *Elizabethan Puritan Movement*, 51.   [124] Add. MS 27632, f. 50v.

[125] Quoted in Collinson, *Elizabethan Puritan Movement*, 68.

[126] Pilkington was arguably the strongest episcopal ally of the nonconformists in the early 1560s, not only permitting vestiarian nonconformity in his own diocese of Durham but writing in defense of the nonconformists to the Earl of Leicester in 1564. See David Marcombe, "A Rude and Heady People: the

insisted that vestments harmed the cause of the gospel and Robert Crowley, one of the nonconformists' leaders in London, justified their disobedience by explaining that they would only wear the vestments when "it may manifestly appeare unto us, that the same may helpe forwarde, and not pull downe, staye or hinder the building up of the Lordes temple."[127] From the crown's perspective this was not their prerogative – it was to "go before the laws, or beyond the laws," as Bacon had put it in 1559 – but the nonconformists saw this as a matter of obeying God before man. John Barthlet, who was suspended for nonconformity in March 1566 and continued to preach under suspension, stridently took the position that the queen ought to be thankful to the nonconformists for having taken the lead in reforming the church.[128] In his published defense of the nonconformist cause, Barthlet quoted a letter by the Polish reformer Jan Laski (a vigorous supporter of John Hooper's vestiarian nonconformity during Edward VI's reign) that defended the willingness of people to "runne before" the magistrate in these matters: "I knowe our Magistrates godlines, wysedome and forwardnes to be such, that when he shall depelye waye, and well considar the daunger and inconvenyence of these ceremonyes, *he wyll rejoyce that there be some that desire to runne before in the law of the Lord, and to prepare and make the waye radye for other*, that he may revoke and brynge all thynges to the sinceritye and perfection of the Apostles ordre."[129] We are accustomed to seeing the *repression* of nonconformity in the vestiarian crisis as leading the newly minted puritans to reassess their view of royal and episcopal authority and embrace increasingly radical views, but we should recognize that the crisis itself was produced by individuals who had *already* reassessed the nature of royal authority and seized authority for themselves.

A willingness to reform without tarrying for the magistrate was taken to its furthest level, of course, by the separatists. The earliest separatist congregation was formed in London in 1567–1568 as a direct response to the vestiarian controversy and the suspension of nonconformist ministers. The

local community and the Rebellion of the Northern Earls," in David Marcombe (ed.), *The Last Principality: Politics, Religion and Society in the Bishopric of Durham, 1494–1660* (Nottingham, 1987), 132; J. H. Primus, *The Vestments Controversy* (Kampen, 1960), 83, 87–88; Collinson, *Elizabethan Puritan Movement*, 73; Lansdowne MS 19, f. 2; Hastings Robinson (ed.), *The Zurich Letters*, 2nd edn. (Cambridge, 1846), 262. As Marcombe has noted, however, while Pilkington defended nonconformists, he was not necessarily opposed to wearing vestments himself: see David Marcombe, "The Dean and Chapter of Durham, 1558–1603" (Doctoral Thesis, Durham University, 1973), 185–196.

[127] Robert Crowley, *A briefe discourse against the outwarde apparell and Ministring garmentes of the popishe church* (Emden, 1566; STC 6079), a4r.

[128] *ODNB*.

[129] John Barthlet, *The Fortresse of Fathers* (Emden, 1566; STC 1040), d1v; emphasis added.

congregation's leaders explained to Bishop Grindal that they had attended their parish churches "so long as we might have the worde freery [sic] preached, and the Sacramentes administred without the preferring of idolatrous geare above it," but when "all our preachers were displaced by your lawe, that would not subscribe to your apparaile and your lawe," they took the provision of true worship into their own hands and, having "remembred that there was a congregation of us in this Citie in Queene Maries dayes," they formed their own congregation where prayer, preaching, and the sacraments could be administered in a godly fashion.[130] As Grindal patiently (although somewhat unenthusiastically) explained to their assembled leaders, they lacked the authority to do this and they were separating themselves from churches "which doe quietlie obeye the Queenes procedinges, & serve God in such good order, as the Queenes grace and the rest *having authoritie and wisedome, have set foorth and established by Acte of Parliament.*"[131] It was precisely this view of the monarch's religious authority, however, that the separatists rejected. When one of the congregation's leaders, a baker and amateur theologian named William White, was rebuked by Grindal in 1569 for holding a fast and exercise without public authority, he responded by arguing that "the people" did not need authorization to follow God's commands.[132] White argued that the people of Ninevah did not wait to obey Jonah's preaching until their king and priests had decided whether it was true. Quite the opposite, "the king of Ninivee did not blame his subjects" for running ahead of him in "well doing," but he and his council instead gladly followed their godly example. If the heathen king of Ninevah responded this way, "how much more ought christian Magistrats to do the like."[133] In a tract about things that "stai the course of the gospell," White complained further about the way in which the bishops and magistrates had arrogated all religious authority to themselves. The doctrine that "none may meddle with these matters, but such as are therunto called, I meane with relegion" was clearly wrong:

> A godly man affirmeth that we ought to see that our faith and religion be grounded on the infallible truth, as well as our magistrats & rulers, and if any thing be not as gods word teacheth, we may lawfully demaund the same of our magistrats: which if it be not graunted, we may do that which God

[130] *A parte of a register* (Middelburg, 1593?; STC 10400), 24–25.
[131] *A parte of a register*, 23; emphasis added.
[132] White was a close associate of John Field and Thomas Wilcox and the author of a preface to the *Admonition to Parliament*. On White, see Collinson, *Elizabethan Puritan Movement*, 116.
[133] Dr Williams's Library, MS Morrice B, p. 602.

requireth in our owne persons, suffering what punishment soever be layed upon us, so it be for well doing.[134]

Having reached this conclusion, White began all over again in a sarcastic tirade that is worth citing at length:

> No doubt to serve God as he willeth is well done: but it must be done of the prechers & magistrats but the commen people must not meddle therewith, till thei go before and lead the way. How if thei will not lead the way? are we discharged? hath none made promise to keepe gods lawes, but princes, preachers & magistrats? or neede not we keepe and do his lawes, except thei comaund us? or shall we be excused by saying, the magistrates would not suffer us to do his [God's] will? or by saying we would have done this, but all the learned were against us? All this will be none excuse for us: it will be sayde to us *search the scriptures for in them you thinke to have eternall life and they are they which testify of me*: and we shall not be judged by our magistrats, by the wordes that thei speak. And Moses chargeth all with keeping of Gods lawes saying: *Harken O Israel*: he sayeth not princes & magistrats onely but whole Israell: so that Israell is still charged for to keepe gods lawes, though prince and magistrats neglect them.[135]

James Pilkington never reached the conclusion that "building the temple" in England required separation from the Church of England, but White's frustrated diatribe could easily have been drawn from the pages of Pilkington's *Aggeus* and its rebuke of even "the simplest and basest man lyvynge" who excused his inaction by saying "we dyd not thys faulte, but our Rulers, or we were not able ta take it in hand, or if they had begon we would have folowed, or suche like fonde excuses. God requires hys house to be buylded, hys woord and religion to be kept and maintayned as well of the lowest as the hyghest, and they whych do not, shall not escape unpunished."[136] White's claims could have just as easily have come from the Marian writings of John Knox or Christopher Goodman. While Knox and Goodman were personae non gratae with Elizabeth for their opposition to female rule and their calls to punish ungodly monarchs, historians of Elizabethan politics have shown that their theories regarding the limits and responsibilities of monarchs would continue to shape the outlook of figures at the heart of the Elizabethan establishment as they dealt with the problem of the succession and the threat posed to Elizabeth and the Protestant nation by Mary Queen of Scots. As this chapter has argued, the expansive notions of religious authority and godly activism that found expression in

---

[134] Dr Williams's Library, MS Morrice B, p. 587.
[135] Dr Williams's Library, MS Morrice B, p. 587.   [136] *Aggeus*, n3r.

Knox and Goodman's resistance theories would also continue to shape Protestant thought and activism under Elizabeth. English Protestants literally saw Elizabeth's accession as a godsend, and when James Pilkington called for reformation in 1560, he depicted the monarch as playing an important and helpful role in establishing true religion. Rather than making the prince the necessary source of religious authority in England, however, he cast the monarch as a powerful partner in a task that God himself laid upon all of his people, a task that must proceed, with or without the monarch's assistance. Elizabeth completely rejected this limited view of her authority – just as she rejected the notion that even her most exalted subjects could demand that she name a successor or execute a fellow monarch – but to her great consternation, many of her most fervent subjects did not.

CHAPTER 5

Revisiting the Troubles at Frankfurt

In 1554–1555, the English exile congregation at Frankfurt was torn apart by a debate over liturgy. The faction known to historians as the "Knoxians" sought to eliminate elements of the 1552 Prayer Book that they considered superstitious, while their opponents the "Coxians" famously proclaimed their desire to "do as they had done in Englande" and to "have the face off an English churche."[1] While a squabble among exiles is hardly unusual, historians have invested *this* squabble with tremendous importance in the history of the English Reformation. The first history of the controversy, a narrative and collection of original documents entitled *A Brieff discours of the troubles begonne at Franckford*, was published in 1574 by a cadre of presbyterians who claimed that the Frankfurt controversy was "the verye originall and beginninge off all this miserable contention" in the Elizabethan church.[2] Ever since, the Troubles have been placed at the beginnings of a major division within English Protestantism, although historians have not always agreed about the nature of that division. The dissenting clergyman

---

[1] Thomas Wood[?], *A Brieff discours off the troubles begonne at Franckford in Germany Anno Domini 1554* (Heidelberg, 1574; STC 25442), 38. While authorship of *A Brieff discours* was traditionally attributed to William Whittingham, Patrick Collinson argued persuasively for Thomas Wood as a more probable author/compiler. Patrick Collinson, "The Authorship of A Brieff Discours off the Troubles Begonne at Franckford," *Journal of Ecclesiastical History* 9 (1958), 188–208. For a highly problematic dissenting position, which posits a heavily redacted text edited by John Field, see Martin A. Simpson, "Of the Troubles Begun at Frankfurt, A. D. 1554," in Duncan Shaw (ed.), *Reformation and Revolution* (Edinburgh, 1967), 17–33. Because this chapter makes an argument about the controversy itself, rather than presbyterians' use of the controversy, quotations from *A Brieff discours* will be drawn from the original letters and documents it reprints; when quotations come from the narrative, they will be noted as such. The "only contemporary account of the church at Frankfort" is "Thorder off discipline in the English churche off Frankforde received," found in LPL MS 2523, ff. 5–7, and likely dating to after 20 September 1555: E. G. W. Bill, *A Catalogue of Manuscripts in Lambeth Palace Library, MSS. 2341–3119 (excluding MSS. 2690–2750)* (Oxford, 1983), 23. For a recent reassessment of the controversy's chronology, which I discovered too late to incorporate into this chapter (but which does not alter my conclusions), see Timothy Duguid, "The 'Troubles' at Frankfurt: a new chronology," *Reformation & Renaissance Review* 14:3 (December, 2012), 243–268.
[2] *A Brieff discours*, 2.

Daniel Neal wrote in his *History of the Puritans* (1732) – with little inter-pretative ambiguity – that "here began the fatal division" between those who sought to maintain the Edwardian liturgy and those who "resolved to shake off the remains of antichrist."[3] Christina Garrett was less partisan but equally dramatic when, noting the re-publication of *A Brieff discours* in 1642, she claimed that "the *Troubles begun at Frankfort* were to close in civil war."[4] Ronald Vander Molen lowered the rhetorical temperature but did not diminish the significance of the controversy when he argued in the 1970s that the "Troubles at Frankfurt" marked the "ideological origins" of the divide between "Anglicans" and "Puritans," with the former committed to a distinctively English form of Protestantism with its own "national church traditions" and the latter preferring an international, biblicist form of Christianity.[5] While eschewing the notion that this controversy had anything to do with "Anglicanism," Patrick Collinson and Diarmaid MacCulloch have also seen the Frankfurt controversy as presaging the divisions within the Elizabethan Church. Collinson argued that the Troubles at Frankfurt "anticipated the alignment of puritans and conform-ists in the Elizabethan Church" by pitting those who demanded strict biblical warrant for church order against those who permitted the use of "things indifferent" and MacCulloch has pointed to the same disagreement over *adiaphora* when writing that the controversy "proved prophetic for the contrasting stances of later years," when "[b]etween conformists and Puritans there lay a great gap of comprehension which the contrasting exclamations of Cox and Knox at Frankfurt had already revealed."[6]

---

[3] Neal, *The History of the Puritans*, vol. 1 (London, 1837), iv. On the role of Frankfurt in seventeenth-century histories of puritanism, see Paul Chang-Ha Lim, *In Pursuit of Purity, Unity, and Liberty: Richard Baxter's Puritan Ecclesiology in Its Seventeenth-Century Context* (Leiden, 2004), 213–214.

[4] Garrett, *The Marian Exiles*, 59.

[5] Vander Molen, "Anglican against Puritan: Ideological Origins during the Marian Exile," 50. Also see Ronald J. Vander Molen, "Providence as Mystery, Providence as Revelation: Puritan and Anglican Modifications of John Calvin's Doctrine of Providence," *Church History* 47:1 (March 1978), 34; Francis J. Bremer, *The Puritan Experiment: New England Society from Bradford to Edwards* (New York, 1976), 8–9. For the claim that the Coxians "wanted their religion to be English, not international," see Everett H. Emerson, *English Puritanism from John Hooper to John Milton* (Durham, NC, 1968), 6. More recently, Dan G. Danner has argued that the Coxians were of "a nationalist and royalist persuasion," while the Knoxians upheld what they viewed as "an international form of Protestantism, a theological ethos founded on the rock of primitive apostolic Christianity." Dan G. Danner, *Pilgrimage to Puritanism: History and Theology of the Marian Exiles at Geneva* (New York, 1999), 21.

[6] Collinson, *Elizabethan Puritan Movement*, 33, 72; MacCulloch, *Later Reformation in England*, 70–71. Elsewhere Collinson has referred to the controversy as "proleptic of later convulsions in the Elizabethan Church": Patrick Collinson, "England and International Calvinism, 1558–1640," in *From Cranmer to Sancroft* (London, 2006), 77. Most recently, John Craig has written that "The divisions that beset the English exiles in Frankfurt and that later became the subject of an important

This chapter revisits the Troubles at Frankfurt, revises our understanding of the controversy itself, and reassesses its relation to later developments within Elizabethan Protestantism. First and foremost, it stresses that the Troubles at Frankfurt took place in a very different political and polemical context than the Elizabethan (or earlier Edwardian) debates over *adiaphora* and religious authority. As a result, the issues at stake and the divide that emerged at Frankfurt were also different. A distinctively "conformist" position was absent among the exiles at Frankfurt and the views of ceremonies adopted by *both* sides in the controversy would later be used by puritans to argue *against* the use of vestments and other traditional ceremonies in the Elizabethan Church. Until it was resurrected in the mid-1570s, moreover, the controversy was conspicuously absent from the vitriolic polemics that puritans and conformists produced against each other during the vestments controversy of the 1560s. Rather than foreshadowing the divide between puritans and conformists, therefore, the positions staked out at Frankfurt are better seen as presaging the widespread commitment of the returning exiles to purge the Elizabethan Church of the "remnants of popery."

English Protestant exiles first arrived in Frankfurt on 17 June 1554. The way had been prepared for their arrival by Valerand Poullain, who was John Hooper's brother-in-law, the pastor of the French Stranger Church at Glastonbury under Edward VI, and still pastor of that same congregation in Frankfurt.[7] Poullain and his French congregation had left England in December of 1553 and settled in Frankfurt on 18 March 1554.[8] When the English exiles arrived three months later, the Frankfurt Senate granted them shared use of a church with Poullain's French congregation, under the condition that they "shulde not discent from the frenchmen in doctrine, or ceremonyes, least they shulde thereby minister occasion off offence, and willed farther, that before they entred their churche, they shulde approve and subscribe the same confession off faith, that the frenche men had then presented."[9] The English quickly discovered that "they were not so stricly bownde ... but that iff the one [congregation] allowed off the other it was

---

tract printed anonymously in 1574 clearly linked the later Elizabethan debates about the prayer book and ceremonies to the experiences of the exiles." Craig, "The growth of English Puritanism," in Coffey and Lim (eds.), *The Cambridge Companion to Puritanism*, 37.

[7] In a letter sent to W. P. on 29 April 1554, John Hooper asked that letters be forwarded to his wife who currently "is at Franckford in high Almayne." Coverdale (ed.), *Certain most godly, fruitful, and comfortable letters*, 146.

[8] Pettegree, *Foreign Protestant Communities*, 115–116; William Muss-Arnolt, "Puritan Efforts and Struggles, 1550–1603: A Bio-Bibliographical Study. I," *American Journal of Theology* 23:3 (July 1919), 351–352.

[9] *A Brieff discours*, 6. The quotations in this paragraph come from the narration.

sufficient."[10] The English congregation decided to employ the English order, but with substantial revisions: they added new prayers, a confession, and metrical psalms and omitted the use of the surplice, litany, certain aspects "touchinge the ministration off the Sacraments . . . as superstitious and superfluous."[11] Having confirmed this order by general consent, they chose a minister and deacons on 29 July 1554.

The "Troubles" began when the Frankfurt congregation sent a letter to other English exiles at Strassburg, Zurich, Wesel, and Emden on 2 August 1554.[12] This extraordinary letter is of the utmost importance in understanding the ensuing controversy, but it has received relatively little attention in discussions of the Troubles. The letter began by apprising the other exiles of the situation at Frankfurt, where the magistrates and people were "very favorable towards us and lovinge . . . no man is againste us, muche love, no grudge, glad to please, lothe to annoie us."[13] At Frankfurt, the English were able to "serve god in puritie off faith, and integritie off lyfe" in a church that they boldly claimed was "subjecte to no blemishe, no, nor so muche as the evell off suspition (from the whiche fewe churches are free) we maie preache, minister, and use Discipline, to the true settinge forthe off gods glorie, and good ensample to others."[14] The Frankfurt exiles claimed that this arrangement was far superior to what the English experienced elsewhere in Europe, since the magistrates and people of Frankfurt "have graunted that thinge, whiche amonge others and in other cities, we coulde not obtaine nor durste allmoste hope for."[15] They asked their scattered countrymen to remember how they had previously "reasoned together in howe to obtaine a churche, and shall we nowe drawe backe as unmindfull off gods providence, whiche hathe procured us one free from all dreggs off superstitious ceremonies?"[16]

In proclaiming their freedom from the "dreggs off superstitious ceremonies," the Frankfurt congregation was inviting controversy. By ordering the exiles to follow a church order acceptable to Poullain's French congregation – which used an order and liturgy derived from Calvin – the Frankfurt magistrates had mandated the establishment of an English Church that would be very different from the Edwardian Church of England. In Frankfurt, God had finally provided the English with (in the words of Thomas Wood, the Elizabethan compiler of *A brieff discours*) "a churche in a strange lande wherein they might heare gods worde truly preached, the

---

[10] *A Brieff discours*, 6.　　[11] *A Brieff discours*, 7.
[12] *A Brieff discours*, 8–13. The letter was signed by John Stanton, William Williams, William Hammon, John Makebray, William Whittingham, Thomas Wood, and Michael Gill.
[13] *A Brieff discours*, 8.　　[14] *A Brieff discours*, 8–9.　　[15] *A Brieff discours*, 8.　　[16] *A Brieff discours*, 9.

Sacraments rightly ministred, and Discipline used, which in their owne countrie coulde never be obtained."[17] Indeed, the Frankfurt congregation made a point of this when – after describing the perfection of their church at Frankfurt – they noted "whiche thinge yff we wishe for, let us not refuse it, seinge where we woulde, we coulde not there obtaine it."[18] The Frankfurt exiles were not presenting themselves as simply reconstituting the Church of England abroad, therefore, but as establishing a more perfectly reformed English Church than had ever before been possible.

In this regard, their connection with Poullain and the French exiles was significant. Under Poullain's leadership, the Glastonbury Stranger Church had used an order and liturgy derived from Calvin's Strassburg liturgy, which Poullain had published in London in 1551. As Andrew Pettegree has shown, the leaders of the Edwardian Stranger Churches and English Protestants like Bishop Hooper had hoped that the Stranger Churches would serve as "a radical Protestant community which by its very existence would serve as a constant spur to further reform in the English Church itself."[19] This was hardly lost on the Edwardian establishment, and the Stranger Churches faced substantial opposition, especially from the Bishop of London, Nicholas Ridley, who continually harassed the London Stranger Churches and energetically attempted to obtain their conformity to the English rite. The Frankfurt congregation's association with Poullain and the former Glastonbury Stranger Church would not have been lost on their fellow exiles scattered across Europe, and when combined with their claims to inhabit a church "without blemish," the barely implicit criticism of the Edwardian Church of England would have been clear.

Having explained their situation, the Frankfurt congregation announced that it was their "duty" to call all other English exiles to form a united church at Frankfurt. It was common for the English exiles to express a desire for a united congregation, but this call for unity was provocative in many respects.[20] First, the Frankfurt congregation wrote as if the other English exiles had forsaken the visible church entirely, rehearsing a variety of arguments to convince them that membership in a visible church was absolutely necessary. God established the church with external order and

---

[17] *A Brieff discours*, 7.   [18] *A Brieff discours*, 8.   [19] Pettegree, *Foreign Protestant Communities*, 35.
[20] The Strassburg and Zurich congregations also expressed their desire for a unified congregation in 1554. In 1556, the exile James Pilkington wrote that "it is agreeable and almost necessary to our exiles, that all we English should meet together in the same church," while the exile Thomas Lever wrote in August 1557 of his hopes that the English would join in "one spot, where it is still permitted us freely, sincerely, and openly to acknowledge and worship Christ." Quoted in Simpson, "Of the Troubles Begun at Frankfurt," 29.

policy, they argued, not merely for the "rude and symple," but for all people "exceptinge no man."[21] Likewise, the Scriptures were given to Christians not for personal reading only but also for public proclamation by teachers appointed to offices within the visible church. As the Frankfurt congregation explained the situation to John Knox when inviting him to be their minister, the English exiles "wander abroad as loste sheepe withowte anie gide."[22] Astonishingly, the Frankfurt congregation claimed in their 2 August 1554 letter that the other exiles were forsaking Christ, for "many off us, (we speake it to our shame) as if we had already forgotten the ende of our creation, are plunged in earthlye affections, and worldlye respectes, so that throughe oure infirmities, this excellente benefit [at Frankfurt] is like to be frustrate."[23] Indeed, the letter presumed that the other exiles would prove resistant to the invitation from Frankfurt, preemptively expressing hope that "no respecte off commoditie there, nor yet feare of burthen here maie once move you to shrink from your vocation," which was to join the Frankfurt congregation.[24] The scattered exiles were accused of pursuing preferment, learning, vocation, and private comfort, all of which threatened to provide a "selie excuse" for refusing the journey to Frankfurt.[25] Frankfurt warned the other exiles that if they did not "esteeme in time the worthenes off gods benefits," they would suffer the same fate as those who refused the summons in Christ's parable of the Great Feast (Matthew 22) and were cast into the darkness with weeping and gnashing of teeth.[26] Crucially, the Frankfurt exiles claimed that this negligence was doing great damage to the evangelical cause at home, since "our adversaries, who sekinge ever to obscure goddes glorie, maye easelie cavell at this dissipation" of the exiles.[27] In fact, the scattered exiles were encouraging Nicodemism: the Frankfurt congregation lamented "to our great grieff" that this slander was "scattered in so muche, that in Englande, manie take occasion to remaine in their filthe. And some thinke they maye dissemble, untill a churche be confirmed, perceavinge that this our scatteringe, augmentethe the griefe of persecution, and so throughe our negligence we leese them for whom Christe died."[28]

The second provocative aspect of Frankfurt's proposal was the way it was cast as a divine command that must be obeyed.[29] The 2 August letter stressed that God's providential hand was clearly at work in Frankfurt:

---

[21] *A Brieff discours*, 12. [22] *A Brieff discours*, 20. [23] *A Brieff discours*, 10. [24] *A Brieff discours*, 9.
[25] *A Brieff discours*, 11. [26] *A Brieff discours*, 10. [27] *A Brieff discours*, 12.
[28] *A Brieff discours*, 12–13.
[29] On this point, see Collinson, *Archbishop Grindal, 1519–1583: The Struggle for a Reformed Church* (Berkeley, 1979), 75.

"What more manifeste signe, what plainer declaration, what worde more expresse and lyvely can we have off dewtie and vocation, than when god speakethe in oure hartes by faithe, guidethe us owte off perille throughe his grace, and nowe laste of all offrethe us a restinge place of his exceding mercy."[30] Indeed, the Frankfurt congregation portrayed the establishment of their church as the fulfillment of prophecy, urging the exiles to "fulfyll in oure selves that whiche Esaias forwarnethe that goddes children shalbe as pigions, whiche flee by flocks in to their dovehouse, whiche is the place where the worde of god is preached, the sacraments ministred, and praier used."[31] Given the unmistakable moving of providence, the Frankfurt letter concluded with an uncompromising call to obey the will of God: "Consider brethren, it is gods cause, he requirethe yow, it is your dewtie, necessitie urgethe, time willethe, your father speakethe, children muste obeie, oure enemies are diligente and the adversary is at hande."[32] In a subsequent letter to the as-yet-unresponsive Zurich congregation, Frankfurt expanded on this theme, urging them to attend to "gods callinge" and stating that they would present no more arguments to draw them to Frankfurt, because "the same holie spirit knocketh at the dore off your consciences not only to move yow of oure behalffs, but to admonishe yow, to avoide the inconveniences of talkes, and the offences of oure poore brethern of Englande, whose marveilinge cannot otherwise be satisfied."[33] The obvious implication here was that any hesitation or refusal to join the congregation at Frankfurt would be to deny the workings of providence, constituting either apostasy or a large step in that direction, and certainly a choice that would harm Christians remaining in England. Divine judgment would follow a refusal to join Frankfurt: "Consider what god woulde saie, I have prepared a plentifull and ripe harveste whiche standethe in a redines and waitethe for the mower and I have appointed thee thy taxe. I have geven instrumentes, and all things fit for the labor, yff thow forslowe it, the croppe is in daunger: yff thow loke for oft warning thow declarest great negligence."[34] Frankfurt urged their fellow exiles to "hyde your talent no longer" and "leave off farther to tempte God," and join them.[35]

If the Frankfurt exiles expected that their missive would be met with enthusiasm – and, as noted earlier in this chapter, it seemed that perhaps they did not – they severely miscalculated. As Patrick Collinson noted, the Frankfurt exiles "were nonentities," while the Strassburg exiles represented the "rump of the Edwardian establishment," a group that saw themselves as

[30] *A Brieff discours*, 9. [31] *A Brieff discours*, 12. [32] *A Brieff discours*, 13.
[33] *A Brieff discours*, 17–18. [34] *A Brieff discours*, 11. [35] *A Brieff discours*, 11–12.

the natural leaders of the Protestant diaspora.[36] The letter's tone was highly offensive, and M. M. Knappen expressed confusion over the fact that it was "a peremptory summons, couched in hortatory and holier-than-thou language of a call to repentance. On first reading it has a strange ring for a message from one set of exiles to others who have also left their country, rather than betray their faith."[37] There were also more substantive reasons, however, for the coolness with which Frankfurt's letter was greeted by the other exiles.

For one thing, the Frankfurt congregation's claim to have received special providential favor likely touched a sensitive nerve. Signs of God's providence played a crucial role for the Marian exiles in legitimating their decision to leave their country. There were good arguments both for and against fleeing persecution, and the decision to go into exile was especially difficult for ministers who would be leaving congregations behind. While many ministers went into exile, some like Rowland Taylor had refused to flee and deliver their congregations into the jaws of the "popish wolf" by fleeing the country, and some ministerial exiles were stricken with guilt over their decision to flee.[38] Thomas Bentham, one of the signees of the Zurich congregation's response to Frankfurt's 2 August 1554 letter, later returned to England to become the minister of the London underground congregation, where he would write to Thomas Lever that "while I was in Germany at liberty of body, having sufficient for it for the time, I was yet many times in great grief of mind and terrible torments of hell and now, being here [in London], every moment of an hour in danger of taking and fear of bodily death, I am in mind most quiet and joyful."[39] In the midst of this anxious situation, discerning signs of providential favor was a particularly powerful way for the exiles to reassure themselves that God approved of their flight.

It is not surprising, therefore, that the Zurich and Strassburg exiles bristled at Frankfurt's claims to have received special providential favor, asserting that they also had received abundant signs of God's favor. The Zurich exiles responded two months later with evident irritation to the Frankfurt congregation's claims regarding providence, informing Frankfurt at the outset that God happened to be at work in their city "aswell."[40] They had felt the "exceadinge goodnesse off god towardes us" in the presence of supportive magistrates and in their opportunities for study and learning in Zurich, so

---

[36] Collinson, *Archbishop Grindal*, 73–74.   [37] Knappen, *Tudor Puritanism*, 121.
[38] Quoted in Jonathan Wright, "Marian Exiles and the Legitimacy of Flight from Persecution," *Journal of Ecclesiastical History* 52:2 (April 2001), 224.
[39] Quoted in Wright, "Marian Exiles," 223.   [40] *A Brieff discours*, 14.

that "when god oure mercifull father shall so think good, we maie be bothe faithfull and skilfull dispensers theroff."[41] While the Zurichers wanted to *help* the Frankfurt congregation, they asked Frankfurt to consider carefully whether the value of their presence at Frankfurt would outweigh the value of their studies at Zurich. Were the Frankfurt exiles to "geve occasion to breake oure godlie feloshippe, to hurte our studies, to dissolve oure exercises, and utterly to everte [i.e., to upset] our godly purposes, ye have to answere even unto him whiche is a faithfull and a juste Judge, and will geve to everie man accordinge to his dedes."[42] Judging from an undated sermon delivered at Strassburg by Edwin Sandys, who would be a signee of the Strassburg congregation's 23 November 1554 response to Frankfurt's summons and who would later be an active supporter of Cox throughout the Troubles, the Strassburg exiles believed that God was actively working on their behalf as well.[43] Their physical and spiritual needs had been so completely met at Strassburg, a city in which everything was "so strangely and almost miraculously ministered and brought unto our hands, as doubtless we could never have found here, if the Lord himself had not gone before, as it were, to make ready and to provide for us? O what tokens of mercy and special favour hath our kind and gracious Father shewed us in this our exile and distress for his gospel, in these our sorrowful and afflicted times!"[44]

Another aspect of Frankfurt's letter that clearly wounded the other exiles was the accusation that they were contributing to the epidemic of Nicodemism in England by pursuing lives of ease, rather than forming a united English exile church. The Zurich exiles complained about how the Frankfurt congregation was

> burtheninge us so sore with your necessitie, that ye think our shrinking back in this behalff shulde argue want off charitie, keepe manie in Englande still whiche else would willingly come foorth, and shewe oure selves careles off that congregation whose edefyinge and winninge to Christe we onely pretend to seeke. These are great causes, but touchinge us nether so truly objected, so firmely grounded, nor yet so aptlie applied, but that as sounde reasons on our partes might fully answere the same.[45]

On one level, the recipients of Frankfurt's letter surely took issue with this accusation because they had been extremely active in attempting to

[41] *A Brieff discours*, 14–15. [42] *A Brieff discours*, 15.

[43] Sandys was also a signatory of Cox's 5 April 1555 letter to Calvin, explaining their side of the controversy. David Laing (ed.), *The Works of John Knox* (Edinburgh, 1855), 4.57.

[44] Edwin Sandys, *The Sermons of Edwin Sandys, D.D.*, ed. John Ayre (Cambridge, 1841), 296. Unfortunately, the sermon is undated.

[45] *A Brieff discours*, 14–15.

combat Nicodemism among their former friends and congregants in England. Robert Horne, a member of the Zurich congregation that rebuffed Frankfurt's initial 2 August 1554 letter and later an active supporter of Cox during the controversy at Frankfurt, had translated and published two of Calvin's anti-Nicodemite *Quatre Sermons* shortly after his escape from England in 1553.[46] In his preface, Horne recounted how he undertook this labor in self-defense and out of pastoral feeling. Horne was being slandered by the papists in England, who would "not cease yea out of their pulpetes, with bosting & gloriouse wordes to carp & sclandre me for my sodein departure, as though ther by they had vanquished & overcome gods truth whiche i had set forth."[47] The English people were being told that the Protestant exiles had fled because they were unable to defend the doctrine they had preached, and Horne was deeply afraid that his former congregation might "be brought in doubt of the veritie therof as though i my self shold have forsaken it & ther by be offended, and be brought from god."[48]

The exiles at Strassburg were also working to combat dissimulation and apostasy among Protestants remaining in England, a state of affairs that they found deeply troubling. As Peter Martyr had written to Bullinger in April 1554, "It is indeed a most distressing and remarkable fact, that we perceive those very persons in that kingdom, whom you would have considered the most resolute, now wavering, and even yielding."[49] In August 1554, exactly at the time when the Frankfurt summons would have arrived, an anti-Nicodemite pamphlet by Thomas Sampson was being printed in Strassburg, addressed to Sampson's former parishioners in London.[50] Sampson, who expressed frustration regarding the Troubles at Frankfurt in a February 1555 letter to Calvin but would eventually join Cox at Frankfurt in 1555, denounced dissembling in this pamphlet and commanded his former flock to "kepe your selfes undefiled frome all Popishe leaven."[51] Sampson may also have been one of the exiled ministers at Strassburg who assisted John Ponet in producing a confession of faith in

---

[46] Horne was a signatory of Cox's 5 April 1555 letter to Calvin, explaining their side of the controversy. Laing (ed.), *The Works of John Knox*, 4.57.

[47] Jean Calvin (trans. Robert Horne), *Certain homilies of M. Joan Calvine conteining profitable and necessarie, admonition for this time, with an Apologie of Robert Horn* (Wesel?, 1553; STC 4392), a5r-v.

[48] Calvin (trans. Horne), *Certain homilies*, a5v.

[49] Martyr to Bullinger, 3 April 1554, in Hastings Robinson (ed.), *Original Letters Relative to the English Reformation* (Cambridge, 1847), 515.

[50] Sampson, *A letter to the trew professors of Christes Gospell*.

[51] Laing (ed.), *The Works of John Knox*, 4.53–54, 4.57; Sampson, *A letter to the trew professors of Christes Gospell*, b3v-b4r.

1554, addressed to "the Lordes of England, and al the commons of the same," which was being distributed in London before the beginning of Parliament in October 1554.[52] Noting that "our adversaries raile upon us behynde oure backes callyng us Heretyckes, Scismatickes, &c.," the ministers were writing this confession to prove "that we shute styl at the olde marke of Gods worde, neither recanting nor revokyng that whiche we have learned in the schole of God and taught amongst you."[53]

The Zurich and Strassburg exiles' efforts to combat Nicodemism shed light not only on their hostility to the Frankfurt congregation's claims but also on their resistance to the liturgical reforms that the original Frankfurt congregation had made. Running throughout the exiles' anti-Nicodemite texts was an intense anxiety that Catholic preachers and polemicists were successfully discrediting the Edwardian Church of England by accusing Protestants of inconstancy. This concern was well founded: Catholics were indeed ridiculing Protestants by contrasting the constancy of Catholic doctrine and liturgy with the frequent changes that had occurred during Edward VI's reign. James Brooks preached at Paul's Cross in 1553 that Protestants had made "every yere, yea every month almost a new faith" during the previous regime, and Protestant mutability and inconstancy was a recurring theme in the widely reported April 1554 examinations of Cranmer, Ridley, and Latimer.[54] Cranmer was mocked for "making every yere a new fayth," while Latimer was told that "you could not tel what you might have: Ye altered and changed so often your Communions and your altars . . . [you] were never constant in any one thyng," all of which was to be expected, since heretics "make everye yeare and every moneth a faith."[55] Bishop Bonner would later accuse John Philpot of having "every yeare a newe faith," and Catholic printed polemics would hammer Protestants for the liturgical inconstancy of the preceding reign.[56] As John Standish would put it, "scantly two of them have in all poyntes wel agreed together," and the only thing Protestants could agree on was "to destroye utterlye all unitie and

[52] *The Humble and unfained confession of the belefe of certain poore banished men* (London?, 1554; STC 5630), a1r. On the text's distribution, see Garrett, *Marian Exiles*, 254.

[53] *The Humble and unfained confession*, b1r-v.

[54] James Brooks, *A sermon very notable, fruictefull, and Godlie made at Paules crosse the. xii. daie of Novembre* (London, 1553; STC 3838), d6r.

[55] Foxe, *The Unabridged Acts and Monuments Online* (1576 edition) [Accessed: 02.06.14].

[56] Foxe, *The Unabridged Acts and Monuments Online* (1576 edition) [Accessed: 02.06.14]. Also see John Gwynneth, *A Declaracion of the state, wherin all heretikes dooe leade their lives* (London, 1554, STC 12558), 44r-v; John Proctor (trans.), *The waie home to Christ and truth leadinge from Antichrist and errour* (London, 1554; STC 24754), b2v-b3v.

comely order."[57] Richard Smith highlighted disagreement between Peter Martyr Vermigli and Bishops Cranmer and Ridley as proof that "the spirite of unite & peace was not with them" and he claimed that Martyr "agreeth not with him selfe."[58]

In the early years of Mary's reign, therefore, the constant liturgical innovation and internal squabbling of Protestants was an oft-repeated Catholic punchline. According to Marian Catholics, as William Wizeman pithily put it, "facial hair, married clergy and worshipping novelties were the only things upon which Protestants agreed."[59] The exiles at Zurich and Strassburg clearly feared that this critique was working as a powerful solvent on the commitment of Protestants remaining in England. Their response to this challenge, indeed their duty toward former parishioners unto whom "some pece of pastorall cure dothe yet reste in my harte" (as Thomas Sampson wrote), was to defend the doctrine and ministry they had exercised in the Edwardian Church of England.[60] This was also, of course, what the imprisoned leaders of the Edwardian Church were currently doing. As Cranmer announced in his very public September 1553 repudiation of the Mass, he and Peter Martyr were prepared "to defend, not onely the common Prayers of the Churche, the ministration of the Sacramentes and other rites and ceremonies: but also all the doctrine and religion set out by our said soveraigne Lord kyng Edward the vi. to be more pure and accordyng to Gods word, then any other that hath ben used in England these 1000. yeares."[61] With Cranmer in prison and facing the stake, defending his prayer book was a way of showing "solidarity with a leader in chains."[62]

These were the circumstances in which Frankfurt's blustery letter arrived, therefore, with its boasts regarding providential favor, the establishment of a fully reformed church "free from all dreggs off superstitious ceremonies," and its criticism of the other exiles for not doing enough to prevent Nicodemism.[63] Not only was all of this clearly offensive to the

---

[57] John Standish, *A discourse wherin is debated whether it be expedient that the scripture should be in English for al men to reade that wyll* (London, 1554; STC 23207), a6r.

[58] Richard Smith, *A bouclier of the catholike fayth of Christes church* (London, 1555; STC 22816), bk. 1, a1v, 1v; bk. 2, c2v.

[59] William Wizeman, "Martyrs and Anti-martyrs and Mary Tudor's Church," in Freeman and Mayer (eds.), *Martyrs and Martyrdom in England, c.1400–1700*, 173.

[60] Sampson, *A letter to the trew professors of Christes Gospell*, a2v.

[61] Foxe, *The Unabridged Acts and Monuments Online* (1576 edition) [Accessed: 02.06.14].

[62] Euan Cameron, "Frankfurt and Geneva: The European Context of John Knox's Reformation," in Mason (ed.), *John Knox and the British Reformations*, 66.

[63] *A Brieff discours*, 9.

other exiles; it reflected a substantively different understanding of what exactly the exiles ought to be doing. The exiles at Zurich and especially Strassburg were "engaged in practical measures for the vindication and perpetuation of the Edwardian achievement."[64] By contrast, the Frankfurt congregation seems to have believed that their main task as exiles – and the most effective tactic for drawing Protestant Nicodemites forth from their dissembling ways – was to finish the work left undone during Edward's reign and to establish a fully reformed church abroad that would serve as a homing beacon for English exiles. Aiming to create a sort of English Geneva, the Frankfurt exiles envisioned their new city as the future headquarters of the English Protestant diaspora. Indeed, Calvin himself would commend this strategy to them in January 1555. In a letter to Knox and Whittingham regarding their use of the Prayer Book, Calvin wrote that the accession of Mary required that "a churche muste be set up in an other place, where ye maie freely make an order againe, whiche shall be apparent to be moste commoditious to the use and edification off the churche."[65] If Frankfurt's adversaries "feare the evell rumor in Englande, as though they had fallen from that Religion which was the cause off their banishment, they are farre deceived." Moving beyond the halfway house of the Edwardian Church of England and establishing "true and sincere Religion" in exile would "compell them that theire remaine [in England], faithfully to consider in to what deepe gulff they have fallen For there downefall shall more grevously wounde them, when they perceyve your goinge forewarde beionde mid course, from the whiche they are turned."[66]

In sum, the exiles at Frankfurt and the exiles at Zurich and Strassburg had substantially different understandings of their mission as exiles, as well as sharply diverging ideas about what was causing the godly to dissemble en masse in England. How could the exiles best further the gospel and the English Reformation: by creating a destination-church that explicitly depicted itself as the completion of the incomplete Edwardian Reformation, or by defending the Edwardian Church of England against the potentially devastating critiques of their Catholic enemies?

This disagreement formed the context for the "Troubles at Frankfurt" regarding the use of the 1552 Prayer Book, and it is to the Troubles that we now turn. The debate is typically treated as a continuation of the debate regarding Scripture and *adiaphora* that had erupted under Edward VI

---

[64] Collinson, *Archbishop Grindal*, 73.   [65] *A Brieff discours*, 35.   [66] *A Brieff discours*, 36.

between John Hooper and Bishops Cranmer and Ridley. Hooper had refused to be consecrated as Bishop of Gloucester if forced to wear the traditional episcopal vestments, deploying a wide range of arguments that denounced the garments as popish, idolatrous, and offensive to "weaker brethren." Ridley and Cranmer rejected Hooper's arguments, claiming that because the vestments were *adiaphora*, or "things indifferent," their use could be lawfully enjoined by royal authority for the sake of good order in the church.[67] These competing notions of religious authority have been seen as continuing to divide English Protestants at Frankfurt, where the Knoxians pursued biblical purity and the Coxians were "unwilling to surrender the perception of a visible Church defined by the mark of loyalty to devotional forms established by law."[68] On this standard account of the controversy, the troubles at Frankfurt were the bridge that connected the ceremonial skirmishing of Edwardian Protestantism with the far more explosive ceremonial debates between puritans and conformists under Elizabeth. Frankfurt, according to A. G. Dickens, was "the battleground of those controversies left unsolved by the reign of Edward VI, and soon to be revived under Elizabeth."[69]

The political and polemical situation at Frankfurt in 1554, however, was rather different from either Edwardian or Elizabethan England.[70] In Edwardian and Elizabethan England, church order and liturgy were not determined by individuals or local congregations, but were instead regulated by the monarch exercising his or her Royal Supremacy over the Church. As the 1552 Prayer Book explained, "no man ought to take in hand, nor presume to appoynct or alter any publique or common order in Christes churche, except he be lawfully called and aucthorized thereunto."[71] After Mary's first Parliament abolished the Edwardian religious legislation in

---

[67] For Ridley's arguments, see Aubrey Townsend (ed.), *The Writings of John Bradford* (Cambridge, 1853), 373–395. Cranmer's 2 December 1550 letter to Martin Bucer implied that the vestments were acceptable because they were sanctified by God, ordained by the magistrate, and used for order: *Work of Thomas Cranmer*, 319.

[68] Heal, *Reformation in Britain and Ireland*, 333.

[69] Dickens, *The English Reformation*, 345. Also see Ryrie, *The Age of Reformation*, 191–192; MacCulloch, *Later Reformation in England*, 70–71; Marshall, *Reformation England*, 120; Craig, "The Growth of English Puritanism," 37; Collinson, *Elizabethan Puritan Movement*, 72; Vander Molen, "Anglican Against Puritan," 45; Scott A. Wenig, *Straightening the Altars: The Ecclesiastical Vision and Pastoral Achievements of the Progressive Bishops under Elizabeth I, 1559–1579* (New York, 2000), 75; Cross, *Church and People*, 107.

[70] As Diarmaid MacCulloch has pointed out, the Edwardian and Elizabethan polemics regarding conformity only superficially took place in a similar context. Appeals to conformity and royal authority under Edward were made in the context of "a revolution on the march," whereas under Elizabeth they were a call "to obey Elizabeth's unchanging settlement." MacCulloch, *The Boy King*, 196.

[71] *The boke of common praier* (1552), a3v.

December 1553, however, it was no longer possible to argue for conformity to the Prayer Book on the basis of obedience to the Supreme Head or adherence to English law.[72] In rejecting Mary Tudor's authority, moreover, the Marian exiles had removed themselves from the legal and political framework within which they had been attempting to reform the church since Henry VIII's break with Rome.

The exiles were not living in a total vacuum of civil authority, however, and it would overstate the case to claim – as Christina Garrett did – that the exiles were "living in a foreign land *outside the limits of any effective jurisdiction.*"[73] While the exiles had not sworn allegiance to their new cities, they nevertheless were subject to the authority of the local magistrates. Given the Frankfurt Senate's demand for conformity to the French congregation's order and given the exiles' critical stance toward elements of the Edwardian Church, the original Frankfurt congregation found themselves in the novel position of being able to defend deviation from the Prayer Book by pleading the need to obey the magistrate. The ground had therefore shifted dramatically from the vestiarian debate surrounding Hooper, in which defenders of conformity like Ridley and Cranmer had been "brilliantly successful in consistently keeping the spotlight on the question of authority, rather than on the issue of corruption and bad examples for weaker brethren which was the preferred ground for [Stranger Church leader Jan] Laski and Hooper."[74] In Frankfurt, the tables were turned: the Frankfurt exiles employed arguments like Ridley and Cranmer's about obedience to magistrates in things indifferent *against* using the Prayer Book, while the Zurich and Strassburg congregations deployed arguments about offense and weaker brethren in order to *defend* the use of the Prayer Book.

In responding to Frankfurt's 2 August 1554 letter, for instance, Zurich made it clear that they would join the Frankfurt church if and only if Frankfurt would agree to "use the same order off service concerninge religion whiche was in Englande laste set forthe by kinge Edward," stating that they were "fully determined to admitt and use no other."[75] Strassburg

---

[72] Prayer Book services became illegal on 20 December 1553; see David Loades, *Mary Tudor: A Life* (Oxford, 1989), 208. It is worth noting, however, that John Hales would later contend that the Marian religious legislation was technically illegal and that the Edwardian settlement therefore retained the force of law. Foxe, *The Unabridged Acts and Monuments Online* (1583 edition) [Accessed: 02.06.14]. There is no evidence of this argument, however, in the sources surrounding the Frankfurt controversy.

[73] Garrett, *The Marian Exiles*, 18.   [74] MacCulloch, *Thomas Cranmer*, 481.

[75] *A Brieff discours*, 18, 16.

likewise wrote in November 1554 that they trusted in the Frankfurt exiles' "good conformitie and ready desiers in reducinge the Englishe churche now begun there, to it former perfection off the laste, had in Englande, so farre as possiblie can be atteined."[76] For reasons we have already explored, the Zurich and Strassburg congregations both strongly emphasized the spiritual harm that Frankfurt's actions would inflict on weaker brethren remaining in England. Zurich followed their statement regarding the Prayer Book with the hope that the Holy Spirit would help Frankfurt to "confounde papistrie, set forthe gods glorie, and shewe suche light in the face off the worlde, that bothe the wicked maie be ashamed, havinge no juste cause off reproche, and also oure weake brethren confirmed and woone to the truthe."[77] At a latter date, the Zurich congregation evidently argued that Frankfurt's liturgical deviance would also offend Christians remaining in England because it would increase the "bands" of their suffering brethren by "deface[ing] the worthie ordinances and lawes" of Edward VI.[78] Strassburg employed a similar tack, responding to Frankfurt on 23 November 1554 with hope that the city magistrates would permit them

> to use our religion accordinge to that godly order settforthe and receaved in England … least by muche alteringe off the same we shulde seeme to condemne the chieff authors theroff, who as they nowe suffer, so are they moste redie to confirme that facte with the price off their bloude and shulde also bothe geve occasion to our adversaries, to accuse oure doctrine of imperfection, and us of mutablitie, and the godly to dowte in that truthe wherin before they were perswaded, and to hinder their comminge hither whiche before they had purposed.[79]

Their sentiments surely reflected the view of their fellow exile Peter Martyr Vermigli, Cranmer's close friend and defender, who wrote in April 1554 that "those who do not feel themselves smitten by the swords of the ungodly in their brethren, are not to be regarded as members of the body of Christ."[80]

Frankfurt's responses attempted to minimize these concerns and persistently stressed their obligation to obey the Frankfurt magistrates. Frankfurt rejected Zurich's arguments in a November 1554 letter, denying the

---

[76] *A Brieff discours*, 22.   [77] *A Brieff discours*, 16.

[78] *A Brieff discours*, 21. These quotations come from Frankfurt's 15 November 1554 response to Zurich and the visit of Thomas Chambers as its representative.

[79] *A Brieff discours*, 22–23. Protestant separatists under Mary were not only avoiding Catholic services, but scrupulously observing the rites and ceremonies of the 1552 Prayer Book: B. R. White, *The English Separatist Tradition: From the Marian Martyrs to the Pilgrim Fathers* (Oxford, 1971), 8.

[80] Robinson (ed.), *Original Letters*, 516. Also see Diarmaid MacCulloch, "Peter Martyr and Thomas Cranmer," in Emidio Campi (ed.), *Peter Martyr Vermigli: Humanism, Republicanism, Reformation* (Geneva, 2002), 173–201.

possibility of offense by claiming that only the ignorant did not know that the Edwardian fathers altered many things "uppon considerations off circumstances." Frankfurt also emphasized that they were constrained by obedience to local authorities, having "shewed oureselves most conformable in all thinges that standethe in our powers."[81] There were some "onprofitable ceremonies" in the Prayer Book that, "althoughe they were tollerable (as some are not) yet beinge in a strange common wealthe, we coulde not be suffred to put them in use, and better it were they shulde never be practised, then they shulde be the subversion off oure churche, whiche shulde fall in great hassard by usinge them."[82] With some irritation, they complained that the use of the Prayer Book seemed to be Zurich's "full scope and marke."[83] Frankfurt likewise dismissed Strassburg's arguments in a December 1554 response, denying any condemnation of the Prayer Book's authors and insisting that the Prayer Book itself taught that ceremonies may be justly "altered and chaunged," all the while stressing the need to obey magistrates by not introducing "certeine Ceremonies whiche the order off the countrie will not beare."[84] Frankfurt roundly dismissed the notion that "the not full usinge off the booke" would "cause the godly to dowte in that truthe wherin before they were perswaded, and to staye theyr comminge hither."[85] If this were true, it would reveal the ignorance of English Protestants who "for breach off a Ceremonie will refuse suche a singuler benefit," but it more likely was a lie and an erroneous report spread by "false brethern, who, to hinder this worthie enterprise, spare not to sowe in everie place, store off suche poore reasons."[86]

These arguments did not anticipate "the alignment of puritans and conformists in the Elizabethan Church," as has been often been claimed.[87] Nor does it seem that the Zurich and Strassburg exiles were expressing "a nationalist and royalist persuasion" or "already beginning to regard the peculiar forms of the royal church with affection, if not reverence," or striving "to maintain a sense of religious identity while in exile."[88] The Strassburg and Zurich congregations did not demand continued use of the Prayer Book on the basis of obedience to authority in things indifferent. Instead, they defended the Prayer Book because nonconformity would do great harm to fellow Protestants remaining in England and give encouragement (and ammunition) to Catholics as they sought to destroy Protantism. Far

---

[81] *A Brieff discours*, 21.   [82] *A Brieff discours*, 21.   [83] *A Brieff discours*, 20–21.
[84] *A Brieff discours*, 25.   [85] *A Brieff discours*, 25.   [86] *A Brieff discours*, 25.
[87] Collinson, *Elizabethan Puritan Movement*, 33.
[88] Danner, *Pilgrimage to puritanism*, 21; Knappen, *Tudor Puritanism*, 128; Wenig, *Straightening the Altars*, 76.

from anticipating future conformist defenses of the Prayer Book, these claims – as we will see in the next chapter – would become commonplace puritan arguments *against* conformity to the Prayer Book under Elizabeth. Conversely, the Frankfurt congregation defended their deviation from the Prayer Book by consistently stressing the obligation to obey the local magistrates and by asserting that offense was not genuinely given by their church order, but only wrongly taken. Again, rather than anticipating future puritan attacks on conformity, these were precisely the sorts of arguments that Elizabethan conformists like Matthew Parker and John Whitgift would make when demanding conformity to the Book of Common Prayer.

All of this highlights the importance of political context in shaping these polemics. The Knoxians' emphasis on obedience was the product of congenial political circumstances, something Elizabethan puritans would attempt to recreate for years to come in Parliament, rather than the product of an unflinching commitment to obedience and magisterial control over *adiaphora*. Through skillful political maneuvering, the Coxians were able to gain the support of the Frankfurt Senate in March 1555 for "the full use of the English book," and the Knoxians lost their most powerful argument against the full use of the Prayer Book. Even before they lost magisterial support, however, Knox was already also deploying a sweeping biblical justification for departing from the Prayer Book alongside calls for obedience to the magistrate. Frankfurt's 3 December 1554 letter to Strassburg insisted that they did not "discente" from those facing martyrdom in England, but they also insisted that they would only use the Prayer Book "so farre as gods worde dothe assure it and the state off this countrie permit."[89] If the narrator of *A Brieff discours* is to be trusted, Knox was justifying his refusal of the Edwardian Prayer Book in December 1554 by claiming that "there were thinges in it placed (as he saied) onely by warrant of mans authoritie and no grownde in godds worde for the same, and had also a longe tyme verye superstitiously in the masse byn wickedly abused."[90] Knox preached an aggressive sermon denouncing the Prayer Book after the arrival of Cox, asserting that "by the worde off God we muste, seeke oure warrant for the establishing off religion, and withowt that to thruste nothinge into anie Christian congregation."[91] The Prayer Book contained "thinges bothe superstitious, unpure, and unperfect," so Knox "would not consent that off that churche it shulde be received."[92] When the Knoxians appealed to the Frankfurt senate after the arrival of the Coxians in 1555,

---

[89] *A Brieff discours*, 25–26.   [90] *A Brieff discours*, 27.   [91] *A Brieff discours*, 38.
[92] *A Brieff discours*, 38.

moreover, they explained that "in the prolixe and Ceremonious booke of the liturgie of Englande, be manie thinges (that we maie speake no worse off it) not moste perfecte" and they thought that "it seemed beste to reduce it to the perfecte rule off the scriptures" and the French congregation.[93] In his own later account of the controversy, Knox explained that he had once held "a good opinion of the Book," although he thought "it ought not in all points to be observed" – an opinion, it must be noted, that Knox also attributed to the Coxians.[94] After seeing men defend the entire book, however, and "by contemplation of our estate, which requireth all our doings to have open defence of the Scriptures, (especially in God's service to admit nothing without God's Word,) I was driven away from my first opinion."[95] As Euan Cameron has summed it up, Knox's view was that "one should allow only such worship as could be proved to be scriptural, rather than abolish only what was explicitly contrary to Scripture."[96]

But while the "Knoxians" at Frankfurt came to argue against the Prayer Book in ways that would be characteristic of radical puritans under Elizabeth, Cox and his followers did not adopt the "conformist" position on these issues, especially in the months after they wrested control away from Knox and Whittingham. The *Troubles* narrator recorded that after Cox and his followers gained control of the Frankfurt congregation in March 1555, the Frankfurt magistrates "graunted them the full use off the Englishe booke commaunding and chardginge him [Cox] therfore not to medle any more to the contrary."[97] Yet curiously, despite this order, the Coxians did not reestablish Prayer Book worship in its entirety and in fact they adopted many of the same changes made by the Knoxians.[98] As the Coxians explained in a letter to Calvin in April 1555, "neither are we so entirely wedded to our country, as not to be able to endure any customs differing from our own; nor is the authority of those fathers and martyrs of Christ so much regarded by us, as that we have any scruple in thinking or acting in opposition to it."[99] They explained to Calvin that

> when the magistrates lately gave us permission to adopt the rites of our native country, we freely relinquished all those ceremonies which were regarded by

[93] *A Brieff discours*, 41.   [94] Laing (ed.), *The Works of John Knox*, 4:43.
[95] Laing (ed.), *The Works of John Knox*, 4:43.   [96] Cameron, "Frankfurt and Geneva," 62.
[97] *A Brieff discours*, 45.
[98] On 26 March 1555, Adolphus Glauburg informed Whittingham that the magistrates had commanded "the full use off the Englishe booke commaunding and chardginge him therfore not to medle any more to the contrary." *A Brieff discours*, 45. This point is missed in Cameron, "Frankfurt and Geneva," 66.
[99] Laing (ed.), *The Works of John Knox*, 4:56. The letter was signed by Richard Cox, David Whitehead, Richard Alvey, Thomas Becon, Edwin Sandys, Edmund Grindal, John Bale, Robert Horne, Thomas Lever, and Thomas Sampson.

our brethren as offensive and inconvenient. For we gave up private baptisms, confirmation of children, saints' days, kneeling at the holy communion, the linen surplices of the ministers, crosses, and other things of the like character. And we gave them up, not as being impure and papistical, which certain of our brethren often charged them with being; but whereas they were in their own nature indifferent, and either ordained or allowed by godly fathers for the edification of our people, we notwithstanding chose rather to lay them aside than to offend the minds or alienate the affections of the brethren.[100]

The Coxians did not necessarily object to altering the Prayer Book, in other words, but they *did* object to the manner and terms in which the Knoxians had condemned it. The crucial point here was that the Coxians were very publicly treating these ceremonies as *adiaphora* whose use was to be governed by the rules of edification, not as superstitious remnants of popery. In a later letter to Calvin, written on 20 September 1555, they explained that they retained certain ceremonies "as knowing them to be very godly: this, however, has never been done by us in a precise manner; for we have abandoned some of them for the sake of your friends, which might at that time have been piously adopted."[101] Indeed, the Coxians were ultimately willing to tolerate individual nonconformity within the Frankfurt congregation on ceremonial matters. Thomas Cole was a Knoxian who had remained in Frankfurt after the majority of the faction left Frankfurt in September 1555 for Basel and Geneva. When Cole wrote to the departed Knoxians, he denounced the Coxians and gleefully reported the problems that they were facing, but he nevertheless had to admit to his friends that the Coxians tolerated his scruples and "permit me to my conscience as touchinge their ceremonies."[102]

This seeming reversal by the Coxians has been widely noted, but it has not been adequately explained.[103] M. M. Knappen commented that the Coxians did this "to placate the Puritan party," but does not explain why they were willing to placate the Knoxians at this point – when the bulk of them had already departed – and yet not earlier.[104] More recently, Euan Cameron has argued that the Coxians' lack of "consistency" suggests that "the ideological differences between Knox and his Frankfurt adversaries were really fewer and slighter than the rhetoric employed suggests," and that the conflict was instead a more personal one between Knox and Cox, since the Coxians "were willing to make changes, without compulsion, once Knox was out of the way, to which they would not consent while still

---

[100] Robinson (ed.), *Original Letters*, 753–754.   [101] Robinson (ed.), *Original Letters*, 757.
[102] *A Brieff discours*, 60.   [103] See Collinson, *Elizabethan Puritan Movement*, 33.
[104] Knappen, *Tudor Puritanism*, 131.

under his apocalyptic glare."[105] While Cameron is certainly right that personal hostilities played a role in the Troubles at Frankfurt, the account of the controversy presented earlier in the chapter suggests that the Coxians' willingness to alter "indifferent" aspects of the Prayer Book after gaining control of the Frankfurt congregation was not inconsistent with their opposition to Frankfurt's original innovations. Their main concerns had been about the effects that the Frankfurt congregation's reforms would have on Protestants remaining in England. By claiming to be a providential and perfectly reformed church and claiming that the Edwardian Church had been popish, the Knoxians were actively harming their evangelical brothers and sisters remaining in bondage in England and giving fodder to papist critics. As Cox and his supporters wrote to Calvin, they did not have "such a mean opinion of the judgments of our countrymen, who resisted ungodliness even unto blood, as that by reason of the clamours of individuals, possessing no weight whatever, *we should brand them with the foulest marks of papistical impiety*."[106] The Coxians were willing to alter aspects of the Prayer Book, but by stressing that these alterations were only to "things indifferent," they did so in a way that did not undermine either the Edwardian Reformation or their former ministry within it.

Cox and company were quite right to be concerned about how the exiles' actions would be perceived back in England, where *any* deviation by the exiles from the Edwardian Church of England could and would be interpreted as a rejection of that reformation. During a 1556 interrogation, the future martyr John Careless proclaimed his allegiance to the second Edwardian Prayer book, only to be asked "thy second boke is also in divers points condemned of heresie at Frankeford among the brethren there, which boke wyll you allowe you?" Careless's interrogator was not referring to the changes that had been introduced by Knox and his congregation, but to "master Cox himself and other that wer preachers in kyng Edwardes tyme, they have disproved your second boke in divers points, & have now made a third boke: how say you which of these thre bokes wil you allow now?" Careless's response stressed that only things indifferent had been altered:

> neither maister Cox, nor anye other of our godly preachers that be fledde unto Franckford, have condempned that booke in any point as repugnaunt to the worde of god, though perchaunce they have altered som thing therein,

---

[105] Cameron, "Frankfurt and Geneva," 67–68. Cameron suggests that Cox may have "never forgiven Knox for persuading the Privy Council to insist on the insertion of the 'Black Rubric' which explained away kneeling at Communion, into the 1552 book" (68).

[106] Robinson (ed.), *Original Letters*, 757; emphasis added.

according to the usage of that countrey where now they are: and I have not demed in my article but the Church of Christ hath authoritie to enlarge or diminish any thyng in the same good booke, so farre forth as is agreeable to the scriptures.[107]

By insisting that they had only changed "things indifferent" in the Prayer Book, rather than claiming to have purged it of superstitious popery, the Coxians had worked hard to make a response like this possible.

Accepting the existence of *adiaphora* did not make the Coxians proto-conformists. As many scholars have shown in great detail, puritans like Edward Dering, Thomas Cartwright, and Laurence Chaderton all accepted the notion of "things indifferent" in both theory and practice. Unlike Elizabethan conformists like John Whitgift, however, these moderate Puritans did not argue that the magistrate was therefore free to order "things indifferent" however he or she desired, but that the use of *adiaphora* should be subject to Pauline rules governing expedience and edification.[108] It was precisely this sort of rationale that the Coxians employed at Frankfurt. The conformist stance on "things indifferent" was predicated on the notion that *adiaphora* were to be ordained by the magistrate purely for order and that people should be made to conform as a matter of conscientious obedience to divinely appointed authority. Archbishops Parker and Whitgift would in principle reject puritan claims to be "offended" by indifferent ceremonies during Elizabeth's reign, arguing that since indifferent ceremonies were not commanded as things necessary for salvation, no offense could be legitimately taken. A conformist take on *adiaphora* and the Frankfurt controversy can be clearly seen in a letter from Bishop Ridley to Edmund Grindal, written shortly before Ridley's martyrdom in October 1555. Ridley, the hammer of the Edwardian vestiarian controversy, gave his blessing to the changes that the Coxians had made to the Prayer Book after expelling the Knoxians:

> Where ye say, ye were by the Magistrates required gently to omit such things in your Book as might offend their people, not as things unlawful, but to their people offensive, and so ye have done, as to the having of surplice and kneeling; truly in that, I cannot judge, but that both ye and the Magistrates have done right well; for I suppose in things indifferent, and not commanded or forbidden by God's Word, and wherein the customs of divers countries be diverse, the man of God, that hath knowledge, will [not] stick to forbear the

---

[107] Foxe, *The Unabridged Acts and Monuments Online* (1563 edition) [Accessed: 02.06.14].

[108] Lake, *Moderate puritans*, esp. 20, 47, 138, 244–246; John S. Coolidge, *The Pauline Renaissance in England: Puritanism and the Bible* (Oxford, 1970); Ethan H. Shagan, "The Battle for Indifference in Elizabethan England," in Racaut and Ryrie (eds.), *Moderate Voices in the European Reformation*, 122–144.

custom of his own country, being those where the people therewith will be offended; and surely if I might have done so much with our Magistrates, I would have required Mr Alasco [Laski] to have done no less when he was with us.[109]

This was a straightforwardly "conformist" reading of the situation: with regard to "things indifferent," the local magistrates possessed the authority to determine which indifferent ceremonies their English visitors would use. Ridley's caustic comment regarding Jan Laski is a perfect example of this view. Laski and the Stranger Church in Edwardian London had explicitly been granted the right to use a liturgy and order that differed from the Church of England. This displeased Ridley, their ostensible diocesan in London, and their legal exemption from conformity did not stop Ridley from continually working "to harass their independent establishment" and impose conformity to the English rite.[110] But the Coxians' reasons for modifying the Prayer Book were not those given by Ridley. Indeed, the Frankfurt magistrate had permitted them to use the Prayer Book in its entirety, but the Coxians chose to alter it *themselves* in order to avoid the offense of their *English* brethren.[111]

An exchange of letters at the end of the Marian exile has often been invoked as yet more proof that the Frankfurt controversy had opened up a clear ideological divide between proto-puritans and proto-conformists. With the death of Mary in 1558, Knox's congregation at Geneva attempted to mend the divisions that had been created by the controversy at Frankfurt, hoping that the exiles could work together to establish a perfectly reformed Church of England under the new queen. The Knoxians at Geneva wrote to Frankfurt that "what so ever offence hathe byn heretofore either taken or geven: it maie so cease and be forgotten ... we for oure partes freely remitt all offences and most intirely imbrace yow oure deare brethren."[112] But like their 2 August 1554 letter, this proposed unity was again conditional: the exiles should stop contending with each other "either for superfluous Ceremonies or other like trifles from the whiche god off his mercy hathe delivered us."[113] This was, of course, to beg the central question that had divided the exiles in the first place and to invite the same sort of controversy all over again. If they got their way, Protestant unity in the first days of the Elizabethan reign would be on the

---

[109] Laing (ed.), *The Works of John Knox*, 4:62.   [110] MacCulloch, *Thomas Cranmer*, 477.
[111] Robinson (ed.), *Original Letters*, 753–754.
[112] *A Brieff discours*, 188. The letter, dated 15 December 1558, was signed by Christopher Goodman, William Williams, John Pullain, Miles Coverdale, Anthony Gilby, William Bevoyes, John Knox, Frances Withers, William Whittingham, John Bodliegh, and William Fuller.
[113] *A Brieff discours*, 187.

Genevans' terms. The Frankfurt exiles – only four of whom had been present at the time of the original controversy – wrote to the Genevans that "we truste that bothe true religion shall be restored, and that we shall not be burthened with unprofitable ceremonies. And therefore, as we purpos to submit oure selves to such orders as shall be established by authoritie, beinge not of themselves wicked, so we would wishe yow willingly to do the same."[114] On the basis of this oft-quoted sentence, this letter has been read as a "tartly" conformist response to the Genevan puritans, as an aftertaste of the "Troubles" and a foretaste of the Elizabethan vestments controversy.[115] But the Frankfurt exiles had more to say. After informing the Genevans that they intended to submit to the ceremonies established by authority if they were not wicked (itself a notable qualification), the Frankfurt congregation further insisted that these ceremonies must be edifying: "if anie shalbe intruded, that shalbe offensive, we, upon juste conference and deliberation upon the same at oure meetinge with yow in Englande (whiche we truste by gods grace will be shortly) wil brotherly joine with yow to be sewters for the reformation and abolishinge of the same."[116] This part of the Frankfurt congregation's reply – which is ignored in almost every discussion of this letter – was not proclaiming the conformist stance that Parker and Whitgift would eventually defend.[117] Quite the contrary, it anticipated nothing better than the broad-based pursuit of "further reformation" beyond the Elizabethan settlement in the early years of the 1560s. Indeed, the list of signatories was headed by none other than James Pilkington.

How did contemporaries view the Troubles at Frankfurt and its significance? When the Knoxian congregation departed for Geneva in defeat, they had constructed a narrative in which they were the heirs of Bishop Hooper and were likewise being persecuted by purported brethren for their devotion to the gospel.[118] It was by no means inevitable, however, that these hostilities

---

[114] *A Brieff discours*, 189.

[115] William P. Haugaard, *Elizabeth and the English Reformation: The Struggle for a Stable Settlement of Religion* (Cambridge, 1968), 31. As Collinson puts it, "It was as if they foresaw precisely the situation which would arise in 1565": *Elizabethan Puritan Movement*, 72.

[116] *A Brieff discours*, 189–190.

[117] See the treatment of this letter in Knappen, *Tudor Puritanism*, 165; Haugaard, *Elizabeth and the English Reformation*, 31; Collinson, *Elizabethan Puritan Movement*, 72; David Loades, "The Sense of National Identity Among the Marian Exiles (1553–1558)," in David Loades and Katherine Walsh (eds.), *Faith and identity: Christian political experience* (Oxford, 1990), 107; N. M. Sutherland, "The Marian Exiles and the Establishment of the Elizabethan Régime," *Archiv für Reformationsgeschichte* 78 (1987), 278; Claire Cross, *Church and People: England 1450–1660*, 2nd edn. (Oxford, 1999), 110. The notable exception is Wenig, *Straightening the Altars*, 78.

[118] *A Brieff discours*, 39–45.

would continue without "anie end," as the Knoxians had predicted they would in March 1555. Calvin urged the Coxians at the end of May 1555 to "applie your selves to make them amendes for the faulte committed" and "to purge diligentlie what so ever remainethe off this breache," expressing hope that the Troubles would "be buryed in perpetuall forgetfullnes."[119] The controversy would continue throughout the summer and autumn of 1555, but after the Knoxians left Frankfurt there were indeed efforts to heal the divisions that had been created. Jane Dawson has recently discovered a letter that reveals "a strained attempt at reconciliation" between Christopher Goodman and Cox in 1557, although it seems to have failed miserably, with Goodman taunting Cox from Geneva by telling him that "'if you desire to know with precision what it is to follow Christ, come to us,'" and Cox offering an "extremely frosty" response.[120] But other attempts at reconciliation seem to have borne better fruit. John Jewel wrote to William Whittingham and Goodman in Geneva to apologize for his actions and when the former Knoxians at Geneva wrote to Frankfurt on 15 December 1558, offering and seeking forgiveness for past offenses, they expected a positive response "as bothe by good experience we have proved, and also have receaved by your letters."[121] The response from the remaining Frankfurt congregation was, as we have seen, far more conciliatory than it has often been depicted.

When the exiles returned to England, the hagiographers of the 1560s did not dredge up the memory of the Troubles at Frankfurt in 1554–1555. Instead, as Patrick Collinson has shown, they actively suppressed it. Foxe's *Acts and Monuments* and Coverdale and Bull's 1564 collection of the martyrs' letters sanitized Ridley's letter to Grindal in October 1555, removing the aforementioned passage in which Ridley criticized Knox's behavior at Frankfurt.[122] In a gesture of some restraint, Knox himself discussed the Troubles at Frankfurt sparingly when writing his *History of the Reformation in Scotland* in the early 1560s, and he chose not to name his opponents, men who – just a few years earlier – had been denounced for seeking his blood.[123] Conciliation like this might be expected at the beginning of the new reign as Protestants sought to present a united front

---

[119] *A Brieff discours*, 53.
[120] Goodman to Cox, 14 March 1557, quoted in Jane E. A. Dawson, "John Knox, Christopher Goodman and the 'Example of Geneva,'" in Polly Ha and Patrick Collinson (eds.), *The Reception of Continental Reformation in Britain* (Oxford, 2010), 129.
[121] *A Brieff discours*, 188.   [122] These omissions are detailed in Collinson, *Grindal*, 76, 319n28.
[123] David Laing (ed.), *The Works of John Knox*, vol. 1 (Edinburgh, 1846), 232. Knox did name his opponents in an unpublished account of the controversy, later printed by Calderwood (see Laing (ed.), *The Works of John Knox*, 4.41–49).

and to obscure the various divisions that had emerged during Mary's reign among exiles, prisoners, and martyrs.[124] With the outbreak of the vestments controversy and open hostility between newly minted "puritans" and the bishops in the mid-1560s, however, the unity of English Protestantism had unmistakably fractured. Even with the gloves off and Protestants denouncing each other in print, however, the Troubles at Frankfurt were conspicuously absent from the intra-Protestant polemics of the 1560s and early 1570s. Anthony Gilby, who had been an active supporter of Knox at Frankfurt and then a leading member of the Genevan congregation, did not invoke the "Troubles" in the vituperative anti-vestiarian polemics he wrote during the 1560s. When casting about for historical precedents for the present situation, Gilby instead pointed to Protestants like Hooper, Latimer, and Bradford who refused to wear vestments under Edward VI.[125] He did not then proceed to draw a line from the disputes between Hooper and Ridley, to Knox and Cox at Frankfurt, and then down to the present-day dispute over the vestments. Instead, Gilby wrote as if the Edwardian controversy over these issues had reached a resolution under Mary. Gilby claimed that even Ridley, the chief Edwardian supporter of vestments, had admitted to Hooper during Mary's reign that he had been "deceived" and "at his death calleth them, *abhominable and foolishe, & to fonde for a vice in a playe.*"[126] Gilby further claimed that the bishops' support for the vestments was of recent Elizabethan origin, since during Mary's reign "All these things were abhorryd as popishe supersticions, and Idolatries, amonge our gospellers both bishops & others, when they were under gods roddes in poverte. But how thei now have learnid courtely devinite, to grounde all apon

---

[124] On this topic, see Thomas Freeman, "Dissenters from a dissenting Church: the challenge of the Freewillers, 1550–1558," in Marshall and Ryrie (eds.), *The Beginnings of English Protestantism*, 154–155.

[125] Anthony Gilby, *A Pleasaunt Dialogue, Betweene a Souldior of Barwicke, and an English Chaplaine* (Middelburg?, 1581; STC 11888), g8r-v. Cf. MacCulloch, *Further Reformation in England*, 70.

[126] Gilby, *A Pleasaunt Dialogue*, g8v. Here Gilby was drawing on two sources, first an undated Marian letter from Ridley to Hooper that had recently been published in 1564 (*Certain most godly, fruitful, and comfortable letters*, 44–47). Second, Gilby was recounting Foxe's account of Ridley's refusal to wear a surplice when his captors prepared to ritually degrade him, which depicted a scene in which Ridley's captors forced him into the "surples, with all the trynkettes appertayning to the masse," as "Doctor Ridley did vehemently invey against the Romyshe Byshop, and all that folyshe apparell, calling him Antichriste, and the apparell folyshe and abhominable, yea to fond for a vice in a play": Foxe, *The Unabridged Acts and Monuments Online* (1563 edition) [Accessed: 02.06.14]. For similar treatments of this material during the vestiarian controversy, see *An answere for the tyme* (Rouen?, 1566; STC 10388), 133–134; Crowley, *A briefe discourse*, c2v. The Plumbers Hall separatists would also make this argument about Ridley when interrogated by Bishop Grindal in 1567: *A parte of a register*, 32.

policie?"[127] This was also the line taken by the former Genevan exile Percival Wiburn in 1570, when he wrote that "all such Bishops as fled in Queene Maries time, or els taried here under the crosse, had cast of, renounced, and forsaken all this trumperie, for the which the peace is nowe disturbed, and afterwarde for their promotion sake, put them on agayne."[128] While puritans were willing to point to earlier divisions between English Protestants, the controversy at Frankfurt in 1554–1555 was absent from these polemically charged readings of recent history. It was as if it had never happened.

There are a variety of reasons why early Elizabethan puritans might not invoke Frankfurt as the "verye originall and beginninge off all this miserable contention," as A Brieff discours would later do in 1574.[129] First, linking their opposition to the vestments under Elizabeth with the Troubles at Frankfurt would indelibly associate their stance with resistance theorists like John Knox and Christopher Goodman, as well as with Jean Calvin. Given Elizabeth's white-hot hatred of Knox and Goodman, and her coolness towards Calvin and Geneva, highlighting these associations could hardly help the godly's cause as they appealed to the monarch to pursue further reformation.[130] The fact that A Brieff discours off the troubles begonne at Franckford tied the puritan cause to such men surely seemed like an own-goal to anti-puritans like Richard Bancroft, as it provided useful evidence for his argument that puritanism was a foreign, seditious force that had infected English Protestantism abroad during Mary's reign.[131] Second, the factional affiliations that developed at Frankfurt did not coincide with the puritan/conformist divisions of Elizabeth's reign – a point that has been previously noted with some surprise, given the traditional interpretation of the controversy and its significance.[132] Vocal critics of the vestments in the 1560s included former Knoxians like William

---

[127] Gilby, To my lovynge brethren that is troublyd abowt the popishe aparrell (Emden, 1566; STC 10390), b2r.

[128] Percival Wiburn, "A comfortable epistle written (as it is thought) by Maister D. W. Doctour of Divinitie, in his owne defence, and the brethren that suffer deprivation for the popish ceremonies urged by the Bishops, about the yere 1570," in A parte of a register, 11.

[129] A Brieff discours, 2.

[130] See Bruce Gordon, Calvin (New Haven, CT, and London, 2009), 263–264; Pettegree, Marian Protestantism, 146–150.

[131] For Bancroft's discussions of Frankfurt, see Richard Bancroft, A Sermon Preached at Paules Crosse (London, 1588; STC 1347), 55–56; Daungerous Positions and Proceedings (London, 1593; STC 1344.5), 39–40; A Survay of the Pretended Holy Discipline (London, 1593; STC 1352), 44–48. Also see Peter Heylyn's account in Aerius Redivivus: or, the History of the Presbyterians (Oxford, 1670; Wing H1681), 14–18, 239–241.

[132] As Patrick Collinson noted, the letter sent to Calvin justifying the actions of the Coxians was signed by "two such puritans of the future as Thomas Lever and Thomas Sampson!" Archbishop Grindal, 78.

Whittingham and Anthony Gilby, as well as former Coxians like Thomas Lever and Thomas Sampson. As these figures attempted to make common cause against the vestments in the mid-1560s, what would they have had to gain by drawing attention to the fact that they had been opponents only a few years hence?

But putting these polemical concerns to the side, we might ask whether Elizabethan puritans like Lever or Sampson would even have viewed the controversy at Frankfurt as "the very originall and beginninge" of the controversy over vestments in which they found themselves embroiled during the 1560s. Lever and Sampson had sided with Cox and had signed the 5 April 1555 letter to Calvin explaining that they had abandoned (among other things) the surplice "not as being impure and papistical, which certain of our brethren often charged them with being" but as things indifferent, the use of which would not in that circumstance serve to edify "the brethren."[133] How did that disagreement with the Knoxians prefigure their disagreement with Archbishop Parker, who was insisting that the Queen could compel them to wear vestments as a sign of obedience to royal authority and denying that "things indifferent" commanded by the monarch could ever be legitimately offensive? When Sampson wrote to Bullinger about the vestments in February 1566, it was tellingly not to inform him that the troubles at Frankfurt had erupted again, but that "there has now been revived that contest about habits, in which Cranmer, Ridley, and Hooper, most holy martyrs of Christ, were formerly wont to skirmish."[134]

Nor did Frankfurt play a role in the conformist polemics surrounding the vestiarian controversy in the 1560s. Archbishop Parker's rebuttal to the nonconformists in 1566 mentioned Hooper and Ridley and reprinted correspondence surrounding their conflict under Edward VI, but it did not mention the Troubles at Frankfurt.[135] Conformists like Parker also had good reasons for discussing the Edwardian debates over vestments rather than the Troubles at Frankfurt. For Parker, the fundamental issue at stake was the need to obey the Supreme Governor when she commanded the use of things indifferent. Frankfurt took place in an entirely different political context, in which both the Knoxians and Coxians determined for themselves how their congregation would use *adiaphora*, a situation that Parker was trying to combat in the 1560s. Had the Coxians seized control and then

---

[133] Laing (ed.), *The Works of John Knox*, 4:56.

[134] Sampson to Bullinger, 16 February 1566, in Robinson (ed.), *The Zurich Letters* (1846), 212. Sampson went on to write that "The state of the question, however, is not in all respects the same," but he did not elaborate on this point.

[135] Matthew Parker, *A briefe examination for the tyme* (London, 1566; STC 10387), ******1v, ******2v; a1r-d4v.

established Prayer Book worship in its entirety, or submitted themselves wholly to the direction of the Frankfurt magistrates, this would have perhaps been useful to the Elizabethan conformists, but their willingness to depart from strict conformity to the Prayer Book would not have aided Parker's cause. It was hardly accidental that the Coxians' subsequent departures from the Prayer Book were silently omitted in Richard Bancroft's stridently conformist account of the Frankfurt controversy.[136]

It does not appear to be until the early 1570s, therefore, that the Troubles at Frankfort were publicly identified as a precursor of the "contention" in the Elizabethan Church.[137] The controversy was discussed in an October 1573 sermon by John Mullins, who had been a signatory of Zurich's initial rebuttal in October 1554 and later a member of the Frankfurt congregation after Cox's victory.[138] Mullins was now the conformist Archdeacon of London and a chaplain to the Queen, and when discussing the troubles besetting the Elizabethan Church of England, he mentioned "a hotte contention ... abowte theis matters" that had occurred at Frankfurt.[139] A year later, *A Brieff discours* was published by Thomas Wood with the explicit aim of creating "a respectable pedigree for Puritanism" by tracing the current controversies within the Church of England back to the Marian exile.[140] In response to Mullins and John Young, who had imputed "the cause off all these troubles to the ambitious heades off certeine speciall persons, who shoulde (as hathe bene at Paules crosse bothe publickly and very furiously declared) stirr upp this striffe in the churche for that they could not attaine to Bishopprikes when as other enjoned them," *A Brieff discours* would show that the present-day divisions predated the distribution of episcopal spoils (such as they were under Elizabeth).[141] Significantly, the book was described as revealing a great secret that had been hidden until Mullins had revealed it, something that Wood had kept "almoste by the space off theis twentie yeres in secret," and that he worried about revealing to the public eye. Indeed, the verse on the title page of *A Brieff discours* was Mark 4:22 (from the Geneva translation, naturally), "For there is nothinge hid that shall not be opened neither is there a secreat but that it shall come to light."[142] Such sentiments surely would have been out of place if the

---

[136] Bancroft, *A Survay of the Pretended Holy Discipline*, 46–47.
[137] Cox alluded to the troubles in 12 Feburary 1571 letter to Rudolph Gualter in Hastings Robinson (ed.), *The Zurich Letters* (Cambridge, 1842), 235.
[138] Garrett, *Marian Exiles*, 234–235.   [139] *A Brieff discours*, 3.
[140] On the context of the text's compilation, see Collinson, "The Authorship of A Brieff Discours," 193–197.
[141] *A Brieff discours*, 2.   [142] *A Brieff discours*, a1r.

Troubles at Frankfurt had been widely regarded as a formative moment in recent ecclesiastical history. Mullins and Wood both were very much charting new ground here by identifying the Troubles as the origin of the Elizabethan controversies. A good indication of the novelty of Wood's approach is the fact that when Walter Travers narrated the history of the English Reformation, in a book published on the same press and as part of the same presbyterian propaganda campaign in 1574, his account of Mary's reign made no mention of any trouble at Frankfurt.[143]

This is not to say that the Troubles at Frankfurt had been forgotten until 1573. Clearly Thomas Wood remembered vividly, although he thought best not to publicize the affair and he waited two decades before bringing Frankfurt to bear on the Elizabethan troubles faced by those who were "reviled and taunted, skoffed at and termed by theis odious names off precisian, puritain, contentious, seditious, rebell, traitor and what not."[144] Lessons had been learned from the troubles, such as those recounted in an August 1558 letter from Christopher Goodman to Peter Martyr Vermigli. While Goodman expressed some regret over his part in the "Frankfort controversy," he nevertheless believed that it had been profitable. First, it caused him to leave Frankfurt for the "happy agreement and solid peace" he had found as pastor (alongside Knox) of the Genevan congregation, which would not have happened if the "other party . . . had been permitted to contaminate the purity of religion with the dregs of popery which they wished to force upon us."[145] The second lesson Goodman learned from Frankfurt was that "it is right never to spare our most bitter enemies the papists, so also according to our ability should we remove the ignorance of our brethren."[146] This defense of the truth would "incur the dislike of many, and sometimes too that of their friends," but "it has ever been the property of truth to be viewed with hatred by the generality."[147] While insisting that "moderation and charity may be preserved between brethren as far as possible," Goodman insisted to Martyr that "in the cause of religion, as you know, no third party is allowed, but we are required therein always to be either hot or cold, and must either gather or scatter . . . we may boldly contend for the truth, whether it be against open enemies, or against those who wish to be called

---

[143] Travers (trans. Cartwright), *A full and plaine declaration*, 3–5, 15–16.   [144] *A Brieff discours*, 194.

[145] Robinson (ed.), *Original Letters*, 769. As Jane Dawson has recently shown, the departure from Frankfurt loomed large in Goodman and the Genevan congregation's emphasis on a purely biblical worship and strict congregational discipline: Dawson, "John Knox, Christopher Goodman and the 'Example of Geneva,'" 126.

[146] Robinson (ed.), *Original Letters*, 769.   [147] Robinson (ed.), *Original Letters*, 769.

brethren."[148] This was a damning indictment of the Coxian party at Frankfurt – "those who wish to be called brethren" – and sounded a tone that had not been heard at the beginning of the exile, but would be heard again shortly as Protestants turned against each other in the 1560s.

When Protestants fought about "things indifferent" in the first decade of Elizabeth's reign, however, the situation and the terms of the debate would be very different than they were in Frankfurt during 1554–1555. The Queen viewed the religious settlement of 1559 as permanent, but the vast majority of Protestants expected and pursued further reformation in the early 1560s.[149] Some of the returning exiles viewed the traditional ceremonies and ornaments that the Elizabethan settlement had retained as idolatrous and entirely unacceptable; others argued that they were theoretically permissible but should be removed because of the spiritual damage they did to "weaker brethren" and "obstinate papists" alike. These views would be met with hostility from the queen and, when matters came to a head in the vestments controversy in the mid-1560s, with a conformist defense of the Elizabethan settlement that insisted that these concerns about offense and spiritual damage were completely irrelevant when the Queen mandated the use of *adiaphora* by law. The ensuing conflict was not without precedent in the history of the English Reformation, but that precedent did not lay in the city of Frankfurt.

---

[148] Robinson (ed.), *Original Letters*, 769–770.
[149] MacCulloch, *Later Reformation in England*, 29–30; Marshall, *Reformation England*, 129–130; Ryrie, *The Age of Reformation*, 200–201.

CHAPTER 6

Catholics and the Elizabethan vestments controversy

On 26 March 1566, more than one hundred London ministers were summoned to Lambeth Palace to face Archbishop Matthew Parker and Bishop Edmund Grindal. The ministers had been called to the Archbishop's residence in hope of settling what historians have come to call the Elizabethan vestments controversy. The controversy swirled around the legal requirement for the Church of England's ministers to wear a square cap and surplice, a white linen gown with drooping sleeves. Both of these garments were part of the traditional uniform of the Catholic clergy, and few English Protestants had any enthusiasm for the "popish rags." Since the beginning of Elizabeth's reign, many Protestant ministers had refused to wear these garments, and even though this was illegal, certain bishops had tacitly permitted and even licensed the practice. On 25 January 1565, Elizabeth had chided Parker and the bishops for their laxity and demanded the enforcement of the laws governing clerical vestments.[1] Parker's ensuing efforts would produce a furor, especially in London. Prominent Protestant clergymen were deprived and imprisoned, some ministers refused to admit clergy who wore the surplice into their churches, conforming ministers faced jeering and sometimes violent crowds, and both sides waged a very public and acrimonious pamphlet battle in the summer and autumn of 1566. At Lambeth, Parker had hoped to settle the matter with a minimum of debate. The choice facing the

---

[1] On Elizabeth's early frustrations, see the 12 August 1561 letter from Cecil to Parker in John Bruce and Thomas Perowne (eds.), *Correspondence of Matthew Parker* (Cambridge, 1853), 148–149; for the queen's 25 January 1565 letter to Parker, see *Correspondence of Matthew Parker*, 223–227. There is some debate about whether the push for conformity in 1565 originated with the queen or with Parker himself; for the latter, see Primus, *The Vestments Controversy*, 93–94; for the former, see Haugaard, *Elizabeth and the English Reformation*, 212–213. For the suggestion that the push for vestiarian conformity was connected with Elizabeth's marital negotiations with the Archduke Charles of Austria, see Susan Doran, *Monarchy and Matrimony: The courtships of Elizabeth I* (London and New York, 1996), 94–95.

assembled London ministers was made exceedingly clear when former non-conformist Robert Cole was presented as a living mannequin bedecked in the required uniform, and Parker directed the assembled ministers to come forward and simply state whether they would conform: "Be brief: make no words."[2]

Both then and now, the vestments controversy has produced a sea of words. A fixture in histories of the English Reformation, the vestments controversy was a formative moment in the religious and political history of early modern England.[3] The word "puritan" was coined during the controversy as a term of abuse for the vestments' opponents, and it was out of the vestments controversy that puritanism emerged as a movement in Elizabethan England. What was at stake? Patrick Collinson encapsulates the scholarly consensus in describing the controversy as "essentially a debate about the limits of public authority in the sphere of 'things indifferent' – *adiaphora* – and about the definition of the *adiaphora* themselves."[4] On this interpretation, the debate was about whether the vestments were things indifferent, and if so, about who possessed the authority to determine their proper use. While the most radical opponents of the vestments insisted that they were *not* indifferent, but rather inherently idolatrous, most of the newly minted puritans agreed that the vestments were *adiaphora*. They also insisted, however, that things indifferent must be used in accordance with Scriptural rules about "edification" and avoiding "offense," a condition that severely limited the magistrate's power to command the use of *adiaphora*.[5] Many "conformists" would have preferred to abolish the vestments, but they took the view that the queen possessed full and ultimate authority to command the use of things indifferent. *Adiaphora* like vestments were to be ordained by the magistrate for the sake of external order in the church, and their use was a matter of obedience to divinely appointed authorities.

This chapter argues that – as with the Troubles at Frankfurt – we still have much to learn about this controversy, the issues it raised, and the ways in which it divided English Protestants. But first, before we can even begin to consider what Protestants had to say about the vestments, we have to listen to English Catholics. Catholic voices are almost entirely absent from

---

[2] Quoted in Collinson, *Elizabethan Puritan Movement*, 76.
[3] For representative examples, see Collinson, *Elizabethan Puritan Movement*, pt. 2; Marshall, *Reformation England*, 130–131; Craig, "The Growth of English Puritanism," 37; and most recently, Zlatar, *Reformation Fictions*, 136–143.
[4] Collinson, *Elizabethan Puritan Movement*, 71.
[5] The fullest and best discussion of this is found in John S. Coolidge, *The Pauline Renaissance in England: Puritanism and the Bible* (Oxford, 1970).

existing accounts of the vestments controversy, which treat it as a wholly Protestant affair.[6] Yet the first printed salvoes in the Elizabethan vestments controversy were not written by English Protestants, but by English Catholics.

In November 1559, the Protestant divine John Jewel preached what came to be known as the "challenge sermon," in which Jewel challenged "papists" to produce a single sentence from scripture, the church fathers, or the early church councils in support of a wide array of Catholic doctrines. English Catholics quickly rose to the challenge, and the result was a deluge of printed polemics from Catholic exiles in the Low Countries. A. C. Southern counted more than sixty texts produced during the 1560s in reaction or counter-reaction to Jewel's challenge.[7] While hardly unknown to historians, this extensive polemical exchange has not been considered in connection with the vestments controversy. This is surprising, given that as the vestments controversy exploded in 1565–1566, the polemical output of English Catholics was peaking, with forty-four titles produced by the exiles between 1564 and 1568.[8]

There is ample evidence that Catholic polemic was being widely distributed and widely read in England during the 1560s.[9] The Catholic exile Nicholas Sander estimated that approximately 20,000 copies of Catholic polemical works were distributed in England during the first two decades of Elizabeth's reign.[10] Even allowing for exaggeration, it is clear that Catholic works were widely available across the country. At the start of Archbishop Parker's push for conformity in March 1565, he wrote to Secretary Cecil that Catholic books were "plentifully had in the court from beyond the sea," and there is evidence to show that Catholic polemics were being read in private homes in London, at the universities (especially Oxford), and in the north, where then-Archbishop of York Edmund Grindal's 1571 visitation specifically inquired about persons possessing or distributing Catholic literature by "Harding, Dorman, Allen, Saunders, Stapleton, Marshall, or any of

---

[6] A few historians have noted Catholic comments on vestments in passing, but have treated these comments as external to the controversy, in which Catholics are seen to play no role: see Collinson, *Elizabethan Puritan Movement*, 35; Leonard J. Trinterud (ed.), *Elizabethan Puritanism* (New York, 1971), 6–8; Peter Iver Kaufman, *Thinking of the Laity in Late Tudor England* (Notre Dame, IN, 2004), 98.

[7] A. C. Southern, *Elizabethan Recusant Prose, 1559–1582* (London, 1950), 66.

[8] Southern, *Elizabethan Recusant Prose*, 31.

[9] Peter Milward, "The Jewel-Harding Controversy," *Albion* 6:4 (Winter 1974), 328–329; Christopher Highley, *Catholics Writing the Nation in Early Modern Britain and Ireland* (Oxford, 2008), 37–38.

[10] Southern, *Elizabethan Recusant Prose*, 36.

them, or by any other Englishe Papist."[11] Indeed, Peter Milward has noted
that the polemical exchange between Bishop Jewel and the Catholic exile
Thomas Harding seems to have been so widely known that Nicholas
Sander's contribution to the debate in 1565 did not bother to quote
extensively from their works, explaining that they were "extant in most
mens handes."[12] Of course, thanks to the formal conventions of early
modern polemics – which took great care to reprint the opponent's text
accurately, interspersed with rebuttal – anyone with access to Bishop Jewel's
impeccably legal *A Replie unto M. Hardinges Answeare* (1565) could also read
the entirety of Harding's attack on the Church of England. This was a point
of concern for Protestants, and in 1572 Bishop Parkhurst of Norwich
expressed skepticism about the advisability of making Jewel's latest book
available in parish churches, as it "might be a great occasion to confirm the
adversaries in their opinions. For they having not wherewith to buy
Harding's book, should find the same already provided for them; and
were like unto the spider, sucking only that might serve their purposes."[13]

While modern scholars have sometimes understandably tended to view
the Protestant-Catholic polemics of the 1560s as a "repetitive, sterile
exchange of pamphlets back and forth," this was certainly not the way
that contemporaries viewed them.[14] Protestants felt real anxiety about the
exiles' books, and the Elizabethan regime sought to repress and rebut
Catholic literature, with the government sponsoring Protestant rejoinders
and specific Catholic authors being denounced from the pulpit at Paul's
Cross.[15] Catholic polemics could be perceived by Protestants as frighten-
ingly effective, and perhaps rightly so, given that the bulk of the English
population were not committed Protestants. Protestant controversialists
like Thomas Norton denounced not only the polemicists themselves

---

[11] Parker to Cecil, 3 March 1565, *Correspondence of Matthew Parker*, 233. Grindal quoted in Highley, *Catholics Writing the Nation*, 37. On the ownership and use of the Catholic exile polemics by Catholic priests in Sussex, see Roger B. Manning, *Religion and Society in Elizabethan Sussex* (New York, 1969), 44–45. On the reading of Catholic polemics at Oxford, see Jennifer Loach, "Reformation Controversies," in James McConica (ed.), *The History of the University of Oxford*, vol. 3 (Oxford, 1986), 386. Elsewhere in the north, Bishop Pilkington wrote to Cecil in March 1565 to warn that Catholic literature from Louvain could be found in Durham: Lansdowne MS 8, f. 215v.

[12] Quoted in Milward, "The Jewel-Harding Controversy," 332.

[13] Quoted in Southern, *Elizabethan Recusant Prose*, 43.

[14] C. Coppens, "Challenge and Counterblast: The Book as a Weapon in the English Controversy during the Second Half of the Sixteenth Century," in *Antwerp, Dissident Typographical Centre: The Role of Antwerp Printers in the Religious Conflicts in England (16th Century)* (Antwerp, 1994), 47.

[15] Southern, *Elizabethan Recusant Prose*, 34; also see Matthew Racine, "A Pearle for a Prynce: Jerónimo Osório and Early Elizabethan Catholics," *Catholic Historical Review* 87:3 (2001), 407. On the denunciation of Catholic polemicists from Paul's Cross in 1565–1566, see Bodleian Tanner MS 50, ff. 25v, 27r, 32r, 34v, 41v, 44v–45r.

but also those in England who "receive these goodly bookes, sprede them abroad, rede them in audiences and corners, commend them, defend them, geve them great praises for learning and substantialnesse, as matters unanswerable, they amplifie them, they set them out."[16] The enormous volume of Catholic print was also troubling to Protestants. In his 1565 response to a book by the Catholic exile Thomas Dorman, Alexander Nowell wrote of the "havocke of bookes" that "came sodenly abroad," and while he claimed that it was "simple soules" that "may muche mervell at suche plentie of Englishe bookes," Nowell and his learned Protestant associates seem to have been equally amazed.[17] Describing the Catholic books as "dartes" thrown at Bishop Jewel's "head" and the Church of England, Nowell described the pressures that Protestants faced from both friend and foe to respond quickly in print, since the lack of an answer would be interpreted as meaning that "thei were not answerable."[18] This was certainly how Bishop Jewel felt about the many responses elicited by his challenge sermon, writing that he was "always battling with these monsters," and lamenting to Heinrich Bullinger and Lewis Lavater in a February 1566 letter that "Here I am again pelted at. What would you have? He [Thomas Harding] must be answered."[19]

It is abundantly clear, therefore, that Catholic polemics had real power in early Elizabethan England and that they loomed large in the minds of English Protestants. There is also evidence that many of the leading participants in the vestiarian controversy were reading and responding to Catholic polemics in the 1560s. John Barthlet was a lecturer at St Giles Cripplegate in London and one of the ministers suspended for nonconformity by Archbishop Parker at Lambeth in March 1566. In the wake of his suspension, Barthlet published two works: *The Fortresse of the Fathers* (1566), probably the most aggressive published piece of nonconformist polemic elicited by the vestiarian controversy; and *The Pedegrewe of Heretiques*

[16] Norton, *A warning agaynst the dangerous practises of Papistes*, g1r. Also see Highley, *Catholics Writing the Nation*, 38.

[17] Alexander Nowell, *A Reproufe, written by Alexander Nowell, of a booke entituled, A proufe of Certayne Articles in Religion denied by M. Juell, set furth by Thomas Dorman, Bachiler of Divinitie* (London, 1565; STC 18741), quotes at a2r, b1r, a2r.

[18] Nowell, *A reproufe*, a4r. Dorman's rejoinder to Nowell would indeed savage the Protestant for answering his book only partially and slowly: Thomas Dorman, *A disproufe of M. Nowelles Reproufe* (Antwerp, 1565; STC 7061), *1r–v.

[19] Jewel to Bullinger and Lavater, 8 February 1566, in Robinson (ed.), *The Zurich Letters* (1842), 148. Norton and Nowell's comments bring an important aspect of Elizabethan religious polemics into focus. As Jesse Lander has recently pointed out, the fact that sixteenth-century polemics appeared in print "create[d] the imagined possibility, if not the reality, of a vast and potentially distant readership," and produced the assumption that polemics "*must* be answered." Jesse M. Lander, *Inventing Polemic: Religion, Print, and Literary Culture in Early Modern England* (Cambridge, 2006), 15–16.

(1566), an anti-Catholic polemic. The latter work attacked in detail a translation by the Catholic exile Richard Shacklock of a text by Stanislaus Hosius – one of the most famous Catholic theologians in Europe – and also criticized translations by Shacklock's fellow exiles Lewis Evans and Thomas Stapleton.[20] Another example is provided by Oxford's Lady Margaret Professor of Divinity, James Calfhill. Calfhill was linked with the leaders of nonconformity at Oxford, Thomas Sampson and Laurence Humphrey, and he was a vocal critic of vestiarian conformity in London during 1565–1566.[21] In the midst of the vestiarian controversy, Calfhill published *An aunswere to the Treatise of the crosse* (1565), a response to a 1564 book by the Catholic exile John Martiall.[22] In addition to attacking Martiall's treatise, Calfhill discussed several of "the famous Pamphlets that come from Lovain," including works by Thomas Harding, Thomas Dorman, John Rastell, Thomas Stapleton, and Lewis Evans.[23] More examples could be given, but the point is that Catholic polemics were being read not only by Bishop Jewel and Archbishop Parker but also by many of those who would lead the opposition to vestments in 1565–1566.

What were these Catholic polemics about? For the most part they focused on the usual points of doctrinal contention in Reformation Europe, especially the Eucharist, purgatory, justification by faith, papal supremacy, and the nature of religious authority. In the course of debating these issues, and especially these last two points, Catholic polemicists had much to say about which ceremonies should be used in Christian worship and who possessed the authority to make this determination – questions which stood at the heart of the vestments controversy. Catholic authors argued that the Roman Catholic Church had been given almost unlimited authority from Christ to institute, alter, or abolish ceremonies for Christian worship. Thomas Harding, the leading Catholic polemicist of the 1560s, wrote that "Christ hath scarcely commaunded any outward thing, the moderation, qualifying, and ordering whereof, he hath not

---

[20] John Barthlet, *The Pedegrewe of Heretiques* (London, 1566; STC 1534). Shacklock's translation was *A Most Excellent Treatise of the begynnyng of heresyes in oure tyme* (Antwerp, 1565; STC 13888). Shacklock's tranlation of Hosius had already received public criticism in a 11 November 1565 sermon at Paul's Cross by Thomas Cole, who would be another leading London nonconformist: Tanner MS 50, f. 27r.

[21] *ODNB*; also see Brett Usher, "The Deanery of Bocking and the Demise of the Vestiarian Controversy," *Journal of Ecclesiastical History* 52:3 (July 2001), 434–455.

[22] Calfhill, *An Aunswere to the Treatise of the Crosse* (London, 1565; STC 4368); John Martiall, *A Treatyse of the Crosse* (Antwerp, 1564; STC 17496).

[23] Quotation at Calfhill, *An Aunswere*, 119r; on the Catholic polemics, see a2v-a3r, 156v. Calfhill also attacked Dorman in his Paul's Cross sermon of 10 February 1566; Tanner MS 50, f. 41v.

lefte to his churche, as according to the condition of the tyme, it hath ben sene most expedient for the common preferment and edifying of the same."[24] On ceremonial matters, therefore, "every man is bownde to folow the order of the churche."[25] These ceremonies could be changed, but Catholics like Harding denounced Protestants for thinking that they had the authority to institute such changes: ceremonies could only be altered by the Roman Church, which made these decisions about *adiaphora* "for thavoyding of unreverence, periles, offences, and other weighty and important causes."[26] Those who abolished traditional ceremonies or used ceremonies in a way that contradicted the Roman Church's use were therefore "auctoures of schisme, and breakers of unitie."[27] From this perspective, the observance or rejection of Catholic ceremonies was heavily freighted with implications concerning one's relationship with the Roman Catholic Church. The observance of the Church's ceremonies was an important sign of allegiance; conversely, the rejection of the Church's ceremonies was an act of schism.

Taking this view of the matter, Catholics chose to gloss the use of traditional ceremonies by Protestants as a gesture of unity with Rome and even as a sign that Protestants intended to end their schism. This line of argument can be found in a 1565 translation by Richard Shacklock of a text by the Polish Cardinal Stanislaus Hosius.[28] In the book, Hosius discussed the bitter battles that Lutherans had recently waged over ceremonies in the wake of Charles V's Interim. The Lutherans had been fighting about "orders or cerimonies" that were "*indifferentia*, that is, thinges which of theyr owne nature be suche, that it skylleth nothyng to soule healthe, whether one leave them or receave them."[29] The ceremonies in question were not essential for salvation, therefore, but "these outewarde cerimonies have thys propertye, that where so ever they be observed a lyke of all men, they be wytnesses of a certayne agreement and consent."[30] The use of "things indifferent" was important, therefore, because it was a way of signaling unity with others who also used them. Given this theoretical explanation of ceremonies and their value, Hosius provided an intriguing interpretation of the Lutheran debates over ceremonies. Hosius wrote that the "neuters" or "Adiaphoristes" of Wittenberg, led by Philip Melanchthon, "thought good to take away certayne new orders, which he [Martin Luther] had brought in and to restore most of the olde

---

[24] Thomas Harding, *An Answere to Maister Juelles Chalenge* (Louvain, 1564; STC 12758), 37v.
[25] Harding, *An Answere*, 36v.   [26] Harding, *An Answere*, 47v.   [27] Harding, *An Answere*, 47v.
[28] Stanislaus Hosius (trans. Richard Shacklock), *A Most Excellent Treatise of the begynnyng of heresyes in oure tyme. . .The hatchet of heresies* (Antwerp, 1565; STC 13888).
[29] Hosius, *A Most Excellent Treatise*, 59v-60r.   [30] Hosius, *A Most Excellent Treatise*, 60r.

orders."³¹ Melanchthon and the Wittenberg Adiaphorists allegedly restored traditional Catholic ceremonies because they "thought good to consent to the Christians, that by them [the indifferent ceremonies] they myght gyve it oute to be understanded, that they began a lyttell to inclyne from Luther to Christ, and that they myght put the world in hope" that they would return to the embrace of the Catholic Church.³² On Hosius's reading of recent Lutheran history, therefore, Melanchthon's decision to use traditional Catholic ceremonies was glossed as an intentional signal to the Catholic world that the Philippists sought a graduated return to orthodoxy and reunion with the Church. Hosius noted that Melanchthon and the Adiaphorists had faced intense opposition from Gnesio-Lutherans like Matthias Flacius, who claimed that the restoration of Catholic ceremonies marked a return to popery. According to Hosius, the Gnesio-Lutherans had grasped the point perfectly. Flacius was correct to see the "wearing of a surplesse" as "the first parte of the myserable wedge" that would restore Catholicism in Germany and he rightly "smelled that wyndowes were made to conveye in the Papacye, which sholde followe after them."³³ Hosius's only disagreement with Flacius was about whether this was really such a miserable thing, asking "is it so greate a faulte to buylde windowes for the Pope his supremacie, and not to make wyndowes for Sathanisme, that is Dyvellyshe doctryne to entre in?"³⁴

Hosius applied this lesson from the Lutherans later in the text when he advised the king of Poland against abolishing the use of certain indifferent ceremonies in the Polish church. While the king received many requests "that there sholde be an alteration in thinges (as some men thought) indifferent, you could be persuaded by no meanes to do it, least you myght seme to gyve a token of youre going backward from the Christian religion left unto you of youre forefathers, and of youre bending forwarde to Sathanisme."³⁵ These indifferent things might "seme to some man to be of lesser importaunce," and things that no one "sholde styck to graunte the takyng away of them," but even granting that "there were no faute in cutting of those thinges" because they were *adiaphora*, it was still a very bad idea to eliminate them.³⁶ Those who sought their abolition were aiming to break up the unity of the Roman Catholic Church: they "desire division in men, and not in suche thinges, as they know well inoughe, pertayne nothing to soule

³¹ Hosius, *A Most Excellent Treatise*, 59v.   ³² Hosius, *A Most Excellent Treatise*, 60r.
³³ Hosius, *A Most Excellent Treatise*, 64v, 61r-v.   ³⁴ Hosius, *A Most Excellent Treatise*, 61v.
³⁵ Hosius, *A Most Excellent Treatise*, 63r-v.   ³⁶ Hosius, *A Most Excellent Treatise*, 63v.

healthe."[37] While licit, eliminating indifferent ceremonies used by the Roman Catholic Church would separate the Polish kingdom from the rest of Christendom, and "in cutting of a mans his owne selffe from all the rest of Christendome, is suche a greate trespasse, that al other synnes compared to it, seme but a mote weyghing in balaunce with a myll poste."[38]

Hosius originally wrote in 1557 to the king of Poland, but for his translator Shacklock and his English readers in 1565, the implications for events in England would have been clear. Indeed, later in the treatise, Shacklock made the comparison explicit in a marginal comment explaining that while the Lutherans were fighting over the "surplesse," "our Protestantes" in England were fighting over "wering of a Prestes cap."[39] Hosius provided Shacklock with a framework whereby the use of Roman Catholic ceremonies was glossed as goodwill toward Rome, a desire for unity with the Pope, and even an openness to healing Protestant schism. This line of argument would be even more directly applied to the retention of Catholic ceremonies in the Elizabethan Church by Bishop Jewel's archenemy, Thomas Harding. Harding's *Confutation* (1565) of Jewel's *Apologie of the Church of England* (1562) began by praising Elizabeth's "good inclination towards the auncient and catholike religion, which the authours of that Apologie with an odious terme do call papistrie."[40] According to Harding, Elizabeth was displaying a pattern of behavior that revealed her favorable feelings toward Roman Catholicism. Elizabeth maintained a crucifix in her chapel, silenced the "lewd mouth" of a preacher who had denounced it, heard "the sobrest preachers" and a Good Friday sermon on the real presence, permitted her subjects to read defenses of the Catholic faith, refused to heed "hote preachers" who called for "sharp persecution," and most recently showed her "earnest zeale and travail to bring (if it might be) those disordered ministers unto some order of decent apparell, which yet they want the reason tapply them selves unto."[41] He was not alone, so he claimed, in drawing this conclusion from Elizabeth's behavior, as "very many others your loving and faithfull subjectes ar with the same provoked to conceive

---

[37] Hosius, *A Most Excellent Treatise*, 63v.   [38] Hosius, *A Most Excellent Treatise*, 63v.
[39] Hosius, *A Most Excellent Treatise*, 71r. It is a curious feature that much of the Catholic commentary on the vestiarian controversy focused on the cap, while Protestant commentary tended to focus on the surplice.
[40] Thomas Harding, *A Confutation of a Booke Intituled An Apologie of the Church of England* (Antwerp, 1565; STC 12762),*2v.
[41] Harding, *A Confutation*, *2v-*3r. For other examples of how Elizabeth's retention of a crucifix could be glossed as a crypto-Catholic gesture, see Martiall, *A Treatyse of the Crosse*, a2v; Dorman, *A Disproufe*, *3r.

comfort and hope of a better estate for matters of religion to be sene in the church of England."[42]

In the mid-1560s, therefore, Catholic polemicists were glossing the queen's push for vestiarian conformity as a sign of royal favor toward Catholicism and as a hopeful portent of things to come. At the same time, the fact that some Protestants were refusing to obey royal commands regarding vestments opened up a polemical goldmine for English Catholics, enabling them to accuse all Protestants of disobedience and position themselves as the truly obedient subjects of the queen. This theme was sounded again and again in the Catholic polemics published in 1565. Lewis Evans reported from Antwerp that leading Protestants like Thomas Sampson, Laurence Humphrey, and Thomas Cole were refusing to wear the cap prescribed by the queen. Disobedience on this quotidian matter revealed the Protestants' deep hatred of good order and obedience, proving "therefore (good people) yt is the false preachers of England, which beareth her no good wyl, yt is they, that for the wearing of a cappe, will comptrole her majesties most gracious mynde, & commaundement, yt is their dreamyng disobedience, which dothe defye her lawes, and yt is their churlyshe hateful hartes, that murmure, and grudge against her majesties proceadinges."[43] Thomas Dorman used vestiarian nonconformity to highlight Protestant hypocrisy: while Protestants defended the Royal Supremacy against papal authority, "even in a matter of no greater importance then is the wearing of a square cappe, they refuse the ordre of the supreme governour in all thinges and causes (as in wordes they call her) ecclesiastical and temporall."[44] For Dorman, the fact that Protestants "grudgeth against the princes ordinaunce in matters indifferent and of small importance, no greater then of a square cap" was equivalent with Knox's *First Blast*, the revolution in Scotland, and the wars of religion in France as evidence for the rebellious qualities of "that unhappy vermine the protestants."[45] William Allen exploited vestiarian nonconformity in 1565 to depict the Protestant clergy as disorderly beasts, gleefully asking "What a doo had the magistrates to make these wylde men go in priestelyke apparell, to kepe theire Rotchettes, to observe sum steppe of antiquitye in theire maners?"[46] Shacklock went furthest along these lines

---

[42] Harding, *A Confutation*, *3r.

[43] Lewis Evans (trans.), *Certaine Tables sett furth by the right Reverend father in God, William Bushopp of Rurimunde* (Antwerp, 1565, STC 15653), e5r-v. Evans would later convert to Protestantism and repudiate this claim in his anti-Catholic polemics of the later 1560s.

[44] Dorman, *A Disproufe*, *2v.   [45] Dorman, *A Disproufe*, 173r.

[46] William Allen, *A Defense and Declaration of the Catholike Churchies Doctrine, touching Purgatory, and prayers for the soules departed* (Antwerp, 1565; STC 371), 237v.

in 1565, claiming that the Protestants were prepared to depose the queen over the vestments, rhyming "The body is rebellion: wherefore can you tell? / For a cap they be redy their Prince to expell."[47]

Catholic polemicists exploited vestiarian nonconformity not only to demonstrate Protestant disobedience but to accuse Protestants of courting popularity, that most damning political accusation of the era. Thomas Harding wrote in 1565 that the nonconformists had shown no regard for "her Majesties commaundement, nor their Metropolitans decree."[48] While the next parliament was expected to pass a bill "that all and singuler spirituall persons shall weare square cappes and syde gownes, as hath ben accustomed," Harding predicted that "many of you shall refuse to obey this order."[49] Why did Protestants refuse to obey church, crown, and parliament? To win "the peoples praise of your constancie, that is to saye, of your stoutnes, of your stourdines, of your upright and stiffenecked disobedience."[50] They did it because they would "lever seme to the people, whom they use for their clawbackes, and to whose judgement they stand or fall, stout champions of their owne gospell, [rather] then meeke folowers of Christes gospell. Such mighty Samsons, such constant Laurences, your joyly gospell breedeth."[51]

It is clear that Catholics were active and aggressive contributors to the increasingly public debate over the Church of England's stance on vestments, *adiaphora*, and the exercise of religious authority. Catholics were able to gloss the queen's demand for vestiarian conformity as a Catholicizing gesture and they exploited vestiarian nonconformity to paint Protestants as disobedient, seditious troublemakers. To appreciate the impact these claims could have and the concern they generated among English Protestants, it is important to remember the climate of religious ambiguity that pervaded early Elizabethan England.[52] The window into the queen's soul is

---

[47] Preface to Hosius, *A Most Excellent Treatise*, a2v. This line of reasoning could also be found in the wake of the controversy. Thomas Stapleton wrote in 1567 that while Protestants claimed to support the doctrine of the Royal Supremacy, "so farre it serveth some of them, and the moste zealouse of them, that nowe their Prince, though *Supreme governour and judge in al causes Ecclesiasticall,* may not by *Gods worde,* appointe them as much as a Surplesse or Cope to be worne in the Churche, or Priestlike and decent apparell to be worne of them otherwise." By using their own interpretation of "Gods Woorde" to limit the prince's authority, Protestants ultimately rejected all authority and revealed their revolutionary designs. Thomas Stapleton, *A Counterblast to M. Hornes Vayne Blaste Against M. Fekenham* (Louvain, 1567; STC 23231), 70r.

[48] Harding, *A Confutation*, 147r.   [49] Harding, *A Confutation*, 292v.

[50] Harding, *A Confutation*, 146v.

[51] Harding, *A Confutation*, 147r. Here Harding was referring to Thomas Sampson and Laurence Humphrey, the leaders of vestiarian opposition at Oxford.

[52] For a good account of the "unsettled" state of religion in the early 1560s, see Jones, *The Birth of the Elizabethan Age*, ch. 3.

notoriously opaque and the motives behind Elizabeth's religious policies were and are difficult to gauge. As many scholars have pointed out, Elizabeth seems to have preferred to leave aspects of her religious settlement intentionally vague in an attempt to minimize domestic opposition and to keep her foreign policy and marital options as open as possible. In the course of negotiations regarding marriage to the Archduke Charles in early 1565, for example, the regime stressed the conservative aspects of the Church of England's worship and its retention of Catholic ceremonial. In the following year, Elizabeth dispatched Archbishop Parker's *Advertisements* (1566), which laid out the ceremonial and vestiarian policy of the Church of England as an indication of its conservatism. Indeed, the public push for vestiarian conformity was a crucial aspect of the negotiations over the match with the Archduke.[53] But the conservative elements in the Elizabethan Church may also have represented something more than tactical maneuvering by the queen. Expressing skepticism about Norman Jones's claim that Elizabeth was "'as Protestant as Jewel, Grindal or Cox,'" Patrick Collinson argued that "her religious conservatism was so consistently manifested, applied with such apparent conviction, that it is hard to believe that it went against the grain of her own beliefs and tastes."[54] Significantly, much of the evidence that Collinson went on to cite in support of Elizabeth's conservatism was also cited by the Catholic exiles as signs of the queen's favor toward their religion.

The point here is not, of course, that Elizabeth really was a crypto-Catholic, or that Protestants really were rabid revolutionaries. The point is that the story that the Catholics exiles were telling – of a Catholicizing queen constrained by heretical councilors who were prepared to unleash revolution over the wearing of a cap – was entirely plausible in the ambiguous years of the mid-1560s and could not be simply shrugged off by English Protestants.[55] In 1564, the Privy Council had advised against admitting the papal nuncio, in part because rumors of his arrival had encouraged

---

[53] Doran, *Monarchy and Matrimony*, 76, 82. Doran emphasizes that in these negotiations Elizabeth was insistent that the Archduke not be permitted to practice Catholicism in England, with the queen arguing that the conservatism of the Church of England would make it an acceptable Church for the Archduke. Elizabeth's push for vestiarian conformity was also highlighted in Anglo-Spanish diplomatic exchanges in the 1560s; I would like to thank Michael Questier for this point.

[54] Patrick Collinson, "Windows in a Woman's Soul: Questions about the Religion of Queen Elizabeth I," in *Elizabethan Essays*, 109–110.

[55] Even in 1570, after the papal excommunication of Elizabeth and the Northern Rebellion, Thomas Norton specifically complained about how Catholic polemicists claimed that "they be such that holde the same religion which the Quene doth not only hold, but also advise, commaund & procure to be holden." Norton, *A warning agaynst the dangerous practises of Papistes*, f4v.

many "to disperse abrode false & slanderous reports of the Quenes Majesties disposicion to chaunge hir religion & the governaunce of this Realm (a thing very false)."[56] In June 1565, the Council expressed concern that "the Adversaries of Religion" were "takyng occasion to fortifie their ffaction" from the queen's command for vestiarian conformity. The Council recommended that the queen clarify her intentions and that the push for conformity be moderated if the papists continued their polemical campaign.[57] Neither of these recommendations were followed, and a month later, Bishop Robert Horne (Winchester) noted that the papists were "endeavouring, by some of their writings dispersed among the people, to bring themselves into power and us into odium, having obtained a handle of this kind, (small enough indeed,) through the controversy lately arisen among us about square caps and surplices."[58] The vestments controversy of 1565–1566 gave English Catholics the perfect opportunity to make a strong case for what the English Church could (and should) become and to position themselves as its most loyal servants. English Protestants had to answer.

How did this Catholic polemical maneuvering influence puritan responses to the vestments? Critics of the vestments were deeply concerned by the ways in which the English people were interpreting the queen's insistence on conformity. As one anti-vestiarian pamphleteer put it, the queen had good intentions for the vestments, but "the end which the commander propoundyth, dothe not folowe, but accordinge to the diversitie of them that use them, and them that judge of them."[59] Starting from this assumption, puritans found it deeply troubling that Catholics were so openly pleased by the queen's efforts to force Protestant clergy to wear caps and surplices. Using the simplest oppositional logic, this fact alone was enough to condemn the policy for a puritan like Anthony Gilby, who explained that "we ar assured that we seke Gods glory, and our adversaries [those enforcing conformity] may see, yf they can se any thinge, that this thinge that they seke is not for gods glory, seing the papistes the enemyes of God, doe so

[56] CUL MS Mm 1.49, p. 29.

[57] SP 12/36, ff. 149v–150r. On this meeting, see Haugaard, *Elizabeth and the English Reformation*, 218–219.

[58] Horne to Gualter, 17 July 1565, in Robinson (ed.), *The Zurich Letters* (1842), 142. Horne went on to explain that the "papists cried out, that there is not among us that unanimity in religion which we profess to have; but that we are guided by various opinions, and unable to remain in any fixed purpose."

[59] *To the Reader. To my faithful brethren* (Emden, 1566; STC 10391), a[iii]4r. As another anti-vestiarian pamphleteer put it, "wee deni not but that they are reteynid of a good intent, but wee see that an evill end doth followe of the restoring of them." *An answere for the tyme*, c1r.

desyre yt and glory in yt."[60] A happy papist was a bad thing in and of itself
for puritans like Gilby – who proclaimed "let us never give them any cause
of Joye, thoughe we shoulde dye for yt"[61] – but there were other reasons why
happy papists were a sign of trouble. Thomas Sampson, who would be
deprived for nonconformity in 1565, repeated a view that had been common
among earlier English Protestants when he argued that godly behavior was
supposed to be discomfiting to papists: even in the use of things indifferent
Christians must not "seeme thereby to consente to theyr [the papists']
blasphemios heresies."[62] It was a Protestant axiom that papists considered
vestments to be essential for Christian worship and that they attributed a
superstitious, idolatrous holiness to the garments. According to the anti-
vestiarians, this opinion was so firmly rooted that the use of vestments by
Protestants could do nothing but confirm "ther supersticius opinion, of
these things," and encourage them to "sticke still in their popishe puddle."[63]
Worse yet, the "popish preistes" who constituted the bulk of the
Elizabethan clergy allegedly continued to wear the vestments "for the
same end, they did in poperie," enabling them to keep "a litill spice of
thier Masse" and confirming lay papists in their belief that "the servis of god
hathe grete nede of them."[64] As an anonymous puritan pamphleteer put it
around 1570, papists would say that the Pope must be "a godly wise man" if
Protestants chose to use his garments "to preserve their religion and common wealth."[65]

More insidiously, puritans claimed that the retention of this small part of
Catholic ceremonial by Protestant clergy would lead the ignorant people to
think that *all* popery was good. Adopting the voice of the people, one anti-
vestiarian pamphleteer told the bishops that "if yow walked in the countrie,
yow shold heare the comon voice saye. *Poperie is not so evil as they make it for
then they wold never commaund these things so streightlie to be observed.* Yow
shold heare: *neyghbore played wee not a wise part, whan wee kept our Masse
clothes & bookes, for by the masse neyghboure wee shall have all again, one
daye.*"[66] In other words, one of the main problems with the vestments was
that they were providing a reason to hope for the future restoration of
popery in England. William Whittingham, former member of the original
Frankfurt congregation and now Dean of Durham Cathedral under Bishop
Pilkington, wrote that the papists "laughe, and triumphe to se us thus delt

[60] Gilby, *To my lovynge brethren*, b1r.   [61] Gilby, *To my lovynge brethren*, a4v.
[62] Sampson to Leicester, ca. 1565, BL Egerton MS 2836, f. 32r.
[63] *An answere for the tyme*, c3v; Crowley, *A briefe discourse*, c4r.   [64] *An answere for the tyme*, c11r-v.
[65] "Certaine Questions," in *A parte of a register*, 41.   [66] *An answere for the tyme*, h6v; emphasis added.

wythe, not ashamyd here upon to bragg, that they truste that the rest of theyr thynges wyll folow."[67] The use of the vestments – especially by the vast numbers of unreconstructed papists who continued to serve as priests in the Church of England – would convince papists that nothing had changed after all. As Thomas Lever complained to Bullinger in July 1560, "the prebendaries in the cathedrals, and the parish priests in the other churches, retaining the outward habits and inward feeling of popery, so fascinate the ears and eyes of the multitude, that they are unable to believe, but that either the popish doctrine is still retained, or at least that it will shortly be restored."[68] This argument against the vestments reached the pinnacle of emotional intensity when anti-vestiarians claimed that the regime's policy was giving hope to Protestants' greatest remaining persecutor from Queen Mary's days, the "blodie bucher" and "monster" Edmund Bonner.[69] For Anthony Gilby, who expressed disgust that the imprisoned Bonner was even being fed, it was deeply troubling to hear reports "that Butcher *Boner* saide: They beginne to taste of our Pottage, they will shortelie fall to the flesh."[70] How could the vestments be edifying if, as John Barthlet claimed, "Keapinge of olde rites maketh Boner and the wicked hope well"?[71]

It was not only the use of vestments themselves that allegedly pleased Catholics but also the way in which nonconformists and tender Protestant consciences were being treated. Humphrey and Sampson, the leaders of nonconformity at Oxford, had been specifically invoked by Catholic polemicists as the figureheads of Protestant contention and disobedience. In the wake of Archbishop Parker's refusal to tolerate their nonconformity in 1565, Humphrey wrote to the episcopal commissioners lamenting that he had been handled in a way that "harted our Adversaries." Had the issue remained private and nonconformists been permitted to quietly resign rather than be publicly deprived, then the papists would not "have accused (in their seditious books) the Protestants for contention."[72] Sampson was also clearly angered by Catholic responses to the controversy, writing to Bullinger on 16 February 1566 that the "inflexible" approach of the authorities "is very gratifying to our adversaries at Louvaine, for they praise these

---

[67] William Whittingham, *To my faithful brethren* (Emden, 1566; STC 10389), a3r.
[68] Thomas Lever to Bullinger, 10 July 1560, Robinson (ed.), *The Zurich Letters* (1842), 85.
[69] Gilby, *To my lovynge brethren*, a4r.
[70] Gilby, *A Pleasaunt Dialogue*, k4r. This text was written in May 1566, and parts of it circulated in that year, but the work as a whole was not published until the 1570s.
[71] Barthlet, *The Fortresse of Fathers*, E1r.   [72] SP 12/36, f. 146r.

things up to the skies."[73] Gilby complained that England's "Gospellers . . .
spoileth another of liberty and living, and the papistes live quietly indeed, &
laugh in their sleeves."[74]

In responding to these arguments invoking Catholic opinion, conformists like Archbishop Parker simply denied that Catholics were actually
talking or thinking like this. If they were, it was the puritans' fault, not
the queen's. In *A briefe examination of the tyme* (1566), generally attributed
to Parker, the Archbishop doubted "Whether the blynde papiste, the weake
papiste, and simple Ghospeller (as you tearme them) have these opinions
nowe advouched," suggesting that "it is rather phantasied of some, then
beleved of the best part. Peradventure you shewe what you have taught
them to suppose of these matters, and therfore trustyng that they have
learned theyr lesson, you conclude thus of every one of theyr myndes."[75]
According to Parker, everyone knew why the queen had actually commanded the use of vestments and it was only the puritans who were willfully
misunderstanding her intentions and the reactions of the population.

In response, the puritans simply pointed to the writings of Harding and
other Catholic exiles as incontrovertible evidence to the contrary. One
anonymous response to Parker asked "what better profe, can you have
then experiens. Remember what Harding writith in this matter, in his
preface before the answear to the Apologie, enquire what the Papistes say
abrod, *yf these thinges be good, all poperie, is not evill, wee trust that other
thinges will follow shortly* &c." This was offered as definitive, empirical proof
that "obstinat Papistes are confirmed, in erro[r]s, by retianinge this apparell."[76] Harding's claims about Elizabeth and the vestments were repeatedly
cited by anti-vestiarian writers to clinch their case. One pamphlet proclaimed "What the Papists judge of us, maye easely be seene by this, that
Harding for the retayning of those Popishe cerymonies, conteynith hope
that popery shalbe restoryd." If a learned papist like Harding could draw
this conclusion, "what the ignorant people judge of the reamnants of
papistri retaynyd, wyse men may well consyder."[77] Anthony Gilby also
invoked Harding, writing that the retention of vestments could not be a
good policy if it caused "the enemies, *Harding* & his fellowes to triumphe,

---

[73] Sampson to Bullinger, 16 February 1565, Robinson (ed.), *The Zurich Letters* (1842), 153.
[74] Gilby, *A Pleasaunt Dialogue*, e4v.
[75] *A briefe examination for the tyme*, ******1r. A similar argument can be found in a brief manuscript
     tract, entitled "A short reply to a smale treatise of late entituled: A briefe awnswer to a pamphlete,
     latelie sett furthe in printe, by a Proctor of the popish apparayll," LPL MS 2007, f. 146r.
[76] *An answere for the tyme*, c6r; emphasis added.   [77] *To the Reader. To my faithfull brethren*, b2r-v.

and to waite for an overthrowe of both partes."[78] The Catholic exiles' public embrace of the queen's vestiarian policy could hardly have been better calculated to fan the flames of controversy among English Protestants.[79]

When puritans fretted about the ways in which the vestments would be perceived, Catholic opinion was only part of a larger equation. Critics of the vestments also wrote about how "Christians" perceived their use, especially recent converts who were still "weak" and "simple gospellers." On one level, the anti-vestiarians had the same fears about "weak" Christians as they did about papists. One anti-vestiarian pamphlet argued that the "Novice in Christ" was not doctrinally strong and remained heavily dependent on the example of the Protestant clergy. If those clergymen put on Catholic vestments, the "simple Christians" who did not yet understand the doctrinal niceties of *adiaphora* and Christian liberty would be "by us beaten back to superstition, from which they were before making hast to flye."[80] On another level, the puritans claimed that wearing the vestments would harm fellow Protestants because it would be an inappropriate use of Christian liberty. In short, the anti-vestiarians claimed that strong Christians, like themselves, understood that Christian liberty permitted them to use "things indifferent" like vestments. "Weak" Christians, however, were not fully convinced of their Christian liberty in things like vestments, and legalistically saw them as inherently wicked. To wear the vestments in the presence of these weaker brethren would produce dire consequences. Some weaker brothers and sisters would be driven away from the Church and might form sects; perhaps more dangerously, others might violate their consciences by attending services that they believed to be idolatrous (due to the use of vestments). This would be a heinous sin, and the anti-vestiarians constantly repeated the various biblical warnings against wounding weak consciences. The London ministers wrote that wearing vestments would bring down "that heavie cursse, which our Saviour hath pronounced against all suche as laye stumbling blocks in theyr brothers wayes."[81] Christ's words in Matthew 18 were quoted incessantly by the anti-vestiarians: "Take heede that ye offende not one of these little ones that beleve in me. Wo unto that man by whom offences come. It were better for that man, that a milstone were tyed about his necke, and he cast into the

---

[78] Gilby, *A Pleasaunt Dialogue*, e4r; also see k4r.

[79] There is an interesting comparison to be drawn here with Stephen Gardiner's calculated decision to express approval of the 1549 *Book of Common Prayer*. See MacCulloch, *Thomas Cranmer*, 486–487.

[80] Crowley, *A brief discourse*, a4v. Also see the brief nonconformist response to Parker, printed by Neal, *History of the Puritans*, 1.141–142.

[81] Crowley, *A brief discourse*, a5r.

deepe of the sea, than that he shoulde offende one of the least that beleve in me."[82]

While this fear of offense led many ministers into nonconformity, others struck compromises with the authorities that mollified their concerns regarding weaker brethren. When Richard Turner, Simon Clark, and Robert Pownolds pledged their conformity at the Chapterhouse in Canterbury in September 1566, they did so with the following requests: first, that they be released from wearing the square cap entirely; second, that they be released from conformity when "travelynge abrode to preache, as in respect of the greate offence that therby may growe unto many"; and third, that their nonconformity be tolerated until they had the opportunity to preach in the cathedral and "use some perswations by doctrine to the people, for theire quyetnes concernynge our conformytie."[83] Turner, Clark, and Pownolds conformed on the condition that their actions would not harm their congregations – hence their refusal to wear vestments in places where they had less control over how their actions were interpreted. We can see a similar dynamic at work in the pledged conformity of George Withers to Archbishop Parker. Withers had been a vocal opponent of the surplice at Cambridge, but by May 1565 he was willing to conform because "the townesmen of Burie, whose offence I chiefly feared have ben earnestlye in hande withe me rather to weare a cappe then to forsake them promisinge more over never the more to regarde it or esteame it for my wearinge of it."[84] This assurance removed Wither's concern that his conformity would be "an offence unto the godlie" or a "stommblinge blocke & an occasion of fallinge" to those who might doubt the gospel he had preached were he to wear the surplice.[85]

In sum, the newly minted "puritans" argued that papists and weak Protestants alike were interpreting the use of vestments in ways that damaged them spiritually. Wearing vestments – except possibly in carefully controlled situations – would not edify, but only "pull downe, staye or hinder the building up of the Lordes temple, which is his Church or congregation."[86] This line of reasoning would be at the heart of puritan

---

[82] Crowley, *A brief discourse*, a6v.
[83] LPL MS 3470, f. 17r. They also requested that they might be permitted to preach together on the subject of their conformity, so "that the offence maye be the lesse to us warde, the burden therof wilbe more easly borne of us, then if one of us alone, should be compelled to do the same."
[84] Inner Temple Library, Petyt MS 538/47, f. 320r.   [85] Petyt MS 538/47, f. 320r.
[86] Crowley, *A briefe discourse*, a4r. In addition to being concerned about the impact of the vestments on those who observed their use, the anti-vestiarians were also concerned with their impact on the wearers themselves; see Ann Rosalind Jones and Peter Stallybrass, *Renaissance Clothing and the Materials of Memory* (Cambridge, 2000), 4.

hostility to the use of vestments and other ceremonies in the Church of England for decades to come, but while the moniker "puritan" was new in the 1560s, this way of thinking about religious ceremonies would not have struck early Elizabethan Protestants as new or unusual in the least. Indeed, precisely this sort of reasoning and rhetoric had been central to the anti-Nicodemite arguments that dominated Protestant literature during Mary's reign, as Protestants grappled with the question of how they ought to respond to the restoration of Catholicism.

When read side by side, the arguments found in anti-Nicodemite literature and anti-vestiarian literature are virtually indistinguishable. Anti-Nicodemites and anti-vestiarians were both deeply concerned with how ceremonial behavior would be perceived by others: for both, the intentions were ultimately less important than the consequences. Both the anti-vestiarians and the anti-Nicodemites offered extensive analyses of how "papists" and "protestants" perceived religious acts. The Mass-going Protestant layman, like the vestment-wearing Protestant minister, was warned that papists would interpret his behavior as support for Catholicism and a step forward (or rather backward) toward reunion with Rome. As Peter Martyr Vermigli put it concisely in his *Treatise of the Cohabitacyon of the faithfull with the unfaithfull*, translated into English and published in 1555, the papists would say to themselves "these gospellers do comme to our masses, which they wold not do yf our masses wer so evell as thei call them: wherfor we may persevere and continue in our old purpose."[87] John Bradford equated attendance at mass with bearing false witness against one's neighbor, since it would be "wyttenessynge the masse to be a true servyce of god and a badge of hys churche, wher there owne conciences saye they lye and so condemneth them," and therefore make the dissembler guilty of murdering his neighbor's soul.[88]

Of course, the Nicodemite who attended Mass was regarded as harming not only papists but also "weaker brethren" who witnessed the act of dissembling. As Sampson put it in 1554, when a Protestant dissembled by attending the Mass, "a double stomble blocke is geven whiche even in things indifferent is to be avoyded," in that idolaters are confirmed in their superstitions and the "weake brother" is offended.[89] While anti-Nicodemite authors insisted that the Mass was idolatry rather than *adiaphora*, they nevertheless regularly applied Pauline ethical rules for the use of "things

[87] *A Treatise of the Cohabitacyon*, e4r. [88] Bradford, *The Hurte of Hering Masse*, c6r-v, e1v.
[89] Sampson, *A letter*, b5v.

indifferent" to the Mass.[90] Going to Mass offended weaker brethren, who did not grasp their liberty in things indifferent, when they were "boldened" to act against the testimony of their consciences. Hooper wrote that "by a dissemblers halting & playing of both handes, ['the weaker sort'] embraceth both in body and in soule, the evil that he abhorreth in hys hart."[91] This was a great evil "to make a doubtful conscience or striving against knowledge to do any thing that is not godly," and Hooper invoked Christ's words from the gospel of Matthew that "it were better a milstone were hanged about such an offenders necke, & cast into the sea . . . For those weaklinges that we make to stomble, Christ died, as S. Paul sayth, God defend we should confyrme any mans conscience in evil."[92] This message and these texts were repeated throughout anti-Nicodemite admonitions: attending mass would offend weaker brethren, encourage them to violate their consciences, and drive them back to popery.[93] In John Bradford's evocative phrase, it would "laye a Pyllow & Cusshen under there knees & elbowes to hold on styll & so to encrease goddes further vengeaunce."[94]

As we have already seen, these arguments were used time and again against wearing vestments. The continuity between the two campaigns was even made explicit in an autumn 1565 sermon at Paul's Cross when the preacher invoked the Marian martyrs in reference to the current debate over *adiaphora*.[95] The preacher recounted how many Protestants had died under Mary for conscience's sake, not only for the sake of their own souls, but to avoid harming their brethren who would be tempted to deny the truth. If Protestant preachers and bishops had renounced the truth under Mary, the preacher claimed, they would have "hindered many within this Realme and caused them allso 2 denye Christ."[96] This bold and dangerous proclamation of the truth "ought not to be only in the principall poynts of religion, *but allso in indifferent thinges*, if so beit I shall therby hurt the conscience of my neghbor."[97] This argument elevated conscientious

---

[90] Hooper, "A letter," in Coverdale (ed.), *Certain most godly, fruitful, and comfortable letters*, 161.

[91] Hooper, "A letter," 160–161.   [92] Hooper, "A letter," 161.

[93] Cf. the virtually identical admonitions in John Philpot, "A letter which he sent to the Christian congregation, exhortyng them to refrayne themselves from the Idolatrous service of the papistes, and to serve god wyth a pure and undefiled conscience after hys worde," in Coverdale (ed.), *Certain most godly, fruitful, and comfortable letters*, 220; Musculus, *The Temporysour*, d3v; *A Treatise of the Cohabitacyon*, e4r; Bradford, *The Hurte of Hering Masse*, c7r-c8r.

[94] Bradford, *The Hurte of Hering Masse*, d4v.

[95] This sermon is contained in Tanner MS 50, which contains a chronological series of notes on Paul's Cross sermons during 1565–1566. Unlike all of the other sermons in the volume, this one has no heading (rendering its author unidentifiable), but the date can be conjectured by the preceding and following sermons: 24 September 1565 and 14 October 1565.

[96] Tanner MS 50, f. 20r.   [97] Tanner MS 50, f. 20r.

scruples over "things indifferent" – and in the autumn of 1565 in London, who in the audience would not think of vestments? – to the same level as the Marian martyrs' willingness to defend the gospel with their lives. Once again, we see how the anti-Nicodemite anxieties that had obsessed the hotter sort of Marian Protestants were continuing to shape the activism of Elizabethan puritans as they opposed the "remnants of popery" remaining within the Church of England.

Unlike the puritans, Archbishop Parker was quite clear that there was an enormous difference between the reigns of Mary and Elizabeth. When Parker responded to the nonconformists in 1566, he conceded that their arguments about avoiding offense would have carried some weight in a different time, but that they were now out of date. Parker wrote that "In indifferent thynges, if lawe, for common tranquilitie have prescribed no order what ought to be done, a Christian man ought to have a great regarde of his neyghbours conscience, accordyng to S. Paules doctrine."[98] Likewise, if the use of vestments was commanded as a *necessary* element of worship – as it had been under Queen Mary – then they should not be used, in order to testify to Christian freedom. But according to Parker, neither of these circumstances currently existed under Queen Elizabeth, "For (thankes be to God) we dwell not among the Babilonians and Chaldies, we have in our Church no publique worshyppyng of Idolles, no Heathenishe or idolatrical sacrifice, as were in some place of the citie of Corinth, whose societie & contagion we ought to avoyde."[99] Elizabeth had commanded the use of vestments by law, not as necessary things, but quite clearly as "things indifferent" to be used without superstition for the sake of order, comeliness, and unity. In this situation, the biblical rules that the "precisans" pointed to about Christian liberty, things indifferent, and avoiding offense no longer applied: obedience was now the primary concern, and offense would be given by disobeying the monarch's command. This was – and would be – the well-known conformist case in a nutshell. As Cecil put it in 1565 letter, external things like vestments "ar of none other value but to make a demonstration of obedience, and to render a testimonie oof unity."[100] Indeed, Parker went so far as to argue that it was unnecessary for the English people to think about or even understand why the vestments were being commanded. They only needed to obey, since "oftentymes the Subject ought to obey in thynges not forbydden by God, and commaunded by lawe, though he do not playnly perceyve eyther for what good end they

[98] *A briefe examination*, ***3v.   [99] *A briefe examination*, ***4r.   [100] Petyt MS 538/38, f. 55v.

are required, or to what ende they wyll come: as dayly experience in common wealthes do shewe."[101] It was preposterous to insist that the queen's subjects "understande as much as the Prince and councell knoweth and intendeth" before they obeyed commandments, as this would "set the subject at his choyse."[102]

Parker's approach effectively sidestepped the entire puritan approach to the vestments. As J. S. Coolidge put it, while the puritans were deeply concerned with edification and talked constantly about the "offense" that vestments would cause, the conformists took the view that such "[p]sychological complexities cease where law 'takes order' . . . The good Pauline text, 'Let every soul be subject unto the higher powers' (Rom. 13:1), cuts this Gordian knot in Tudor England."[103] The puritans, unsurprisingly, were shocked by the claim that Pauline teaching regarding *adiaphora* was now irrelevant in Elizabethan England. One rejoinder to Parker urged him to consider "how shamfully you do erre" in claiming that "lawes pretending common tranquillitie maye prescribe an order contrarie to the ordar of charite commaunded of the holie goste, by his instrument S. Paull: binding all ages, places, and personnes. Where doth S. Paull, or anie part of holie writt teache such doctrine"?[104] While Parker's arguments about *adiaphora* and obedience were not without precedent – similar claims had been advanced by Thomas Starkey under Henry VIII and by Thomas Cranmer against John Hooper under Edward VI[105] – the attempt to replace offense with obedience departed significantly from the ways in which even Elizabeth's bishops had treated *adiaphora* in the recent past.[106] In 1559, several bishops and leading divines wrote to the queen, seeking to persuade her to abolish the use of altars in the Church of England.[107] The authors argued that altars were technically illegal because the Book of Common Prayer specified the use of "a table" and that tables had more support in Scripture and patristic sources, but they

---

[101] *A briefe examination*, ****3r.   [102] *A briefe examination*, ****3r.

[103] Coolidge, *The Pauline Renaissance in England*, 43. "The English situation is like what Paul's would have been if an edict had gone out from a benevolent emperor requiring, for the sake of good order, that Christians should always eat meats offered to idols."

[104] *An answere for the tyme*, d7v.

[105] Starkey, *A preface to the Kynges hyghnes*; for Cranmer's views, see "Of Ceremonies why some be abolished, and some reteigned," in *The booke of common praier* (London, 1549; STC 16275), t4v-t6r; MacCulloch, *Thomas Cranmer*, 411–412.

[106] Drawing on different evidence, Brett Usher has also emphasized Parker's divergence from his episcopal brethren in his campaign for conformity: Usher, "The Deanery of Bocking."

[107] "Certeyne reasons to be offred to the Quenes Majesties consideracion why it is not convenient that the Comunion shulde be mynystred at an Altere," ca. 1559, LPL MS 2002, ff. 107–109. This document is printed in John Strype, *Annals of the Reformation* (Oxford, 1824), 1:1:237–241. Patrick Collinson has argued that Edmund Grindal was the author of this document: *Archbishop Grindal*, 100.

nevertheless admitted that altars were *adiaphora* and "a thinge whiche in some other tyme might be tollerated."[108] As such, their main argument was not that altars were strictly prohibited, but that "at this tyme the continuance of Altares shulde bring merveilous inconveniences."[109] The bishops based their stance on the ways in which various segments of the English population perceived altars and on the potential they had for offense. Since many of the "godly mynded" rejected altars as "ordenunces and devises of man not commaunded in goddes worde," their retention would "minister an occasion of offence and division amongst the godly mynded."[110] This might even lead some to separate from the established church, since the bishops expected that thousands who had embraced the gospel "will absteine from receiving the communion at an Altare, whiche in the ende maye growe to occasion of greate schisme and division amonge your people."[111] Conversely, the bishops argued that the Catholic clergy who remained within the Church of England greatly desired the retention of altars, because altars aided them in simulating the mass and confirming "the simple in their former errours."[112] Rather than arguing that the queen could simply nullify the potential for offense by commanding the use of altars for the sake of order and unity, the bishops saw offense and charity as ongoing concerns and deployed arguments that would shortly be used against wearing vestments. In other words, while Parker was following in the footsteps of distinguished predecessors in the English Reformation when he replaced offense with obedience as the overriding concern with regard to the use of *adiaphora*, we need to recognize that the "conformist" position represented a controversial course in the mid-1560s.

In the only monograph on the vestments controversy, J. H. Primus argued that the differing emphases on offense and obedience led puritans and conformists to simply talk past each other in the controversy.[113] This, however, is not entirely true. Parker not only attempted to deny the anti-vestiarians' premises; he also attempted to refute them on their own terms by arguing that the use of vestments would *not* harm the English population in the various ways that the anti-vestiarians claimed. Rather, they would actually be a powerful tool for converting Catholics into true Christians. The argument is worth quoting at length:

> *You woulde have us thynke that the receyvyng of these orders doth not edifie, because (as you imagine) the obstinate papiste shalbe confirmed in his opinion. This thyng is easyer and oftener saide of you, then proved as yet. For truely*

---

this may be a meanes rather to wynne the adversaries from theyr errours, when they see us without superstition or any necessitie, turne those thinges to good uses, which they fowly abused, and heare us condemne in open preachyng, that which they set so much by. And uppon this cause it seemeth, the Apostles used long after Christes ascention the Ceremonies of Moises, and that in the Temple, to wynne to Chryst the obstinate Jewes. The histories Ecclesiasticall also have divers experiences, howe much our auncient fathers increased Christes Churche by such godly policie. Hence it was, that they plucked not downe all the Jewyshe Sinagoges and Heathenyshe Temples, but turned them to the service of God: that they altered theyr feast dayes: that they chaunged their rites to Godlye purposes. And that this myght be done, it appeareth by S. Augustine to *Publicola*, saying: *Cum vero ista vel in honorem veri dei convertuntur, hoc de illis fit, quod de ipsis hominibus, cum ex sacrilegis et impiis in veram religionem mutantur.* When these thinges be converted unto the honour of the true God, it is of them as it is of the parties them selves, whan they were before committyng sacrilege and impietie, nowe they be converted into true religious persons.[114]

Rather than viewing vestments as a cipher, as merely a means of showing obedience, Parker was arguing here that their use had positive merits and that the Protestant appropriation of vestments could play a key role in the conversion of English Catholics.[115] Like medieval Christian missionaries who felled sacred trees to construct churches, English Protestants would appropriate and repurpose objects of Catholic superstition for the true service of God. Parker was not the only bishop to express hope that the Protestant use of Catholic externals might lead to conversions. In a February 1564 letter to Parker, Bishop John Scory (Hereford) had expressed hope that the use of Catholic vestments by Protestant preachers might lead Catholics to credit their evangelical message. Scory wrote that he hoped that "all soche as in my diocese ar cownted and called papists maye as redely thinke all on thing in doctrine and religion according to the truth of christs gospell with us, as we ar redey to agre in the owteward apparell of cappes gownes and typpets with them: an then shall god be glorified, and the Q. majestie honored and gladded."[116]

While it is well known that puritans feared the "offense" that would be given by vestments, it has not been recognized that the leading early

---

[114] *A briefe examination,* ***iv.

[115] Parker's argument even went beyond what his successor at Canterbury, Archbishop Whitgift, would argue against Thomas Cartwright in the 1570s regarding the ability of ceremonies to edify *"per accidens."* See Lake, *Anglicans and Puritans?,* 19, 46, and esp. 65: "He [Whitgift] never claimed that the ceremonies in question edified or had any religious significance at all." Also see John Ayre (ed.), *The Works of John Whitgift* (Cambridge, 1851), 1.71–72.

[116] Harley MS 6990, f. 64v.

Elizabethan defender of the vestments defended their use as a valuable weapon in the Church of England's evangelical arsenal. When making this argument, Parker was not denying the relevance of the puritans' concerns regarding edification and offense: he was instead arguing that they were simply mistaken about the effect vestments would have on Catholics. These were radically different understandings of how Protestants should relate to England's Catholic majority and represented a disagreement as significant as the one regarding scriptural and royal authority.

While historians have not focused on this aspect of Parker's defense of the vestments, it hardly went unnoticed by his contemporaries. Opponents of the vestments were horrified by Parker's claims. The notion that the use of vestments would assist in the conversion of papists was, as we have seen, the mirror opposite of everything the anti-vestiarians had been arguing (and, as they frantically pointed out, the opposite of everything English Catholics had been saying as well). *An answere for the tyme* (1566) directly addressed Parker's invocation of Augustine and the policy of Christianizing pagan rituals in order to win converts, claiming that Augustine

> utterly, misliked the pollicie, answering: *quaeritis*, &c. do yow aske me houe the pagans may be wonne? how they may be called to salvacion? forsake thier solemnites, let goe their toies, and then yf they agree not to our tru[t]he, let them be ashamed, of their fewnes. Yf wee could agree: with Augustine and forsake the popishe toyes, and trinkettes, with in shorte space no doubt the Papistes which now swarve, wold shrinke in the wetting and wax so few, that they wolde be ashamed of their litle nomber.[117]

The whole notion that apparel could be used "to winne the adversaries" was utterly opposed by "godes word."[118] Instead, only the complete repudiation of popish ceremonies would drive papists from their superstitions. It was also, in this author's opinion, a fundamentally new claim for a Protestant to make. Bucer and Peter Martyr may have argued during Edward VI's reign that Hooper ought to wear the vestments, but they urged him to "bear with the things tollerable for a tyme, wishing the utter abolishing of them. This man defendith them as good orders, profitable to edifie, and therfore mete to be retayned still."[119] What was so objectionable about Parker's arguments, in other words, was that he had invested them with positive value, such that their future abolition became unnecessary. They were here to stay, and "further reformation" was not only unnecessary, but undesirable.

---

[117] *An answere for the tyme*, c6v. Anthony Gilby repeated this response almost verbatim in *A Pleasaunt Dialogue*, g8r.
[118] *An answere for the tyme*, c6r. [119] *An answere for the tyme*, a3v-a4r.

The anti-Nicodemite ethos again provides an important context for this part of the anti-vestiarian case. Marian anti-Nicodemites had insisted that the only way to convert "simple" and "ignorant" papists was to repudiate their worship: even the smallest compromise was sinful and uncharitable because it did not adequately proclaim to papists the wickedness of their religion. This common anti-Nicodemite argument was applied extensively to the use of "things indifferent" in the 1562 translation of Johann Wigand's *De Neutralibus et Mediis, Grosly Inglyshed, Jacke of both Sydes*. Wigand, a Gnesio-Lutheran who (like Matthias Flacius) opposed the policies of Lutherans like Melanchthon regarding *adiaphora*, denounced any attempt to use *adiaphora* as a means to unite Protestants and Catholics.[120] The text proclaimed that "the order is moste filthily turned up syde down, when the agrement or conformytye of externall matters is fyrst sought at their handes, which have most sluttishly soiled those things with horrible supersticions & blasphemyes, and powred them full as it were of deadly poison."[121] Agreement must *first* be forged on doctrine, and then agreement on the external forms of worship would follow. This had been the position of the anti-Nicodemites toward Catholic ritual during the reigns of Henry VIII and his eldest daughter and it would be the position of the puritans toward vestments and other "remnants of popery" under Elizabeth.

As we have seen, Parker had a very different view of how externals might play a role in the evangelistic mission of the Church of England. It is possible that Parker was making the strongest possible case for a policy he did not entirely support, but we can gain insight into Parker's mindset by examining an encounter he had two years earlier with a group of high-ranking French Catholics.[122] In May 1564, the queen commanded Parker to entertain the French ambassador and his delegation on their journey to the court to finalize the Treaty of Troyes. Parker reported back on the meeting in June, writing to Cecil that the Ambassador and his companions had been particularly interested to learn about "the order and using of our religion." In talking with them, Parker discovered that the French were severely misinformed about the Church of England, thinking that "we had neither *statas preces*, nor choice of days of abstinence, as Lent, &c., nor orders

[120] On Wigand's career and theology, see Ronald E. Diener, "Johann Wigand, 1523–1587," in Jill Raitt (ed.), *Shapers of Religious Traditions in Germany, Switzerland, and Poland, 1560–1600* (New Haven, CT, and London, 1981), 19–38.

[121] Wigand, *De Neutralibus*, L4r.

[122] On Parker and the push for liturgical reform in the Convocation of 1562–1563, see David Crankshaw, "Preparations for the Canterbury provincial convocation of 1562–3: a question of attribution," in Susan Wabuda and Caroline Litezenberger (eds.), *Belief and Practice in Reformation England* (Aldershot, 1998), 60–93.

ecclesiastical, nor persons of our profession in any regard or estimation, or of any ability, amongst us."[123] Parker "beat that plainly out of their heads," and the French were very pleased to learn "that in ministration of our Common Prayer and Sacraments we use such reverent mediocrity, and that we did not expel musick out of our quires, telling them that our musick drowned not the principal regard of our prayer."[124] Friday evening's dinner provided Parker with the perfect opportunity for an evangelistic object lesson: the Archbishop arranged for a fish supper to be prepared and explained to the French that "it was rather in the respect of their usage at home than for that we used so the Friday or other such fasting days, which we observe partly in respect of temperance and part for policy, not for any scrupulosity in choice of days."[125] All in all, the Frenchman "noted much and delighted in our mediocrity, charging the Genevians and the Scottish of going too far in extremities."[126] Indeed, the French "professed that we [the English] were in religion very nigh to them," not least in mutual hostility to the pope, and Parker responded by saying that "I would wish them to come nigher to us, grounding ourselves (as we do) upon the apostolical doctrine and pure time of the primitive Church."[127] In conclusion, Parker expressed hope to Cecil that "this ambassador may be a great stay in his country for the better supposing of us hereafter."[128]

Parker's account of this meeting reveals him experimenting with a particular diplomatic and evangelistic strategy toward Roman Catholics – the sort of strategy that the author of *De Neutralibus* had denounced as "up syde down" – and records his impressions of that strategy's efficacy.[129] The French objected to the "extremities" that characterized the religion of Jean Calvin and John Knox, but they came to think favorably about the Church of England (or at least so they said) when they learned more about its ceremonies and recognized similarities with the Roman Catholic Church. Parker used a "thing indifferent" [ab]used by Catholics – fasting on Fridays – to show "respect" for his visitors' religious practice, but also as an opportunity to teach the French the true (Protestant) use of Christian liberty in "things indifferent" like fasting. Ultimately, Parker was convinced that the Church of England's ceremonies and their outward similarity to the religion to which the Catholics

---

[123] Parker to Cecil, 3 June 1564, in *Correspondence of Matthew Parker*, 215.
[124] *Correspondence of Matthew Parker*, 215.   [125] *Correspondence of Matthew Parker*, 216.
[126] *Correspondence of Matthew Parker*, 215.   [127] *Correspondence of Matthew Parker*, 216.
[128] *Correspondence of Matthew Parker*, 216.
[129] On Parker's failed efforts to convert leading Roman Catholic clergymen in 1559, see Louise Campbell, "A Diagnosis of Religious Moderation: Matthew Parker and the 1559 Settlement," in Racaut and Ryrie (eds.), *Moderate Voices in the European Reformation*, 32–50.

were accustomed made the Catholics favorably disposed to the worship of the Protestant Church of England in a new way, and Parker hoped this might lead them to be open to Protestant belief as well.

When Parker defended the use of vestments in the Elizabethan Church, therefore, he brought with him the belief that the use of traditional ceremonies coupled with clear teaching on Christian liberty could be an effective evangelistic tool. The great threat to the edification and conversion of England was not the vestments, but rather the extremists, the vocal nonconformists (many of whom were literally friends of Geneva's Calvin and Scotland's Knox) whose incendiary rhetoric and disobedience were bringing the Church of England into disrepute and undermining its ability to edify the queen's subjects, especially her Catholic subjects. When Parker responded to the Catholic polemics addressing the vestiarian controversy, therefore, he chose to focus on rebutting their accusations of Protestant disobedience and division.[130] Parker in *A briefe examination* responded not only to nonconformists but also to the "Englishe Lovanistes" with their "fawning flatterie prefaces" and "bookes so fast and hastyly sent over in great numbers."[131] Parker wrote that "the adversaries of true religion [the papists] can winne no great rejoyce at these mens [the puritans'] oversightes, as beyng but a very fewe, and counted in deede none of the sincere and learned protestauntes, howsoever for a tyme they seemed to be amongest us. For though they be gone out from us, yet they were belyke never of us."[132] This was a harsh repudiation of putative brethren and a brutally simple rejoinder to Catholic accusations of Protestant disunity and disloyalty.[133] Parker was wholeheartedly agreeing with the Catholic exiles that Protestant nonconformists were seditious popularity-seekers, but simultaneously neutralizing and deflecting this attack by disowning the nonconformists entirely. Parker went on to write that the Catholic exiles should not "delyght them selves with any hye rejoysinges, as though the Prince woulde for disprovyng of a fewe counterfaites, dislyke the whole state of the rest of the Cleargie." Just as the rest of the apostles were not "discredited, though Judas fell out from them," neither were the English clergy besmirched by these false brethren.[134]

---

[130] For Parker's early concern about how Catholics were exploiting the controversy, see Parker to Grindal, 30 January 1565, in *Correspondence of Matthew Parker*, 228.

[131] *A briefe examination*, *4r-v. [132] *A briefe examination*, *4r.

[133] In part, this was tit for tat: in *A brief discourse*, the London nonconformists had first made the bold claim that "the earnest soliciters of this matter . . . are not, neyther were at anye tyme Protestantes: but when tyme woulde serve them, they were bloudy persecuters, & synce tyme fayled them, they have borne back as much as lay in them" (c5r).

[134] *A briefe examination*, *4r-v.

This chapter has attempted to revise our understanding of a much-studied episode in English history. It has shown how Catholics played an important and hitherto unrecognized role in the vestments controversy, glossing the Church of England's retention of vestments as a sign of the queen's crypto-Catholicism and powerfully exploiting nonconformity as proof of Protestants' inherently disloyal and disobedient nature. By emphasizing the role played by Catholics in what previously has been considered an intra-Protestant dispute, this chapter contributes to a growing body of scholarship that aims to restore English Catholics to their proper place in the "mainstream" history of early modern England.[135] It sheds light on the role played by flesh-and-blood Catholics (and not merely the abstract specter of popery) in shaping Protestant thought and identity in early modern England. Catholic voices played an important role in shaping puritan views of the vestments, disproving (in their view) the regime's claims that the English people understood that the vestments were ordained only as a matter of order, and proving the puritan claim that the vestments were harming the cause of the gospel. Parker's encounters with Catholics seem to have played a role in shaping his alternative vision of the vestments (and other traditional ceremonies) as potent means of converting Catholics into true Christians. When Parker aggressively disowned the nonconform-ists and expelled them from the Protestant fold, he was not only retaliating against puritan attacks on the bishops but also attempting to parry Catholic attempts to exploit the divisions within English Protestantism for their own purposes. Catholics were not only important participants in the vestiarian debate, therefore; their involvement played a crucial role in shaping intra-Protestant polemics and intensifying hostilities between Protestants. At the moment when the word "puritan" was being coined by Catholic polem-icists, puritanism was not so much "one half of a stressful relationship."[136] Instead, it was only one part of a multifaceted argument with other Protestants and with Roman Catholics.

---

[135] For representative examples, see the essays in Ethan H. Shagan (ed.), *Catholics and the 'Protestant nation': Religious politics and identity in early modern England* (Manchester, 2005); Michael C. Questier, *Catholicism and Community in Early Modern England: Politics, Aristocratic Patronage and Religion, c. 1550–1640* (Cambridge, 2006); Peter Lake, "A Tale of Two Episcopal Surveys: The Strange Fates of Edmund Grindal and Cuthbert Mayne Revisited: The Prothero Lecture," *Transactions of the Royal Historical Society* 18 (2008), 129–163; Peter Lake and Michael Questier, *The Trials of Margaret Clitherow: Persecution, Martyrdom and the Politics of Sanctity in Elizabethan England* (London, 2011).

[136] The phrase is Patrick Collinson's, in *The Birthpangs of Protestant England*, 143.

CHAPTER 7

The battle for English Protestantism

When Bishop Edmund Grindal examined a group of separatists in 1567 who had left the Church of England because they refused to hear ministers who wore a surplice, he challenged them by asking, "There be good men and good martyrs that did weare these thinges in K. Edw. dayes: doe you condemne them?"[1] Grindal's question pointed to a basic problem that would bedevil puritans for decades to come. When puritans criticized the Church of England and called for further reformation, their opponents pointed to heroic martyrs – like John Hooper, Hugh Latimer, Nicholas Ridley, and Thomas Cranmer – who had worn vestments, occupied episcopal office, and written the Prayer Book. According to Henry Howard, presbyterians like Thomas Cartwright should be prepared "to enter the field, not against D. Whitgifte," but against martyrs like Cranmer and Ridley, who had not only been content to serve as bishops and to strictly observe every aspect of the Book of Common Prayer, but who had "sealed with their bloud the testimonie of their conscience."[2] By anointing the Elizabethan Church with the blood of the martyrs, conformists were not only drawing on a virtually unassailable source of authority but also pointing to the "recent and superficial origin" of the puritan movement and condemning it as "the invention of an insignificant and youthful *coterie*" – a damning accusation in a culture that venerated antiquity and abhorred novelty.[3] The puritans faced a powerful historical challenge. How would they respond to it? How did their calls for "further reformation" fit into the history of the English Reformation?

In theory, the puritans had an easy answer at hand when they were rebuffed with the examples of figures like Cranmer and Ridley. As Zelotes told Atheos in George Gifford's famous *The Countrie divinitie* (1581),

---

[1] *A parte of a register*, 32.
[2] Henry Howard, *A Defense of the Ecclesiasticall Regiment of Englande, defaced by T. C. in his Replie agaynst D. Whitgifte* (London, 1574; STC 10393), 41; also see 189–191.
[3] Collinson, "The Authorship of A Brieff Discours off the Troubles Begonne at Franckford," 194; also see Lake, *Anglicans and Puritans?*, 27.

"the worde of God is the onelie rule, and wee must followe our forefathers no further then they follow the word of God. You must not followe David, nor Abraham in every thing they did."[4] It was relatively easy to make this argument about Catholic forefathers or about biblical personae, but it was much more difficult to admit that the martyrs immortalized in the pages of Foxe's *Acts and Monuments* had been guilty of upholding popery. As the author of *A Second Admonition to Parliament* starkly put the objection in 1572, the presbyterians' opponents "say that we in thys do uncover our fathers privities, and would wishe us to forbeare so to do."[5] As we have seen in preceding chapters, there was a need to maintain Protestant solidarity in the face of a steady stream of English Catholic polemic that poured vitriol on martyrs like Cranmer and Ridley, depicted them as debauched arch-heretics, and pointed to divisions among Protestants as proof that they were heretical purveyors of falsehood.[6] Elizabethan Catholic authors often made this argument by pointing to the recent history of the English Reformation and its constantly shifting theology and liturgy, creating a further problem for puritans who aimed to change the Church of England yet again. Writing in 1565, for example, the Catholic exile Thomas Stapleton pointed out that the form of communion used in the Elizabethan Church of England "differeth as much from the first order of communion used in King Edwardes time, as the *Lutherans* do from the *Zuinglians*," because the 1549 Prayer Book "bothe allowed the real presence in the Sacrament as Luther did, and used also many olde ceremonies of Christ his church" and the Elizabethan liturgy (based on the revised 1552 Prayer Book) "denieth the reall presence, as *Zuinglius* and *Calvin* do, and rejecteth the ceremonies of the Masse."[7] This enabled Stapleton to pit Edwardian Protestants against Elizabethan Protestants – in effect, against themselves – arguing that "by the judgement of all the ghospellers in Kinge Edwardes time, and of the stinking martirs of that age, our communion now practised in England is

---

[4] George Gifford, *A Briefe discourse of certaine points of the religion, which is among the common sort of Christians: which may bee termed the Countrie Divinitie* (London, 1581; STC 11845), 4v.

[5] *A Second Admonition to the Parliament*, *3r. The reference here was to the story of Ham and Noah in Genesis 9:20–27.

[6] See, among many examples, Harding, *An Answere to Maister Juelles Chalenge*, 39r; Harding, *A Confutation*, 140v; Dorman, *A Disproufe*, 103v–104r; Hieronymus Osorius, *A Learned and Very Eloquent Treatie, writen in Latin . . . wherein he confuteth a certayne Aunswere made by M. Walter Haddon against the Epistle of the said Bishoppe unto the Queenes Majestie* (Louvain, 1568; STC 18889), 28v–29r.

[7] Fridericus Staphylus (trans. Thomas Stapleton), *The Apologie of Fridericus Staphylus Counseller to the late Emperour Ferdinandus, &c.* (Antwerp, 1565; STC 23230), 8r. The quotations come from Stapleton's preface.

hereticall, and against the pure doctrine of the ghospel."[8] As we saw in the previous chapter, Protestants were tremendously concerned about this sort of Catholic polemic, and there was a heavy burden on them to deflect these charges of internal division and to defend the unity and continuity of English Protestantism.[9]

Some Puritans were nevertheless willing to take the plunge and criticize early English Protestants, almost without reservation, for failing to establish a proper church polity and discipline. William Fulke's *A Brief and Plain Declaration* (written in the first flush of presbyterian political agitation in 1572, but not published until 1584) defined the present historical moment as the first instance in the course of the English Reformation when a full reformation of church polity had been sought, stating that "the present age may see & judge, what is the uttermost of our desire, concerning reformation, which hitherto for lacke of such a publike testimoniall, hath been subject to infinite slaunders."[10] Fulke described his book as a testimony to future generations that "the truth in this time, was not generallye unknowen nor untestified, concerning the right regiment of the church of god . . . that our example shold not be prejudicial unto them: as the example of our Godly fathers (which in thys poynt neglected their duetie) hath beene prejudiciall unto us."[11] Responding in 1572 to the accusation that the presbyterians were like Ham, delighting in their father Noah's nakedness, the presbyterian author of the *Second Admonition* did not deny that their fathers were naked, but insisted that "we woulde, and doe what we can, to cover thys shame with a ryght cover, that is with a right reformation, and that do we going backward, as men lothe and sorye to heare of the nakednesse, and desirous to cover it, that our fathers (if they wil be our fathers) may no longer shew their shame."[12] Nevertheless, "the deformities have continued long, and are manifestly intollerable, where against we are

---

[8] Staphylus (trans. Stapleton), *The apologie*, 8v.

[9] Conformists were also ready to define Protestant criticisms of the Church of England as crypto-popery: Whitgift's first response to the *Admonition* took the fact that both the presbyterians and the papists criticized the Church of England and its ministry, sacraments, and liturgy to prove that there was "no great difference betwixt them and the Papistes, & I thinke verily they both conspire togither." John Whitgift, *An answere to a certen Libell intituled, An admonition to the Parliament* (London, 1573; STC 25429), 331. It was immaterial, Whitgift claimed, that these two groups were criticizing the Church on different grounds.

[10] William Fulke, *A Briefe and plaine declaration, concerning the desires of all those faithfull Ministers, that have and do seeke for the Discipline and reformation of the Church of Englande* (London, 1584; STC 10395), 147.

[11] Fulke, *A briefe and plaine declaration*, 147. On generational rhetoric in the English Reformation, see Alexandra Walsham, "The Reformation of the Generations: Youth, Age and Religious Change in England, c. 1500–1700," *Transactions of the Royal Historical Society* 21 (2011), 93–121.

[12] *A Second Admonition*, *3v.

commaunded to cry out," rather than "studie and endevor to please men."[13] Neither author was willing to name names in print, but in private it seems presbyterians were not so concerned to cover their fathers' nakedness. As one presbyterian noted in a handwritten list of anti-episcopal talking points and jokes, "Cranmer & Ridle[y] with manie churches [were] like Salomon with his manie wives &c."[14]

Separatists, unsurprisingly, were willing to be far harsher in public. Having rejected the Church of England as a false church, the separatists could show little compunction in also rejecting its martyrs, or rather "pseudomartyres" as Henry Barrow provocatively referred to them.[15] The Edwardian Church of England, which these pseudo-martyrs had defended, fared little better. The group of separatists examined by Bishop Grindal in 1567 responded to the statement that "we holde the reformation that was in King *Edwardes* dayes" by replying

> You buylde much of K. *Edwardes* time. A very learned man as anie is in the Realme, I think you can not reproove him, writeth these wordes of K. *Edwardes* time. I will let passe to speake of *King Henries* time, but come to K. *Edwardes* time, which was the best time of reformation: all was driven to a prescript order of service, peesed and patched out of the popishe portasse, of mattins, masse, and Even-song: so that when the minister had done his service, he thought his duetie done, to be short, there might no Discipline be brought into the Church.[16]

The separatist Robert Browne went even further in 1582, depicting Edward's reign as a period of escalating popery: "The Popes olde house was destroyed in Englande, and they are called to builde him a newe. In the time of King *Edward* the 6. they began such a building. They had gotte the Popishe tooles, but they coulde not holde them. God was mercifull by the rodde of Queene Marie, and dyd beate such evill weapons out of their handes, yet these have gotte againe that false popish government."[17]

There were ways, however, in which puritans could criticize the actions of the bishop-martyrs and yet at the same time fully excuse their failures. Walter Travers argued that England's rejection of disciplinary reform was

---

[13] *A Second Admonition*, *3v.
[14] LPL MS 453, f. 39r. This was the forty-first in a lengthy list of anti-episcopal talking points, which can be dated to the period after the Marprelate Tracts based on the inclusion of the joke "Of the two bad [,] better it were to be a simple martinist then a Grigorie martinist" (f. 38r).
[15] Henry Barrow, *A Brief Discoverie of the False Church* (1590), in Carlson (ed.), *The writings of Henry Barrow, 1587–1590*, 284.
[16] *A parte of a register*, 33–34.
[17] Robert Browne, *A Treatise upon the 23. of Matthewe* (1582), in Carlson and Peel (eds.), *The writings of Robert Harrison and Robert Browne*, 219.

sinful at the present day in a way that it had not been before. While the Antichristian institutions and offices of the pre-Elizabethan church were "heynous, yet because they came off ignorance might the rather obteine some pardon."[18] Now, in the light of the presbyterian pamphleteering of the early 1570s, the discipline "hathe made her selfe knowen unto us" with such clarity and self-evident truth that it "may perce the eyes even off men that are blinde."[19] To reject the discipline in Elizabethan England was now to reject manifest truth – in other words, the very definition of a heretic – and would bring harsh judgment from God. As B. R. White, Stephen Brachlow, and Peter Lake have discussed, this argument reflected a willingness among puritan authors in the 1570s to describe the English Reformation as an organic process and to assert that they had received a fuller knowledge of divine truth than their early English Protestant predecessors.[20] As Thomas Cartwright had put it a year earlier, English Protestants "have growne in the knowledge of the truth," whereas while previously they were only "able to leape over a hedge, we should now have our feete so prepared by the gospell, that they should be as the feete of a hynde, hable to surmount even a wall if neede were."[21] Speaking about the Marian martyrs, the Plumber's Hall Separatists claimed in 1567 that "We condemne them not," but "we would goe forward to perfection, for we have had the Gospell a long time amonest us."[22] This argument was not only made to explain away the lack of discipline in the Edwardian Church of England, but also its use of ceremonies that the puritans now deemed idolatrous. In Anthony Gilby's *A Pleasaunt Dialogue, Betweene a Souldier of Barwicke, and an English Chaplaine* (written in 1566), the chaplain expressed surprise that some ministers refused to wear vestments, since "in K. Edwardes dayes, this apparell was used of godlie men."[23] The Puritan solider replied that Edward's time "was but the firste shewe of the light, whereof thou talkest. Wee muste growe to further perfection."[24]

Even a separatist like Henry Barrow – who had spoken contemptuously of "pseudomartyres" in 1590 – could choose to talk this way about the martyred bishops of the Edwardian Church of England when it was to his

---

[18] Travers, *A full and plaine declaration*, a3r.   [19] Travers, *A full and plaine declaration*, a3r, b1r.

[20] Lake, *Anglicans and Puritans?*, 25–26; Stephen Brachlow, *The Communion of Saints: Radical Puritan and Separatist Ecclesiology 1570–1625* (Oxford, 1988), ch. 2; and White, *The English Separatist Tradition*, 16–18.

[21] Thomas Cartwright, *A Replye to an answere made of M. Doctor Whitegifte Againste the Admonition to the Parliament By T.C.* (Hemel Hempstead?, 1573; STC 4712), 7.

[22] *A parte of a register*, 32.   [23] Gilby, *A Pleasaunt Dialogue*, g8r.   [24] Gilby, *A Pleasaunt Dialogue*, g8r.

advantage.[25] While the bishops regularly invoked the Marian martyrs against presbyterians, presbyterians could also invoke the martyrs when battling separatists, demanding that the separatists admit the martyrs died in vain if the Church of England was (as the separatists claimed) a false church. In a 1590 pamphlet, for instance, George Gifford demanded to know whether the separatists "have greater light then eyther *Ridley, Cranmer, Howper, Bradford, Philpot, Taylor,* and other had?"[26] Barrow's rejoinder in 1591, true to form, denounced "the false ministerie or their corrupt ministration, adulterate sacraments, etc." which he described as "accursed in God's sight."[27] But later in his text, Barrow explained that the sin of these martyrs was accidental and excusable:

> The godly martyres so lately escaped out of that smokie fornace of the popish church, could not so clearely discerne, and sodenly enter into the heavenly and beautiful order of a true established church. It is more than one daye's worcke, to gather, to plante and establishe a church aright, much more so manie thowsand severall churches as are supposed in this land. It can be no wonder that those godly men being so unexpert and unexercised in his heavenly worcke, never having lived in, seene, or hearde of any orderly communion of sainctes, anie true established church upon earth of so many hundreth yeeres, ever since the general defection under Antichrist so much foretold of in the Scriptures, no marvaile, I say, if they erred in setting up the frame.[28]

In one neat move, Barrow nullified early English Protestant support for a popish church by classifying it as an excusable sin of ignorance. "The godly may sinne of ignorance, of negligence, of fraylety, yet not therupon untill obstinacie be added unto sinne, cease to be Christians ... We finde them obstinatly to have resisted no part of God's worde or truth he gave them sight of at anie tyme, but to have bene verie faithfull and constant even unto bandes and death in that truth they were come unto."[29] Barrow not only exculpated the martyrs here but praised them for having followed their

---

[25] On Barrow's view, see White, *The English Separatist Tradition,* 16–17.

[26] Gifford, *A Short Treatise,* 100.

[27] Henry Barrow, *A Plaine Refutation of M. G. Giffardes reprochful booke, intituled a short treatise against the Donatists of England* (1591), in Carlson (ed.), *The Writings of Henry Barrow, 1590–1591,* 280–281.

[28] Barrow, *A Plaine Refutation,* 323–324.

[29] Barrow, *A Plaine Refutation,* 323–324. John Canne would make a similar argument in *A Necessitie of Separation From the Church of England* (Amsterdam, 1634; STC 4574), when he claimed that Marian martyrs like Hooper and Bradford knew "corruptions to be in their *worship & ministrie,*" but that they did not fully appreciate the "kinde and degree" of these corruptions as later *"Nonconformists"* had done. Had they possessed this fuller knowledge and "known that these things were unlawfull and antichristian, and their *Church government* taken wholly from the *Pope*: I beleeve they would not have joyned in spirituall communion therewith" (191).

consciences according to the knowledge God had permitted them. Indeed, stressing their steadfastness in the face of danger enabled Barrow to claim the martyrs for the separatists and to wield them as a club against Gifford and the presbyterians. On Barrow's view, the presbyterians *knew* that the Elizabethan Church was antichristian, but unlike the Marian martyrs, the presbyterians were rank dissemblers and Nicodemites who refused to risk their lives and their livings to do what God required.[30]

In sum, Elizabethan presbyterians and separatists both attempted to legitimate their calls for reform by promulgating an essentially progressive account of the English Reformation in which God only slowly and gradually brought his elect out of popery.[31] The puritans themselves, conveniently enough, found themselves on the cutting edge of enlightenment according to this historical schema. The virtue of this approach – as White, Brachlow, and Lake have pointed out – was that it enabled these Elizabethan dissidents to criticize the failure of the martyrs to enact a full reformation, but at the same time exculpate them of wrongdoing and permit a celebration of their steadfast faith. When writing in this mode, presbyterians could affect a fascinating fusion of both antiquity and novelty. While presbyterians always claimed that their view of church government was the most ancient form, dating back to the Scriptures and the earliest church, in their own day they could also boldly claim that it was the most *avant-garde*, representing the newest stage in the unfolding work of the Holy Spirit in England. Thomas Cranmer himself had employed this sort of argument to explain away the English clergy's continuing affirmation of transubstantiation after the break with Rome, and it was perhaps only fitting that his ecclesiastical descendants would return the favor.[32]

---

[30] This is a theme throughout Barrow's *A Plaine Refutation*, but see especially 281–282.

[31] For yet another example, see the presbyterian bill presented to parliament in 1587, which explained that Henry VIII had reformed the church "as much as for the knowledge of that time was possible," and that Edward VI had introduced further reforms "attainyng unto a clearer knowledge of the true worship of god, by the further increase of that heavenlie light" but had been unable to reform the church fully "by reason of the innumerable deformities and corruptions, which he found yet remayning in the church, And allso of the shortnes of his Raigne" (Dr Williams's Library, MS Morrice B, p. 247). Since the beginning of Elizabeth's reign, "the light of gods florious gospell increasing dailie, by meanes of your highnes long, peaceable and blessed raigne, learned and zealous men have aswell out of the holie word of god as by the example of other best reformed churches, observed divers imperfections corruptions and repugnancies" (Dr Williams's Library, MS Morrice B, p. 248).

[32] Cranmer explained that "although the auctoritie of Rome was then newely ceassed, yet the darknes and blyndnesse of errours and ignoraunce that came frome Rome, styll remayned and overshadowed so this Realme, that a great noumbre of the parliament had not yet their eies opened to see the truthe": Thomas Cranmer, *An Answer*, 285–286. Earlier in the text, Cranmer made the same sort of argument to explain away aspects of Luther and Bucer's eucharistic theology that he currently rejected (16).

At times, then, the puritans depicted their movement as being of relatively recent vintage. But it has not been recognized that puritans could simultaneously tell a very different story about early English Protestantism, identifying "puritan" ancestors among the heroes and martyrs of the early English Reformation. Perhaps the most obvious figure for puritans to latch on to was William Turner, who was one of the living links between the Henrician radicals of the 1530s and 1540s and the Elizabethan radicals of the 1560s.[33] Up until his death in 1568, Turner had a well-deserved reputation for aggressive nonconformity and for his hostility toward the bishops. Bishop Berkeley complained in a March 1563 letter to Cecil that Turner, his Dean at Wells, had spoken against bishops from the pulpit, asking "who gave them autoritie, more over me, then I over them: eyther to forbidd me preachinge, or to depryve me: unless they have yt from their holy father the pope," while Archbishop Parker wrote to Cecil in April 1565 that Turner "hath enjoyned a comon adulterer to do his open penance in a square prests cap."[34] Unsurprisingly, therefore, Turner was praised by puritan authors for having suffered persecution at the hands of the Elizabethan bishops and he was lauded by the presbyterian compiler of *A Brieff discours off the troubles begonne at Franckford* as one of "the moste auncientest fathers of this oure owne countrie" who refused to "yelde or consent" to the popish abominations the bishops were forcing on the English clergy.[35]

Turner was praised by fellow puritans not merely for taking godly stands against the corruptions of the Elizabethan Church, however, but for the arguments he had made in the 1540s about the use of "popishe ceremonies, & ungodly tradiciones" in the Henrician Church.[36] The retention of traditional ceremonies in the Elizabethan Church of England was, of course, a massive point of contention for Elizabethan puritans, who regularly enumerated the hundreds of "popish remnants" that still remained.[37] As we saw in the preceding chapter, one of the standard puritan arguments against the use of traditional ceremonies and ornaments in the

---

[33] On the intellectual continuities between Turner's Henrician writings and the thought of Elizabethan puritans, see Knappen, *Tudor Puritanism*, 59–69; Jones, *William Turner*, 2–3, 17, 40, 138–141, 164, 201. My focus here is not on identifying ideological continuities per se, but rather on the ways in which Turner's writings were invoked and used by Elizabethan puritans.

[34] Lansdowne MS 8, f. 6r; Lansdowne MS 8, f. 141r.

[35] *A Second Admonition*, 25; *A Brieff discours*, 215.

[36] Turner, *The Rescuynge of the Romishe Fox*, b2v. On these arguments, see the discussion of Turner in Chapter 1.

[37] Gilby's *Pleasaunt Dialogue* contained "a short table" with "120. particular corruptions yet remaining in our saide Church, with sundrie other matters, necessarie to be knowen of all persons" (a1r).

Church of England was that Catholics viewed these things superstitiously (i.e., as inherently holy and as a necessary part of the worship of God and, therefore, necessary for salvation) and that they therefore must be abolished to testify to the doctrine of justification by faith alone. Conformists responded that the prince could command the use of traditional ceremonies and nullify any possible superstition by explicitly proclaiming that they had no holiness and were used purely for the sake of policy, order, and unity in the church. Puritans saw this as useless at best – papists would view them superstitiously no matter what the prince intended – and it became a central plank in the puritan critique that popish remnants could not be retained in the name of "policie."[38] When Anthony Gilby made this argument in 1566, he went out of his way to praise Turner as its originator:

> That olde Doctor Turner (reverende in other nations abroad for his great learning, and amongste the Godly at home, for his great zeale, his travailes, his perils so long sustayned, and his great constancie) did almoste thirtie yeares ago espie, and bewray unto the worlde, the crafte of Satan, that laboured to make poperie policie, and so to goe aboute to cure the wounde of the beast, which being in it self uncurable, shold yet in another beast be cured: who shoulde doe all things that the first beast could doe before him, and so, after a sort shoulde cause men to worship the first beast, whose deadly wounde, was in this seconde healed. His invention was pretie and pleasaunte, *of the croppeeared Foxe* [margin: "The name of D. Turners Booke"], who now was become the Kinges beast, and the Kinges game, that no man might hunt it: wherein he worthilie reproved that foolish policie.[39]

Gilby did not think that Turner had been ignorant or blinded by the mist of popery during the reign of Henry VIII. Quite the contrary, he had been exceptionally clear-sighted.

Turner's Henrician writings were not only being cited as a historical precedent by Elizabethan Puritans; they were also being mined for arguments. In a vitriolic reply to a sermon by Bishop Jewel, the puritan agitator William White and the presbyterian ringleader Thomas Wilcox (coauthor of the *Admonition to Parliament*) repeated word for word (and without attribution) the arguments made by Turner in the 1540s against canon law and popish ceremonies.[40] White and Wilcox discussed Jewel's claim that

---

[38] Gilby, *To my louynge brethren*, b3r; Gilby, *A Pleasaunt Dialogue*, e1v.

[39] Gilby, *A Pleasaunt Dialogue*, d7r-v. Here Gilby could have been referring to either Turner's *The huntyng & fyndyng out of the Romishe fox* or *The Rescuynge of the Romishe Fox*, as this language could be found in both.

[40] Cambridge University Library (CUL) MS Ee 2.34, ff. 15–18. For another copy, headed "Certaine griefs justly conceived of B Jewell's sermon with a brief Answer to some parte therof written by W. W. and drawne into forme by T. W.," see Doctor Williams's Library, MS Morrice B, pp. 605–609. White

clothing and forms abused by papists (like clerical vestments) had not been irrevocably tainted thereby, instead remaining "the good creatures of god" and free for Christians to use in the church.[41] By contrast, White and Wilcox claimed that the vestments had been given their "fasshion and forme" from Antichrist, and argued that the idea that the queen's commandment could annul these Antichristian properties was as ridiculous as

> if the Turke shold decree by lawes statuts and edits that all the ceremonies of moyses law as offering of calves Incense, oyle, and flower, and all Aarons attire should no more be taken for moyses ceremonies and Arons attire, but for his ceremonies and his attire, shold not moyses Ceremonies continuewe moyses ceremonies still and Arons holye garments continuewe Arons garments still, we think yea.[42]

Here, they were loosely quoting (and geographically relocating) Turner's *The huntyng & fyndyng out of the Romishe fox* (1543), where he wrote "If the kyng of denmark shuld set out a proclamation that all the ceremonies of Moses law as offering up of calves and frankincens shuld nomore becalled & taken for Moses ceremonies but for hys shuld not Moses ceremonies continue Moses ceremonies still for all the proclamation? I think so."[43] When White and Wilcox wrote that "no proclamacon law or statute dispossesse Antechrist the pope from his ceremonies ordinancs constitucons and attire, but loke what ceremonies ordinances constitutions and attire weare this xx^tie yeares agoo shalbe his ceremonies ordinancs constitucions and attire still though a Thowsand proclamacons should command the contrarye," they were again quoting Turner's statement in 1543 that "Then is theyr no proclamation that can disposses the the [sic] pope of hys ceremonies and constitutiones but the ceremonies & ordinances whiche was hys xii yere ago shall be hys ceremonies and ordinances still thoge a thousaud proclamationes shuld command the contrari."[44]

Turner was not the only Henrician evangelical who was being pressed into service for the puritan campaign for further reformation. *A Second Admonition to the Parliament* (1572) invoked as a precedent Henry Brinkelow's *The complaynt of Roderyck Mors*, first published in 1542, twice in 1548, again in 1560, and later to be partially reprinted (ominously) in

was also familiar with Turner's later writings, invoking Turner by name in a letter to Bishop Grindal in 1569 as an authority for the commonplace puritan argument that the bishops were placing greater emphasis on the enforcement of human laws and traditions than they were on God's laws. Dr Williams's Library, MS Morrice B, p. 604. White's loose quotation of Turner in the letter seems to have been from *The Hunting of the Fox and the Wolfe* (London, 1565; STC 24357), d1r.

[41] CUL MS Ee 2.34, f. 17v. [42] CUL MS Ee 2.34, f. 17v.
[43] Turner, *The huntyng & fyndyng out of the Romishe fox*, b8r.
[44] CUL MS Ee 2.34, f. 17v., *The huntyng & fyndyng out of the Romishe fox*, b8r.

1642.[45] Brinkelow's *Complaynt* was, in many respects, a congenial text for presbyterians: it claimed that every bishop was a little pope and urged Henry VIII that if he wished to "bannish for ever the antichryst the pope out of this reame, ye must fell downe to the grounde those rotten postes the bishops, which be cloudes without moisture."[46] Brinkelow went on to denounce the bishops' positions as temporal lords, to reject their civil jurisdictions, and to call for the confiscation of all episcopal wealth and an end to all degrees of clergy "but priestes and Bisshoppes as it was in the primative church."[47] Brinkelow – or rather his *nom de guerre* Roderike Mors – and William Turner would both reappear in rather elevated company in an anti-episcopal petition to the Parliament of 1587, listed alongside Calvin, Beza, Bullinger, Knox, and Hooper as historic opponents of the bishops.[48] Two years earlier, another Henrician evangelical – Richard Tracy – was assimilated to the puritan cause. In 1544, Tracy had called for the abolition of "Lordlye Bishops," an end to ecclesiastical courts, and an end to the employment of bishops in civil offices and royal service. Puritans were demanding the same things in 1585 when an unknown puritan discovered Tracy's *A supplication to our moste soveraigne Lord kynge henry the eyght* (1544) and republished it with new marginalia to ensure that readers recognized the applicability of Tracy's critiques to the Elizabethan Church: "Lordship of Bishops against Gods word in king Henrys days ergo nowe," "Lord bishops not sent from God," and "Annas and Cayphas exercising the office of civil magistrates judged Christ to death: so doo our Bishops."[49] Yet another puritan rediscovered Tracy's book in 1604 and intended to republish it as a way of turning the attention of the English people – and especially of their new king – to the evils of episcopacy, nonresidence, and pluralism. While the book was never reprinted, a manuscript copy of the new title page and preface found its way into Archbishop

[45] *A Second Admonition*, a2r.
[46] Henry Brinkelow, *The complaint of Roderyck Mors, somtime a gray Fryre, unto the parlament house of Ingland hys naturall countrey* (London, 1548?; STC 3760), g6v.
[47] Brinkelow, *The complaint of Roderyck Mors*, g8v.
[48] Dr Williams's Library, MS Morrice B, f. 128r. The petition's author(s) seem to have been aware that Rodericke Mors was a pseudonym, referring to "A learned man undre the name of Rhodoricke Mors." Also see Albert Peel (ed.), *The Seconde Parte of a Register* (Cambridge, 1915), 2.210.
[49] Richard Tracy, *A Supplication to our Moste Sovereigne Lorde Kyng Henry the eight* (London?, 1585; STC 24166). Apart from the new marginalia, nothing distinguished this Elizabethan edition from the 1544 edition. An early nineteenth-century reader of the copy owned by the Folger Shakespeare Library evidently thought this was a Henrician text until he or she read one of the new marginalia that mentioned "her Majestie," writing in pencil underneath that "The Book appears therefore to have been reprinted in Q. Eliz Time" (d2r). For these new marginalia, see Tracy, *A Supplication* (1585), c5v, c6v.

Bancroft's library.[50] The author, an avowed presbyterian "gentill man" and former Marian exile who had "ben in the reformed churches," thought this book provided strong support for the presbyterian cause and claimed that "whatsoever he speaketh of the dominion of the popish Bishoppes, non residentes & idoll preestes, is allso most true of ours."[51]

Brinkelow and Tracy were not, of course, the only early English Protestants whose writings were available to Elizabethan readers. In addition to surviving Henrician and Edwardian texts, and excerpts found in Foxe's *Acts and Monuments*, the collected works of William Tyndale, Robert Barnes, and John Frith were edited and published by Foxe in 1573; John Bale's massive commentary on Revelation, *The Image of Both Churches*, was reprinted in 1570; five editions of works by John Hooper were printed in London during the 1580s; and editions of Hugh Latimer's collected sermons were printed during every decade of Elizabeth's reign, and again under James I and Charles I.[52] Thomas Cartwright would draw on Foxe's 1573 edition of Tyndale, Barnes, and Frith in his defense of the *Admonition to Parliament* against John Whitgift in the later 1570s. When Cartwright penned *The second replie* (1575), he momentarily went beyond claims about the presbyterians having received "further light" by invoking William Tyndale and Robert Barnes in support of the central presbyterian claim that every congregation should have its own bishop/minister. Cartwright quoted Tyndale's critical account in *The practyse of Prelates* of how bishops, driven by ambition and greed as the church grew wealthier, "*made them substitutes, which they called preistes, and kept the name of Bishop unto them selves,*" perverting the original office of bishop and creating the system of episcopal hierarchy.[53] A few pages later, Carwright quoted statements by Barnes and John Hooper on this same issue.[54] Cartwright quoted

---

[50] LPL MS 806/2, ff. 127–135. The book's new title was to be "A supplication to Kinge Henrie the eight of noble memorie. Wherin, the lordships of Bishops, with ther pluralitans & idoll preests ar set forth in ther true colours, which was printed Anno 1544, and now newly sett forth, for the speciall use of our tyme ... Anno 1604" On the manuscript's provenance, see Richard Palmer, *A Catalogue of the Tenison Manuscripts (MSS 639–928d)* (at Lambeth Palace Library), 294.

[51] LPL MS 806/2, ff. 129v–132r.

[52] John Foxe (ed.), *The Whole workes of W. Tyndall, John Frith, and Doct. Barnes, three worthy Martyrs, and principall teachers of this Churche of England* (London, 1573; STC 24436); for Bale, see STC 1301; for Hooper, see STC 13743, 1219, 13756.5, 1221, 13751; for Latimer's sermons, see STC 15276–15283.5 (1562, 1572, 1575, 1578, 1584, 1596, 1607, 1635, 1636).

[53] Thomas Cartwright, *The second replie of Thomas Cartwright: agaynst Maister Doctor Whitgiftes second answer, touching the Churche Discipline* (Heidelberg, 1575; STC 4714), 521.

[54] Hooper was already a puritan favorite by the later 1570s, having been praised by the author of *A Second Admonition* and by other puritans for the stance he had taken on vestments under Edward VI. See Crowley, *A briefe discourse*, c2v; *A Second Admonition*, 35. On the basis of an undated Marian letter from Nicholas Ridley to Hooper, puritans claimed that Ridley had eventually come around to

Barnes's claim that "*I will never believe, nor can never believe, that one man maie by the lawe off God, be bishop off twoo or three cyties, yea off an whole contrey: for that yt is contrary to the doctrine of S. Paul, which writing unto Titus, commaundeth that he should ordeine a bishop in every towne,*" and Hooper's claim that "*the bishop should be bishop but of one citie . . . A great pitie it is to see, how far the office off a bishop is degenerated, from the originall in the scripture . . . there were more to doo for the best off them in one cytie, then he could doo. They know the primitive church had no such bishops untill the time off Silvester the first, &c.*"[55] Cartwright not only noted that Barnes and Hooper were "twoo of the moste famous men, which our lande browght forth thes manie yeares," but he also sought to associate their martyrdoms with the presbyterian movement when he cryptically remarked that one of these two martyrs "amongst other thinges, suffred also for this cause nowe in hande."[56]

Hooper's writings also proved useful to Cartwright when he defended the *Admonition*'s insistence that clergy must not hold civil offices. One of Whitgift's retorts to this claim had been the fact that Cranmer, Ridley, and Hooper had "consented unto" this practice. According to Cartwright, Whitgift was factually mistaken on this point: Hooper did not consent to this practice, but rather "it is manifest that he did flatly condemn it."[57] In his commentary on the Ten Commandments, Hooper had written that "*the Bishops for the space of 400 yeares after the Apostles, although they were more able then ours, did meddle with no civil affaires*" and "sharply taunteth our Bishop which meddleth with boeth offices, when one is *more then he is able, with al his diligence, to discharge, and impossible that he should doe boeth*: and that *if the Magistrate wil employ a Bishop in civil affaires, he owght to discharge him of his Ministery.*"[58] Cartwright immediately made the now-familiar progressive argument that "Yf M. Cranmer and Ridley did exercise boeth," then it was only because the "Sun of the gospel" had not yet

---

Hooper's view of the vestments, a claim that conformists staunchly contested. See chapter 5, fn. 126. For conformist interpretations of Ridley's stance, see Parker, *A briefe examination*, ******2v; Howard, *A defense of the ecclesiastical regiment*, 41–42.

[55] Cartwright, *The second replie*, 526–527. In the margin Cartwright cited, "In M. Foxes booke of Barnes, Tindall, &c. fol. 216. or there about. M. Hooper upon the 8. commaund. pag. 90." Hooper's commentary on the Ten Commandments was first published at Zurich in 1549 and then republished multiple times during Edward VI's reign: see STC 13746, 13749, 13750, 13750.5.

[56] Cartwright, *The second replie*, 526. These puritan invocations of Barnes have not been discussed in recent work on Barnes's posthumous reputation: Alec Ryrie, "'A saynt in the deuyls name': Heroes and Villains in the Martyrdom of Robert Barnes," in Freeman and Mayer (eds.), *Martyrs and Martyrdom in England c. 1400–1700*, 144–165; Maas, *The Reformation and Robert Barnes*.

[57] Thomas Cartwright, *The rest of the second replie of Thomas Cartwrihgt: agaynst Master Doctor Whitgifts second answer, touching the Church discipline* (Basel, 1577; STC 4715), 30.

[58] Cartwright, *The rest of the second replie*, 30.

dispersed the clouds of popery, but while this exculpation served a formal purpose, it rang somewhat hollow coming immediately after his praise of Hooper for condemning the clergy's civil occupations.[59] While Cartwright depicted *some* early English Protestants as fumbling their way through the dissipating smoke of popery, he was also keen to note that some had already seen the light.

Cartwright's introduction of Tyndale, Barnes, and Hooper into the self-referential world of presbyterian polemic marked the beginning of what would become a sustained and increasingly elaborate attempt to create an early English Protestant pedigree for the presbyterian movement. The most organized effort along these lines began in the late 1580s, orchestrated by the circle of presbyterians associated with the notorious Martin Marprelate tracts: John Udall, John Penry, and Job Throckmorton.[60] Udall sought to enlist early English Protestants as supporters of the presbyterian cause in *A Demonstration of the trueth of that Discipline*, printed late in the summer of 1588 at East Molesey by Penry and Robert Waldegrave, shortly before the first Marprelate tract was printed on the same press.[61] In defending the presbyterian claim that every congregation was to have one bishop with "equall authoritie in their severall charges, & in the generall governement of the Churche," Udall reproduced Cartwright's quotations from Barnes and Hooper to make the same point.[62] Udall left East Moseley before Waldgrave and Penry began to print the Marprelate tracts, but Penry and

---

[59] Cartwright, *The rest of the second replie*, 30.

[60] Joseph Black has commented on the use of early English Protestants in the Marprelate tracts, but here I expand on Black's discussion by showing that the circle of Puritans behind Marprelate had experimented with this strategy before the Marprelate tracts and would continue and indeed expand their efforts in the years after the Marprelate tracts. See Joseph L. Black (ed.), *The Martin Marprelate Tracts: A Modernized and Annotated Edition* (Cambridge, 2008), xxix–xxx; on the relationship between Udall, Penry, and Throckmorton and their role in the Marprelate project, see xxxiv–xlviii.

[61] John Udall, *A Demonstration of the trueth of that Discipline, which Christe hath prescribed in his worde for the governement of his Church, in all times and places, untill the ende of the worlde* (East Molesey, 1588; STC 24499); Black (ed.), *The Martin Marprelate Tracts*, l–li.

[62] Udall, *A Demonstration*, 52. While Hooper's commentary on the Ten Commandments had been reprinted by Waldegrave in 1588 and, given Udall's presence with Waldgrave at East Molesey in 1588, he presumably had direct access to the freshly printed text, internal evidence makes it almost certain that Udall copied these quotations directly from Cartwright's *Second replie*. Udall acknowledges his dependence on existing presbyterian literature in the preface (*A Demonstration*, c4v), but his direct dependence on Cartwright's *Second replie* for these quotations is demonstrated by an error Udall made when attributing the quotation from Barnes. With an imprecision that modern scholars struggling to find a reference will recognize, Cartwright had attributed Barnes's quotation to "M. Foxes booke of Barnes, Tindall, &c. fol. 216. or there about" (it was actually on p. 210). When Udall quoted the same passage from Barnes, he attributed the quotation to "Acts and Monuments. fol. 216" (*A Demonstration*, 52). Udall's confusion regarding exactly which book by Foxe this quote came from, combined with his use of the same page number supplied by Cartwright, clinches the case.

Throckmorton – or, rather, Martin Junior – continued the strategy of invoking early English Protestants in the fifth Marprelate pamphlet, *Theses Martinianae* (July 1589).[63] Martin Junior claimed that "the hierarchy of bishops, in their superiority over their brethren, and their civil offices, hath been gainsaid and withstood by the visible church of God successively and without intermission for these almost 500 years last past."[64] Like Cartwright had done, Martin directly challenged the conformists' ownership of the Marian bishop martyrs by asserting that "this cause of overthrowing the state of lord bishops, and bringing in the equality of ministers, is no new cause, but that which hath been many years ago held and maintained, even in the fire, by the holy martyrs of Christ Jesus."[65] Martin proceeded to demonstrate this case with theses drawn from "the doctrine which the blessed martyrs of Christ Jesus Master Tyndale, Master Doctor Barnes, and Master Frith taught" before their martyrdoms in the reign of Henry VIII.[66] According to Martin, "this wicked government of bishops was an especial point gainsaid by the servants of God in the time of King Henry the eight, and Queen Mary," and he directly attributed the deaths of "the holy martyrs" to "the withstanding whereof."[67] By claiming that the martyrs had really been on the presbyterian side, Martin Junior was inverting rather than dodging the argument that the conformists had been wielding for decades against the puritan critics of the Church of England.

In reality, as Joseph Black has shown in his meticulous edition of the Marprelate tracts, Martin Junior based his subsequent theses on Tyndale's writings.[68] Thesis 57, for instance, quoted Tyndale's claim in his "*Practise for Prelates*" (first published in 1530) that "it is not possible that naturally there can be any good lord bishop."[69] Sometimes Martin took a statement of principle from Tyndale, applied it to the circumstances of the Elizabethan Church, and then stated what he assumed Tyndale would

[63] Recognizing the development and elaboration of this new line of historical argument in *Theses Martinianae* qualifies the conventional wisdom that the Marprelate tracts "made no original contributions" to the presbyterian platform, with Marprelate's originality laying instead "in his polemical aggressiveness, not his ecclesiology" (Black, *The Marprelate Tracts*, xix). On this point, also see Lander, *Inventing Polemic*, 89–90; Ritchie D. Kendall, *The Drama of Dissent: The Radical Poetics of Nonconformity, 1380–1590* (Chapel Hill and London, 1986), 173–176; Joad Raymond, *Pamphlets and Pamphleteering in Early Modern Britain* (Cambridge, 2003), 27–28; Lake and Questier, *Antichrist's Lewd Hat*, 509.

[64] *Theses Martinianae* in Black (ed.), *The Martin Marprelate Tracts*, 152.

[65] *Theses Martinianae* in Black (ed.), *The Martin Marprelate Tracts*, 152.

[66] *Theses Martinianae* in Black (ed.), *The Martin Marprelate Tracts*, 152.

[67] *Theses Martinianae* in Black (ed.), *The Martin Marprelate Tracts*, 152.

[68] See Black (ed.), *The Martin Marprelate Tracts*, 269–271.

[69] *Theses Martinianae* in Black (ed.), *The Martin Marprelate Tracts*, 153.

have said. Thesis 59, for instance, claimed that "our bishops are none of the Lord's anointing, but servants of the Beast," which Black suggests was based on Tyndale's statement in *The Obedience of a Christian Man* (not quoted by Martin) that "Bishops and priestes that preach not, or that preach, ought save Gods word, are none of Christes, nor of hys annoyntyng: but servauntes of the beast whose marke they beare."[70] Over the course of nearly forty theses, Martin used Tyndale to argue that a bishop (i.e., parish minister) should be restricted to preaching alone (Thesis 64); that "all civil rule and dominion is by the word of God flatly forbidden unto the clergy" (Thesis 67); that "bishops ought to have no prisons wherein to punish transgressors" (Thesis 71); that the Church Fathers "knew of no authority that one bishop should have above another, neither thought, or once dreamed, that ever any such thing should be" (Thesis 73); that the word "priest" was popish (Theses 75–77); that "there ought to be no other manner of ecclesiastical censure but that which is noted, Matt. 18:15, 17, which is, to proceed from a private admonition, to one or two witnesses, and thence to the church, that is, not to one, but unto the governors of the church, together with the whole congregation" (Thesis 81); that people should refuse to appear in the bishops's courts and ignore their prohibitions on preaching (Theses 83, 85, 86); and that non-preaching clergy, pluralists, and nonresidents must be abolished (Theses 91–92).[71] By the time Martin was finished, it appeared that Tyndale, Barnes, and Frith were practically presbyterians.

In invoking and quoting Tyndale, Barnes, and Frith, Martin Junior was not merely arguing that these luminaries of Henrician Protestantism would have been critics of the Elizabethan Church. Instead, he was also making the far more sweeping and unusual claim that "this doctrine of theirs is now to be accounted the doctrine of the church of England," and that the English people were bound by statute law "to disavow and withstand the places and callings of lord bishops."[72] The argument went like this: when the writings of Tyndale, Barnes, and Frith had been republished in Elizabeth's reign by John Foxe, they had been published *cum privilegio*. According to Martin Junior, this meant that the doctrine they taught "is also to be accounted the doctrine of faith and sacraments in the church of England, and so is approved by statute."[73] Hence, before his nearly forty theses from

---

[70] *Theses Martinianae* in Black (ed.), *The Martin Marprelate Tracts*, 153; *Obedience* quoted from 269n28.
[71] *Theses Martinianae* in Black (ed.), *The Martin Marprelate Tracts*, 153–155.
[72] *Theses Martinianae* in Black (ed.), *The Martin Marprelate Tracts*, 152.
[73] *Theses Martinianae* in Black (ed.), *The Martin Marprelate Tracts*, 153.

Tyndale, Martin Junior wrote that "upon these former grounds we may safely hold these conclusions following, and are thereby allowed by statute, and her Majesty's prerogative."[74] As Black notes, this was "a dubious argument, even by the standards of Renaissance polemic," and conformist critics like Matthew Sutcliffe simply dismissed it, writing in 1595 that "the words *Seene & allowed*, which are prefixed before divers pamphlets have no other force, then to signifie that they are allowed to bee printed, not allowed for law or trueth."[75] Black suggests that Martin's argument on this point "might not have been made entirely in earnest," but while this is certainly plausible given the Marprelate family's consistently jocular tone, it was certainly more than a joke.[76] Other evidence suggests that the men behind Marprelate, as well as those influenced by him, took this argument quite seriously and were willing to stake much upon it. In 1593, Penry and Francis Johnson made this argument in letters sent to Burghley while imprisoned in the Fleet. Penry wrote to Burghley in April 1593 that

> If this statute of 23 Eliz. be against such boks as reprove the church govern-
> ment by L: ArchB[s] and B[s], then it accompteth the former profession and
> wryting of the holie martirs As of M[r] Wicliffe, Thorpe, Swinderby. L:
> Cobham, Tindall, Frith &c. the profession and practise of the reformed
> churches, of the noble Kings of Ffraunce and Scotland together with the
> wrytings of Ma[r] Calvin Beza and others, to be within the compasse of
> sedisious wordes and rumors uttered againste the Queenes most excellent
> Majestie and to the stirring up of rebellion amongst her subjects, And so the
> printing publishing and selling of theis bookes is also within the compasse of
> this statute, whereas manie of theis bookes are seene and allowed and
> published by her Majesties royall priviledge.[77]

---

[74] *Theses Martinianae* in Black (ed.), *The Martin Marprelate Tracts*, 153.
[75] Quoted in Black (ed.), *The Martin Marprelate Tracts*, 144. Also see Sutcliffe's critique of this claim in *An Answere to a Certaine Libel* (London, 1592; STC 23450), 69, 159.
[76] Black (ed.), *The Martin Marprelate Tracts*, 144.
[77] Lansdowne MS 75, f. 54r. Penry had also made the same argument in *A Treatise Wherein is Manifestlie Proved, That Reformation and Those that sincerely favor the same, are unjustly charged to be enemies, unto hir Majestie, and the state* (Edinburgh, 1590; STC 19612), published after the seizure of the Marprelate press, and written in neither Martin's persona nor his satirical style. Here Penry wrote that Lollards and "Our owne martyrs as M. Tindall, M. Barnes, M. Hooper, have so disliked this government of Bb. as no men more. This doctrine of theirs being according unto the worde, they sealed with their blood, and is now acknowledged the doctrine of our church" (i2v). The argument reappeared in *A petition directed to her most excellent Majestie* (Middelburg, 1592; STC 1521), attributed to either Penry or Throckmorton, where the author discussed sermons of Hugh Latimer that argued against bishops holding civil office, concluding: "His Sermons contayning this matter, are publikelie to bee solde with authoritie, testified in these wordes: *Seene and allowed according to the order of the Queenes injunctions*. And *Matthew Sutcliffe* saieth, That bookes which passe with this approbation, do conteyne nothing contrarie to the State of this realme. Therefore it were straunge that the Seekers

Francis Johnson made the same argument to Burghley in 1593, claiming that if it violated the law to "reprove the ecclesiasticall ministery and government of archbyshops, lord bishops, archdeacons, deanes, etc.," then works like Tyndale's *Obedience of a Christian Man* and *The Practice of Prelates*, Frith's *Antithesis between Christ and the Pope*, Foxe's *Acts and Monuments*, and the printed confessions of foreign Reformed churches should also be illegal.[78] Tyndale and Frith "helde that archbishops, lord byshops, archdeacons, deanes, officialls, parsons, vicars, and the rest of that sorte are the disciples of Antechriste, yea, very Antechrists themselves," yet their books were "allowed by publicke authoritye and printed by priviledge of Her Majestye."[79] However unpersuasive this argument might seem to modern and (at least some) Elizabethan readers, it seems doubtful that Penry and Johnson would have sought assistance from one of the most powerful men in England using an argument that they intended as a joke. As they knew, and as Penry learned the hard way in May 1593, they were arguing for their lives.

This effort to provide a historical pedigree for the presbyterian movement did not end with Martin Junior. After the authorities tracked down the Marprelate press, and Penry and Waldgrave fled to Scotland, the former Marprelate conspirators continued to search for presbyterian precedents in the history of the English Reformation.[80] In a 1590 pamphlet defending presbyterianism against Richard Bancroft, Penry again sent Tyndale into the field to do battle against clerical hierarchy: "it would be knowne, what account M. Bancroft maketh of that notable martyr M. Tindale, which speaking of priests and Bb. hath these words: ther is presbyteros, which same is saith he, imediatly after called a Bishop: and in the same place, all that were Elders or priests (if they so will) were called Bishops also, though they have devided the name now."[81] Penry further invoked Tyndale to criticize Bancroft's defense of the title "priest" for the Church of England's ministers, arguing that Bancroft was allying himself with papists like Sir Thomas More rather

> then with M. Tindale, and the most sincere professours in the world at this day, in abrogating that popishe name, and using the worde Minister, or Elder in the steade thereof . . . the reader shal learne out of M. Tindale,

of Reformation should suffer as felons, for writing against the civill offices of Bishops against their authoritie in the Parliament, in the Councell, and such like civill places, seeing writings to that effect be seene solde and allowed as not prejudiciall to our estate, neither diffamatorie to hir Majestie" (38).

[78] Leland H. Carlson (ed.), *The Writings of John Greenwood and Henry Barrow, 1591–1593* (London, 2003), 464. For the original text, see Lansdowne MS 75, ff. 52–53.

[79] Carlson (ed.), *The Writings of John Greenwood and Henry Barrow, 1591–1593*, 463, 465.

[80] For the chronology, see *ODNB*.

[81] John Penry, *A Briefe Discovery of the Untruthes and Slanders (Against the True Governement of the Church of Christ) contained in a Sermon, preached the 8. of Februarie 1588 by D. Bancroft* (Edinburgh, 1590; STC 19603), 52.

who in his obedience of a Christian man sayth, that the worde Sacerdos, should have had another name in english, then priest, but that Antichrist hath deceived us with unknowne and strange termes, to bring us into superstitious blindnes, as for the word presbyteros saith he (both in this place, and against Moore in the place above cited) it ought in English, to bee translated Elder.[82]

Aligning themselves with glorious martyrs like Tyndale not only granted legitimacy to the presbyterians, therefore; it also enabled them to associate their opponents with full-blooded papist persecutors like More.

Penry was also attempting to expand his repertoire of historical precedents for "the cause" while in Scotland. In a second pamphlet published in exile from Edinburgh, Penry began with a request to his readers:

> M. D. Haddon delivered in Parliament [margin: "Anno 12. or 13 Elizab."] a Latine book concerning church discipline, written in the dayes of king Ed. 6. by M. Cranmer, & Sir John Cheek knight &c. This book was committed by the house to be translated unto the said M. Hadon, M. George Bromely, M. Norton, &c. If thou canst good reader help me, or any other that labour in the cause unto the said book: I hope (though I never saw it,) that in so doing thou shalt doe good service unto the Lord and his Church.[83]

Penry was referring to the *Reformatio Legum Ecclesiasticarum*, compiled in 1553 by Cranmer and leading members of the Edwardian Protestant establishment, which aimed to create a new legal and institutional framework for the Church of England. The project failed to gain support before Edward VI's death but, as Penry knew, it was revived in the parliament of 1571, discussed, and then dropped. While apparently unaware of its contents at the time, Penry presumably thought that if it had been rejected by parliament (as several of his own parliamentary petitions for the discipline had been), it would surely provide support for "the cause."

This historical strategy reached a new pitch in *A petition directed to her most excellent Maiestie*, first published in 1591 and then republished the following year. The text has been variously attributed to either Throckmorton or Penry, but whichever one was the true author, the pamphlet is clearly a product of the Marprelate circle.[84] *A petition* continued

---

[82] Penry, *A Briefe Discovery*, 52–53.

[83] Penry, *A Treatise Wherein is Manifestlie Proved*, ¶2v. This pamphlet included a range of quotations from late medieval figures, drawn largely from the writings of John Bale and Foxe's *Acts and Monuments*. Other purported supporters of the discipline were invoked without supporting documentation, like Martin Luther, of whom Penry said his views were "sufficiently knowne" (i2v).

[84] *A petition directed to her most excellent Maiestie* (1591; STC 1522a), reprinted the following year (STC 1521). All subsequent quotations are taken from the 1592 edition.

to adduce early English Protestant precedents and, to a greater extent than Marprelate or Penry had done in previous texts, provided extensive quotations to support its claims. John Wyclif, who was referred to as "that famous protestant,"[85] was quoted extensively: clergy "*may not rule like civill Lordes . . . no Prelate ought to have any prison to punishe offendours*" and "*no King should impose uppon any Bishop or Curate any secular matter.*"[86] Most ominously for the bishops, *A petition* quoted Wyclif's claim that "*It is lawfull for Princes to take from ministers their temporall livings, if they get a habite or custome in abusing them.*"[87] The Lollard William Swinderby was quoted from Foxe's *Acts and Monuments* as holding that "*the more Lordship a Priest hath, the neerer he is to Antichrist,*" and *Piers Plowman* and Chaucer were also quoted for opposition to lordly bishops.[88] After these late medieval "protestants," the now familiar cast of early English evangelicals also appeared. The "renowmed professor of the Gospell Maister *Tindall*" was quoted as writing "*That it was a shame of all shames, and a monstrous thing, that Bishops should deale in civill causes.*"[89] Like Cartwright had done, *A petition* continued the strategy of linking the martyrdom of these evangelicals with their hostility to bishops, pairing Barnes's claim that it violated divine law for a man to "*be Bishop of two or three cities, or of a whole Countrie*" with the marginal gloss "*Barnes against Ll. Bishops. He witnessed this article with his bloud.*"[90] John Hooper – identified only as a martyr, with no mention of the fact that he was also a bishop – was boldy cited as a Protestant who wrote "against the protestant Bb. under King *Edwarde* the sixt," especially against the service of bishops in civil offices: "*If he be so necessarie for the Court that in civill causes he can not bee spared, let him use that vocation and spare the other. It is not possible he should doe both well. It is a great oversight in Princes thus to charge them with two burthens.*"[91] If Hooper were alive at the present day, the author noted, "hee might peradventure (if some had their will) be martyred once againe."[92]

A new luminary was added to the list as well: Hugh Latimer, easily the most famous preacher of the English Reformation and the only Marian martyr who could rival Cranmer and Ridley in prestige. *A petition* quoted and glossed Latimer over the space of three pages, beginning with Latimer's resignation of his bishopric in the early 1540s. Latimer had been "a Bishop in King Henrie the eight his time, but he gave over his Bishoprike (as also *Shaxton*, Bishop of Salisburie did at the same time) being divested of his Bishoplike habite, *he skipped for joy* (as Maister Foxe reporteth) *feeling his*

---

[85] *A petition*, 49. [86] *A petition*, 34. [87] *A petition*, 49. [88] *A petition*, 34–35.
[89] *A petition*, 35. [90] *A petition*, 35. [91] *A petition*, 35–36. [92] *A petition*, 36.

shoulders so light, and being discharged (as he said) *of so heavie a burthen.*"[93] *A petition* then proceeded to quote extensively from Latimer's Edwardian sermons, which had been republished in 1584, quoting especially his criticisms of lordly bishops and his attacks on the temporal duties of the clergy: "*Let the Priest preache, and let the Noble man handle temporall matters.*"[94] There was no question in the author's mind about which side Latimer would have joined had he lived to see the Elizabethan Church: "Thus Puritan-like wrote Father Latimer, the famous martyr, yet hee was never esteemed a troubler of the state, a Mar-prince, and a diffamer of the Kinge, though in deede he was a *Mar-bishop and Mar-prelate.*"[95]

A petition aimed not only to reveal these Henrician and Edwardian "puritans" and "Marprelates" to its audience, however, but more broadly to craft a narrative of the English Reformation in which Elizabethan puritans represented the traditional English mainstream from which the bishops and their supporters had allegedly departed. According to *A petition*, English law and England's bishops had until recently demanded further reformation. Henry VIII had known that the ecclesiastical laws of England "were corrupt" and had established a commission to sift the good from the bad and create a new ecclesiastical law. If Penry was indeed the author of *A petition*, he had finally obtained the copy of the *Reformatio Legum Ecclesiasticarum* that he had been seeking because he wrote (with corresponding page numbers listed in the margin) that "They collected into one booke many good things . . . which are directly contrarie to the practise and orders of the moderne Bishops."[96] As Cranmer had overseen this commission, this proved that conformist efforts to sanctify the current ecclesiastical order with Cranmer's memory were illegitimate, because "D. Cranmer & the former Bb. mislike many things in our present state."[97] Indeed, in Cranmer's *Book of Common Prayer* "there is prescribed a *Commination* to bee used at a certeine time in the yeare: not to continewe ever, but till an *order of Discipline practised in the primitive Church be restored*, which were greatly to bee wished, as the authours of that booke doe saye. Yet this Commination standeth, and the Discipline there mentioned, is yet wanting."[98] This only further proved that "*The lawe expecteth another kinde of discipline then is yet used.*"[99]

Cranmer was not the only bishop to be enlisted against the Elizabethan bishops, however, as the author explained that "Touching the state of

---

[93] *A petition*, 36.   [94] *A petition*, 37.   [95] *A petition*, 37–38.
[96] *A petition*, 4. It had been published in 1571 (STC 6006).   [97] *A petition*, 4.   [98] *A petition*, 5.
[99] *A petition*, 5.

Bb. divers who nowe most egerlie defende [the bishops], when they were nearest to God, that is, in miserie & anguishe of soule, did speake against it: but afterwarde inclining to the worlde, with their conditions they altered their opinions."[100] The greatest polemical effect was achieved by citing "The writings of the Bb. them selves" as a prime reason why presbyterians supported government by elders.[101] *A petition* quoted John Aylmer, an anti-puritan hammer in the 1580s as Bishop of London and sharply ridiculed by Martin Marprelate, who had written in 1559 (before becoming a bishop) that bishops should give up the bulk of their wealth to the queen and that civil and ecclesiastical offices should not be confused.[102] Bishop Bullingham of Gloucester was given similar treatment for statements he had made before becoming a bishop, leading the author of *A petition* to conclude that "This doublinge by such as defende the Hierarchie, must needs cast great doubtes in the hartes of all men."[103] *A petition* devoted particular attention to the anti-Catholic polemics of bishops like Jewel, Nowell, and Bilson. Writing against Catholics, Nowell had claimed "*that Christ refused pompe, riches and dominions, when the Divell offered them. Hee denyed his kingdome to be of this worlde, and forbad his trew Disciples the possession of such riches and worldly dominions, as the Pope nowe claymeth. In another place, Christ forbad his Ministers all Dominion and worldly governement,* Mat. 20. And againe, *S. Peter forbiddeth Ministers to exercise Dominions or Lordship over their flockes.*"[104] The author claimed that "This manner of reasoning against the papistes hath incensed me vehemently against L. Bb. If these reasons be not good, Maister *Jewell,* Maister *Nowell,* and D. *Bilson* have much to answere."[105] The irony of this was that when the Catholic exile Thomas Dorman had written a pamphlet against Nowell in 1565, Dorman had warned Nowell that "you harpe so muche upon this string of making bisshoppes and priestes equall" when attacking papal supremacy, that "if youre Archebishoppes and bishoppes loke not in time: I thinke those goodfelowe ministres, shoemakers, wevers, tinkers, broomemen, coweherdes, fidlers etc, whome youre bishoppes have made equall to you that be

---

[100] *A petition*, 7.   [101] *A petition*, 15.

[102] *A petition*, 7–8. The quotations were taken from Aylmer's 1559 defense of Elizabeth and had been previously deployed in the early 1570s by the presbyterians Thomas Wilcox and William White, who claimed that they did not desire "any other thing" but the implementation of Aylmer's critique of the bishops' "pompus lyvinges and lordlye tytles": CUL MS Ee 2.34, f. 16v.. This was an accusation against Aylmer that would stick. Patrick Simon would cite this passage from *A Petition* in his *Informations, or a protestation, and a treatise from Scotland. Seconded with D. Reignoldes his letter to Sir Francis Knollis. And Sir Francis Knollis his speach in Parliament. All suggesting the usurpation of papal bishops* (1608; STC 14084), 69–70.

[103] *A petition*, 9.   [104] *A petition*, 10–11.   [105] *A petition*, 11.

inferiour ministres, yow of youre goodnes will shortly make equall to youre bishoppes and archebishoppes."[106] Dorman died in 1577, but he would have been delighted to learn that Nowell's chickens had come home to roost.

For puritans, this historical strategy had distinct advantages over the alternatives. In 1641, John Milton would unflinchingly call Cranmer and Ridley "halting and time-serving *Prelates*," who along with Latimer "suffer'd themselvs to be the common stales to countenance with their prostituted Gravities every Politick Fetch that was then on foot, as oft as the Potent *Statists* pleas'd to employ them."[107] Few Elizabethan puritans, writing with the Marian fires still smoldering in the Protestant imagination, were willing or wanted to say such things about the Oxford martyrs. While claims to have received "greater light" enabled puritans to implicitly criticize but not condemn figures like Cranmer and Ridley, it also effectively abandoned the early English Reformation – and the prestige of its martyrs – to their conformist opponents. As Thomas Freeman has noted, the importance of martyrology in early modern England ensured that "Each English confession and denomination viewed its past through a martyrological lens that magnified persecution, suffering and heroism."[108] Identifying a different set of Protestant martyrs as their spiritual ancestors enabled presbyterians to offer a stronger response to the reproach offered by martyr-bishops like Cranmer and Ridley. Rather than simply deflecting these examples, the ability to cite distinguished English martyrs who had called archbishops "Antichrists" enabled presbyterians to respond in kind and turn the conformists' rhetoric back around against them. As one presbyterian put it, to affirm that "the hierarchie now used in England . . . is right as it should be" would require him to condemn not only the leading Reformed divines on the continent as "heritiks" but also "Mr Tindall D. Barnes Latimer Hooper Bradford &c which have bine hitherto taken for blessed martires."[109] At a

[106] Dorman, *A Disproufe*, 72v-73r.
[107] John Milton, *Of Reformation Touching Church-Discipline in England: And the Causes that hitherto have hindred it* (London?, 1641; Wing M2134), 10. Also see the condemnations levied in Henry Hickman, *Plus Ultra, or, Englands Reformation, Needing to be Reformed. Being an Examination of Doctor Heylins History of the Reformation of the Church of England* (London, 1661; Wing H1913), 22; Smectymnuus, *An Answer to a Booke Entituled, An Humble Remonstrance* (London, 1641; Wing M748), 102–103.
[108] Freeman, "Over their Dead Bodies," 31. Scholars have discussed how the compilation and publication in 1593 of John Field's register of "persecuted" Puritans was an imitation of Foxe's *Acts and Monuments* (a comparison drawn even at the time by the bishops), but the evidence presented here suggests that the puritan martyrological project was even more extensive, with some puritans trying to claim virtually the entire company of early English Protestant martyrs as proponents of their cause.
[109] LPL MS 453, f. 39r.

time when the political support that presbyterians had enjoyed was rapidly eroding, it was a remarkable (and desperate) attempt to reclaim legitimacy.

This historical strategy seems to have crossed the highly permeable boundary between presbyterianism and separatism along with its proponent John Penry. By 1593, Penry had joined the separatist congregation in London and quickly found himself in prison. When Penry was examined on 10 April 1593 about his participation in separatist services, one of his examiners Henry Fanshaw said, "It is strange unto me, that yow hold such opinions (Penry) as none of the learned of this age, or any of the martyrs of former times mainteined. Can yow shew any writers, either old or new, that have bene of your judgement?" Perhaps no one was better prepared to answer this question, of course, and Penry proceeded to name Wyclif, several prominent Lollards, and then Tyndale, Lambert, Barnes, and Latimer, who were "the lordes most blessed witnesses of this latter age."[110] As noted earlier in this chapter, Penry and Francis Johnson also claimed precedents among Henrician Protestants in letters to Cecil, with Johnson insisting that his congregation's separation from the Church of England had "expresse warraunte and commandment" from Scripture, the confessions of other Reformed churches, and "the testimony of many faithfull and worthie martirs in former ages," specifically "Mr. Tindall, Mr. Frithe, Mr. Wickliffe, etc."[111]

Penry was executed in May 1593 for his involvement with the Marprelate Tracts, but Johnson would remain in prison until April 1597. While in prison, Johnson published a lengthy defense of separation against the criticisms of the puritan minister Arthur Hildersham. To bolster his case against the Church of England, Johnson devoted three pages to quoting George Joye's commentary on the Old Testament book of Daniel, first published in 1545 and then twice republished in 1550. Joye explained that Antichrist was at work in the Church of England during the 1540s, elevating his own "law and tradition to be observed above Gods lawes," suppressing the true gospel, making holy days, filling the church with Antichristian "rites, ceremonies, and traditions," trying to thrust Christ together with the

---

[110] *The Examinations of Henry Barrowe John Grenewood and John Penrie, before the high commissioners, and Lordes of the Counsel. Penned by the prisoners themselves before their deathes* (Dort?, 1596?; STC 1519), c3r.

[111] Johnson to Burleigh, 2 June 1593, in Carlson (ed.), *The Writings of John Greenwood and Henry Barrow, 1591–1593*, 437–438. Christopher Hill noted this citation of Tyndale by Johnson, though he misdated it to 1590: Christopher Hill, "William Tyndale and English History," in *Intellectual Origins of the English Revolution Revisited* (Oxford, 1997), 312.

Pope, and a range of other abominations.[112] To Johnson, Joye was critiquing precisely the problems that he had identified in the Elizabethan Church of England: "Thus wrote and judged those blessed servants of God long synce. And as now we see these things were truly said of the prelates and other Clergy of that age, howsoever few then durst or would professe it: so certainely the ages to come will see it to have ben truly found in the Prelacy and other ministery of this age, notwithstanding that few now dare or will acknowledg it."[113] Here Johnson used Joye's critique of the Henrician Church to provide historical depth to his own stance, but by defining Joye as one a "few" voices crying in the wilderness, he also legitimated the minority position of separatists like himself and his congregation.

After his release from prison, Johnson served as the pastor of the English separatist congregation in Amsterdam, and in this capacity he would again turn to early English Protestants for aid in his 1600 pamphlet exchange with the non-separating puritan Henry Jacob.[114] Johnson was persistently annoyed by Jacob's constant invocation of the martyrs against the separatists, asking Jacob "whether every of your Replies have not this for their foundation and undersong, *M. Cranmer M. Ridley, &c.* as if for our faith and worship of God, we should turne from the living God to dead men."[115] Johnson stressed the authority of Scripture and made a series of arguments that Cranmer and Ridley – notwithstanding their errors committed in ignorance – were in fact closer in spirit to the separatists than to the Elizabethan Church.[116] But near the end of his reply, Johnson set aside his attempt to enlist Cranmer and Ridley and focused instead on "speaches and testimonies" of other martyrs.[117] Johnson wrote that "William Tindall and John Frith published, *That Archbishops, Lordb. Archdeacons, Deanes, Officials, Parsons, Vicars, and the rest of that sort, are the disciples of Antichrist, yea very Antichrists themselves,*" and elsewhere he quoted Tyndale's claim that Augustine, Jerome, Cyprian, Chrysostom, and Bede "*knew of none authority that one Bishop should have above another, neyther thought or once dreamed that ever any such should be.*"[118] Johnson recycled the quotations from Hooper about bishops in the primitive church that had appeared in Cartwright, Udall, and Penry's writings and then added to this now

[112] Johnson, *A Treatise of the Ministery*, 24–25.   [113] Johnson, *A Treatise of the Ministery*, 25–26.
[114] Francis Johnson, *An Answer to Maister H. Jacob His Defence of the Churches and Ministery of England* (Amsterdam?, 1600; STC 14658).
[115] Johnson, *An Answer to Maister H. Jacob*, 10.
[116] Johnson, *An Answer to Maister H. Jacob*, 29–30, 40–41, 48–49.
[117] Johnson, *An answer to Maister H. Jacob*, 162.   [118] Johnson, *An answer to Maister H. Jacob*, 164, 183.

established package of precedents several new quotations from John Bale, who was a fellow "exile for the testimonie of Jesu."[119] Bale's *Image of Both Churches* was quoted repeatedly: "*What other els* (saith he) *is Pope, Cardinal, Metropolitan, Primate, Archbishop, Diocesan, Archdeacon, Officiall, Chauncelour, Commissarie, Deane, Prebend, Parson, Vicar, and such like, but very names of blasphemy? For offices they are not appoincted by the holy Ghost, nor yet once mentioned in the scriptures.* This John Bale held and published. Then which, what can be more full and evident against you?"[120] Johnson followed this immediately with another quotation from Bale:

> *To receive the beastes marke in their forheads and hands, is both to agree to such decrees, traditions, lawes, constitutions, actes, and proclamations, as they under those titles have made onely for their owne covetousnes and pompe, and neither for the glory of God, nor yet for the right maintenance of the Christian common wealth: And also to be sworne to the same, to subscribe to it, to give counsel or ayde to it, to mainteine it by learning, to minister in it, to execute under it, to accuse, punish, and put to death for it, or to thinke it lawfull and godly, with such like.*[121]

To Johnson, this was a clear condemnation of any participation in the Elizabethan Church of England and a clarion call to separation.

Johnson and Penry were not alone among the separatists in invoking early English Protestants to support separation from the Church of England. When the ex-separatist Peter Fairlambe rebutted the arguments of a Mr. Bernhere in 1606, he criticized Bernhere's invocation of (among others) the Lollards and John Hooper "as friends to your cause," and proceeded to deny that their statements had any relevance for the contemporary situation.[122] John Robinson quoted John Hooper to support his view of the congregation's role in excommunication in *A Justification of Separation from the Church of England* (1610), writing that "*Mr Hooper* . . . in his Apology writes, that *excomunication should be by the Bishop, & the whole Parish, & that Pauls consent, & the whole Church with him did excommunicate the incestuous man.*"[123] In the 1611 separatist

---

[119] Johnson, *An answer to Maister H. Jacob*, 162.

[120] Johnson, *An answer to Maister H. Jacob*, 162–163.

[121] Johnson, *An answer to Maister H. Jacob*, 163.

[122] Peter Fairlambe, *The Recantation of a Brownist. Or A Reformed Puritan* (London, 1606; STC 10668), e2r–f1v; quotation at e2v.

[123] John Robinson, *A Justification of Separation from the Church of England* (Amsterdam, 1610; STC 21109), 210. Robinson seems to have been quoting very loosely, and with some additions, from Articles 73–75 of *A briefe and cleare Confession of the Christian faith*, which was in fact an English translation by Hooper of Jean Garnier's *Briefve et claire confession de la foy chrestienne, contenant cent articles, selon l'ordre du symbole des apostres*. The first time this appeared under Hooper's name was in

pamphlet *Mr Henry Barrowes Platform*, Miles Micklebound argued against "the Ministerie of Arch and Lordbishops," citing the works of the Brownists, Laurence Chaderton, John Wyclif, John Bale, Robert Barnes, and John Hooper.[124]

Early English Protestants would continue to prove useful to opponents of episcopacy more broadly in the early seventeenth century. Thomas Whetenhall's *A Discourse of the Abuses Now in Question in the Churches of Christ* (1606, reprinted 1617) reproduced numerous quotations from Scripture, the church fathers, and "by the lights of the Gospell, and blessed Martyrs of late in the middest of the Antichristian darknes."[125] These "lights" and "Martyrs" included leading continental Reformed divines and early English Protestants like Bale, Barnes, Becon, Cranmer, Hooper, John Lambert, Latimer, Lever, Ridley, and Tyndale.[126] Whetenhall also included several passages from the most radical Henrician text on the subject of church government, Tristram Revel's translation of François Lambert's *Farrago Rerum Theologicarum*, which Whetenhall noted had been "dedicated unto the most Noble Queene *Anne* mother to our late Soveraigne Queene *Elizabeth*."[127] Revel's translation was not unknown to Elizabethans – he was mentioned in Holinshed's *Chronicle* (1577) and was quoted at length in a manuscript digest of anti-episcopal authorities dating from the late 1580s or 1590s – and it would go on to be cited by several Jacobean opponents of episcopacy.[128] Quotations from Revel's translation would appear alongside passages from Tyndale, John Lambert, Bradford, Hooper, and Bale in *An Answere to a Sermon Preached* (1609), an anonymous challenge to George Downame's defense of *iure divino* episcopacy that adduced a variety of "our owne writers & Martyrs" alongside

---

John Baker, *Lectures of J.B. vpon the xii. Articles of our Christian . . . Also hereunto is annexed a briefe and cleare confession of the Christian faith . . . Written by that learned and godly martyr J.H. sometime Bishop of Glocester in his life time* (London, 1581; STC 1219).

[124] *Mr Henry Barrowes Platform* (London?, 1611, STC 1525), a8v-b1v; quote at a8v.

[125] Thomas Whetenhall, *A Discourse of the Abuses Now in Question in the Churches of Christ* (1606; STC 25332), *1r; reprinted 1617 (STC 25333).

[126] Whetenhall's extracts are indexed in his "Table of the Authors Alleaged in this Discourse," in *A Discourse*, *4r-v.

[127] Whetenhall, *A Discourse*, 75.

[128] Raphael Holinshed, *The Firste volume of the Chronicles of England, Scotlande, and Irelande* (London, 1577; STC 13568b), 1613, where Revel was included among evangelical authors in the reign of Henry VIII. The digest, which can be found in LPL MS 453, included a wide range of patristic and contemporary theologians, and quoted from Revel's translation at ff. 78v and 91v. It also included extracts from William Tyndale (ff. 54v, 66r, 88r, 151v), Robert Barnes (f. 89r), John Hooper (ff. 54v, 66r), Hugh Latimer (f. 66r), Thomas Lever (f. 80v), William Turner's translation of Urbanus Rhegius's *A comparison betwene the Olde learnynge & the Newe* (f. 89v), Thomas Becon (f. 142v), John Bale (f. 146v), and Miles Coverdale (f. 151v).

continental Protestants to refute Downame's views.[129] Like Whetenhall had done, the author of *An answere* noted that it had been dedicated to Queen Anne and proceeded to quote its claim that every parish should have its own bishop, chosen (and potentially deposed) by the parish.[130] The references to early English Protestants found in *An answere* were subsequently borrowed by Alexander Leighton in *An Appeal to the Parliament; or Sions Plea against the Prelacie* (1628/9).[131] In repeating these precedents, however, Leighton seems to have confused François Lambert with the Henrician martyr John Lambert, expressing shock that Downame "houldeth it an unworthie speech in holy Lambert, that Honourable martyr: *that a Pastor may be Censured by his Church.*"[132] Nearly a hundred years later, the earliest printed call in the English Reformation for congregationalist church government had been transformed into a wholly English call to arms, hallowed by the flames of another Lambert's martyrdom.

Tyndale himself was made to speak afresh against the bishops in a 1641 pamphlet entitled *Newes from Heaven both Good and True Concerning England,* which recounted a conversation in heaven between Tyndale and John Bradford about the "stirs and discords there are at this time in our native Countrey *England,* betwixt Superiors, and Inferiours."[133] The conversation opened with Bradford entreating Tyndale to give advice to the English people, which a friend of Bradford's would in turn relate "to some godly brother of ours yet in the flesh," since "your works are very hard to be found and those that have them do not raed [sic] them so oft as they should."[134] Tyndale spoke on a variety of topics and came out as an opponent of Archbishop Laud when asked, "is it not meet that the King should make use of them they call spirituall Lords for his Counsellors?"[135] Tyndale responded, "O no by no meanes, for is it not a shame above all shames and a monstrous thing, that no man should be found able to govern a worldly Kingdome save *Bishops & Prelates,* that are appoynted to preach the Kingdome of God, which Kingdome *Christ* saith is not of this World?

---

[129] *An Answere to a Sermon Preached the 17 of April* (Amsterdam, 1609; STC 20605), 159–165, quote at 162. Polly Ha has noted quotations from Tyndale and Barnes in a manuscript reply to Downame and another early seventeenth-century presbyterian manuscript: Ha, *English Presbyterianism, 1590–1640,* 89.

[130] *An Answere to a Sermon Preached,* 162–163.

[131] Alexander Leighton, *An Appeal To the Parliament; or Sions Plea against the Prelacie* (Amsterdam, 1628/9?; STC 15429), 13.

[132] Leighton, *An Appeal,* 285. François Lambert had not been martyred.

[133] *Newes From Heaven Both Good and True Concerning England ... Being a Dialogue between Mr. Tindall and Mr. Bradford, two famous English Martyrs* (London, 1641; Wing F15), a2r.

[134] *Newes From Heaven,* a2r.   [135] *Newes From Heaven,* a2v.

The truth is deare brother, to preach Gods word is too much for halfe a man one man therefore cannot well do both for no man can serve two Masters."[136]

The historical strategy of assimilating early English Protestants to the puritan cause reached its maximalist expression in the writings of William Prynne in the early 1640s. In *A Terrible Out-Cry Against the Loytering Exalted Prelates: Shewing the danger, and unfitnesse of Conferring them in any Temporall Office or Dignity* (1641), John Hooper and Hugh Latimer were quoted at great length, both to the effect that bishops could not serve in civil occupations and fulfill their spiritual duties.[137] In Prynne's *The Antipathie of the English Lordly Prelacie, Both to Regall Monarchy, and Civill Unity* (1641), he offered dozens of pages of lengthy quotations from early English Protestants to prove the Antichristian nature of "the Prelates Lordly jurisdiction over their fellow-brethren, contrary to Christs institution: the greatnesse of their wealth and temporall possessions; their admission to temporall Offices of greatest authority and trust: their sitting as Peeres in Parliament, and Judges in some temporall Courts; their residence in or about the Court, and advancement to be Counsellors of State."[138] After a host of Lollards, Prynne then quoted books or English translations by – among others – Tyndale, Frith, Barnes, Richard Tracy ("The nameless Author of a Supplication to King *Henry* the eight, printed 1544"), John Lambert, William Marshall's translation of Luther's *"The Image of a very Christian Bishop"* from 1536, William Turner (a.k.a. "William Wraghton"), Henry Brinkelow ("Roderick Mors"), John Bale (a.k.a. "Henry Stallbridge"), Simon Fish, Bucer, Zwingli (*The image of both Pastors*, translated by Veron in 1550), Hooper, and Latimer.[139]

Unsurprisingly, these attempts to claim early English Protestants for the presbyterian and separatist causes did not go uncontested. In the early 1590s, Matthew Sutcliffe wrote in response to both Udall's *A Demonstration of the trueth of that Discipline* and to Penry/Throckmorton's *A petition directed to her most excellent Majestie*, employing a variety of strategies to respond to the presbyterians' historical claims. First, Sutcliffe sometimes argued that these early English Protestants were either ignorant of the truth or simply wrong. Sutcliffe claimed not to know whether Robert Barnes had really said "I will never beleeve one can be bishop over two or three cities, or a whole

[136] *Newes From Heaven*, a2v.
[137] William Prynne, *A Terrible Out-Cry Against the Loytering Exalted Prelates* (London, 1641; Wing W389), 2–5.
[138] William Prynne, *The Antipathie of the English Lordly Prelacie, both to Regall Monarchy, and Civill Unity* (London, 1641; Wing P3891A), 307–308.
[139] Prynne, *The Antipathie*, 363–429.

countrey by the law of God," but he did know that if Barnes *had* actually said this, he was ignorant of the fact that *"Titus* was bishop of *Candie, Ignatius* of *Syria*, with infinite moe out of the Fathers and Councils." Had Barnes known these facts, "he would bee of another beliefe."[140] With regard to the claims made by *A Petition* about Aylmer and Bullingham's statements about bishops at the start of Elizabeth's reign, Sutcliffe wrote in 1592 that Aylmer's comments were an "oversight" and an "error," while Bullingham too had "erred" and corrected himself subsequently with "repentance."[141] When George Downame replied to his anonymous critic's invocation of Tristram Revel's 1536 translation of François Lambert, he too claimed that Lambert's statements were "a very unadvised speech if it be truely alledged," but insisted that nevertheless he was not "disallowing the government of the church by orthodoxal BB."[142]

This claim about "orthodoxal" bishops points to the second main sort of response to the puritan historical project. In responding to Udall, Sutcliffe also claimed that if Barnes had erred, it was explicable, insofar as "[m]any things slipped such men upon hatred to popish bishops."[143] According to Sutcliffe, Penry and Udall were guilty of anachronism when they applied these early English Protestant quotations to the present day because early English Protestants had been writing against papists, and their criticisms therefore could not be applied to Elizabeth's Protestant bishops or the institutions and structures of the now-Protestant Church of England. Sutcliffe therefore deflected Hooper's statement that "In the primitive Church they had no bishops as we have" by saying that "He speaketh of bishops under the Popedome," and if hypothetically he had been speaking about Protestant bishops, "the speach might very well be spared."[144] Sutcliffe demanded that "the libeller (if he can) bring forth one place, which is not meant of papisticall bishops," and complained that "it is a shamefull course, though greatly pleasing these mens humors, to take that which good men spake against pompous and tyrannicall Bishops that governed at pleasure, and gave over preaching altogether: and to apply the same against Bishops, that neither so excell in wealth ... nor in power ... & are not popish tyrants, but preachers of the gospell."[145] Making the same point in a different way, Richard Bancroft complained

---

[140] Matthew Sutcliffe, *A Remonstrance: or Plaine Detection* (London, 1590; STC 20881), 139.
[141] Sutcliffe, *An Answere to a Certaine Libel*, 17.
[142] George Downame, *A Defence of the Sermon Preached* (London, 1611; STC 7115), 4.161.
[143] Sutcliffe, *A Remonstrance*, 139.   [144] Sutcliffe, *A Remonstrance*, 139.
[145] Sutcliffe, *An Answere to a Certaine Libel*, 159, 68–69. This was Downame's constant refrain as well, writing that John Bradford's criticism of bishops pertained to "Popish BB. as minister not, but Lord

that the advocates of the Discipline were misconstruing the complaints they were reprinting: "Let a man cast downe his head, but for a day, like a bulrush, and give a grone or two in the behalfe of that kingdome: and by and by he is snatched up above the man in the moone, and may passe amongest them for an illuminated Elder."[146] In reality, Bancroft insisted, early English Protestants knew nothing of the puritans' "Consistoriall beliefe," and only through "paynted colours, and Sophisticall shewes" could they be enlisted as allies.[147]

Sutcliffe's third main response argued that earlier English Protestants had complained about *abuses* and *misbehavior* in the Church rather than fundamentally rejecting the institutions and structures of the Church themselves. Those early Tudor authors "inveigh against the manners of men, and corruptions of those times," and "it is one thing to desire the reformation of some one abuse, and another to desire the subversion both of all ecclesiastical governors, and lawes, which cannot be without a dangerous innovation of state ... the course of the proceeding of those that have spoken against mens manners, and some one lawe, is farre different from these mens doings and writings, that strive for the new kingdome of the Consistorie."[148] Surveying the writings of "*Wickleffe, Suinderby, Tindall, Hooper, Barnes, Latimer,* and others whom he chargeth with speaking against the state of the Church, and common wealth," Sutcliffe denied that any of them prove that these men "call our lawes antichristian, nor disgrace the governement of the prince, nor condemne the superioritie of bishops ... nor ever sought to have a new found governement established in the church."[149] Far from seeing Latimer as a proto-puritan – let alone a proto-Marprelate – Sutcliffe thundered that "there can bee nothing more unlike, then bishop *Latimers* booke, and *Cartwrightes* replies defacing the bishops."[150]

In sum, Sutcliffe accused his puritan interlocutors of making false claims and anachronistically reading complaints about popish abuses as criticisms of the institutions, offices, and practices of the Elizabethan Church of England. The goal was to deprive the puritans of any claim to historical continuity with the early heroes of the English Reformation. Sutcliffe's claims meshed perfectly with the histories of puritanism that were being written by conformists in the later 1580s and early 1590s, which

it," rather than "orthodoxal Bishops," and that when John Bale denounced titles like "Metropolitanes" and "Diocesans" as Antichristian, "he cannot be understood as speaking of these offices in the true church, but as they are members of Antichrist." Downame, *A Defence*, 4.162.

[146] Bancroft, *A Survay*, 357.   [147] Bancroft, *A Survay*, 358.
[148] Sutcliffe, *An Answere to a Certaine Libel*, 67–68.
[149] Sutcliffe, *An Answere to a Certaine Libel*, 67.   [150] Sutcliffe, *An Answere to a Certaine Libel*, 159.

reasserted puritan novelty and aimed to place puritans outside of the mainstream of English Protestantism. In the midst of a response to the first three Marprelate tracts in 1589, Thomas Cooper provided a brief narrative of the English Reformation that emphasized that "this maner of government that now is used, was by law confirmed as good and godly" during the reign of Edward VI by "*bishop Cranmer, Ridley, Latimer,* and many other, which after sealed their doctrine with their blood," and by men like Coverdale and Hooper who "were contented to use the office, authority, and jurisdiction of bishops, the one at *Exeter,* the other at *Glocester.*"[151] It was not "untill about the tenth yeere of her Majeisties raigne" that "curious devises" against the government of the Church of England appeared.[152] This assault on the discipline of the Church of England was a wholly Elizabethan development, designed and supervised by Satan, that aimed to undermine the true church gradually and that for "the space of these fifteene or sixteene yeeres, hath exceedingly growen, betweene the Ministers and Preachers of England."[153]

The definitive conformist account of the origins of puritanism was, of course, Richard Bancroft's well-known *A Survey of the Pretended Holy Discipline* (1593), "[t]he first history of the Elizabethan Puritan movement."[154] Bancroft positioned his history as a rejoinder to (among many other Puritan texts) Throckmorton/Penry's *A Petition,* whose author he called "crased," "franticke," a "light headed cockbraine," and worthy to receive "the garland for crying" against the government of the Elizabethan Church.[155] Rejecting the notion that the puritans were the heirs of England's earliest Protestants, Bancroft located the origins of puritanism firmly in the city of Geneva.[156] The "malecontents" (like John Hooper) who had begun to trouble the Edwardian Church of England were obeying their Protestant Pope, Jean Calvin, who had "written sundry letters into *England* to some suche like effect."[157] During the Marian period, other English exiles were "assaulted with the orders of *Geneva,*" and Bancroft described their

---

[151] Thomas Cooper, *An Admonition to the People of England* (London, 1589; STC 5682), 79.

[152] Cooper, *An Admonition,* 80.   [153] Cooper, *An Admonition,* 126.

[154] Peter Lake, "The historiography of Puritanism," in Coffey and Lim (eds.), *The Cambridge Companion to Puritanism,* 346.

[155] Bancroft, *A Survey,* 5, 236, 360, 5.

[156] This was also an Elizabethan Catholic talking point. The serial convert Lewis Evans (writing as a Catholic) sought to disassociate Elizabethan Protestantism from earlier English Protestantism when he wrote in 1565 (in the midst of the vestments controversy) that the new Elizabethan ministers adhered to what he called "*Geneva* faith" that was "not yet full seaven yeares of age" – dating, in other words, to the end of the Marian exile in 1558. Lewis Evans, *A brieve Admonition vnto the nowe made Ministers of Englande* (Antwerp, 1565; STC 10589), a5r.

[157] Bancroft, *A survay,* 44.

"intoxication" and "giddinesse" with Calvinist church polity.[158] This "*disciplinarian* canker" and Calvinist "infection" was then carried back into England at Elizabeth's accession by the returning Genevan exiles, who remained umbilically connected to Geneva's Theodore Beza, where it produced decades of parliamentary agitation, secret presbyterianism, and ultimately separatism.[159] So thoroughly Genevan was puritanism that Bancroft dubbed it "Genevating," insisting that "if my life lay uppon it, I could not finde, that there was ever in the world, anie such platforme of Discipline, as is now urged, by the patrones and defenders of it, before maister *Calvin* devised it, and with much trouble set it up, at the last in *Geneva*."[160] From Bancroft's perspective, puritanism was a foreign disease that had been contracted under Edward VI, incubated among the Marian exiles at Geneva, and then proceeded to ravage Elizabethan England upon the exiles' return.

The fact that Elizabethans were unable to agree about what early English Protestants said about bishops and church government should not be surprising, certainly no more so than the fact that they were unable to reach any consensus on what the Bible or the Church Fathers taught about these subjects. Indeed, what appears at first to have been a historical dispute was actually shot through with theological assumptions and disagreements. Take, for instance, Sutcliffe's claim that the presbyterians were quoting Tyndale and other early English Protestants out of context, given that the latter had been denouncing popish rather than Protestant bishops. This was a common way of insulating the Elizabethan Protestant episcopate from Henrician Protestants' harsh words regarding bishops: in 1573, for instance, Foxe rather significantly re-titled Tyndale's vicious *The practyse of Prelates* (1530) as *The practise of popishe Prelates* and *The practise of papisticall Prelates*.[161] In making this argument, however, Sutcliffe was actually begging the biggest question at stake between conformists and presbyterians in Elizabethan England: Was the polity of the Elizabethan Church of England godly/Protestant or ungodly/popish? Whereas Sutcliffe clearly thought the former, presbyterians thought the latter, incessantly claiming that the government of the Church of England was "Antichristian" and that the bishops were

---

[158] Bancroft, *A survay*, 44–45.   [159] Bancroft, *A survay*, 44.   [160] Bancroft, *A survay*, 51, 70.

[161] These titles appeared, respectively, in the table of contents and the body of the text: *The Whole workes*, a1v, 340. See John A. R. Dick, "Revisions in *Mammon* and *Prelates*," in John T. Day, Eric Lund, and Anne M. O'Donnell (eds.), *Word, Church, and State: Tyndale Quincentenary Essay* (Washington, DC, 1998), 307–321.

"popish prelates."[162] John Penry claimed that Richard Bancroft was probably a crypto-papist and, at the very least, was permitted to preach and publish "popery unreprooved" even though England publicly had "profession of the gospell."[163] The Plumbers Hall Separatists claimed in 1567 that those "which were burned in Qu. Ma. time, died for standing against poperie, as we nowe doe."[164] Indeed, some presbyterians argued that England in the early 1570s or 1600s was exactly analogous to England in the early 1540s, so of course texts from that period applied to Elizabethan Protestants.[165] The presbyterian who hoped to republish Richard Tracy's 1544 *Supplication* to Henry VIII directed his audience to read the book and then "consider, what it desireth to be reformed, & what lett it complaineth of, & compare that tyme to our tyme thinge with thinge, circumstance with circumstance," all of which would show that what was said then of "popish Bishoppes . . . is allso most true of ours."[166] When puritans and conformists read early English Protestant statements about bishops and the government of the church, their theological assumptions and contemporary perceptions led them to see exactly what they wanted to see.

When Elizabethan presbyterians claimed to find fellow "puritans" in the reign of Henry VIII, they were indeed guilty of many of the intellectual crimes that conformists like Sutcliffe and Bancroft had identified. Tyndale and Latimer were *not* presbyterians, and while figures like Hooper and Bale may have criticized aspects of episcopacy in certain contexts, they were then willing to accept bishoprics and exercise episcopal power in others. It was fundamentally anachronistic, moreover, to assimilate early English evangelicals to the presbyterian or separatist cause: with the notable exception of William Turner, none of the evangelicals that the presbyterians loved to invoke lived to see the Elizabethan Church, and there was no way of knowing how they would have responded to the enormously complex and rapidly shifting dynamics of Elizabethan England. But if the presbyterians and separatists failed to prove that they were the true heirs of the English Protestant tradition, so too did the conformists. The conformists' attempt to cast early English Protestantism in their own image was plagued with similar problems and they had to explain away virulently anti-episcopal

---

[162] Presbyterians could also acknowledge a difference between popish bishops and the Church of England's bishops, but use that distinction to argue that the faults exhibited by popish bishops (like "lordeship of bishopes") were "much mor to be condempned in the proffesores of the gosspell." LPL MS 453, f. 41v.

[163] Penry, *A Briefe Discovery*, 35.   [164] *A parte of a register*, 32.   [165] See *A Second Admonition*, h2r.

[166] LPL MS 806/2 f. 130v.

stances and sweeping calls for further reformation among early English evangelicals that bore little resemblance to their own views. Ultimately, when Elizabethans looked to the past and attempted to identify the true nature of English Protestantism, what they discovered – though they could not or would not recognize this fact – was that English Protestantism had no one true nature. Early English Protestants, like the Scriptures and the early church, did not speak with one clear voice and did not share a single vision of reformation, the church, or godly life. Early English Protestants could not be made to adjudicate the disputes over church government in the Elizabethan Church for they had been divided about these issues themselves.

Conclusion

Reformation Unbound has traced the development of radical Protestant thought along two of the most important faultlines in the history of English Protestantism. Sixteenth- and seventeenth-century English Protestants would be sharply divided over the external forms of the Church of England and the extent to which its liturgy, ceremonies, government, and discipline were in need of reform. They disagreed about whether such things were matters of biblical prescription or "things indifferent" left up to human regulation, and even among Protestants who agreed that such matters were *adiaphora*, disagreements developed about who ought to regulate them and about the criteria for determining their proper use. It was in these intense debates over *adiaphora* and ecclesiology that, as Patrick Collinson put it, "the geological fault-line between Anglicanism and Nonconformity, Church and Chapel, began."[1] There were also serious "contradictions between the principle and claims of the all-inclusive national Church, and the religious self-awareness of the godly people, the virtuoso minority whose practice of religion was prodigious." These contradictions produced calls for increased discipline within the national church, but they also produced disruptive social behavior as the self-styled godly minority sought to differentiate and segregate themselves from "the 'reprobate', 'carnal' majority." This tension too would have enormous consequences for English history and "[i]t was the English Reformation and the Reformed English Church itself which struck this reef of contradiction."[2]

We tend to treat the emergence of these tensions and the development of radical positions on these issues as later developments in the history of the English Reformation, associated above all with the development of puritanism. This book has argued, however, that these tensions – along with radical visions of "further" reformation and godly life in the world – had been part of the English Reformation from its very beginnings. It has shown that

---

[1] Collinson, *English Puritanism*, 16.   [2] Collinson, *The Birthpangs of Protestant England*, 20–21.

sharply contrasting visions of the church had already formed in the reign of
Henry VIII: calls for a revolutionary restructuring of the church's government, offices, and functions according to biblical guidelines did not await
the coming of the presbyterians in the 1570s, but had been issued by
evangelicals in the late 1520s and 1530s. These calls for radical ecclesiastical
reform were based on a view of biblical authority that differed significantly
from that advanced by other evangelicals and by the Henrician regime,
which retained many elements of the pre-Reformation church as matters of
royal "policy" and argued that the crown possessed sweeping powers to
define and determine the use of "things indifferent" in the Church of
England – a view that was already being openly criticized and rejected by
radical evangelicals in the 1540s.

But while these disagreements about religious authority, *adiaphora*, and
the shape of a reformed church were present from the start of the English
Reformation, they were neither constant nor unchanging. Debate about
church government was largely muted during the reign of Edward VI and
the debate over *adiaphora* that did develop during the Edwardian reformation did not then simply continue among the Marian exiles at Frankfurt,
who did not – as is commonly thought – divide into "puritan" and
"conformist" camps when they argued about whether they should use the
Book of Common Prayer. The unique circumstances of Mary's reign led the
Protestant exiles to think about religious ceremonies in distinctive ways,
creating in many an all-consuming fear that they would deny Christ and
inflict immeasurable spiritual harm on others by even being present at
popish ceremonies. Mary's reign also produced radical views of religious
authority among the Protestant vanguard, who implicitly or explicitly
invested the godly *themselves* with the responsibility to establish true worship, regardless of their prince's inclinations. After Mary's death, Queen
Elizabeth and conformists would once again assert that the monarch
possessed supreme authority over the church, and they would demand
obedience without question regarding the use of "things indifferent" –
claims that were hardly unprecedented in the history of the English
Reformation. But these (and more expansive) conformist claims now
stood in a new and starker tension with radical trends in recent Protestant
thought – trends, as we have seen, that were continuing to shape the
thought of the hottest Elizabethan Protestants.

The book has also traced profound tensions regarding the nature and
consequences of godly identity in the early decades of the English
Reformation. In stark contrast to visions of the reformation and the national
church that envisioned the establishment of peace and unity among the

English people, some Henrician evangelicals insisted that the reformation would bring not "peace, but a sword." Envisioning Christian life in highly confrontational ways, they argued that godly preaching and living would inevitably produce conflict with the worldly, and claimed that earthly peace for the godly would only be purchased at the cost of betraying the gospel. Protestants had ample opportunity to experience conflict after Mary's accession, and while the majority quietly conformed to the Marian Church, the most radical Protestants denounced Nicodemism as a damnable betrayal of the gospel and insisted that the godly must not even *appear* to live at peace with idolatry. These anti-Nicodemite anxieties and demands for a confrontational Christian witness utterly dominated the worldview of the Marian exiles, and this book has shown ways in which they would persist within Elizabethan Protestantism as well, driving puritan calls for ceremonial nonconformity, separatist withdrawal from the "popish" Elizabethan Church, and visions of godly life that encouraged social segregation and manifest hostility to the sinfulness the pervaded Elizabethan society.

Altogether, the analysis presented in the preceding chapters has important implications for the way we understand Elizabethan puritanism and its place in the history of English Protestantism. On one level, *Reformation Unbound* sheds new light on the development of puritanism by revising our understanding of central episodes in its early history, not least by drawing attention to the important role played by Catholics during the 1560s in exacerbating already existing tensions between English Protestants over the use of "things indifferent." It also sheds new light on the development of puritan self-understanding, revealing the extensive ways in which some puritans came to identify themselves (and their program of reform) with many of the most famous figures in the early history of the English Reformation. On another level, it argues that continuities existed between radical puritanism and earlier radical thought, showing how anti-Nicodemite attitudes and radical views of authority within Marian Protestantism would evolve and continue to shape the thought and activism of Elizabethan puritans. Most broadly, though, by expanding our understanding of the intellectual boundaries of early English Protestantism, it renders some developments within Elizabethan puritanism much less unusual than we have hitherto thought. The presbyterian platform that emerged in the early 1570s, for example, was a novel development in many ways and marked a sharp escalation in hostilities between the most radical puritans and the Elizabethan Church. The earliest presbyterians did not derive their ideas from early English Protestants and, as Peter Lake notes, "[o]nly a fool would seek to deny the importance of the Genevan example or of the direct influence of foreign divines like Calvin and Beza on Elizabethan presbyterianism."[3] But when viewed in relation to the radical evangelical visions of a reformed Church from the reign of Henry VIII – with their denunciations of clerical hierarchy and diocesan episcopacy, among other things – even some of the most radical elements of the presbyterian platform begin to look far less like new directions in the intellectual history of English Protestantism. In various ways, then, *Reformation Unbound* ultimately enables us to re-situate radical puritanism in the history of English Protestantism, putting it not at the beginning of a long and divisive history of Protestant disagreement regarding reform and godly identity, but in the middle of a history that reached back to the beginnings of the English Reformation itself.

[3] Lake, *Anglicans and Puritans?*, 3–4.

Bibliography

MANUSCRIPTS

Bodleian Library, Tanner MS 50
British Library, Add. MSS 19400, 27632, 32091
British Library, Cotton MS Cleopatra E vi
British Library, Egerton MS 2836
British Library, Harley MSS 416, 422, 425, 6990
British Library, Lansdowne MSS 8, 17, 28, 75
British Library, Royal MS 17 B xxxv
Cambridge University Library, MSS Ee 2.34, Mm 1.49
Dr Williams's Library, Morrice MS B
Emmanuel College Library, Cambridge, MS 261
Inner Temple Library, Petyt MSS 538/38, 538/47
Lambeth Palace Library MSS 453, 806/2 2002, 2007, 2523, 3470
National Archives, SP 6/3, SP 12/36

PRINTED WORKS

Allen, William, *A Defense and Declaration of the Catholike Churchies Doctrine, touching Purgatory, and prayers for the soules departed* (Antwerp, 1565), STC 371
Anon., *An answere for the tyme* (Rouen?, 1566), STC 10388
    An Answere to a Sermon Preached the 17 of April (Amsterdam, 1609), STC 20605
    The examinations of Henry Barrowe John Greenwood and John Penrie, before the high commissioners, and Lordes of the Counsel. Penned by the prisoners themselves before their deaths (Dort?, 1596?), STC 1519
    The Humble and unfained confession of the belefe of certain poore banished men (London?, 1554), STC 5630
    The Institution of a Christen Man (London, 1537), STC 5163
    Mr Henry Barrowes Platform (London? 1611), STC 1525
    A Necessary Doctrine and erudicion for any chrysten man, set furth by the kynges majestye of Englande (London, 1543), STC 5176
    Newes From Heaven Both Good and True Concerning England ... Being a Dialogue between Mr. Tindall and Mr. Bradford, two famous English Martyrs (London, 1641), Wing F15

A parte of a register (Middelburg, 1593?), STC 10400

A petition directed to her most excellent Majestie (Middelburg, 1592), STC 1521

*A pretye complaynt of Peace that was banyshed out of dyvers countreys & brought by
   Welth in to England* (London, 1538), STC 5611

A proclamacyon of the hygh Emperour Jesu Christ, unto all his faythfull Chrysten
   (London, 1534), STC 14561a

A Second Admonition to the Parliament (Hemel Hempstead?, 1572), STC 4713

To the Reader. To my faithful brethren (Emden, 1566), STC 10391

Bale, John, *A brefe chronycle concernynge the examincacyon and death of the blessed
   martyr of Christ syr Johan Oldecastell* (Antwerp, 1544), STC 1276

   *The epistle exhortatorye of an Englyshe Christyane unto his derelye beloved contreye of
   Englande against the pompouse popyshe Bysshoppes therof* (Antwerp, 1544?), STC
   1291a

   The first examinacyon of Anne Askewe (Wesel, 1546), STC 848

   The Image Of bothe churches (London, 1548), STC 1297

   The lattre examinacyon of Anne Askewe (Wesel, 1547), STC 850

   The vocacyon of Johan Bale to the bishoprick of Ossorie in Irelande (Wesel?, 1553),
   STC 1307

   Yet a course at the Romyshe foxe (Antwerp, 1543), STC 1309

Bancroft, Richard, *Daungerous Positions and Proceedings* (London, 1593), STC
   1344.5

   A Sermon Preached at Paules Crosse (London, 1588), STC 1347

   A survay of the Pretended Holy Discipline (London, 1593), STC 1352

Barlow, Jerome and William Roy, *Rede me and be nott wrothe* (Strassburg, 1528),
   STC 1462.7

Barlow, William, *A dyaloge descrybyng the orygynall ground of these Lutheran faccyons*
   (London, 1531), STC 1461

Barnes, Robert, *A Critical Edition of Robert Barnes's A Supplication Vnto the Most
   Gracyous Prince Kynge Henry the. VIIJ. 1534*, ed. Douglas H. Parker (Toronto,
   2008)

   A supplicacion unto the most gracyous prynce H. the. viii (London, 1534), STC 1471

   *A supplicatyon made by Robert Barnes doctoure in divinitie, unto the most excellent
   and redoubted prince kinge henrye the eyght* (Antwerp, 1531?), STC 1470

Barthlet, John, *The Fortresse of Fathers* (Emden, 1566), STC 1040

   The Pedegrewe of Heretiques (London, 1566), STC 1534

Baylor, Michael G. (ed. and trans.), *The Radical Reformation* (Cambridge, 1991)

Bigod, Francis, *A treatise concernynge impropriations of benefices* (London, 1535?),
   STC 4240

Bilson, Thomas, *The True Difference Betweene Christian Subjection and Unchristian
   Rebellion* (Oxford, 1585), STC 3071

Black, Joseph L. (ed.), *The Martin Marprelate Tracts: A Modernized and Annotated
   Edition* (Cambridge, 2008)

Bradford, John, *The hurt of hearyng Masse* (London, 1580), STC 3495

   The Hurte of Hering Masse (London, 1561), STC 3494

   The Writings of John Bradford, ed. Aubrey Townsend (Cambridge, 1853)

Bray, Gerald (ed.), *Documents of the English Reformation* (Cambridge, 2004)
(trans. and ed.), *Tudor Church Reform: The Henrician Canons of 1535 and the Reformatio Legum Ecclesiasticarum* (Woodbridge, 2000)

Brinkelow, Henry, *The complaynt of Roderyck Mors, somtyme a gray fryre, unto the parliament howse of Ingland his natural cuntry* (Strassburg, 1542), STC 3759.5

The complaint of Roderyck Mors, somtime a gray Fryre, unto the parlament of house of Ingland hys naturall countrey (London, 1548?), STC 3760

The lamentacyon of a Christen against the Citye of London (Bonn, 1542), STC 3764

Brooks, James, *A sermon very notable, fruictefull, and Godlie made at Paules crosse the. xii. daie of Novembre* (London, 1553), STC 3838

Browne, Robert, *A Treatise of reformation without tarying for anie* (Middelburgh, 1582), STC 3910.3

Bullinger, Heinrich and Jean Calvin, *Two Epystles* (London, 1548), STC 4080

Two Epystles One of Henry Bullynger . . . another of Jhon Calvyn . . . whether it be lawfull for a Chrysten man to communycate or be pertaker of the Masse of the Papystes, wythout offendyng God and hys neyghboure, or not (Antwerp, 1544), STC 4079.5

Calfhill, James, *An Aunswere to the Treatise of the Crosse* (London, 1565), STC 4368

Calvin, Jean, "Apology of John Calvin, to Messrs the Nicodemites upon the Complaint that they make of his too great rigour (1544)" trans. Eric Kayayan, *Calvin Theological Journal* 29 (1994), pp. 346–363

Certain homilies of m. Joan Calvine conteining profitable and necessarie, admonition for this time, with an apologie of Robert Horn (Rome [i.e. Wesel?], 1553), STC 4392

Commentaries of that divine John Calvine, upon the Prophet Daniell (London, 1570), STC 4397

Commentaries on the Twelve Minor Prophets by John Calvin, trans. John Owen. (Grand Rapids, 1950)

An epistle both of Godly Consolacion and also of advertisement (London, 1550), STC 4407

Foure Godlye sermons agaynst the pollution of idolatries (London, 1561), STC 4438, 4438.5

Foure Sermons of Maister John Calvin, Entreating of matters very profitable for our time . . . Translated out of Frenche into Englishe by John Fielde (London, 1579), STC 4439

The Mynde of the Godly and excellent lerned man M. Jhon Calvyne, what a faithfull man, whiche is instructe in the Worde of God, ought to do, dwellinge amongest the Papistes (Ipswich, 1548), STC 4435, 4435.3, 4435.5, 4435.7

A Sermon of the famous and Godly learned man, master John Calvine, chiefe Minister and Pastour of Christs church at Geneva, conteining an exhortation to suffer persecution for followinge Jesus Christe and his Gospell (London, 1581), STC 4439.5

The Sermons of M. John Calvin Upon the Fifth Booke of Moses called Deuteronomie (London, 1583), STC 4442

Two godly and learned Sermons (London, 1584), STC 4461

Canne, John, *A Necessitie of Separation From the Church of England* (Amsterdam, 1634), STC 4574

Carlson, Leland H. (ed.), *The Writings of Henry Barrow 1587–1590* (London, 2003)

(ed.), *The Writings of John Greenwood 1587–1590* (London, 2003)

(ed.), *The Writings of Henry Barrow 1590–1591* (London, 2003)

(ed.), *The Writings of John Greenwood and Henry Barrow, 1591–1593* (London, 2003)

Cartwright, Thomas, *A Replye to an answere made of M. Doctor Whitegifte Againste the Admonition to the Parliament By T.C.* (Hemel Hempstead?, 1573), STC 4712

The rest of the second replie of Thomas Cartwrihgt: agaynst Master Doctor Whitgifts second answer, touching the Church discipline (Basel, 1577), STC 4715

The second replie of Thomas Cartwright: agaynst Maister Doctor Whitgiftes second answer, touching the Churche Discipline (Heidelberg, 1575), STC 4714

Champneys, John, *The Harvest is at Hand, wherin the tares shall be bound and cast into the fyre and brent* (London, 1548), STC 4956

Colet, John, *The sermon of doctor Colete, made to the Convocacion at Paulis* (London, 1530), STC 5550

Cooper, Thomas, *An Admonition to the People of England* (London, 1589), STC 5682

A briefe exposition of such Chapters of the olde testament as usually are redde in the Church at common praier (London, 1573), STC 5684

Coverdale, Miles (ed.), *Certain most godly, fruitful, and comfortable letters of such true Saintes and holy Martyrs of God* (London, 1564), STC 5886

A confutacion of that treatise, which one John Standish made agaynst the protestacion of D. Barnes (Zurich, 1541?), STC 5888

A faythfull and true pronostication upon the yere. M. CCCCC.xlviii (London, 1547), STC 20423

A faythful & true pronostoication upon the yeare. M.CCCCC.xlix (London?, 1548?), STC 20424

(trans.), *The original & sprynge of all sectes & orders by whome, whan or were they beganne* (Southwark, 1537), STC 18849

Cranmer, Thomas, *An Answer . . . unto A crafty and sophisticall cavillation devised by Stephen Gardiner* (London, 1551), STC 5991

The boke of common praier (London, 1552), STC 16284.5

The booke of common praier (London, 1549), STC 16275

Certayne Sermons, or Homelies, appoynted by the kynges Majestie (London, 1547), STC 13640

The Work of Thomas Cranmer, ed. G. E. Duffield (Philadelphia, 1965)

Crowley, Robert, *A briefe discourse against the outwarde apparell and Ministring garmentes of the popishe church* (Emden, 1566), STC 6079

Dorman, Thomas, *A Disproufe of M. Nowelles Reproufe* (Antwerp, 1565), STC 7061

A Proufe of Certeyne Articles in Religion, Denied by M. Juell sett furth in defence of the Catholyke beleef (Antwerp, 1564), STC 7062

Downame, George, *A Defence of the Sermon Preached* (London, 1611), STC 7115

Drant, Thomas, *Two Sermons preached* (London, 1570), STC 7171

Elton, G. R., *The Tudor Constitution: Documents and Commentary*, 2nd edn. (Cambridge, 1982)

Evans, Lewis, *A brieve Admonition vnto the nowe made Ministers of Englande* (Antwerp, 1565), STC 10589

(trans.), *Certaine Tables sett furth by the right Reverend father in God, William Bushopp of Rurimunde* (Antwerp, 1565), STC 15653

Fairlambe, Peter, *The Recantation of a Brownist. Or A Reformed Puritan* (London, 1606), STC 10668

Field, John and Thomas Wilcox, *An Admonition to Parliament* (Hemel Hempstead?, 1572), STC 10848

Field, John, *Certaine Articles, collected and taken (as it is thought) by the Byshops out of a litle boke entituled an Admonition to the Parliament, wyth an Answere to the same* (Hemel Hempstead?, 1572), STC 10850

Fox, Edward, *The true dyfferens betwen the regall power and the Ecclesiasticall power*, trans. Henry Stafford (London, 1548), STC 11220

Foxe, John, *The Acts and monuments of John Foxe* (New York, 1965), vol. 5

(ed.), *The Whole workes of W. Tyndall, John Frith, and Doct. Barnes, three worthy Martyrs, and principall teachers of this Churche of England* (London, 1573), STC 24436

The Unabridged Acts and Monuments Online (HRI Online Publications, Sheffield, 2011). http://www.johnfoxe.org

Frith, John, *A boke made by John Frith prisoner in the tower of London* (Antwerp, 1533), STC 11381

A mirroure to know thyselfe (Antwerp, 1536?), STC 11390

A myrroure or lokynge glasse wherin you may beholde the sacramente of baptisme described (London, 1548), STC 11391

A pistle to the Christen reader; The Revelation of Antichrist; Antithesis (Antwerp, 1529), STC 11394

The Work of John Frith, ed. N. T. Wright (Appleford, 1978)

Fulke, William, *A Briefe and plaine declaration, concerning the desires of all those faithful Ministers, that have and do seeke for the Discipline and reformation of the Church of Englande* (London, 1584), STC 10395

Gifford, George, *A Briefe discourse of certaine points of the religion, which is among the common sort of Christians: which may bee termed the Countrie Divinitie* (London, 1581), STC 11845

A Plaine Declaration that our Brownists be full Donatists (London, 1590), STC 11862

A Short Treatise against the Donatists of England, whome we call Brownists (London, 1590), STC 11869

Gilby, Anthony, *An answer to the devillish detection of Stephane Gardiner* (London?, 1547/8), STC 11884

A Commentarye upon the prophet Malachy (London?, 1553), STC 11885.5

A Commentarye upon the Prophet Mycha (London, 1551), STC 11886

To my lovynge brethren that is troublyd abowt the popishe aparrell (Emden, 1566), STC 10390

A Pleasaunt Dialogue, Betweene a Souldior of Barwicke, and an English Chaplaine (Middelburg?, 1581), STC 11888

Goodman, Christopher, *How Superior Power Oght to be Obeyd* (Geneva, 1558), STC 12020

Gwynneth, John, *A Declaracion of the state, wherin all heretikes dooe leade their lives* (London, 1554), STC 12558

Hall, Edward, *The union of the two noble and illustre famelies of Lancastre & Yorke* (London, 1548), STC 12722

Harding, Thomas, *An Answere to Maister Juelles Chalenge* (Louvain, 1564), STC 12758

  A Confutation of a Booke Intituled An Apologie of the Church of England (Antwerp, 1565), STC 12762

Henry VIII, *A proclamation, concernynge rites and ceremonies* (London, 1539), STC 7791

Heylyn, Peter, *Aerius Redivivus: or, the History of the Presbyterians* (Oxford, 1670), Wing H1681

Hickman, Henry, *Plus ultra, or, Englands reformation, needing to be reformed being an examination of Doctor Heylins History of the reformation of the Church of England* (London, 1661), Wing H1913

Holinshed, Raphael, *The first volume of the chronicles of England, Scotlande, and Irelande* (London, 1577), STC 13569

Hooper, John, *An Answer unto my lord of wynchesters booke* (Zurich, 1547), STC 13741

  A declaration of Christe and of his offyce (Zurich, 1547), STC 13745

  Whether Christian faith maye be kepte secret in the heart (London?, 1553), STC 5160.3

Hosius, Stanislaus, *A Most Excellent Treatise of the begynnyng of heresyes in oure tyme ... The hatchet of heresies*, trans. Richard Shacklock (Antwerp, 1565), STC 13888

Howard, Henry, *A Defense of the Ecclesiasticall Regiment in Englande, defaced by T. C. in his Replie agaynst D. Whitgifte* (London, 1574), STC 10393

Humphrey, Laurence, *De Religionis Conservatione et Reformatione Vera*, trans. Janet Karen Kemp in "Laurence Humphrey, Elizabethan Puritan: His Life and Political Theories" (West Virginia University, Ph.D. Dissertation, 1978)

Jewel, John, *Certaine Sermons preached before the Queenes Majestie, and at Paules crosse* (London, 1583), STC 14596

Johnson, Francis, *An Answer to Maister H. Jacob His Defence of the Churches and Ministery of England* (Amsterdam?, 1600), STC 14658

  A Treatise Of the Ministery of the Church of England. Wherein is handled this question, Whether it be to be separated from, or joyned unto (n.p., 1595), STC 14663.5

Joye, George, *An Apologye made by George Joye to satisfye (if it maye be) w. Tindale* (London, 1535), STC 14820

  The exposicion of Daniel the Prophete (Antwerp, 1545), STC 14823

  Jeremy the Prophete, translated into Englisshe (Antwerp, 1534), STC 2778

  The letters which Johan Ashwel Priour of Newnham Abbey besids Bedforde, sente secretely to the Bishope of Lyncolne (Antwerp, 1531?), STC 845

A present consolation for the sufferers of persecucion for ryghtwysenes (Antwerp, 1544), STC 14828

Knox, John, *The Appellation of John Knox* (Geneva, 1558), STC 15063

The Copie of an Epistle Sent by John Knox one of the Ministers of the Englishe Church at Geneva unto the inhabitants of Newcastle, & Barwike. In the end wherof is added a briefe exhortation to England for the spedie imbrasing of Christes Gospel hertofore suppressed & banished (Geneva, 1559), STC 15064

A Faythfull admonition made by John Knox (Emden, 1544), STC 15069

History of the Reformation in Scotland, ed. William Croft Dickinson (Edinburgh, 1950), vol. I.

A Percel of the vi Psalme expounded (London?, 1554), STC 15074.4

On Rebellion, ed. Roger A. Mason (Cambridge, 1994)

The Works of John Knox, ed. David Laing (Edinburgh, 1855), vols. I, 4.

Lambert, François, *The summe of christianitie gatheryd out almoste of al placis of scripture, by that noble and famouse clerke Francis Lambert of Avynyon*, trans. Tristram Revel (London, 1536), STC 15179

Lant, Richard *A compendyous treatyse of sclaundre* (London, 1545), STC 24216a

Latimer, Hugh, *Certayn Godly Sermons* (London, 1562), STC 15276

Frutefull Sermons (London, 1575), STC 15278

The seconde Sermon (London, 1549), STC 15274

Sermons by Hugh Latimer, ed. George Corrie (Cambridge, 1844)

Sermons and Remains of Hugh Latimer, ed. George Corrie (Cambridge, 1845)

Leighton, Alexander, *An Appeal To the Parliament; or Sions Plea against the Prelacie* (Amsterdam, 1628/9?), STC 15429

Lever, Thomas, *A fruitfull Sermon made in Poules churche at London in the shroudes the seconde daye of February* (London, 1550), STC 15543

A Sermon preached at Pauls Crosse, the xiiii day of December (London, 1550), STC 15546.3

A Sermon preached the thyrd Sonday in Lent before the Kynges Majestie and his honorable Counsell (London, 1550), STC 15547

Luther, Martin, *On the Bondage of the Will in Luther and Erasmus: Free Will and Salvation*, ed. E. Gordon Rupp and Philip S. Watson (Louisville, 1969)

A faithful admonition (London, 1554), STC 16981

The images of a verye Chrysten bysshop, and of a couterfayte bysshop, trans. William Marshall (London, 1536?), STC 16983.5

Martin Luther's Basic Theological Writings, ed. Timothy F. Lull (Minneapolis, 1989)

Lydgate, John, *This lyttell treatyse compendiously declareth the damage and Destruction in Realmes caused by the Serpente of Division* (London, 1535), STC 17027.5

Marsilius of Padua, *The defence of peace: lately translated out of laten in to englysshe*, trans. William Marshall (London, 1535), STC 17817

Martiall, John, *A Treatyse of the Crosse* (Antwerp, 1564), STC 17496

Matthew, Simon, *A Sermon made in the cathedrall churche of saynt Paule at London* (London, 1535), STC 17656

Milton, John, *Of Reformation Touching Church-Discipline in England: And the Causes that hitherto have hindred it* (London?, 1641), Wing M2134

More, Thomas, *The Complete Works of St. Thomas More* (New Haven, CT and London, 1969–1981), vols. 5–6, 8

Morison, Richard, *A Remedy for Sedition* (London, 1536), STC 18113.7

Musculus, Wolfgang, *The Temporysour* (Wesel?, 1555), STC 18312

Nichols, John Gough (ed.), *Narratives of the Days of the Reformation* (London, 1859)

Norton, Thomas, *A warning agaynst the dangerous practises of Papistes* (London, 1569), STC 18685.7

Nowell, Alexander, *A Reproufe, written by Alexander Nowell, of a booke entituled, A proufe of Certayne Articles in Religion denied by M. Juell, set furth by Thomas Dorman, Bachiler of Divinitie* (London, 1565), STC 18741

Ochino, Bernardino, *Certayne Sermons of the ryghte famous and excellente Clerk Master Barnardine Ochine* (London, 1551), STC 18766

Osorius, Hieronymus, *A Learned and Very Eloquent Treatie, writen in Latin ... wherein he confuteth a certayne Aunswere made by M. Walter Haddon against the Epistle of the said Bishoppe unto the Queenes Maiestie* (Louvain, 1568), STC 18889

Parker, Matthew, *A briefe examination for the tyme* (London, 1566), STC 10387
Correspondence of Matthew Parker, ed. John Bruce and Thomas Perowne (Cambridge, 1853)

Peel, Albert (ed.), *The Seconde Parte of a Register* (Cambridge, 1915)

Peel, Albert and Leland H. Carlson (ed.), *The Writings of Robert Harrison and Robert Browne* (London, 2003)

Penry, John, *A Briefe Discovery of the Untruthes and Slanders (Against the True Governement of the Church of Christ) contained in a Sermon, preached the 8. of Februarie 1588 by D. Bancroft* (Edinburgh, 1590), STC 19603
A Treatise Wherein is Manifestlie Proved, That Reformation and Those that sincerely favor the same, are unjustly charged to be enemies, unto hir Majestie, and the state (Edinburgh, 1590), STC 19612

Pilkington, James, *Aggeus and Abdias Prophetes* (London, 1562), STC 19927
Aggeus the Prophete declared by a large commentarye (London, 1560), STC 19926.3
The burnynge of Paules church (London, 1563), STC 19931
A Godlie Exposition Upon Certeine Chapters of Nehemiah (Cambridge, 1585), STC 19929
The Works of James Pilkington, B.D., ed. James Scholefield (Cambridge, 1842)

Ponet, John, *A Shorte Treatise of politike power* (Strassburg, 1556), STC 20178

Proctor, John (trans.), *The waie home to Christ and truth leadinge from Antichrist and errour* (London, 1554), STC 24754

Prynne, William, *The Antipathie of the English Lordly Prelacie, both to Regall Monarchy, and Civill Unity* (London, 1641), Wing P3891A
A Terrible Out-Cry Against the Loytering Exalted Prelates (London, 1641), Wing W389

Rhegius, Urbanus, *A comparison betwene the Olde learnynge & the Newe. Translated out of Latyn in Englysh by Wyliam Turner* (London, 1537), STC 20840.5

Ridley, Lancelot, *An exposition in the epistell of Jude the apostel of Christ* (London, 1538), STC 21042

Robinson, Hastings (ed.), *Original Letters Relative to the English Reformation* (Cambridge, 1847)

(ed.), *The Zurich Letters* (Cambridge, 1842, 2nd edn. 1846)

Robinson, John, *A Justification of Separation from the Church of England* (Amsterdam, 1610), STC 21109

Roy, William, *A Brefe Dialoge bitwene a Christen Father and his stobborne Sonne*, ed. Douglas H. Parker and Bruce Krajewski (Toronto, 1999)

Russell, Thomas (ed.), *The Works of the English Reformers: William Tyndale and John Frith* (London, 1831)

Sampson, Thomas, *A letter to the trew professors of Christes Gospell, inhabitinge in the Parishe off Allhallowis, in Bredstrete in London, made by Thomas Sampson, sometyme their Pastore* (Wesel?, 1554), STC 21683

Sandys, Edwin, *The Sermons of Edwin Sandys, D.D.*, ed. John Ayre (Cambridge, 1841)

Sarcerius, Erasmus, *Common places of scripture ordrely and after a compendious forme of teachyng set forth*, trans. Richard Taverner (London, 1538), STC 21752.5

Smectymnuus, *An Answer to a Booke Entituled, An Humble Remonstrance* (London, 1641), Wing M748

Smith, Richard, *A bouclier of the catholike fayth of Christes church* (London, 1555), STC 22816

Solme, Robert, *Here begynnyth a traetys callyde the Lordis flayle* (Basel, 1540), STC 22897

Spangenberg, Johann, *The sum of divinitie drawen out of the holy scripture*, trans. Robert Hutten (London, 1548), STC 23004.5

Standish, John, *A discourse wherin is debated whether it be expedient that the scripture should be in English for al men to reade that wyll* (London, 1554), STC 23207

Staphylus, Fridericus, *The apologie of Fridericus Staphylus*, trans. Thomas Stapleton (Antwerp, 1565), STC 23230

Stapleton, Thomas, *A Counterblast to M. Hornes Vayne Blaste Against M. Fekenham* (Louvain, 1567), STC 23231

Starkey, Thomas, *A preface to the Kynges hyghnes* (London, 1536), STC 23236

Strype, John, *Annals of the Reformation* (Oxford, 1824), vol. 1

Sutcliffe, Matthew, *An Answere to a Certaine Libel* (London, 1592), STC 23450

A Remonstrance: or Plaine Detection (London, 1590), STC 20881

Swinnerton, Thomas, *A Litel Treatise ageynst the mutterynge of some papistis in corners* (London, 1534), STC 23551.5

A mustre of scismatyke bysshoppes of Rome (London, 1534), STC 23552

J.T., *An Apologie or defence agaynst the calumnacion of certayne men* (Wesel?, 1555), STC 23619

Taverner, Richard (trans.), *The confessyon of the fayth of the Germaynes exhibited to the most victorious Emperour Charles the v* (London, 1536), STC 908

Throckmorton, Job, *The state of the Church of Englande, laide open in a conference betweene Diotrephes a Byshop, Tertullus a Papist, Demetrius an usurer,*

Pandochem an Inne-keeper, and Paule a preacher of the worde of God (London, 1588), STC 24505

Tracy, Richard, *A Supplication to our Moste Sovereigne Lorde Kyng Henry the eight* (London?, ca. 1585), STC 24166

A supplycacion to our moste soveraigne lorde Kynge henry the eyght (London, 1544), STC 24165.5

Travers, Walter, *A full and plaine declaration of Ecclesiasticall Discipline owt off the word off God, and off the declininge off the churche off England from the same*, trans. Thomas Cartwright (Heidelberg, 1574), STC 24184

Turner, William, *The Hunting of the Fox and the Wolfe* (London, 1565), STC 24357

The huntyng & fyndyng out of the Romishe fox (Bonn, 1543), STC 24353

The Rescuynge of the Romishe Fox (Bonn, 1545), STC 24355

Tyndale, William, *An answere unto Sir Thomas Mores dialoge* (Antwerp, 1531), STC 24437

An exposicion uppon the v. vi. vii. chapters of Mathew (Antwerp?, 1533?), STC 24440

The exposition of the fyrste Epistle of seynt Jhon with a Prologge before it (Antwerp, 1531), STC 24443

(trans.), *The New Testament: The text of the Worms edition of 1526 in original spelling*, ed. W. R. Cooper (London, 2000)

The obedience of a Christen man (Antwerp, 1528), STC 24446

The practyse of Prelates (Antwerp, 1530), STC 24465

Udall, John, *The Combate betwixt Christ and the Devill* (London, 1588), STC 24492

A Demonstration of the trueth of that Discipline, which Christe hath prescribed in his worde for the governement of his Church, in all times and places, untill the ende of the worlde (East Molesey, 1588), STC 24499

Peters Fall. Two Sermons upon the Historie of Peters denying Christ (London, 1584), STC 24503

Vadian, Joachim, *A worke entytled of the olde god and the news*, trans. William Marshall (London, 1534), STC 25127

Vermigli, Peter Martyr, *A Treatise of the Cohabitacyon of the faithfull with the unfaithfull* (Strassburg, 1555), STC 24673.5

Viret, Pierre, *An Epistle to the Faithfull, necessary for all the children of God: especially in these dangerous dayes*, trans. F. H. (London, 1582), STC 24779

Whetenhall, Thomas, *A Discourse of the Abuses Now in Question in the Churches of Christ* (1606), STC 25332

Whitgift, John, *An answere to a certen Libell intituled, An admonition to the Parliament* (London, 1573), STC 25429

The Works of John Whitgift, ed. John Ayre (Cambridge, 1851) 3 vols.

Whittingham, William, *To my faithful brethren* (Emden, 1566), STC 10389

Wigand, Johann, *De Neutralibus & Mediis, Grosly Englished, Jacke of both sides* (London, 1591), STC 25613

De Neutralibus et Mediis, Grosly Inglyshed, Jacke of both Sydes (London, 1562), STC 25612, 25612.5

Wood, Thomas, *A Brieff discours off the troubles begonne at Franckford in Germany Anno Domini 1554* (Heidelberg, 1574), STC 25442

Wyse, Nicholas, *A consolacyon for chrysten people to repayre agayn the lordes temple* (London, 1538), STC 26063

Zwingli, Huldrych, *The ymage of bothe Pastoures, sette forth by that mooste famouse Clerck, Huldrych zwinglius, & now translated out of Latin into Englishe. By John Veron, Senonoys* (London, 1550), STC 26142

SECONDARY WORKS

Aers, David, "Altars of Power: Reflections on Eamon Duffy's *The Stripping of the Altars: Traditional Religion in England, 1400–1580*" *Literature and History* 3 (1994), pp. 90–105

Alford, Stephen, *Kingship and Politics in the Reign of Edward VI* (Cambridge, 2002)

"A Politics of Emergency in the Reign of Elizabeth I" in *English Radicalism, 1550–1850*, ed. Glenn Burgess and Matthew Festenstein (Cambridge, 2007), pp. 17–36

Avis, Paul D. L., *The Church in the Theology of the Reformers* (Atlanta, GA, 1981)

Bainton, Roland, *The Reformation of the Sixteenth Century* (Boston, 1952)

"The Left Wing of the Reformation" in *Studies on the Reformation* (Boston, 1963), pp. 119–129

Bates, Lucy, "The Limits of Possibility in England's Long Reformation" *Historical Journal* 53:4 (2010), pp. 1049–1070

Bauckham, Richard, "Marian Exiles and Cambridge Puritanism: James Pilkington's 'Halfe a Score'" *Journal of Ecclesiastical History* 26:2 (April 1975), pp. 137–148

Tudor Apocalypse (Appleford, 1978)

Benedict, Philip, *Christ's Churches Purely Reformed: A Social History of Calvinism* (New Haven, CT, and London, 2002)

Bernard, G. W., *The King's Reformation: Henry VIII and the Remaking of the English Church* (New Haven, CT, 2005)

Black, J. William, "From Martin Bucer to Richard Baxter: 'Discipline' and Reformation in Sixteenth- and Seventeenth-Century England" *Church History* 70:4 (December 2001), pp. 644–673

Bossy, John, *Peace in the Post-Reformation* (Cambridge, 1998)

Bowker, Margaret, "The Supremacy and the Episcopate: The Struggle for Control, 1534–1540" *The Historical Journal* 18:2 (June 1975), pp. 227–243

Bowler, Gerald, "'An Axe or an Acte': The Parliament of 1572 and Resistance Theory in Early Elizabethan England" *Canadian Journal of History* 19:3 (December 1984), pp. 349–359

"English Protestants and Resistance Theory, 1553–1603" (London, Ph.D. dissertation, 1981)

"Marian Protestants and the Idea of Violent Resistance to Tyranny" in *Protestantism and the National Church*, ed. Peter Lake and Maria Dowling (London, 1987), pp. 124–143

Brachlow, Stephen, *The Communion of Saints: Radical Puritan and Separatist Ecclesiology 1570–1625* (Oxford, 1988)

Bremer, Francis J., *The Puritan Experiment: New England Society from Bradford to Edwards* (New York, 1976)

Brigden, Susan, *London and the Reformation* (Oxford, 1989)

 New Worlds, Lost Worlds: The Rule of the Tudors, 1485–1603 (New York, 2000)

Burgess, Glenn, *British Political Thought, 1500–1660: The Politics of the Post-Reformation* (Basingstoke, 2009)

Burgess, Glenn and Matthew Festenstein (eds.), *English Radicalism, 1550–1850* (Cambridge, 2007)

Butterworth, Charles C. and Allan G. Chester, *George Joye, 1495?–1553* (Philadelphia, 1962)

Cameron, Euan, *The European Reformation* (Oxford, 1991)

 "Frankfurt and Geneva: The European Context of John Knox's Reformation" in *John Knox and the British Reformations*, ed. Roger A. Mason (Aldershot, 1998) pp. 51–73

Campbell, Louise, "A Diagnosis of Religious Moderation: Matthew Parker and the 1559 Settlement" in *Moderate Voices in the European Reformation*, ed. Luc Racaut and Alec Ryrie (Aldershot, 2005), pp. 32–50

Carleton, Kenneth, *Bishops and Reform in the English Church, 1520–1559* (Woodbridge, 2001)

Clebsch, William A., *England's Earliest Protestants, 1520–1535* (New Haven, CT, and London, 1964)

Coffey, John and Paul C. H. Lim (eds.), *The Cambridge Companion to Puritanism* (Cambridge, 2008)

Collinson, Patrick, *Archbishop Grindal, 1519–1583: The Struggle for a Reformed Church* (Berkeley, 1979)

 "The Authorship of A Brieff Discours off the Troubles Begonne at Franckford" *Journal of Ecclesiastical History* 9 (1958), pp. 188–208

 "Biblical Rhetoric: The English Nation and National Sentiment in the Prophetic Mode" in *Religion and Culture in Renaissance England*, ed. Claire McEachern and Debora Shuger (Cambridge, 1997), pp. 15–45

 The Birthpangs of Protestant England: Religious and Cultural Change in the Sixteenth and Seventeenth Centuries (New York, 1988)

 "The Cohabitation of the Faithful with the Unfaithful" in *From Persecution to Toleration: the Glorious Revolution and Religion in England*, ed. Ole Peter Grell, Jonathan I. Israel, and Nicholas Tyacke (Oxford, 1991), pp. 51–76

 The Elizabethan Puritan Movement (Oxford, 2000)

 "England and International Calvinism, 1558–1640" in *From Cranmer to Sancroft* (London, 2006), pp. 75–100

 English Puritanism (London, 1983)

 "Episcopacy and Quasi-Episcopacy in the Elizabethan Church" in *L'institution et les pouvoirs dans les églises de l'antiquité à nos jours*, ed. Bernard Vogler (Louvain, 1987), pp. 229–238

 "Episcopacy and Reform in England in the Later Sixteenth Century" in *Godly People: Essays on English Protestantism and Puritanism* (London, 1993), pp. 155–189

 "The Monarchical Republic of Queen Elizabeth I" in *Elizabethan Essays* (London, 1994), pp. 31–57

"Separation In and Out of the Church: The Consistency of Barrow and Greenwood" *The Journal of the United Reformed Church History Society* 5:5 (November 1994), pp. 239–258

"Windows in a Woman's Soul: Questions about the Religion of Queen Elizabeth I" in *Elizabethan Essays* (London, 1994), pp. 87–118

Collinson, Patrick, Richard Rex, and Graham Stanton, *Lady Margaret Beaufort and her Professors of Divinity at Cambridge: 1502–1649* (Cambridge, 2003)

Como, David R., "Radical Puritanism, c. 1558–1660" in John Coffey and Paul C. H. Lim (eds.), *The Cambridge Companion to Puritanism* (Cambridge, 2008), pp. 241–258

Coolidge, John S., *The Pauline Renaissance in England: Puritanism and the Bible* (Oxford, 1970)

Coppens, C., "Challenge and Counterblast: The Book as a Weapon in the English Controversy during the Second Half of the Sixteenth Century" in *Antwerp, Dissident Typographical Centre: The Role of Antwerp Printers in the Religious Conflicts in England (16th Century)* (Antwerp, 1994), pp. 31–54

Craig, John, "The growth of English Puritanism" in John Coffey and Paul C. H. Lim (eds.), *The Cambridge Companion to Puritanism* (Cambridge, 2008), pp. 34–47

Crankshaw, David, "Preparations for the Canterbury provincial convocation of 1562–3: a question of attribution" in *Belief and Practice in Reformation England*, ed. Susan Wabuda and Caroline Litzenberger (Aldershot, 1998), pp. 60–93

Cross, Claire, *Church and People: England 1450–1660*, 2nd edn. (Oxford, 1999)

D'Alton, Craig W., "The Suppression of Lutheran Heretics in England, 1526–1529" *Journal of Ecclesiastical History* 54:2 (April 2003), pp. 228–253

Daniell, David, *William Tyndale: A Biography* (New Haven, CT, and London, 1994)

Danner, Dan G., *Pilgrimage to Puritanism: History and Theology of the Marian Exiles at Geneva* (New York, 1999)

Davies, Catharine, *A religion of the Word: The defence of the reformation in the reign of Edward VI* (Manchester, 2002)

"'Poor Persecuted Little Flock' or 'Commonwealth of Christians': Edwardian Protestant Concepts of the Church" in *Protestantism and the National Church*, ed. Peter Lake and Maria Dowling (London, 1987), pp. 78–102

Davies, Catharine and Jane Facey, "A Reformation Dilemma: John Foxe and the Problem of Discipline" *Journal of Ecclesiastical History* 39:1 (January 1988), pp. 37–65

Davis, John F., *Heresy and Reformation in the South-East of England, 1520–1559* (London, 1983)

"The Trials of Thomas Bylney and the English Reformation" *Historical Journal* 24:4 (December 1981), pp. 775–790

Dawson, Jane E. A., "John Knox, Christopher Goodman and the 'Example of Geneva'" in *The Reception of Continental Reformation in Britain*, ed. Polly Ha and Patrick Collinson (Oxford, 2010), pp. 107–135

"Resistance and Revolution in Sixteenth-Century Thought: The Case of Christopher Goodman" in *Church, Change and Revolution: Transactions of the Fourth Anglo-Dutch Church History Colloquium*, ed. J. van den Berg and P. G. Hoftijzer (Leiden, 1991), pp. 69–79

"Revolutionary Conclusions: The Case of the Marian Exiles" *History of Political Thought* 11:2 (Summer 1990), pp. 257–272

"Trumpeting Resistance: Christopher Goodman and John Knox" in *John Knox and the British Reformations*, ed. Roger A. Mason (Aldershot, 1998), pp. 131–153

"The Two John Knoxes: England, Scotland and the 1558 Tracts" *Journal of Ecclesiastical History* 42:4 (October 1991), pp. 555–576

Dick, John A. R., "Revisions in *Mammon* and *Prelates*" in *Word, Church, and State: Tyndale Quincentenary Essay*, ed. John T. Day, Eric Lund, and Anne M. O'Donnell (Washington, DC, 1998), pp. 307–321

Dickens, A. G., *The English Reformation*, 2nd edn. (University Park, PA 1989)

"The Reformation in England" in *The Reformation Crisis*, ed. Joel Hurstfield (New York, 1966), pp. 44–57

Diener, Ronald E., "Johann Wigand, 1523–1587" in *Shapers of Religious Traditions in Germany, Switzerland, and Poland, 1560–1600*, ed. Jill Raitt (New Haven, CT, and London, 1981), pp. 19–38

Dixon, C. Scott, *Protestants: A History from Wittenberg to Pennsylvania 1517–1740* (Chichester, 2010)

Dolff, Scott, "The Two John Knoxes and the Justification of Non-Revolution: A Response to Dawson's Argument from Covenant" *Journal of Ecclesiastical History* 55:1 (January 2004), pp. 58–74

Doran, Susan, *Monarchy and Matrimony: The courtships of Elizabeth I* (London and New York, 1996)

Dowling, Maria, "The Gospel and the Court: Reformation under Henry VIII" in *Protestantism and the National Church*, ed. Peter Lake and Maria Dowling (London, 1987), pp. 36–77

Driedger, Michael, "Anabaptism and Religious Radicalism" in *Palgrave Advances in the European Reformations*, ed. Alec Ryrie (Basingstoke, 2006), pp. 212–231

Duffy, Eamon, "Continuity and Divergence in Tudor Religion" in *Unity and Diversity in the Church*, ed. R. N. Swanson (Oxford, 1996), pp. 171–205

The Stripping of the Altars: Traditional Religion in England c. 1400–c. 1580 (New Haven, CT, and London, 1992)

The Voices of Morebath: Reformation and Rebellion in an English Village (New Haven, CT, and London, 2001)

Durston, Christopher and Jacqueline Eales (eds.), *The Culture of English Puritanism, 1560–1700* (New York, 1996)

Eire, Carlos M. N., "Calvin and Nicodemism: A Reappraisal" *Sixteenth Century Journal* 10:1 (Spring 1979), pp. 44–69

War Against the Idols: The Reformation of Worship from Erasmus to Calvin (Cambridge, 1986)

Elton, G. R., *Policy and Police: The Enforcement of the Reformation in the Age of Thomas Cromwell* (Cambridge, 1972)

Reform and Renewal: Thomas Cromwell and the Common Weal (Cambridge, 1973)

Emerson, Everett H., *English Puritanism from John Hooper to John Milton* (Durham, NC, 1968)

Euler, Carrie E., "Bringing Reformed Theology to England's 'Rude and Symple People': Jean Véron, Minister and Author Outside the Stranger Church Community" in *From Strangers to Citizens: The Integration of Immigrant Communities in Britain, Ireland, and Colonial America, 1550–1750*, ed. Randolph Vigne and Charles Littleton (Sussex, 2001), pp. 17–24

Couriers of the Gospel: England and Zurich, 1531–1558 (Zurich, 2006)

Fox, Alistair, "Prophecies and Politics in the Reign of Henry VIII" in *Reassessing the Henrician Age: Humanism, Politics and Reform, 1500–1550*, ed. Alistair Fox and John Guy (Oxford, 1986), pp. 77–94

Freeman, Thomas S., "'As True a Subiect being Prysoner': John Foxe's Notes on the Imprisonment of Princess Elizabeth, 1554–5" *English Historical Review* 117:470 (February 2002), pp. 104–116

"Dissenters from a dissenting Church: the challenge of the Freewillers, 1550–1558" in *The Beginnings of English Protestantism*, ed. Peter Marshall and Alec Ryrie (Cambridge, 2002), pp. 129–156

"Over their Dead Bodies: Concepts of Martyrdom in Late Medieval and Early Modern England" in *Martyrs and Martyrdom in England, c. 1400–1700*, eds. Thomas S. Freeman and Thomas F. Mayer (Woodbridge, 2007), pp. 1–34

"Providence and Prescription: The Account of Elizabeth in Foxe's 'Book of Martyrs'" in *The Myth of Elizabeth*, ed. Susan Doran and Thomas S. Freeman (Basingstoke, 2003), pp. 27–55

Garrett, Christina, *The Marian Exiles: A Study in the Origins of Elizabethan Puritanism* (Cambridge, 1938)

Gray, Jonathan Michael, *Oaths and the English Reformation* (Cambridge, 2012)

Gordon, Bruce, *Calvin* (New Haven and London, 2009)

de Greef, Wulfert, *The Writings of John Calvin: an Introductory Guide*, trans. Lyle D. Bierma (Grand Rapids, 1993)

Gregory, Brad S., *Salvation at Stake: Christian Martyrdom in Early Modern Europe* (Cambridge, MA, 1999)

Gunther, Karl and Ethan H. Shagan, "Protestant Radicalism and Political Thought in the Reign of Henry VIII" *Past & Present* 194 (February 2007), pp. 35–74

Ha, Polly, *English Presbyterianism, 1590–1640* (Stanford, CA, 2011)

Haigh, Christopher, *English Reformations: Religion, Politics, and Society under the Tudors* (Oxford, 1993)

Reformation and Resistance in Tudor Lancashire (Cambridge, 1975)

Haugaard, William P., *Elizabeth and the English Reformation: The Struggle for a Stable Settlement of Religion* (Cambridge, 1968)

Heal, Felicity, "The Bishops and the Act of Exchange of 1559" *The Historical Journal* 17:2 (June 1974), pp. 227–246

Of Prelates and Princes: A Study of the Economic and Social Position of the Tudor Episcopate (Cambridge, 1980)

Reformation in Britain and Ireland (Oxford, 2003)

Helmholz, Richard H., "Canon Law in Post-Reformation England" in *Canon Law in Protestant Lands*, ed. Richard H. Helmholz (Berlin, 1992), pp. 203–221

Hessayon, Ariel and David Finnegan (eds.), *Varieties of Seventeenth- and Early Eighteenth-Century English Radicalism in Context* (Farnham, 2011)

Highley, Christopher, *Catholics Writing the Nation in Early Modern Britain and Ireland* (Oxford, 2008)

Hill, Christopher, "William Tyndale and English History" in *Intellectual Origins of the English Revolution Revisited* (Oxford, 1997), pp. 312–317

Hillerbrand, Hans J. (ed.), *Radical Tendencies in the Reformation: Divergent Perspectives* (Kirksville, MO, 1988)

"Radicalism in the Early Reformation: Varieties of Reformation in Church and Society" in Hans J. Hillerbrand (ed.), *Radical Tendencies in the Reformation: Divergent Perspectives* (Kirksville, MO, 1988), pp. 25–41

Hodler, Beat, "Protestant Self-Perception and the Problem of *Scandalum*: a Sketch" in *Protestant History and Identity in Sixteenth-Century Europe*, vol. 1, ed. Bruce Gordon (Aldershot, 1996), pp. 23–30

Horst, Irvin Buckwalter, *The Radical Brethren: Anabaptism and the English Reformation to 1558* (Nieuwkoop, 1972)

Hughes, Celia, "Two Sixteenth-Century Northern Protestants: John Bradford and William Turner" *Bulletin of the John Rylands University Library of Manchester* 66 (1983), pp. 104–138

Hume, Anthea, "William Roye's 'Brefe Dialoge' (1527) an English Version of a Strassburg Catechism" *Harvard Theological Review* 60:3 (July 1967), pp. 307–321

Ives, Eric, *The Life and Death of Anne Boleyn* (Malden, MA, 2004)

Jansen, Sharon L., *Political Protest and Prophecy under Henry VIII* (Woodbridge, 1991)

Jones, Ann Rosalind and Peter Stallybrass, *Renaissance Clothing and the Materials of Memory* (Cambridge, 2000)

Jones, Norman, *The Birth of the Elizabethan Age: England in the 1560s* (Oxford, 1993)

The English Reformation: Religion and Cultural Adaptation (Oxford, 2002)

Jones, Whitney R. D., *William Turner: Tudor Naturalist, Physician and Divine* (London and New York, 1988)

Kaufman, Peter Iver, *Thinking of the Laity in Late Tudor England* (Notre Dame, IN, 2004)

Kendall, Ritchie D., *The Drama of Dissent: The Radical Poetics of Nonconformity, 1380–1590* (Chapel Hill and London, 1986)

Kingdon, Robert, "The Episcopal Function in Protestant Churches in the Sixteenth and Seventeenth centuries" in *L'institution et les pouvoirs dans les églises de l'antiquité à nos jours*, ed. Bernard Vogler (Louvain, 1987), pp. 207–220

Kirby, Torrance, *The Zurich Connection and Tudor Political Theology* (Leiden, 2007)

Knappen, M. M., *Tudor Puritanism* (Chicago, 1939)

Lake, Peter, *Anglicans and Puritans? Presbyterianism and English Conformist Thought from Whitgift to Hooker* (London, 1988)

The Antichrist's Lewd Hat (New Haven, CT and London, 2002)

"'A Charitable Christian Hatred': The Godly and Their Enemies in the 1630s" in *The Culture of English Puritanism, 1560–1700*, ed. Christopher Durston and Jacqueline Eales (New York, 1996), pp. 145–183

"Defining Puritanism – Again?" in *Puritanism: Transatlantic Perspectives on a Seventeenth-Century Anglo-American Faith*, ed. Francis J. Bremer (Boston, 1993), pp. 3–29

"The historiography of Puritanism" in John Coffey and Paul C. H. Lim (eds.), *The Cambridge Companion to Puritanism* (Cambridge, 2008), pp. 346–371

Moderate puritans and the Elizabethan church (Cambridge, 1982)

"Presbyterianism, the Idea of a National Church and the Argument from Divine Right" in *Protestantism and the National Church in Sixteenth Century England*, ed. Peter Lake and Maria Dowling (London, 1987), pp. 193–224

"A Tale of Two Episcopal Surveys: The Strange Fates of Edmund Grindal and Cuthbert Mayne Revisited: The Prothero Lecture" *Transactions of the Royal Historical Society* 18 (2008), pp. 129–163

Lake, Peter and Michael Questier, *The Trials of Margaret Clitherow: Persecution, Martyrdom and the Politics of Sanctity in Elizabethan England* (London, 2011)

Lander, Jesse M., *Inventing Polemic: Religion, Print, and Literary Culture in Early Modern England* (Cambridge, 2006)

Laube, Adolf, "Radicalism as a Research Problem in the History of the Early Reformation" in Hans J. Hillerbrand (ed.), *Radical Tendencies in the Reformation: Divergent Perspectives* (Kirksville, MO, 1988), pp. 9–23

Lim, Paul Chang-Ha, *In Pursuit of Purity, Unity, and Liberty: Richard Baxter's Puritan Ecclesiology in Its Seventeenth-Century Context* (Leiden, 2004)

Loach, Jennifer, "Reformation Controversies" in *The History of the University of Oxford*, vol. 3, ed. James McConica (Oxford, 1986), pp. 363–396

Loades, David, *Mary Tudor: A Life* (Oxford, 1989)

"The Sense of National Identity Among the Marian Exiles (1553–1558)" in *Faith and identity: Christian political experience*, ed. David Loades and Katherine Walsh (Oxford, 1990), pp. 99–108

Loewenstein, David, *Treacherous Faith: The Specter of Heresy in Early Modern English Literature and Culture* (Oxford, 2013)

Lucas, Scott, "'Let none such office take, save he that can for right his prince forsake': *A Mirror for Magistrates*, Resistance Theory and the Elizabethan Monarchical Republic" in *The Monarchical Republic of Early Modern England:*

Essays in Response to Patrick Collinson, ed. John F. McDiarmid (Aldershot, 2007), pp. 91–108

Maas, Korey D., *The Reformation and Robert Barnes: History, Theology and Polemic in Early Modern England* (Woodbridge, 2010)

MacCulloch, Diarmaid, "Archbishop Cranmer: concord and tolerance in a changing Church" in *Tolerance and intolerance in the European Reformation*, eds. Ole Peter Grell and Bob Scribner (Cambridge, 1996), pp. 199–215

The Boy King: Edward VI and the Protestant Reformation (New York, 2001)

"England" in *The Early Reformation in Europe*, ed. Andrew Pettegree (Cambridge, 1992), pp. 166–187

The Later Reformation in England, 1547–1603 (Basingstoke, 2001)

"The Myth of the English Reformation" *Journal of British Studies* 30:1 (January 1991), pp. 1–19

"Peter Martyr and Thomas Cranmer" in *Peter Martyr Vermigli: Humanism, Republicanism, Reformation*, ed. Emidio Campi (Geneva, 2002), pp. 173–201

The Reformation (New York, 2003)

"Sixteenth-century English Protestantism and the Continent" in *Sister Reformations: The Reformation in Germany and in England*, ed. Dorothea Wendebourg (Tübingen, 2010), pp. 1–14

Thomas Cranmer: A Life (New Haven, CT, and London, 1996)

MacLure, Miller, *The Paul's Cross Sermons, 1534–1642* (Toronto, 1958)

McGinn, Donald Joseph, *The Admonition Controversy* (New Brunswick, NJ, 1949)

McGrath, Patrick and Joy Rowe, "The Marian Priests Under Elizabeth I" *Recusant History* 17 (1984), pp. 103–120

Manning, Roger B., *Religion and Society in Elizabethan Sussex* (New York, 1969)

Marcombe, David, "The Dean and Chapter of Durham, 1558–1603" (Doctoral Thesis, Durham University, 1973)

"A Rude and Heady People: the local community and the Rebellion of the Northern Earls" in *The Last Principality: Politics, Religion and Society in the Bishopric of Durham, 1494–1660*, ed. David Marcombe (Nottingham, 1987), pp. 117–151

Marshall, Peter, *Reformation England, 1480–1642*, 2nd edn. (London, 2012)

Marshall, Peter and Alec Ryrie (eds.), *The Beginnings of English Protestantism* (Cambridge, 2002)

Martin, J. W., "The Protestant Underground Congregations of Mary's Reign" in *Religious Radicals in Tudor England* (London, 1989)

Mason, Roger A., "Knox, Resistance and the Royal Supremacy" in Mason (ed.), *John Knox and the British Reformations* (Aldershot, 1998), pp. 154–175

Milward, Peter, "The Jewel–Harding Controversy" *Albion* 6:4 (Winter 1974), pp. 320–341

Monta, Susannah Brietz, "Martyrdom in Print in Early Modern England: The Case of Robert Waldegrave" in *More Than a Memory: The Discourse of Martyrdom and the Construction of Christian Identity in the History of Christianity*, ed. Johan Leemans (Leuven, 2005), pp. 271–294

Muss-Arnolt, William, "Puritan Efforts and Struggles, 1550–1603: A Bio-Bibliographical Study I" *American Journal of Theology* 23:3 (July 1919), pp. 345–366

Neal, Daniel, *History of the Puritans*, vol. 1 (London, 1837)

Oates, Rosamund, "Puritans and the 'Monarchical Republic': Conformity and Conflict in the Elizabethan Church" *English Historical Review* 127:527 (2012), pp. 819–843

Parker, Kenneth, *The English Sabbath: A study of doctrine and discipline from the Reformation to the Civil War* (Cambridge, 1988)

Pearse, M. T., *Between Known Men and Visible Saints: A Study in Sixteenth-Century English Dissent* (Cranbury, NJ, 1994)

Pearson, A. F. Scott, *Church & State: Political Aspects of Sixteenth Century Puritanism* (Cambridge, 1928)

Penny, D. Andrew, *Freewill or Predestination: The Battle over Saving Grace in Mid-Tudor England* (Woodbridge, 1990)

Pettegree, Andrew, *Foreign Protestant Communities in Sixteenth-Century London* (Oxford, 1986)

Marian Protestantism: Six Studies (Aldershot, 1996)

Pineas, Rainer, "William Turner's Polemical Use of Ecclesiastical History and His Controversy with Stephen Gardiner" *Renaissance Quarterly* 33:4 (Winter 1980), pp. 599–608

Pragman, James H., "The Augsburg Confession in the English Reformation: Richard Taverner's Contribution" *Sixteenth Century Journal* 11:3 (1980), pp. 75–85

Primus, J. H., *The Vestments Controversy: An Historical Study of the Earliest Tensions within the Church of England in the Reigns of Edward VI and Elizabeth* (Kampen, 1960)

Questier, Michael C., *Catholicism and Community in Early Modern England: Politics, Aristocratic Patronage and Religion, c. 1550–1640* (Cambridge, 2006)

Racaut, Luc and Alec Ryrie (eds.), *Moderate Voices in the European Reformation* (Aldershot, 2005)

Racine, Matthew, "*A Pearle for a Prynce*: Jerónimo Osório and Early Elizabethan Catholics" *Catholic Historical Review* 87:3 (2001), 401–427

Ranson, Angela, "Sincere Lies and Creative Truth: Recantation Strategies during the English Reformation" *Journal of History and Cultures* 1 (2012), pp. 1–18

Raymond, Joad, *Pamphlets and Pamphleteering in Early Modern Britain* (Cambridge, 2003)

Rex, Richard, *Henry VIII and the English Reformation*, 2nd edn. (Basingstoke, 2006)

"New Light on Tyndale and Lollardy" *Reformation* 8 (2003), pp. 143–171

Rupp, E. G., *Studies in the Making of the English Protestant Tradition* (Cambridge, 1947)

Russell, Conrad, "Arguments for Religious Unity in England, 1530–1650" *Journal of Ecclesiastical History* 18:2 (1967), pp. 201–226

Ryrie, Alec, *The Age of Reformation: The Tudor and Stewart Realms, 1485–1603* (Harlow, 2009)

Being Protestant in Reformation Britain (Oxford, 2013)

"Counting sheep, counting shepherds: the problem of allegiance in the English Reformation" in *The Beginnings of English Protestantism*, ed. Peter Marshall and Alec Ryrie (Cambridge, 2002), pp. 84–110

The Gospel and Henry VIII (Cambridge, 2003)

(ed.), *Palgrave Advances in the European Reformations* (Basingstoke, 2006)

"'A saynt in the deuyls name': Heroes and Villains in the Martyrdom of Robert Barnes" in *Martyrs and Martyrdom in England c. 1400–1700*, ed. Thomas S. Freeman and Thomas F. Mayer (Woodbridge, 2007), pp. 144–165

"The Strange Death of Lutheran England" *Journal of Ecclesiastical History* 53: 1 (January 2002), pp. 64–92

Saenger, Paul, "The Earliest French Resistance Theories: The Role of the Burgundian Court" *The Journal of Modern History* 51:4, On Demand Supplement (December 1979), pp. D1245–D1246

Shagan, Ethan H., "The Battle for Indifference in Elizabethan England" in *Moderate Voices in the European Reformation*, ed. Luc Racaut and Alec Ryrie (Aldershot, 2005), pp. 122–144

Catholics and the 'Protestant Nation': Religious Politics and Identity in Early Modern England (Manchester, 2005)

"Clement Armstrong and the godly commonwealth: radical religion in early Tudor England" in *The Beginnings of English Protestantism*, ed. Peter Marshall and Alec Ryrie (Cambridge, 2002), pp. 60–83

Popular Politics and the English Reformation (Cambridge, 2003)

The Rule of Moderation: Violence, Religion and the Politics of Restraint in Early Modern England (Cambridge, 2011)

Shakespeare, Joy, "Plague and Punishment" in *Protestantism and the National Church*, ed. Peter Lake and Maria Dowling (London, 1987), pp. 103–123

Simpson, James, *Burning to Read: English Fundamentalism and its Reformation Opponents* (Cambridge, MA, 2007)

Simpson, Martin A., "Of the Troubles Begun at Frankfurt, A. D. 1554" in *Reformation and Revolution*, ed. Duncan Shaw (Edinburgh, 1967), pp. 17–33

Skinner, Quentin, *The Foundations of Modern Political Thought*, vol. 2, *The Age of Reformation* (Cambridge, 1978)

Smeeton, Donald Dean, *Lollard Themes in the Reformation Theology of William Tyndale* (Kirksville, MO, 1986)

Southern, A. C., *Elizabethan Recusant Prose, 1559–1582* (London, 1950)

Spalding, James C., "The Reformatio Legum Ecclesiasticarum of 1552 and the Furthering of Discipline in England" *Church History* 39:2 (June 1970), pp. 162–171

Stayer, James M., *Anabaptists and the Sword* (Eugene, OR, 1976)

Sutherland, N. M., "The Marian Exiles and the Establishment of the Elizabethan Régime" *Archiv für Reformationsgeschichte* 78 (1987), pp. 253–284

Trinterud, Leonard J. (ed.), *Elizabethan Puritanism* (New York, 1971)

Troeltsch, Ernst, *The Social Teaching of the Christian Churches*, trans. Olive Wyon, 2 vols. (New York, 1960)

Trueman, Carl R., *Luther's Legacy: Salvation and English Reformers, 1525–1556* (Oxford, 1994)

Tyacke, Nicholas, "Anglican attitudes: some recent writings on English religious history, from the Reformation to the Civil War" in *Aspects of English Protestantism, c. 1530–1700* (Manchester, 2001), pp. 176–202

Anti-Calvinists: The Rise of English Arminianism, c. 1590–1640 (Oxford, 1987)

Underwood, William, "Thomas Cromwell and William Marshall's Protestant Books" *The Historical Journal* 47:3 (September 2004), pp. 517–539

Usher, Brett, "The Deanery of Bocking and the Demise of the Vestiarian Controversy" *Journal of Ecclesiastical History* 52:3 (July 2001), pp. 434–455

"Durham and Winchester Episcopal Estates and the Elizabethan Settlement: A Reappraisal" *Journal of Ecclesiastical History* 49:3 (July 1998), pp. 393–406

Vander Molen, Ronald, "Anglican Against Puritan: Ideological Origins during the Marian Exile" *Church History* 42:1 (March 1973), pp. 45–57

"Providence as Mystery, Providence as Revelation: Puritan and Anglican Modifications of John Calvin's Doctrine of Providence" *Church History* 47:1 (March 1978), pp. 27–47

Verkamp, Bernard, *The Indifferent Mean: Adiaphorism in the English Reformation to 1554* (Athens, OH, 1977)

Wabuda, Susan, "Equivocation and Recantation During the English Reformation: The 'Subtle Shadows' of Dr Edward Crome" *Journal of Ecclesiastical History* 44:2 (April 1993), pp. 224–242

"Setting Forth the Word of God: Archbishop Cranmer's Early Patronage of Preachers" in *Thomas Cranmer: Churchman and Scholar*, ed. Paul Ayris and David Selwyn (Woodbridge, 1993), pp. 75–88

Walker, Greg, "Saint or Schemer? The 1527 Heresy Trial of Thomas Bilney Reconsidered" *Journal of Ecclesiastical History* 40:2 (April 1989), pp. 219–238

Walsham, Alexandra, *Charitable hatred: Tolerance and intolerance in England, 1500–1700* (Manchester, 2006)

Church Papists: Catholicism, Conformity and Confessional Polemic in Early Modern England (Woodbridge, 1999)

"'Frantick Hacket': Prophecy, Sorcery, Insanity, and the Elizabethan Puritan Movement" *The Historical Journal* 41:1 (March 1998), pp. 27–66

"The godly and popular culture" in John Coffey and Paul C. H. Lim (eds.), *The Cambridge Companion to Puritanism* (Cambridge, 2008), pp. 277–293

"The Reformation of the Generations: Youth, Age and Religious Change in England, c. 1500–1700" *Transactions of the Royal Historical Society*, Sixth Series, 21 (2011), pp. 93–121

"'A Very Deborah?': The Myth of Elizabeth I as a Providential Monarch" in *The Myth of Elizabeth*, ed. Susan Doran and Thomas S. Freeman (Basingstoke, 2003), pp. 143–168

"'Yielding to the Extremity of the Time': Conformity, Orthodoxy and the Post-Reformation Catholic Community" in *Conformity and Orthodoxy in the English Church, c. 1560–1660*, ed. Peter Lake and Michael Questier (Woodbridge, 2000), pp. 211–236

Walzer, Michael, *The Revolution of the Saints: A Study in the Origins of Radical Politics* (New York, 1972)

Wenig, Scott A., *Straightening the Altars: The Ecclesiastical Vision and Pastoral Achievements of the Progressive Bishops under Elizabeth I, 1559–1579* (New York, 2000)

White, B. R., *The English Separatist Tradition: From the Marian Martyrs to the Pilgrim Fathers* (Oxford, 1971)

Williams, George Huntston, *The Radical Reformation*, 3rd edn. (Kirksville, MO, 2000)

Winters, Roy Lutz, *Francis Lambert of Avignon (1487–1530): A Study in Reformation Origins* (Philadelphia, 1938)

Wizeman, William, "Martyrs and Anti-Martyrs and Mary Tudor's Church" in *Martyrs and Martyrdom in England, c.1400–1700*, ed. Thomas S. Freeman and Thomas F. Mayer (Woodbridge, 2007), pp. 166–179

Wright, Jonathan, "Marian Exiles and the Legitimacy of Flight from Persecution" *Journal of Ecclesiastical History* 52:2 (April 2001), pp. 220–243

Wright, William J., "The Homberg Synod and Philip of Hesse's Plan for a New Church-State Settlement" *Sixteenth Century Journal* 4:2 (October 1973), pp. 23–46

Zagorin, Perez, *Ways of Lying: Dissimulation, Persecution, and Conformity in Early Modern Europe* (Cambridge, MA, 1990)

Zlatar, Antoinina Bevanr, *Reformation Fictions: Polemical Protestant Dialogues in Elizabethan England* (Oxford, 2011)

Index

adiaphora, 1, 7–8, 71, 253, 254
  and church government, 26, 33, 36–37, 47,
    50–51, 53, 54–60
  and the Troubles at Frankfurt, 170–181
  and the vestments controversy, 190, 194–197,
    205–206, 208–213, 214–216
  Catholic views, 194–197
Aers, David, 64
Alford, Stephen, 133–134
Allen, William, 198
Anabaptists, 3, 85
anti-Nicodemism. See Nicodemism and anti-
    Nicodemism
authority, religious, 136–140, 254, Also see
    adiaphora, Royal Supremacy, ch. 4 passim
  and conformists, 209–210
  and puritans, 153–157
  and the Marian exiles, 131–133
  and the Troubles at Frankfurt, 170–181
Avis, Paul D., 17, 53
Aylmer, John, 239, 247

Bacon, Nicholas, 140, 154
Bainton, Roland, 4
Bale, John, 229
  as Bishop of Ossory, 60, 61
  in conformist polemic, 248
  in puritan polemic, 236, 243, 244, 246
  on adiaphora, 55–56
  on bishops, 56–57
  on church government, 21
  on conflict, 96
  on confrontation, 110
  on dissimulation, 101, 103, 104
  on persecution, 73
  on recantation, 102
  on violence against papists, 89–90
Bancroft, Richard
  and the Troubles at Frankfurt, 184, 186
  on early English Protestants and
    presbyterianism, 247–248, 249–250

Barlow, William, 65
Barnes, Robert, 20, 229
  in conformist polemic, 246, 247, 248
  in puritan polemic, 229–230, 232, 237, 241,
    244, 246
  on adiaphora, 71
  on bishops, 20, 23–24, 30–32
  on the clergy's civil occupations, 23–24
  revisions to his Supplicatyon, 32
Barrow, Henry, 119, 120–121, 221, 222–224
Barthlet, John, 154, 193, 203
Bauckham, Richard, 68, 135, 137
Baynton, Edward, 77–78
Becon, Thomas, 244
Bentham, Thomas, 165
Berkeley, Gilbert, 225
Beza, Theodore, 17, 27, 61, 228
Bigod, Francis, 66
Bilney, Thomas, 75–76, 79
Bilson, Thomas, 150, 239
Black, J. William, 18
Black, Joseph, 231–234
Boleyn, Anne, 31, 36
Bonner, Edmund, 168, 203
Bossy, John, 65
Bowker, Margaret, 43
Bowler, Gerald, 133
Brachlow, Stephen, 222
Bradford, John
  in conformist polemic, 247–248
  in puritan polemic, 183, 223, 240, 244, 245–246
  on dissimulation, 102, 103–104, 107, 112, 207, 208
Brinkelow, Henry
  in puritan polemic, 227–228, 246
  on adiaphora, 55
  on separation, 107–108
Brooks, James, 168
Browne, Robert, 119, 144, 221
Bucer, Martin, 16, 18, 40, 213, 246
Bull, Henry, 112, 182
Bullinger, Heinrich, 101, 105

279